Creditworthiness and Reform
in Poland

CENTER FOR GLOBAL BUSINESS
THE SCHOOL OF BUSINESS OF INDIANA UNIVERSITY

Creditworthiness and Reform in Poland

Western and Polish Perspectives

Edited by

Paul Marer
Indiana University

Włodzimierz Siwiński
Warsaw University

Published in association with the Indiana Center for Global Business, and the Polish Studies Center, Indiana University

INDIANA UNIVERSITY PRESS
BLOOMINGTON AND INDIANAPOLIS

$So2$
HC
340.3
$C74$
1988

Manufactured in the United States of America

LIBRARY OF CONGRESS

Library of Congress Cataloging-in-Publication Data

Creditworthiness and reform in Poland: Western and Polish perspectives / edited by Paul Marer and Włodzimierz Siwiński.

    p.   cm.
"Published in association with the Indiana Center for Global Business, Indiana University."
    Includes revised versions of papers originally presented at Conference on the Polish Economy and Debt, 1985, Smithsonian Institution, sponsored by Indiana University School of Business et al.
    ISBN 0-253-31472-0. ISBN 0-253-20477-1 (pbk.)
    1. Poland—Economic conditions—1945- —Congresses. 2. Poland—Economic Policy—1981—Congresses. 3. Debts, External—Poland—Congresses. 4. Poland—Foreign economic relations—Congresses. I. Marer, Paul. II. Siwiński, Włodzimierz. III. Indiana University, Indiana Center for Global Business. IV. Conference on the Polish Economy and Debt (1985: Smithsonian Institution). V. Indiana University. School of Business.
HC340.3.C74 1988
338.9438—dc19
                                         87-26962
                                            CIP

Contents

LIST OF TABLES

LIST OF CHARTS

Contributors

Nicholas G. Andrews — Retired Foreign Service Officer; served as Deputy Chief of Mission, American Embassy, Warsaw (1979-81)

Jack Bielasiak — Associate Professor of Political Science and Director, Polish Studies Center, Indiana University, Bloomington

Carlo Boffito — Professor of Economics, University of Torino; Consultant, Banca Commerciale Italiana, Milan, Italy

Jean F. Boone — Senior Research Assistant in Soviet Economics, Congressional Research Service, The Library of Congress

Michael L. Boyd — Assistant Professor of Economics, University of Vermont, Burlington

Włodzimierz Brus — Professor of Economics, Wolfson College, Oxford University, Oxford, England

Zbigniew Brzezinski — Professor, Center for Strategic and International Studies, Georgetown University, Washington D.C.; former National Security Advisor to the President

Keith Crane — Associate Economist, The Rand Corporation, Santa Monica, California

Michał Dobroczyński — Professor of International Economics, Warsaw University, Warsaw

Gabriel Eichler — Vice President and Country Manager, Vienna Branch, Bank of America; Senior Member, Bankers' Committee on Polish Debt Rescheduling

Zbigniew Fallenbuchl — Professor of Economics, University of Windsor, Windsor, Canada

Gerhard Fink — Director, Vienna Institute for Comparative Economic Studies, Vienna, Austria

Hubert Gabrisch — Research Fellow, Vienna Institute for Comparative Economic Studies, Vienna, Austria

Stanisław Gomulka — Professor, London School of Economics, London

John P. Hardt — Associate Director for Research Coordination, Congressional Research Service, The Library of Congress, Washington D.C.

David C. Holland — Doctoral Candidate in Economics, University of Birmingham, the U.K.; Visiting Scholar, European University Institute, Florence, Italy

Władysław Jermakowicz — Associate Professor of Business, University of Southern Indiana, Evansville; former Department Chair, Institute of Management, Polish Academy of Sciences, Warsaw

Zbigniew Kamecki — Professor of International Economics, Central School of Planning and Statistics, Warsaw

Paul I. McCarthy — Vice President, Chemical Bank of New York

Paul Marer — Professor of International Business, Indiana University, Bloomington

Witold Morawski — Professor of Sociology, Warsaw University; Visiting Professor of Political Science and Polish Studies, Indiana University, Bloomington (1987)

Piotr Mroczkowski — Assistant Professor of Economics, Warsaw University; Visiting Research Associate, Indiana University, Bloomington (1985-86).

Petra Pissulla — Research Scholar, Economic Research Institute, Hamburg University, Hamburg, Federal Republic of Germany

Kazimierz Poznański — Associate Professor of Economics, University of Washington, Seattle

Jim Prust — Division Chief, Eastern Europe, International Monetary Fund, Washington D.C.

Stanisław Raczkowski — Professor, Central School of Planning and Statistics, Warsaw; Chairman of the Polish Planning Commission

Thomas W. Simons Jr. — Deputy Assistant Secretary of State for European Affairs, U.S. Department of State, Washington, D.C.

Włodzimierz Siwiński   Associate Professor of International Economics, Warsaw University, Warsaw; Visiting Professor of International Business and Associate Director of the Polish Studies Center, Indiana University, Bloomington (1984-86)

Benjamin Slay   Doctoral Candidate in Economics, Indiana University, Bloomington; conducted research in Poland during 1983-86

Józef Sołdaczuk   Director, Foreign Trade Research Institute; Professor, Central School of Planning and Statistics, Warsaw

Sarah M. Terry   Associate Professor of Political Science, Tufts University; Fellow, Russian Research Center, Harvard University, Cambridge

Acknowledgments

Many individuals contributed a great deal of time and effort to enable the editors to blend into a cohesive book the thirty-three essays, most of which are original contributions commissioned especially for this volume. We wish to thank our contributors who were gracious enough to put up with our numerous suggestions for revisions.

The antecedent of this volume was a Conference on the Polish Economy and Debt that the editors organized (in behalf of Indiana University's School of Business, Polish Studies Center, and Russian and East European Institute) at the Woodrow Wilson Center for Scholars of the Smithsonian Institution in Washington D.C. on October 21-22, 1985. We acknowledge a grant from the U.S. Department of Commerce to help fund that Conference, and wish to thank *Allen Lenz*, Director of the Department of Commerce's International Trade and Investment Division, for his gracious help in arranging the funding. It is a pleasure also to acknowledge the financial and in-kind contributions of the East European Program of the Woodrow Wilson Center, then under the leadership of *George W. Hoffman*, Acting Secretary of the East European Program.

Valuable financial, logistical, and substantive support for the conference and this publication were provided by the former director of Indiana University's Polish Studies Center, *Timothy Wiles*, and by its current director, *Jack Bielasiak*.

Our special thanks go to those participants in the Smithsonian Conference who made valuable substantive contributions by presenting papers or serving as chairpersons or discussants, but who, for a variety of reasons, did not contribute a chapter to the volume. Their ideas and suggestions are, however, reflected in the chapters in this volume: *Richard T. Davies*, former U.S. Ambassador to Poland; *William Cline* and *John Williamson* of the Institute for International Economics; *Barbara Despiney* of the Économies et Techniques de Planification, Paris; *Bartłomej Kamiński* of the University of Maryland; *Dave Kemme* of Wichita State University; *J.M. Montias* of Yale University; *Mario Nuti* of the European University Institute, Florence; *Stanislaw Rudcenko* of Bankers Trust Company, London; *Krystyna Szymkiewicz* of the Centre d'Économie Internationale des Pays Socialistes, Paris; *Jan Vanous* of PlanEcon, Washington, D.C.; and *Harold Williams* of Kent State University. In addition to these "formal" participants, more than fifty persons from the IMF, the World Bank, the U.S., and foreign governments, as well as specialists from academia, research institutes, and from the business and banking communities attended the conference and made valuable contributions during the discussion.

There is no single person to whom the editors are more indebted, in connection with both the conference and this volume, than *Ellie Valentine* of Indiana University's Polish Studies Center, who worked tirelessly, and with efficiency and initiative, to help organize from Bloomington a conference in Washington D.C. with more than one hundred participants, and who typed and coded many of the chapters and helped coordinate the publication process. *Melanie Kearns* of the School of Business of Indiana University also provided valuable and timely help with the editorial, typing, and coding chores, assisted by *Pamela Stewart*. *Kevin Kenyon* ably edited the volume.

Janet Rabinowitch at the Indiana University Press was most helpful with her suggestions and for seeing the work through its various publication stages.

The publication of this book was made possible by financial support from the Indiana Center for Global Business, School of Business, Indiana University.

Paul Marer
Włodzimierz Siwiński

Glossary

CC	Convertible Currency
CCC	Commodity Credit Corporation
CME	Centrally-Managed Economy
CMEA	Council for Mutual Economic Assistance
CPE	Centrally Planned Economy
CSCE	Conference on Security and Cooperation in Europe
ECU	European Currency Unit
FAZ	Wage-fund tax (see PFAZ)
FTC	Foreign Trade Corporation
FTE	Foreign Trade Enterprise
GATT	General Agreement on Tariffs and Trade
GDP	Gross Domestic Product
GDR	German Democratic Republic
IMF	International Monetary Fund
LDC	Less Developed Country
MDE	Market-Directed Economy
MBFR	Mutual and Balanced Force Reductions
MFN	Most Favored Nation (tariff classification)
MFT	Ministry of Foreign Trade
MMS	Macro-Management System
MTF	Multinational Task Force
MYRA	Multi-Year Rescheduling Agreement
NATO	North Atlantic Treaty Organization
NBP	National Bank of Poland
NMP	Net Material Product
OD	Retention quotas (*odpisy dewizowe*)
OECD	Organization for Economic Cooperation and Development
PFAZ	Wage-fund tax (*Państwowy Fundusz Aktywizacji Zawodowej*)
PUWP	Polish United Workers' Party
ROD	Foreign Exchange Accounts (*rachunki odpisów dewizowych*)
SDR	Special Drawing Rights
SITC	Standard International Trade Classification
WOG	Large Economic Organizations (*Wielkie Organizacje Gospodarcze*)
ZCT	Zero-Coupon Treasury (bond)

Introduction

Paul Marer and Włodzimierz Siwiński

In 1987, Poland was one of the most heavily-indebted countries in the world. Its debt to Western creditors stood at $35 billion. It also owed significant amounts to its Eastern-bloc trading partners, principally the USSR, mostly in transferable rubles, a non-convertible currency. Since 1981 Poland has been unable to service its debt fully, that is, to pay all the interest and to repay the principal as its loans were maturing. Poland has thus lost its creditworthiness.

Poland's inability to meet its schedule of payments in 1981 came as a shock to foreign observers. Until then, creditors believed that central planners in communist countries were in control of their economic destinies, and that if an unusual situation arose to hinder the servicing of an East European country's debt, the USSR—as a lender of last resort—would come to the aid of an ally. These assumptions were shattered by Poland's inability to meet its payment obligations and by the country's 25 percent decline in output during 1981-82—largely because imports had to be cut drastically as debt-servicing difficulties mounted—the worst depression in any industrial country since World War II.

Poland is, therefore, an important case study for understanding why and how central planners, supposedly in control of their nation's economic destiny, could allow economic conditions to deteriorate so substantially.

During 1981-82, when these debt-servicing problems came to the fore, the country's external financial situation was perceived in the West as a major threat to the stability of the entire global financial system. There was apprehension that some banks with large loans to Poland might be forced into bankruptcy, triggering a loss of confidence in the entire Western banking system. A further concern was that other large debtor countries might be encouraged to follow Poland's example.

In retrospect, today we know that the other countries that subsequently joined Poland in not paying their external obligations fully—such as Romania and Yugoslavia in Eastern Europe and Mexico, Brazil, and Argentina in Latin America—did so not because they were encouraged by the actions of Poland but because their own economies were faltering and because they faced unfavorable external circumstances. Today, Poland is just one of many countries in severe economic, financial, and political difficulties. In some ways, its problems, and its possible impact on the stability of the global financial system, have been eclipsed by the problems of the "giant" debtors, like Mexico and Brazil.

Nevertheless, Poland's situation represents a fascinating, by and large still imperfectly understood, and important case study. Poland is one of the world's largest debtors; in the communist world, it is the largest. Its experience helps to illuminate the origins and consequences of the global debt crisis. Although we know that the causes of the debt crisis vary considerably from country to country, and that there is no uniform formula for dealing with the problems of every country, it is of interest to investigate the similarities and the differences between Poland and other heavily-indebted countries. For example, what combination of internal and external factors has been responsible for the accumulation of the large debt of Poland? What are the consequences of the debt crisis in that country? What do creditors suggest Poland should do to regain creditworthiness?

On the issue of what Poland should do, there seems to be a broad agreement inside and outside the country that the introduction of comprehensive economic reforms is essential for improving Poland's economic performance and for regaining creditworthiness. There is less of a consensus on what kinds of reforms are needed, when and how to introduce them, and the likelihood that they can be consistently implemented. There is little agreement also on what would be the most likely economic and political impacts of alternative reform measures, within the relatively short time frame of a few months or over the medium-term horizon of several years.

These and related issues are the focus of this book. This volume may well be the most comprehensive assessment of the economic, political, and sociological aspects of the debt problem, and its possible solution, to be found in a single publication, focusing on a single country. The volume's thirty-three chapters combine the perspectives of several academic disciplines—economics, business, banking, political science, sociology—with the viewpoints of practitioners, such as bankers, government officials, and the staff of the International Monetary Fund (IMF). The contributors represent leading experts from seven countries, including well-known specialists residing in Poland (some mirroring closely the official positions of the authorities, others reflecting more independent positions). The book combines the "big picture" with a wealth of detail and recommendations, some of which break new ground.

Many controversies surround Poland's economic and political future, and the role that international financial institutions, Western governments, and creditor banks should play in trying to shape it. The issues are discussed from a variety of perspectives, objectively and scientifically, with a minimum of jargon, and without pulling any punches.

The antecedent of this volume was a Conference on the Polish Economy and Debt that the editors organized (in behalf of Indiana University's School of Business, Polish Studies Center, and Russian and East European Institute) at the Woodrow Wilson Center for Scholars of the Smithsonian Institution in Washington D.C. on October 21-22, 1985. Thirteen of the thirty-three chapters represent substantially revised versions of the papers that were presented at the Smithsonian conference; twenty of the chapters were commissioned subsequently, to fill specific gaps in our knowledge of facts and understanding of the issues.

The contributions are grouped into six sections, each considering a set of related issues.

Section I is an overview of Poland's economy: the causes and consequences of the crisis, the partial recovery that has occurred between 1982 and 1987, and the economy's near-term prospects.

In Chapter 1, *Jim Prust,* a staff member of the IMF, traces the causes of Poland's economic crisis, describes the progress made through mid-1987 toward recovery, explains the systemic and policy reforms implemented during 1981-86, and outlines the additional measures being considered.

In Chapter 2, *Keith Crane* summarizes the state of the Polish economy and reform in 1987 in relation to the period immediately before and after the imposition of martial law. He describes the primary and secondary policy goals of the Polish authorities, detailing the presumed priorities of various party and government officials, institutions, and social groups. This contribution shows how the clash of opposing ideas and interests, and the leadership style of General Jaruzelski, make it difficult to implement the kinds of economic policies and comprehensive reforms that are needed.

A retrospective assessment of why Poland lost its creditworthiness is presented by the coeditor of the volume from Poland, *Włodzimierz Siwiński* (Chapter 3). He shows what combination of wrong economic policies, inefficiencies of the Polish version of the CPE system, and adverse external developments were jointly responsible for Poland's economic crisis and loss of creditworthiness.

Chapter 4, by *Michael L. Boyd,* documents the surprising role that the agricultural sector has played in the debt crisis; Chapter 5, by *Nicholas G. Andrews,* discusses the domestic ideological and political factors that explain it.

Chapter 6, by *Kazimierz Poznański,* focusing on industry's role, documents that although large-scale purchases of Western machinery and licenses during the 1970s were not directed and absorbed efficiently, those imports, nevertheless, did have a positive impact on the competitiveness of Poland's manufactures exports to the West during the 1970s. But the subsequent (1980-86) steep and prolonged reduction in Poland's machinery imports and cessation of license purchases from the West led, during the 1980s, to a severe decline in Poland's export competitiveness. Without reversing the trend in imports, a further decline in competitiveness is likely, which does not augur well for regaining creditworthiness.

Concluding the economic overview, in Chapter 7 *Zbigniew Kamecki* enumerates the positive developments in Poland's economy since 1982, including a reversal in the decline in output, improved equilibrium on the domestic market, lower inflation, and the transformation of large and persistent trade deficits into sizable surpluses.

The contributions in Section II focus on the political economy of reforms in Poland. *Włodzimierz Brus* (Chapter 8) examines why each of the previous four, more-or-less comprehensive reform attempts had failed and draws two main lessons from it. One is that the ultimate criterion of the authorities for choosing a course of action is the preservation of their power. This can lead to seemingly contradictory actions: supporting a reform to avert the political danger of economic setbacks, while at the same time opposing it because it would curtail the regime's span of control. Brus shows why and how each reform attempt goes through a predictable cycle, and describes its stages.

Chapter 9 summarizes the findings of *Władysław Jermakowicz*, a specialist on comparative economic systems, who suggests a new way to model and quantify systemic changes in the USSR and Eastern Europe. Presenting his results for the first time in English, the author shows both the internal dynamics of reform cycles in Poland and the relationship between reform cycles in the USSR and in several individual East European countries.

Witold Morawski, a leading sociologist from Poland, looks at the relationship between reform and public opinion (Chapter 10). He reports the results of polls conducted that reveal what percent of the population supports, rejects or is neutral vis-à-vis the regime, and the state of public opinion regarding the possibility of introducing comprehensive politico-economic reforms. The author spells out concretely what, in his view, would be a workable reform compromise between society and the authorities.

Focusing on the problem of reform implementation, *Jack Bielasiak*, a political scientist, traces the post-martial-law tension between economic reform and political normalization. Building on Brus' framework, he shows why the resolution of economic problems is repeatedly relegated to the background (Chapter 11).

The topic of the next five chapters is the economic aspects of the reform. *Zbigniew Fallenbuchl's* detailed study of reform implementation points to a dual discrepancy: first, that between the original program and the specific legal provisions enacted to implement it, and, second, between the various legislative acts and the changes actually introduced (Chapter 12).

Next, *Zbigniew Kamecki*, an expert from Poland, elucidates the economic and political difficulties of implementing reforms (Chapter 13), followed by *David C. Holland's* examination of how one of the key institution of the reforms, workers' self-management, has fared before and after 1981 (Chapter 14). The section concludes with two complementary descriptions and assessments of reforms in the foreign-trade sector by *Carlo Boffito* (Chapter 15) and *Benjamin Slay* (Chapter 16).

Several main themes emerge in the section on the political economy of reform. During approximately the last 35 years, Poland has repeatedly gone through cycles of crisis, reform, and stagnation. Therefore, the authorities lack domestic and external credibility with their new reform programs. Only an independent political force could attain credibility. But it is not at all clear that such a force can emerge under the prevailing political system. In its absence, apathy by the general public and opposition by vested interests represent two important obstacles to reform. Thus, even if the authorities were, this time, truly committed to basic reforms, their implementation would be hampered by resistance from managers who would have to take on more risk and responsibility, by the entrenched bureaucracy whose power would be curtailed, and even by some workers who would have less job security.

On discussing reforms, many on the Polish side tend to stress the difficult social conditions and adverse political consequences for the authorities that economic adjustment and reform—both involving further temporary belt-tightening for certain segments of the population— are likely to entail. In their view, this justifies why reforms can be introduced only slowly. By contrast, the emphasis on the Western side (supported by some experts from Poland) is on the need to improve economic efficiency by introducing radical reforms quickly, as the only way to regain creditworthiness, too.

Sections III and IV record a sharp dialogue on Poland's debt situation and prospects between experts from Poland (several serving as key advisors to the authorities) and experts from the West (some in excellent positions to reflect the views of the major creditors to Poland).

In Section III, four contributors from Poland, *Stanisław Rączkowski* (Chapter 17), *Zbigniew Kamecki* (Chapter 18), *Michał Dobroczyński* (Chapter 19), and *Józef Sołdaczuk* (Chapter 20), emphasize three main points. First, that adverse developments in the world economy (skyrocketing interest rates, deteriorating terms of trade, slowdown in Western growth rates, and the economic sanctions on Poland) have contributed in a major way to the country's debt-servicing difficulties. Second, that creditors should appreciate that during 1982-86, Poland generated a total of about $6 billion net capital outflows, made possible in part by the willingness of the East—the USSR first and foremost—to grant Poland substantial new credits, and in part by the substantial economic belt-tightening in the form of lower consumption and drastically reduced investment levels. Third, given Poland's sizable trade surplus with the West, modest growth plans, progress in implementing economic reforms, the decision to join and cooperate with the IMF and the World Bank, and the liberalization of its joint-venture laws, the West should "reward" Poland by granting it additional credits. The new money would be used to finance greater imports, badly needed to improve Poland's debt-servicing capability. Granting new credits would thus be in the economic and financial interests of the West.

The Western side (Chapters 21 through 25), and even some participants from Poland, have a different perspective. While acknowledging the belt-tightening in Poland of the last several years (with some questions about whether that was made voluntarily or was simply unavoidable, owing to a lack of new foreign credits), *Gerhard Fink* and *Hubert Gabrish* (Chapter 21) point out that the adjustment has been insufficient to pay fully even the interest on the debt outstanding. That is, Poland's "current account," although improved, is still in deficit. Bankers consider being current on interest payments, or at least making steady progress in moving in that direction, as a necessary though not sufficient condition for a country to reestablish its creditworthiness.

Western experts acknowledge that the central need of Poland, as of many other countries, is obtaining new money to help finance economic development. But this requires the restoration of creditworthiness, which was lost in the late 1970s and early 1980s as a result of delays in undertaking the needed reforms and adjustments. But creditworthiness cannot be restored simply through limited belt-tightening and debt restructuring. Poland, as other countries, must show evidence of modernization, with improved efficiency and export competitiveness; and its policies must be convincing to lenders. This is why Western contributors ask: have Poland's economic policies and system features changed sufficiently in recent years to give creditors the confidence that it would manage additional loans wisely?

Several contributors present a scathing indictment of Poland's debt-management practices during the 1970s, as revealed by investigations conducted by the authorities in Poland, and confirmed by the first-hand experiences of several of our authors. For example, all information connected with the debt was a carefully-guarded secret. *Gabriel Eichler* of the Bank of America notes that, before 1982, even research institutes that were supposed to analyze and make policy recommendations concerning foreign trade and finance had little information about the country's balance of payments. Moreover, the few Polish bankers who had full information had little or no influence on country's economic policies and programs (Chapter 22). The extreme secrecy on foreign credits is documented by *Sarah M. Terry*, who finds that the decisions were made by a few politically unaccountable persons who kept them so secret that not even members of the Politburo were given opportunities to discuss the debt issue in a meaningful fashion. Evidently, there was no one in the country in a decisionmaking position who could grasp the full implications of the exploding debt crisis until it was too late to prevent it (Chapter 23).

Has the situation improved in recent years?

In terms of compiling and making available information (on the balance of payments and the debt) to foreign creditors as well as inside Poland, it indeed has improved a great deal since 1982, thanks in part to the pressure exerted by the creditor banks. But in many other respects, there has been insufficient progress up to now. For example, Poland's scarce convertible-currency resources are still not allocated efficiently. Access to Western currency is based not on economic criteria, but on the coercive potential of the various ministries and producers. And old-fashioned planning methods are not well suited to bringing about sustainable improvements in the balance of payments. Planning consist largely of setting sectoral target indices for production and consumption. The balance of payments is still more a residual than a high-priority target of the policymakers. Based on this and other considerations, the Western consensus is that Poland must do more to cut its payments deficit, to improve economic efficiency, and to institute a long-term program for recovery and improved export-competitiveness. There is agreement that the introduction of fundamental economic reforms to improve the efficiency of the economy is essential for a sustained improvement in the domestic economy and external finance. Basic economic reform is viewed as an indispensable component of Poland's creditworthiness in the long run.

Several contributors make concrete suggestions about what might be done to improve Poland's debt-servicing capability. For example, *Paul McCarthy* of the Chemical Bank suggests that, under certain circumstances, the West may provide new "collateralized" loans, whose servicing would take priority over servicing the old debt (Chapter 24). *Paul Marer* suggests that Poland might wish to follow the example set by certain developing countries and arrange the conversion of some of its debt into equity (Chapter 25).

Section V explores a range of issues connected with Poland's membership in the IMF and the World Bank. *Piotr Mroczkowski* reviews the stormy early postwar history of Poland's membership in the two organizations (Chapter 26). The contrasting experiences of the Fund and the Bank with Romania (tending in recent years toward conflict) and with Hungary (much more cooperative) are described by *Petra Pissulla*, with implication drawn for Poland (Chapter 27).

The U.S. coeditor of the volume, *Paul Marer*, discusses several fundamental issues connected with Poland's IMF and World Bank membership (Chapter 28). Are the IMF and the World Bank politically willing and bureaucratically capable of insisting that Poland carry out systemic reforms, given that such an approach would be precedent-setting and controversial? Are Fund and Bank programs compatible with the economic system features even of a "reformed" CPE, such as Poland, whose financial markets are at an infant stage of development (which calls into question the feasibility of depending on financial instruments for influencing economic performance), and whose factor and product prices may be arbitrary and inflexible (which call into question reliance on market-mechanism incentives)? And would Poland, if pressured by the Fund and the Bank to implement comprehensive economic reforms, accept such "conditionality"?

The next contribution, by *Stanisław Gomulka*, spells out in detail the kinds of reform steps that the IMF and the World Bank should promote in Poland: financial discipline for enterprises and the creation or development of proper markets for finished and intermediate goods, credit, foreign exchange, and investments (Chapter 29).

One conclusion one may draw from the contributions in this section is that only when the authorities have not only the good intentions, but the power and the commitment to implement a new course, can meaningful external influence be assured. Given the severe domestic and external constraints Poland faces, the expectations of what the IMF and the World Bank could accomplish to improve Poland's economic performance should remain realistic.

The last section (VI) explores Western policy options vis-à-vis Poland. *Thomas W. Simons Jr.*, U.S. Deputy Assistant Secretary of State for European Affairs, provides a historical overview of U.S. policy toward Eastern Europe, identifying the common and changing elements in the long-standing U.S. policy of "differentiation" among the countries of Eastern Europe. He explains why, in spite of the policy's drawbacks, it is the only approach that can achieve sufficient domestic political support in the U.S. (Chapter 30).

Zbigniew Brzezinski, former National Security Advisor to President Jimmy Carter, traces the political and economic environments in the USSR-led "co-stagnation" sphere, spelling out implications for the United States. He concludes that the U.S. may be entering into a phase of unique opportunity to promote its political interests vis-à-vis both the USSR and Poland more effectively than it has up to now (Chapter 31).

Next, *Nicholas G. Andrews*, a former official of the U.S. State Department, assesses the effectiveness of the U.S. sanctions against Poland that were in force between 1982 and early 1987. He concludes that the negative impacts were probably greater than the positive ones and suggests that economic sanctions for political purposes should be used sparingly, only in last-resort situations (Chapter 32).

The last contribution (Chapter 33) is coauthored by *John P. Hardt* and *Jean F. Boone*, two staff members of the Congressional Research Service, who explain why Poland was treated preferentially by the U.S. during much of the postwar period, until the sanctions were imposed. They then detail several new policy initiatives to improve U.S.-Polish relations, some of which were taken during 1986-87, and others that remain possibilities for a future political agenda.

The reader should note that the tables and charts are numbered consecutively through the book. The lists of tables and charts give their locations.

PART I.

Overview of the Polish Economy: Causes and Consequences of the Crisis, Partial Recovery, Prospects

1

Partial Recovery from the Economic Crisis

Jim Prust

Overview

Poland suffered a well-publicized economic crisis in the late 1970s and early 1980s.[1] Its domestic economy fell into disarray and its external finances showed massive payments deficits. To outside observers the most striking feature was an escalating debt problem. Despite attempts from the mid-1970s onward to arrest the deterioration in Poland's economic situation, the debt-service ratio—the share of exports needed to pay the interest on total outstanding debt and to repay the principal due—reached an unmanageable 100 percent by 1980, and the external debt in convertible currencies rose to $24 billion in the same year.

During the early 1970s, the authorities launched a major drive toward investment and modernization, which relied heavily on imports from the West and was financed mainly by foreign borrowing. The resulting unprecedented surge in investment, output, and the standard of living proved unsustainable. Domestic expenditure was allowed to rise much more rapidly than output. The growth of exports, although relatively fast, did not keep pace with that of imports. By the middle of the decade, the trade deficit in convertible currencies reached about $3 billion annually, or the equivalent of 9 percent of gross domestic product (GDP).

From the mid-1970s onward the authorities took steps to restrain the growth of investment and imports. These measures had some effect on the convertible trade balance, but they were of little avail in restraining the current external deficit because of rapidly rising interest payments on a burgeoning external debt. Nonetheless, the cuts in investment and imports led, in a context of increasing shortages, to declining output from 1979 onward. In 1980 the authorities' attempts to raise prices in order to redress a growing financial disequilibrium provoked a major conflict between the labor movement and the government. Implementation of an agreement between the two parties, signed in August 1980, proved contentious. Industrial unrest persisted and output continued on a downward spiral. Meanwhile, the external-payments difficulties intensified and creditor confidence collapsed. Despite a continuing enforced contraction of imports and the start of debt-rescheduling operations, external-payments arrears became substantial.

Chart 1. Poland: Key Domestic Indicators, 1978-86

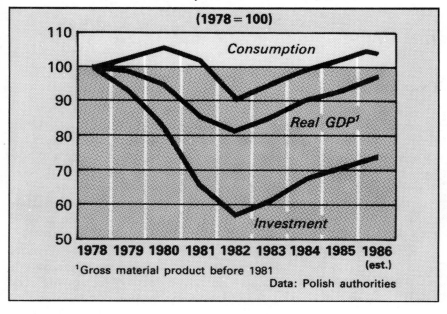

The experience of the 1970s left Poland with its domestic economy in disarray and with an acute external debt-servicing problem. By 1980, the external debt, in convertible currencies, which had been negligible ten years earlier, reached $24 billion—the equivalent of about three times current receipts in convertible currencies—and the debt-service ratio was almost 100 percent. Clearly an excessively rapid growth of demand had contributed to the country's problems. But on top of this, there was a widespread perception that the economy was characterized by more

Chart 2. Poland: Indicators of External Performance in Convertible Currencies, 1978-86

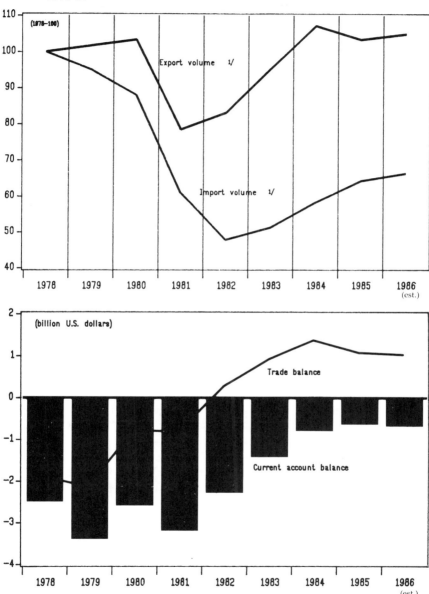

1/Includes trade under bilateral payments agreements with non-CMEAmembers.

Source: Polish authorities.

fundamental defects, including a poor selection of investment projects and undue delays in their completion.

Partial Recovery Since 1982

This was the background for a battery of policy changes and initiatives aimed at a fundamental reform of the economy. A substantial body of legislation was introduced in late 1981 and 1982 that sought to create a more decentralized economic system than had been in place for most of the postwar period. Under the reformed system, enterprises were to enjoy greater autonomy in output, investment, pricing, and other decisions and to ultimately be under the authority of their own workforces. The role of the central authorities would be confined mainly to the setting of macroeconomic targets and using "indirect" policy instruments. As an essential accompaniment, financial discipline was to be strengthened at the enterprise level by making it possible to liquidate unprofitable enterprises. Also, credit policy and the tax system were to be placed on a less discretionary basis.

With greater reliance on financial variables, price reforms were an integral part of the overall reform package. Many administered prices were changed, greatly reducing the need for budgetary subsidies. At the same time other prices were freed from administrative control. As a result, the price level doubled in 1982, which brought about sharp contractions in real incomes and expenditure, in the economy's real stock of liquidity, and in the budget deficit. The exchange system was also substantially modified. A single exchange rate for transactions in convertible currencies was introduced, which was set at a considerably more depreciated level than the average of the various rates that had previously been in effect. Exports were encouraged by means of a scheme whereby exporters could use a certain proportion of their foreign-exchange earnings to finance imports.

Since 1982 there has been a partial improvement in Poland's domestic and external economic situation (see Tables 1 and 2 at the end of the Chapter). After bottoming out in 1982, at a level almost 20 percent below its peak in 1978, gross output recovered fairly rapidly, growing 5-6 percent annually in the next two years. This recovery was led by the coal-mining sector, where the abatement of industrial unrest was a key factor. The growth rate slackened somewhat in 1985, partly as a result of an unusually severe winter. It picked up again in 1986 because of improved labor productivity—to a provisionally estimated 5 percent. Through 1984, the growth of domestic expenditure was held below that of output, and the rate of inflation declined progressively. In 1985-86, policies were relaxed somewhat; in turn, the real foreign balance on goods and services weakened, wage earnings grew rapidly, and inflation increased—to an estimated 17 percent in 1986.

The balance of payments in convertible currencies has improved significantly since 1982. In 1983-84 the improvement was underpinned by the relatively slow growth in domestic expenditure, which permitted a substantial rise in net exports to the convertible-currency area. Exports of coal and other raw materials increased rapidly, and the net deficit on trade in food and agriculture products continued to decline. As a result, the trade surplus grew from $0.3 billion in 1982 to $1.4 billion in 1984. Subsequently, with the short-run possibilities for boosting exports of primary products largely exhausted, export volume has broadly stagnated. The volume of imports, meanwhile, has continued to expand. Consequently, there was a decline in the trade surplus to about $1 billion in 1985-86. Despite the disappointing trade performance, the buoyancy of private transfers has allowed the current deficit to be confined at about $0.6 billion (equivalent to about 1 percent of 1986 GDP). Interest payment obligations in 1986 were $2.7 billion.

External Debt Problems Persist

A continuing current-account deficit, together with a drying up of new capital inflows, has left Poland unable to meet a large proportion of its external debt-service obligations since 1980. Five rescheduling agreements have been signed with commercial banks, providing total debt relief of some $8 billion. The latest, concluded in September 1986, covered maturities of the previously rescheduled debt due in 1986-87. These agreements have typically rescheduled 95 percent of the principal. In addition, under most of the agreements, a proportion of interest payments was effectively recycled through the provision of revolving trade credit facilities.

Three rescheduling agreements have also been concluded with Western official creditors under the auspices of the Paris Club, which provides total debt relief of about $15 billion. After an initial agreement in 1981, there was a hiatus in discussions with these creditors, to whom, by the end of 1984, some $11 billion of arrears and all principal and interest originally due in 1985 were signed during that year. Discussions have been held on the rescheduling of obligations due in 1986, but no agreement has yet been concluded.

In view of the capitalization of interest by official creditors, their share in Poland's total external debt in convertible currencies has risen in recent years. Western official creditors held almost two-thirds of the debt outstanding at the end of 1986 (about $33.5 billion), a large portion of which falls due for repayment in the 1990s. By the same token, the share of the Polish debt that is held by commercial banks has diminished. At the end of 1986, the banks held about 20 percent of the medium- and long-term debt, which had a somewhat shorter average maturity than the debt held by official creditors. Most of the remaining debt consists of claims held by the member countries and institutions of the Council for Mutual Economic Assistance (CMEA), Middle Eastern creditors, and commercial creditors.

Current Issues and Prospects

Despite the progress made in recent years, the Polish economy has not fully recovered from the crisis of the early 1980s. Domestic output remains below its precrisis peak. The standard of living has just about regained its level of the late 1970s, but this has been achieved at the expense of a major shift in the composition of expenditure away from investment. Consequently, the capital stock has become increasingly outmoded. Moreover, the speed with which it can be modernized is limited, because a substantial proportion of investment spending continues to be absorbed by uncompleted projects started in the precrisis years.

Poland's external financial situation is still dominated by difficulties in servicing debt in convertible currencies and by the prospect of heavy debt-repayment obligations extending well into the 1990s. At the same time, Poland is expected to begin reducing its indebtedness in nonconvertible currencies to its CMEA partners.

The challenge facing Polish policymakers is how to achieve both an improved standard of living and the needed modernization of the capital stock while also meeting a larger part of the country's external debt-service obligations. Reconciliation of these objectives will require far-reaching changes in economic policy to improve the economy's efficiency and to increase its export orientation. The economic reform program launched in 1981-82 was viewed as an important means of furthering these objectives. But after a number of significant policy changes were made, this program has proceeded more slowly than originally intended.

As a result, a broad range of prices has remained subject to control, and price distortions persist, notably for energy and various basic materials, foreign exchange, and capital. At the same time, the role of administrative mechanisms has remained substantial in the allocation of both key production inputs and finished goods. Enterprises generally do not yet enjoy the degree of autonomy originally envisaged, nor has it yet proved possible to subject the enterprises to the financial discipline that was to accompany their greater autonomy. Budgetary subsidies have indeed been greatly reduced in recent years, which reduces substantially the overall budget deficit. Even so, the budget remains a mechanism for considerable discretionary intermediation of resources, both through those subsidies that remain and differentiated effective rates of enterprise taxation.

To impart a new impetus to the reform program, the authorities have recently taken a number of measures, and they are well along in the formulation of others. These measures will form a "second stage" of the reform process.

One important aim of the new reform measures is to boost export incentives. An active exchange-rate policy is being pursued, and on February 1, 1987, the zloty was devalued by almost 20 percent against the basket of convertible currencies to which it is pegged; this followed a devaluation of a similar size in September 1986. At the same time, the scheme whereby imports may be financed through the proceeds of retained export has been modified; exporters now have legal ownership of the foreign exchange in question rather than simply having a priority claim on it. Further liberalization in the rules governing the use of retained foreign exchange is being considered. In addition, several institutional and legal steps to encourage foreign trade were taken in 1986, including the introduction of a new law on joint ventures with foreign partners and the establishment of an Export Development Bank.

On the domestic front, the Polish authorities plan further revisions in the price structure. This will entail substantial increases in the prices of energy and other basic materials, and greater freedom in price-setting procedures generally. In addition, the share of raw and basic materials subject to central allocation will be progressively reduced. As flanking measures, tighter financial and income policies are envisaged. In the immediate future, the government's program for 1987 calls for a cut in the rate of budgetary subsidies and the elimination of the budget deficit, a deceleration in the rate of credit expansion, and a reduction in real wages.

All of these measures are necessary to move Poland's economy toward a better balance between demand and supply in the domestic market, to increase its export orientation, and to ensure achievement of the aims of the recently approved Five-Year Plan for 1986-90. Increases in the labor force and in the supply of production inputs are expected to be relatively small during these years. Any growth in output must therefore depend largely on gains in efficiency. For this reason, the targeted annual growth rate in domestic output during the plan period—about 3.5 percent—is moderate by past standards. The growth of aggregate domestic expenditure is to be held somewhat below that of output, and investment is expected to rise faster than consumption.

Note

1. Reprinted, with minor alterations and updating by the author, from *IMF Survey*, February 23, 1987, with permission.

Table 1. Poland: Selected Domestic Indicators, 1980-86

(Percentage change unless otherwise indicated)

Indicator	1980	1981	1982	1983	1984	1985	Prov. 1986
	(In constant prices)						
Gross domestic product	−6.0	−10.0	−4.8	5.6	5.6	3.6	5.1
Consumption	2.1	−3.7	−11.0	5.1	4.6	3.2	4.9
Gross fixed investment	−12.3	−19.1	−13.7	8.8	9.8	4.4	4.3
Consumer prices	9.4	21.2	100.8	22.1	15.0	15.1	17.8
Average monthly wages in the socialized sector	13.4	27.3	51.3	24.5	16.3	18.8	20.4
	(In current prices)						
State budget balance (as a percentage of GDP)	−1.2	−11.4	−2.9	−2.1	−2.2	−1.2	−1.1
Money and quasi-money	13.0	24.0	36.7	14.5	18.7	24.2	25.1

Sources: Compiled by the IMF, based on Central Statistical Office, *Rocznik Statystyczny*, various issues; and data provided by the Polish authorities.

Table 2. Poland: Balance of Payments in Convertible Currencies,[1] 1980-86

Item	1980	1981	1982	1983	1984	1985	Prov. 1986
	(In Millions of U.S. Dollars)						
Current account	−2,586	−3,185	−2,272	−1,412	−774	−618	−665
Trade balance	−790	−822	268	916	1,380	1,088	1,035
Exports	7,364	4,971	4,543	4,806	5,324	5,120	5,316
Imports	−8,154	−5,793	−4,275	−3,890	−3,944	−4,032	−4,281
Services (net)	−2,449	−3,017	−2,858	−2,703	−2,616	−2,470	−2,644
Of which:							
Interest payment obligations[2]	(−2,463)	(−3,316)	(−3,031)	(−2,889)	(−2,729)	(−2,609)	(−2,734)
Transfer (net)	653	654	318	375	462	764	944
Medium- and long-term capital (net)	2,858	666	−3,021	−2,526	−1,844	245	−1,850
Principal repayment obligations[2]	−5,605	−6,037	−6,701	−4,242	−2,758	−2,391	−3,458
Drawings on loans	8,669	4,919	1,474	565	218	261	294
Debt relief[3]	(—)	2,111	2,208	1,154	779	2,387	1,530
Principal	(—)	(1,634)	(2,208)	(1,154)	(779)	(1,559)	(1,443)
Interest	(—)	(477)	(—)	(—)	(—)	(828)	(87)
Credit extended and other capital (net)	−206	−327	−2	−3	−83	−12	−216
Short-term capital and other items (net)	−674	−1,048	336	175	−141	99	−367
Overall balance	−402	−3,567	−4,957	−3,763	−2,759	−274	−2,882
Memorandum items:	(In Billions of U.S Dollars)						
External debt in convertible currencies (end of period)	24.1	25.4	26.5	26.4	26.9	29.7	33.5
Current account balance in nonconvertible currencies	−0.71	−1.21	−0.36	−0.35	−0.51	−0.53	−0.28
	(In Percent)						
Debt service ratio							
Based on accrued obligations	97	167	194	131	93	88	105
Based on actual payments	97	65	44	39	27	35	32
Current account balance in convertible currencies as percent of GDP	−4.6	−5.9	−3.5	−1.9	−1.0	−0.9	−0.9

Source: IMF Staff compilation from data provided by Polish authorities.
[1] Transactions within swing limits under bilateral payments agreements with non-CMEA countries are excluded.
[2] Before debt relief.
[3] Debt relief in a particular year as shown in this presentation refers only to the rescheduling of payments originally due in that year; debt relief in respect of arrears incurred in previous years is not shown. As regards debt relief from western official creditors, payments obligations are considered to have been rescheduled on signature of the relevant multilateral agreements rather than of the bilateral agreements with individual creditor countries.

2

The Economy Five Years After Martial Law

Keith Crane

Macroeconomic Performance

Current economic policy in Poland is partially dictated by the failures of the past. These have been notable. After recording significant increases in output in the early 1970s, the Polish economy suffered a drastic decline in output in both 1981 and 1982 (-12.0 and -5.5 percent, respectively).[1] This is the worst economic performance recorded by any industrial country since World War II. The decline in 1981 was due in part to sharp declines in hard-currency imports, but also because of the rigidities in the distribution system. As the quantity of intermediate goods available declined, the remainder were not allocated to their most efficient uses. Consequently, the decline in output in 1981 was greater than would otherwise have been the case.

Most of the decline took place directly after the declaration of martial law, in the first quarter of 1982. Martial law abruptly curtailed the economic upswing, especially noticeable in coal output, which had begun in October 1981. Part of the drastic fall in output in the first quarter of 1982 can be attributed to the imposition of martial law itself. Transportation and communication systems were subject to rigid controls, and some factories were closed for fairly long periods. The continued reduction in the level of hard-currency imports also contributed to the decline.

Recovery from the 1979-82 Polish recession, although slow, is continuing. Increases in net material product have averaged less than 5

13

percent per year since 1982. This is a low rate of growth for a country emerging from a recession, especially since Polish economic output has yet to regain its previous peak recorded in 1978. Output in all major sectors (industry, agriculture, and construction) has risen since 1982, although most of the rise in output in 1985-86 has occurred in industry, especially the machine-building sector. As noted by Michael Montias, part of these increases consists of "junk" industrialization: the production of machinery which is difficult if not impossible to sell on world markets because foreign substitutes are so much better. Thus the value of this type of production tends to be inflated in Polish statistics.

Because of the limited increases in economic output, consumption and investment have also failed to return to their previous peaks. Per-capita consumption is not expected to reach 1978 levels until the 1990s. Annual increases in real personal consumption between 1983 and 1986 have been moderate, averaging 4 percent per year (per-capita levels have been substantially less). Collective consumption has held up better; it presently exceeds 1978 levels. Investment, although increasing at a more rapid rate than consumption, is still little more than half the level of 1978.

Probably one of the more disappointing areas in macroeconomic policy for the Polish government has been in generating overall macroeconomic equilibrium. Although consumer price inflation has been high by historical standards, averaging 17.5 per year since 1983, the markets for consumer goods, especially automobiles and some other consumer durables, continue to be plagued by shortages. Equilibrium in markets for foodstuffs, on the other hand, has improved. The government has been able to abolish the rationing of a number of foods while maintaining fixed prices.

Another area in which Poland's macroeconomic performance has been disappointing, at least for its creditors, is the ruble and hard-currency current-account balances. The Soviet Union continues to permit Poland to run large deficits in bilateral trade. Poland is now the largest ruble debtor to the Soviet Union in the European CMEA and appears to be the only member which has not been forced to reduce its ruble trade deficit in recent years. Poland's other partners in the CMEA, with the exception of the GDR, are more hard-nosed than the Soviet Union. Their trade with Poland remains roughly in balance, or the deficit is on their side, not Poland's.

Poland has recorded a surplus in hard-currency trade since 1982, but it has never been large enough to pay the interest, let alone the principal due on the hard-currency debt. At their peak in 1985, hard-currency earnings covered 75 percent of interest payments owed; in 1986-87 the percentages were lower. Consequently, its hard-currency current account has remained in deficit. Because of Polish accounting idiosyncracies under which interest owed, but not paid, was not recorded,

Polish statistics did not list the actual size of the deficit until recently. Estimates indicate it has run $600-1,500 million a year since 1982.[2] Poland's creditors have responded to lack of payment by transforming interest into principal. As a consequence, Poland's hard-currency debt now exceeds $31.2 billion; in 1980 it was about $24 billion. My projections of the size of the debt in 1990, which are based on optimistic assumptions, run $36-37 billion.[3]

Economic Reform

The Polish government adopted a number of significant changes in the way it ran the economy after the imposition of martial law. Enterprise councils elected by employees were set up which ostensibly had the power to elect or at least veto the choice of manager (see Chapter 14 by Holland). Enterprises were to become self-financing, which implied that profits were to be pursued or, at the very least, losses avoided; otherwise, the enterprise could be closed. Moreover, the firm's future development was to be contingent on profitability: investment was to be financed from retained profits or bank loans granted on the basis of the expected rate of return. Ministerial controls on managers were to be reduced and, if possible, eliminated; managers were to be independent, accountable to the workers' council, and intent on increasing profits and value-added.

For this system to function efficiently, markets were to play a more important role in the economy. Prices of a large number of non-essential consumer goods and intermediate products were to be set by the market. Competition was to be encouraged. Enterprises were to be allowed to start production outside their traditional areas. Cooperatives, private individuals, local governmental units, and Poles overseas were allowed to set up enterprises in several industrial sectors.

Within this new system the role of the authorities was to change dramatically. Indirect indicators, such as the exchange rate, interest rates, taxes, and subsidies, were to be used to steer the economy. Most importantly, because of the change in the control of enterprises and managers' objectives, the government was no longer to assign plan targets to enterprises. Enterprises were to draw up their own plans, but managerial and employee bonuses were no longer tied to the fulfillment, as was previously the case. Although the role of the government in the economy was not to decline, it was supposed to change radically.

The reform has not been a success; whether it has been a total failure continues to be argued in both Poland and the West. Critics of the reform cite an impressive body of anecdotes and data to show that the reform has not operated as planned. Most telling are the continued role of the associations and ministries in the allocation of inputs and the lack of a rational system for the setting of prices. A very high percentage of inputs (over 50 percent by value) are rationed through quotas rather than distributed by markets. Consequently, an enterprise manager, if he hopes to get a fair share, has to stay within the good graces of the minister, association head, or other bureaucrat who controls these inputs. This state of affairs sharply limits a manager's freedom of action. Associations and branch ministries continue to be interested in output figures rather than profits. Enterprise managers are therefore forced to push for higher production rather than reducing costs or altering their production profile towards more profitable products. Moreover, the economic bureaucracy has tended to preserve the former structure of production, propping up loss-making firms by providing them with investment funds and subsidies and drastically circumscribing the role of the markets in the setting of prices and allocation of resources. Consequently, the efficiency gains which should have been generated by the reform have been much less than one would have expected, given the endemic waste in the Polish economy. On the other hand, some Polish firms have gone bankrupt; cost control and profitability have become more important. Some Polish economists and the leadership argue that there has been a change in managerial outlook.

The other major stumbling block to the reform has been the government's equivocal attitude toward prices. Much like the old system, prices are to provide a "fair" profit to the enterprise, reflecting costs but not demand. Moreover, some prices must be set at "fair" levels, otherwise the products are "too expensive." Consequently, prices of the most "important" consumer goods and raw materials are set by the government and are periodically revised, though only after a political struggle in the case of consumer goods. Manufactured goods are then set on a cost-plus basis, using fixed raw materials prices as a base.

This system continues to give Polish enterprises all the wrong signals. Food-processing plants often face problems of profitability because output prices remain controlled. Manufacturers of machinery and consumer durables have had more leeway in setting prices and have benefited from the fixed prices of their inputs. Consequently they have not faced a profitability squeeze. A decline in demand has yet to hurt enterprises because growth in the money supply, through the payment of subsidies to loss-making firms, has kept nominal demand growing, and price controls have prevented prices from equilibrating demand and supply in many markets. The resulting endemic excess demand has kept almost all enterprises profitable. The lack of a rational system of market-clearing prices has discouraged the government from relying more on profitability indicators in evaluating enterprises and has solidified the position of the branch ministries and associations, allowing them to use their influence to push managers to pursue ministerial rather than enterprise objectives.

The problem has been even more pronounced in the foreign-trade sector. Because of the overvaluation of the zloty, enterprises find hard-currency imports relatively cheap compared to domestically-produced inputs or those imported from the CMEA, when differences in the quality of goods between imports from the two groups are considered. Hard-currency exports are not as lucrative as sales on the domestic market, which is one reason why increases in manufactured exports have been slow and those of machinery have even declined.

On the other hand, some successes can be traced to the reform. The policy of treating private and state-owned farms more evenly and of easing restrictions on private farming while increasing procurement prices has been successful. During the first half of the 1980s, agriculture has performed better than all other sectors. Global output by private manufacturers has doubled in real terms since 1978, while the output of state-owned industry has declined. Anecdotal evidence indicates that some Polish enterprise managers have become more entrepreneurial and cost-conscious, and some workers' councils have a significant voice in running enterprises. Moreover, even if output statistics in the machinery sector have been inflated, productivity increases in Poland over the past four years have been substantial. They have accounted for almost all recorded growth. It would be difficult to explain these improvements without giving some credit to the economic reform, especially as enterprise managers have had somewhat greater freedom to set wages so as to reflect performance and to pursue more profitable areas of production.

Economic Policy and the Polish Government

The Polish government, like all governments, consists of and responds to groups of individuals with competing interests and goals. It is not surprising that it rarely speaks with one voice. Nonetheless, if Western economic leverage is to be effectively applied, some idea of the groups participating in economic policymaking, their goals, interests, and favored policies needs to be formulated so that the potential effects of various Western policy instruments on Polish economic policy can be better assessed.

Although the Poles are now more forthcoming in terms of leaking policy debates to the press, the policy positions and the relative importance of the various groups within the party, the government, and government-sponsored institutions are not always clear. Consequently, much of this section rests on inference and speculation. Nevertheless, the following actors appear to have pushed for policies which have either been adopted or have affected the implementation of official policy.

The First Party Secretary. Wojciech Jaruzelski and other leaders drawn from the military do not appear to have had a strong intellectual influence on the economic reform or the direction of economic policy. It is difficult to garner from their statements specific economic policies which they favor, other than more work discipline and better management. Jaruzelski has reiterated his firm opposition to any return to pre-Solidarity practices. This appears to imply that the government opposes a return to directive planning, as well as corruption—i.e., Jaruzelski strongly supports a different, "reformed" economic system. However, he does not seem to have a preference for a particular mix of markets and price controls on private and public enterprise. His role appears to be that of arbiter of competing policies within the government. This role has been taken over to some degree by Zbigniew Messner, since his appointment as Prime Minister.

The PUWP. It is difficult to find an area where the Polish United Workers Party (PUWP) has left a significant mark on the theoretical foundations of the reform. The Central Committee and the Secretariat appear to reflect the debates within the government concerning the direction of economic policy; both those favoring a more consistent implementation of the reform and those arguing for special dispensations for particular industries are represented on the Central Committee. Neither group is a consistent winner. The party as a whole probably favors tighter central controls, but no group within the party has produced a coherent alternative to the present muddled reform. The policy discussion at the 1986 Party Congress often centered around populist moves: criticizing price "gouging" in the private sector and calling for more discipline and tighter links between wages and output.

The Reformers. Władysław Baka, president of the National Bank, was formerly special minister for the implementation of the reform. His public statements indicate that he has a healthy respect for the market and advocates a greater use of market prices within the Polish economy and a tougher line vis-à-vis loss-making enterprises. He also appears to be aware of the need to rationalize the price system. His views appear to be supported in part by the Ministry of Finance and the Association of Polish Economists.

Both the Ministry of Finance and the Central Bank have important roles in the reform. They have taken over much of the authority previously given to the branch ministries. The Ministry of Finance controls prices and sets tax and subsidy rates. Because it is also concerned with balancing the budget, it places a much greater emphasis on profitability and and a smaller emphasis on investment and production than the branch ministries. These emphases contribute to the push for reform. Because the Central Bank provides the finance for investment, it is concerned with the rate of return of projects and the financial health of enterprises. Thus it has a much stronger interest in efficiency and reform than other governmental agencies.

The Regulators. The Ministry of Finance, in its role as price controller, and the Ministry of Labor, Wages and Social Affairs have been most concerned with wage inflation. They have been active in introducing new regulations and directives to limit wage increases. Many of these regulations are inconsistent with a market-type reform and consequently are detrimental to the prospects of successfully improving the system.

The Metal Eaters. Vice-Premier Szałajda has been identified as a supporter of the heavy-industry lobby. This group is especially concerned with the continued flow of investments to heavy industry. Consequently, these individuals often support recentralization because of the increased likelihood of greater investment in their preferred industrial branches. In recent years several initiatives have emerged from the Ministry of Mining and Power and from the Ministry of Metallurgy and Engineering to recentralize the control of enterprise in their industries. The most recent of these efforts is an attempt to force enterprises in the electronics industry to join a centrally-controlled association.[4]

The New Unions. The new government-sponsored labor unions have, like the party but more successfully, adopted a populist approach. They have argued for continued subsidies and central guarantees on wage rates for particular job categories, a move which would limit enterprise autonomy in setting wages. At times they have also clashed with the workers' councils over prerogatives. They generally oppose greater use of markets and broader autonomy for enterprises and favor price controls on consumer goods.

The Foreign Trade Constituency. The Ministry of Foreign Trade, in conjunction with the Foreign Trade Bank, is the body most concerned with Poland's external balance. The Ministry has pushed for more incentives for hard-currency exports and has played an important role in permitting enterprises to retain hard-currency earnings in special accounts. Enterprise managers are supposedly free to use these accounts as they wish.[5] The Ministry of Foreign Trade has also pushed for continued devaluations of the zloty. It has generally supported efforts to decentralize the economy and rely more on market prices, especially world-market prices.

Primary and Secondary Policy Goals

In 1982 the policy goals of the Polish authorities were obvious. The first was the suppression of Solidarity, which was accomplished by the imposition of martial law, the arrest of most of the organization's leaders, and the breakup of strikes. The next order of business was to increase output. The sharp price increases in January 1982 helped restore equilibrium on some intermediate and consumer-goods markets. Because Polish farmers could now purchase goods that were previously in short supply, this move probably contributed to the increase in agricultural output that was recorded in 1982. Lengthening the work week in the mines, coupled with higher output bonuses, helped increase the production of coal and some minerals and metals. The expansion of the private sector led to a rapid increase in privately-produced output and probably removed some bottlenecks. The introduction of the economic reform may also have contributed to a more rational use of capacity and labor and increased output.

These two policy goals, the suppression of Solidarity and the restoration of economic growth, were achieved by the end of 1982. They have remained the primary goals for the Polish government. However, other and often conflicting secondary goals have since emerged. Government vacillation in choosing among them has contributed to the lack of success of the economic reform and has engendered a series of continuing problems. These secondary goals include:

—Increasing economic efficiency;
—Attaining single digit levels of inflation;
—Attaining market equilibrium;
—Maintaining real wages among politically sensitive groups;
—Preventing unemployment;
—Increasing investment; and
—Servicing the debt.

Single Digit Inflation, Economic Efficiency, and Market Equilibrium. The rapid rates of inflation in recent years (averaging over 20 percent since 1982) have been highly unpopular with most of the people. It is not clear whether this reflects the perception (or reality) of declining real incomes or discontent with fluctuating prices after years of relative price stability. In any event, it is not surprising that reducing the inflation rate has been an important policy goal.[6]

The government has pursued this goal by placing price controls on many consumer goods and attempting to control wage increases through central directives. The Ministry of Finance and the Ministry of Labor, Wages and Social Affairs have been most concerned with wage inflation. They have concentrated on directives to limit wage increases, including regulations that prohibit workers in high demand from changing jobs for higher rates of pay. This regulation has been less than successful. The Ministry of Domestic Trade and Services has shared responsibility for prices with the Ministry of Finance. They have relied heavily on fixed and administrative prices to limit inflation.

Rarely has the government displayed the patience to rely on market forces to lower prices. For example, on February 1, 1982, the first day enterprises were given the leeway to increase prices in the reformed system, newly posted prices for appliances and automobiles were several times higher than before. The next day these prices were promptly halved, not because of market forces but through government intervention.

More recently, some sections of the government, especially the Ministry of Finance and the Central Bank, have focused on market equilibrium as a policy goal. They note the very high efficiency costs of allocating goods through queues, ration cards, and administrative fiat rather than through markets, and that these costs impose a major barrier to more rapid economic growth. They also argue that inflation can be better reduced by decreasing the rate of the creation of money.

Such a policy will encounter substantial political opposition. Inflation has remained high in Poland because the national budget deficit has been large and financed by the creation of money. To close the budget deficit would imply sharp reductions in subsidies, the largest single budget category, or increases in taxes. Because most of the subsidies go to keep down the costs of food, public transportation, energy, and raw materials, a reduction in subsidies would lead to an increase in food or transport prices or large input price increases for enterprises. The former angers consumers; the latter endangers the financial health of numerous manufacturing enterprises and, it is feared, will set off a round of cost-plus inflation as increased input costs are passed along in final output prices.

Another area earmarked for cuts is discretionary subsidies and tax rebates. Because prices in Poland are still subject to controls, enterprise managers can reasonably argue that the financial condition of their enterprise is due to government regulations, not their own inefficiency. This has led to the proliferation of tax exemptions and subsidies; an enterprise's financial performance has come to depend far more on its manager's ability to bargain with the Ministry of Finance into granting an exemption than on improving efficiency.

A fierce political battle is raging over these exemptions. Everyone agrees that they are bad, but no one is willing to dispose of them. Consequently, the Ministry of Finance and the National Bank are under constant pressure to reduce exemptions in general, but to grant them in particular cases. Some progress has been made in making regulations more uniform in 1985 and 1986, but in light of the Hungarian experience, one would have to be very optimistic to believe that exemptions will not continue to characterize the Polish financial system.

Unemployment and a Politically-Determined Wage Structure. One reason why exemptions and enterprise-specific subsidies have been so widespread appears to have been the fear of unemployment on the part of some policymakers in the central government and the desire to placate politically important groups of workers, such as miners and workers in the steel and shipbuilding industries. Unemployment was a concern at the inception of the reform. Early retirement was offered to all Poles working in state-owned enterprises at that time; a large number of Poles took advantage of the offer. Almost immediately enterprises began to complain of labor shortages, and the labor market has been tight ever since.

Unemployment has not been a problem because the central authorities have been loath to threaten firms with bankruptcy. A bankruptcy law was signed only in 1985. The first victim of the law was a small metal-fabricating firm in Zabrze in Upper Silesia. Until 1987 when Budapol, a large construction firm in Warsaw, came under fire, no major firm has been at risk. If the central authorities do decide to impose a "harder budget constraint" on enterprises, this problem may resurface, especially in areas with only a few enterprises or in the case of a large enterprise in financial difficulties. So far the central authorities indicate they will bail out any firm with financial problems whose closure could generate political problems.

A more pressing problem has been wages. The central authorities have intervened repeatedly in the labor market with little regard for economic consequences. At the end of 1982, a year when consumer prices doubled, the government granted a substantial unilateral wage increase which covered almost all workers in the economy (Table 1). Before this increase, equilibrium was beginning to emerge in a number of consumer-goods markets; afterward, shortages reappeared and excess demand increased, but the government felt that the increases in nominal incomes would reduce political unrest. To some extent, it may have been right.

The government has also been adept at targeting specific groups for wage increases. It is no accident that wages in coal mining are higher in real terms than they were before the recession. Workers in other industries in which Solidarity was strong—ferrous metals and transport equipment—have also continued to receive better-than-average treatment in terms of wages. Pensioners, bureaucrats, and social-service workers (teachers, hospital workers, etc.) have experienced the largest declines in real incomes. Although some of the increased differentials between coal miners and other workers may have been economically warranted, political reasons also appear to have been of importance.

Investment. Much of the burden of adjustment to the decline in output and closing the trade deficit has fallen on investment. Levels of investment, in constant prices in 1985, were roughly half those recorded in 1978. Enterprise managers now complain of decapitalization, as machinery and equipment have worn out and not been replaced. Government and party leaders also voice concern about the widening technological gap between Poland and other countries.

The suggested solution to this problem has been the same as that voiced ever since the imposition of central planning in Poland after World War II: more investment. It is one that has not been successful in the past and will probably be unsuccessful in the future. It has been difficult to generate the resources needed for this policy within the confines of the current economic and political system.

The economic reform envisages greater enterprise-management accountability and more self-reliance in terms of investment. If managers believe that the enterprise will be bailed out if the investment goes awry and if managers continue to be rewarded on the basis of the size of the enterprise they manage, rather than profits, the motivation to embark on large, new investment projects will remain strong. This appears to have been the case up to now.

Consequently, the government has had to control the quantity of investments, since demand responds poorly to market signals. Control is exercised through the national bank by vetting loan applications (ostensibly on the basis of their expected rates of return and the financial strength of the enterprise), or through direct investment grants from the budget. The latter, which has been greatly reduced in Hungary, still account for over one-third of investment in Poland. Their continued importance means that the government controls most investment decisions. This state of affairs bodes ill for a surge in the efficiency of capital investment and thus for an acceleration in economic growth.

Servicing the Debt. This policy goal is discussed last because the leadership appears to have given it the lowest priority among the secondary policy objectives. In contrast to the GDR or Hungary, where a concerted effort was made to get their financial houses in order, or in Romania, where debt repayment was given high priority, the Poles are still engaged in reschedulings of both guaranteed and unguaranteed debts. After an initial sharp reduction in the hard-currency account deficit in 1982-83, the deficit has begun to widen again; the debt continues to increase. Although part of the problem is the sheer size of the debt, Poland's recent lack of progress in reducing the current-account deficit probably stems from the low priority given to debt service. This probably reflects the political pressure to improve the standard of living (see Chapter 13 by Kamecki) as well as the readily-available excuse of Western economic sanctions. Moreover, the constituency within the government which has pushed to accord debt service a higher priority appears to be confined to a few individuals within the national bank and the Ministry of Foreign Trade. Other interests have had a much more important voice in government decision making.

Although I perceive little push in Poland to balance the hard-currency current account, the declared policy of reorienting Polish trade toward the CMEA does not appear to have been pursued with any conviction. Hard-currency exports continue to be given a higher priority than ruble exports. Most exports of "hard" goods (coal, foodstuffs, minerals, etc.) continue to go to the West, and factory managers are more highly rewarded for increasing hard-currency exports than ruble exports.

Since 1982, ruble imports have held up much better than hard-currency imports. This is not surprising, due to the Soviet Union's willingness to let Poland run ruble trade deficits. On average, Poland's ruble exports since 1982 have also increased more rapidly than hard-currency exports, but in 1983-84, hard-currency exports posted the more rapid rates of increase. Poland has enacted new joint-venture legislation to encourage Western firms to invest in Poland, and continues to welcome—although in a less friendly fashion than in the immediate aftermath of martial law—the investments of expatriate Poles. These are not actions taken by a government determined to sharply reduce its economic ties with the West. Rather, they reflect Poland's attempts to adjust to its severe balance-of-payments problems.

Notes

1. The figures cited here and below are taken from *Statistical Yearbook,1985* or *Statistical Bulletin* (both in Polish), unless otherwise specified.

2. *East-West*, no. 128, November 28, 1986, p. 8.

3. Keith Crane, *Polish Balance of Payments and Output in 1990: Alternative Scenarios*, P-7157, The RAND Corporation, Santa Monica, 1985.

4. This initiative by the minister of metallurgy and engineering was voted down by the enterprise managers in the industry.

5. During 1982-87 enterprises received the right to repurchase hard currency from export proceeds; since 1987, enterprises own the hard currency. Under the new system, the enterprises can only exercise their former rights of purchase over the course of the next five years. Although enterprises now have stronger legal rights to keep part of their hard-currency earnings, the new rules have actually made it impossible for enterprises to exercise rights to purchase over $1.5 billion of claims built up under the old system.

6. Władysław Baka, "Some Thoughts on the Economy and Sound Money," *Contemporary Poland*, 1986, no. 11, pp. 9-12.

3

Why Poland Lost Its Creditworthiness

Włodzimierz Siwiński

The Polish crisis that began in the late 1970s has been the deepest economic crisis in postwar Europe. Since 1983 we have seen some modest improvement, but the crisis is far from resolution, although there are reasons to believe that in some way it will continue for several years. The solution is constrained by the difficulties that Poland faces in servicing its large foreign debt.

There is no simple explanation for the reasons that caused the deep and prolonged crisis. The basic explanation lies in the unique combination of mistaken economic policies and the inefficiency of the centrally-planned economic (CPE) system. Although adverse external developments aggravated Poland's balance-of-payments position, they are hardly at the root of the problem. There is no doubt that the Polish crisis has its roots in domestic developments.

During the 1960s, economic performance deteriorated, compared with that of the late 1950s and early 1960s. By the end of the 1960s the weaknesses of the traditional CPE system became quite clear.[1] The long-lasting stagnation of personal real incomes, combined with the prospect of the large price increases that were declared in December 1970 by the party leadership, led to labor unrest—for neither the first nor the last time in the postwar period.

The New Economic Strategy of Gierek

Gierek, who replaced Gomułka in 1970 as the party leader, profoundly changed the economic strategy and made its main goal an improvement of the standard of living. To do this, the rate of growth of output had to be accelerated and made more dependent on improvements in productivity rather than on increases in the quantity of inputs. This in turn required economic modernization.

The Polish authorities conceived expansion of economic links with the West as a leading factor in this strategy. The Poles expected imports of Western technology, financed by the Western credits, to increase the production of modern manufactures, stimulate the growth of national income, and increase the standard of living. They also expected that the influx of modern technology would help generate the exports needed for the repayment of foreign credits. Foreign credits supplemented domestic savings and enabled the authorities to simultaneously increase the investment required for modernization and consumption, which are necessary to provide incentives for labor.[2] One economist called this strategy an import- and consumption-led growth.[3]

Economic Policy Misguided

Considering Poland's earlier policies of economic isolation from the West, the new strategy triggered a dramatic shift in foreign economic policy. In substance, the strategy was feasible and promising, as suggested by the experiences of many countries, especially those of the so-called newly industrializing countries. But in Poland, the economic policy based on this strategy was ill-designed and badly implemented.

First, the authorities mistakenly believed that they could implement the strategy without significant changes in the economic system. The attempt to reform the Polish economy undertaken in 1973 was abandoned two years later, and most of the decentralizing measures were canceled. To some degree the retreat reflected the pressure of an economic policy that required too much expansion. This rapid expansion caused inflationary pressures, with all the resulting tensions, shortages, and inefficiencies, and created an inauspicious environment for the introduction of market-oriented reforms.[4] Nevertheless, the decisive factor preventing the economic reform was the lack of political will and the resistance of the party bureaucracy to introduce it. As a result, basic features of the traditional CPE system remained unchanged. It did not support the development of the export of manufactures. Such exports lagged behind Poland's rapidly increasing imports, which, in turn, contributed to increased indebtedness.

Second, the strategy was overexpansionary and exceeded the capacity of the economy to implement it. Rapidly rising domestic expenditure (investments plus consumption) was much higher than domestic production; the large disequilibrium was financed from external sources. In the 1970s capital accumulation increased to more than 30 percent of the national income, reaching 38 percent in 1975,[5] a very high level by the standard of any country. The huge sum of investments exceeded the country's capacity to construct and install the investment projects and contributed to many bottlenecks in the material, especially in the machine-building sectors. As a result, a large number of investment projects were begun but not completed during this period. In 1981 the value of investment projects already begun was 4.4 times the value of total investment spending in the same year.[6] This means that if all investment spending was committed to projects that were already begun, it would have taken more than 4 years to complete them without any possibility of undertaking new projects (assuming an unchanged investment level)! It substantially diminished the efficiency of the whole investment program and reduced Poland's ability to generate export earnings. At the same time, since many investment projects were based on Western technology, Poland was forced to make a large expenditure on licenses, know-how, machinery and equipment, and intermediary inputs.

Consumer spending, prompted by the very high growth rate of personal incomes, also expanded too quickly. During 1970-80 nominal personal incomes increased by more than 200 percent, whereas the national net material product distributed rose only 71 percent,[7] a figure well above planned levels. The ensuing inflation was suppressed through the administrative control of many prices; price increases were tolerated in certain less sensitive areas. The prices of basic products, most notably food, remained stable. Social pressures forced the authorities (in December 1970 by Gomułka and in June 1976 by Gierek) to reverse attempts to raise the price of staples. This caused many shortages and bottlenecks and generated pressure to increase imports and decrease exports. Agriculture, which used to be a large net contributor to the hard-currency trade balance, became a huge drain on the trade balance (as documented in Chapter 4 by Boyd, with the policy background explored in Chapter 5 by Andrews). The overexpansionary strategy induced strains in the balance of payments and generated the large external spending that exceeded the economy's ability to finance it. The temporary solution was the accumulation of foreign debt.

Third, the strategy was poorly coordinated. Effective central coordination is a crucial factor in planned economies, in which the market plays a limited role in the allocation of resources. During the 1970s the authority of the center gradually disintegrated. Fighting among factions within the Party weakened the Party's ability to manage central coordination. Many high-level appointees were neither experts nor good administrators. One result of this was the lobbying of local and sectoral interests, almost without any limit on starting new investments and production projects. The soft budget constraint released them from assuming responsibility for their actions. The informal bargaining processes, characteristic of CPEs generally, assumed extreme importance in Poland; political and personal connections with top decision makers played a more important role than considerations of efficiency.

As a result, the allocation of investments was inappropriate and inefficient. As much as 75-80 percent of investments was devoted to new projects, a policy that neglected the modernization of existing plants. Strong priority was given to the production of investment goods and heavy industry. The electro-machine industry, metallurgy, and energy attracted more than 61 percent of total investments in industry.[8] Low priority was given to export-oriented projects. The strategy, then, was one of import substitution.

The authorities also mismanaged the acquisition of foreign licenses. According to a governmental report, 20 percent of the 428 licenses obtained during 1971-80 were never used, and 10 percent were unjustified in view of domestic alternatives.[9] In many cases the technology was quite inefficient. The flow of new technology was mostly in the form of finished products, thus neglecting subcontractors and intermediary inputs. As a result, the structure of production was unbalanced and could operate only with large imports of intermediate products, aggravating the negative balance of payments. Planners soon lost control over investment outlays, imports, wage increases, technology transfers, and, eventually, the level of foreign debt.

Poland's highest priority was incorrectly assigned to production for the domestic market. A wide range of sectoral priorities was specified: essential consumption goods, motorization, and investment goods generally. At the same time, many sectors were neglected, such as export production, which was often paid lip service but was never at the top of the list. In CPEs, exports are considered a "necessary evil" to pay for imports. For enterprises, exports were never a coveted business. Foreign-trade policy sowed the seeds of its own destruction because it was based on import-led growth without the promotion of exports. During the 1970s, external equilibrium was never the highest priority for economic policy. It was treated, rather, as a residual, determined largely by import needs and the availability of external finance.

Another serious flaw in economic policy was the isolation of the domestic economy from external developments, despite the growing importance of foreign commercial relations. In traditional CPEs the state monopoly on foreign trade checks the direct impact of world markets on domestic producers and consumers. Domestic prices are not related to the foreign market, and external trade is conducted only by authorized state agencies. Therefore, adjustments to developments on foreign markets is not automatic, as in market economies, but can be imposed only through the central planners. In Poland during the 1970s, this adjustment was deliberately delayed for many reasons. Despite rising energy prices and the ensuing Western recession, the excessively high rate of growth of domestic output and consumption were maintained and facilitated by foreign borrowing. The decision was apparently based on a misjudgment of the nature and persistence of the external shocks to the world economy. The adjustment undertaken in the late 1970s was inconsistent, ill-designed, and ineffective. This was due, in part, to the weakening control of the central authorities.

Shortcomings of the Economic System

The policymakers who designed and implemented the wrong economic policy bear the main responsibility for the crisis that erupted in Poland. But behind this policy was an economic system that did not force any adjustment and did not create the right incentives. It is worth noting some of the often-cited causal links to Poland's debt crisis.

The CPE system has no mechanism to generate the efficient allocation of resources. The "soft budget constraint" enables inefficient producers not only to survive but to prosper without any incentives for efficiency.[10] Distorted prices give wrong signals for resource allocation. Firms have insufficient incentives for saving on costs, improving technology, developing exports, or the efficient substitution of imports. Such systemic features hindered the efficient utilization of the large investments, including that of Western technology and foreign credits, and impaired export capabilities.

In CPE systems producers operate in a noncompetitive environment. Enterprises are oriented toward vertical links with the authorities and focus their energies on the management of a highly bureaucratic and politicized bargaining process. On world markets they have to operate in a competitive environment, one with no great distinction between the domestic and global market. This explains why Polish producers have such difficulty with competition on foreign markets and why they prefer to sell on the domestic market.

The CPE system allows enterprises as well as the authorities to ignore, for the time being, the constraints imposed by market forces, because producers and consumers are almost completely isolated from external influences. Domestic prices are not affected by world market prices. No direct market process forces them to adjust to external developments; such an adjustment can be implemented only by central planners. Nevertheless, in the 1970s it was possible to rely on foreign credits to finance the external imbalances and to postpone the necessary adjustment. There was no effective response to the growing foreign debt until it became unmanageable. Then the unwillingness of creditors to extend new money forced a much more costly and painful adjustment than if it would have been undertaken earlier and voluntarily.

External Developments

The "new economic strategy" was adversely affected by a series of external disturbances related to changes of the conditions abroad of price and demand.[11] The increase of oil prices contributed to the deterioration of Polish terms of trade, especially within the Council of Mutual Economic Assistance (CMEA). Nevertheless, the full impact of these shocks was delayed by the price rules of the CMEA. Also, Poland, as a coal exporter, suffered much less than did countries with more limited energy resources.

Polish exports were also hurt by the sluggish demand in the OECD (Organization for Economic Cooperation and Development) countries, especially during the second half of the 1970s, when conditions deteriorated because of the recession and because of the growing competition from the group of newly industrializing developing countries. Poland had a limited capability to respond to the tougher conditions of demand.

During the 1970s the availability and real (inflation-adjusted) costs of credits on the international market favored the borrowers. But the anti-inflationary policy adopted in the U.S. and other developed countries, combined with an increased perception of risk by the lenders, led to large increases in the real rate of interest, which in turn contributed to the mounting burden of debt service. Because of its large foreign debt, Poland suffered very much, as noted in Chapter 20 by So*i*daczuk.

To be sure, external developments can always hurt a country's payment position. Unless a country chooses complete economic isolation and is willing to suffer its adverse consequences, it is not possible to avoid external disturbances. Nevertheless, each country should attempt to absorb external shocks at the lowest possible costs. Polish policymakers did not apply adequate and effective measures to avoid the balance-of-payments crisis that destroyed the country's external creditworthiness. The implications and future scenarios of when and how it will be possible to restore Poland's creditworthiness is the main focus of this book.

Notes

1. Włodzimierz Brus, *General Problems in the Functioning of a Socialist Economy* (in Polish) (Warsaw, 1961).

2. Zbigniew Fallenbuchl, "The Economic Crisis in Poland and Prospect for Recovery," in *East European Economies: Slow Growth in the 1980s*, Selected Papers Submitted to the Joint Economic Committee, U.S. Congress, Vol. 2 (Washington, D.C., 1986).

3. Domenico Mario Nuti, "The Polish Crisis: Economic Factors and Constraints," in Jan Drewnowski, editor, *Crisis in East European Economy* (New York, 1982), p. 30.

4. Włodzimierz Brus, "The Political Economy of Polish Reforms," *Praxis International*, July 1985; and Ibid.

5. *Concise Statistical Yearbook 1985* (in Polish) (Warsaw, 1985).

6. Ibid.

7. Ibid.

8. "Government Report on the State of the Economy," (in Polish) *Trybuna Ludu*, 1981, p. 126.

9. Ibid.

10. Paul Marer, "Economic Policies and Systems in Eastern Europe and Yugoslavia: Commonalities and Differences," in *East European Economies: Slow Growth in the 1980s.*

11. Ibid.

4

Agriculture and the Debt Crisis

Michael L. Boyd

Although agriculture could contribute significantly to the overall development of the Polish economy, it was an important factor in the crisis of the trade deficit of the 1970s and early 1980s. This chapter examines the ways in which the agricultural sector contributed to the general decline in the international financial position of Poland.

During the 1970s, as part of its program to improve the standard of living, the government promoted an increase in livestock production by raising purchase prices from producers. At the same time, it stimulated an increase in the consumption of livestock products by maintaining low prices for consumers. Investment in agriculture suffered in comparison to other sectors; it was directed almost entirely to state farms, and the needs of the more numerous private farmers were neglected. Much of the investment in improved technology went to the construction of large-scale livestock operations, which relied heavily on imports from the West, both for their basic capital stock and for important variable inputs that cannot be grown in Poland, such as fodder concentrates and other feeds.[1] Therefore, the government sought to improve the standard of living—in particular, the level of meat consumption—by an increased reliance on imports. As the supply of foodstuffs could not keep up with the rapidly growing demand, the import of both agricultural goods and agricultural technology increased rapidly to meet the current requirements of consumption.

Until 1974, a combination of good weather and increased incentives resulting from the relaxation of certain restrictions on private farmers led to growth in production and the maintenance of the role of agriculture as, on average, a trade surplus sector. The figures in Table 3 are typical; agriculture contributed three-fourths of Poland's hard-currency trade surplus. The situation began to change in 1975, when a combination of poorly implemented domestic policies and changing global market conditions caused agriculture to become a chronic trade-deficit sector. Hard-currency deficits rose from about $500 million in 1975 to over $2 billion in 1981. (Table 3). The hard-currency deficit in agricultural technology increased until the late 1970s, but the largest increase was in the net import of agricultural products, rising from $520 million in 1975 to over $1.2 billion in 1981. Also, a deterioration in Poland's trade surplus in processed foods indicates how domestic policies led to far greater increases in the final demand for, than in the supply of, foodstuffs.

Table 4 shows the contribution of the large and growing hard-currency deficits in Poland's agriculture-related trade to the increase in its external debt. The last row of Table 4 computes trade deficits that are related to agriculture as a percentage of the annual increments to Poland's hard-currency debt during 1975-81. In 1975, the agricultural trade deficit was 18 percent of the increase in the total hard-currency debt. This figure rose to 25 percent in 1976, to 38 percent in 1978, and soared

Table 3. Poland's Net Exports, Total and Agricultural, 1970 and 1975-81

(Millions of U.S. Dollars)

	1970	*1975*	*1976*	*1977*	*1978*	*1979*	*1980*	*1981*
Total Trade								
Total	−60	−2,254	−2,851	−2,351	−1,976	−1,337	−2,090	−2,320
Agriculture								
Total	−11	−805	−1,039	−1,082	−1,223	−1,373	−2,040	−2,697
Food products	+149	+188	+221	+22	+146	−1	−190	−918
Agricultural commodities	−88	−588	−850	−684	−983	−928	−1,371	−1,303
Investment goods for agriculture	−72	−404	−410	−419	−386	−445	−479	−477
Trade with Non-Socialist Countries								
Total	+147	−2,671	−2,931	−2,154	−1,890	−1,689	−980	+26
Agricultural								
Total	+111	−506	−887	−812	−998	−1,170	−1,526	−2,090
Food products	+168	+159	+195	+44	+164	+13	−100	−666
Agricultural commodities	−43	−520	−854	−659	−926	−918	−1,297	−1,235
Investment goods for agriculture	−14	−144	−228	−196	−236	−264	−129	−189

* Figures may not sum to total due to rounding.

Source: *Statistical Yearbook of Agriculture and Agricultural Economy 1982*[2]

Table 4. Poland's Hard-Currency Debt and the Agricultural Trade Deficit, 1975-81

(Billions of U.S. Dollars)

	1975	*1976*	*1977*	*1978*	*1979*	*1980*	*1981*
1. Total hard-currency debt	7.6	11.2	14.3	16.9	23.1	22.8	24.3
2. Increment to hard-currency debt	2.8	3.6	3.1	2.6	6.2	– .03	1.5
3. Total trade deficit	2.7	2.9	2.2	1.9	1.7	1.0	– .03
4. Agricultural trade deficit	0.5	0.9	0.9	1.0	1.2	1.5	2.1
5. (4)/(2) x 100 (%)	18	25	26	38	19	– 500	140

Sources: Table 3 and Fallenbuchl.[3]

to 140 percent in 1981. Between 1975 and 1981, Poland's cumulative, hard-currency trade deficit from the agricultural sector was $8 billion. During the same period the hard-currency debt increased by $19.5 billion. Thus, policies in or relating to agriculture accounted for 41 percent of the large increment in debt during 1975-81. These figures indicate that the agricultural policies of the Gierek regime, detailed in the next chapter, contributed materially to a decline of the domestic agricultural sector, to an increase in that sector's drain on Poland's international finances, and to the increase in hard-currency indebtedness.

On the other side of the coin we find that improved agricultural policies and performance could play a major role in regaining creditworthiness. That the authorities in Poland are aware of this is suggested by the Rzeszów agreement of 1981. It promotes basic reforms, including continued recognition of the right of private farmers to exist and to have improved access to land, investment funds and machinery, and markets.[4] Although some developments since 1983 indicate the willingness of the authorities to move in these directions, it remains an open question whether a sufficiently strong, long-term commitment to reform will be made that will allow the Poles to realize the full benefits of such changes. Improvements in the agricultural-trade balance during 1983-85 suggest that progress is being made, but we cannot yet make final conclusions.

Notes

1. Zbigniew Landau and Jerzy Tomaszewski, *The Polish Economy in the Twentieth Century* (New York, 1985), pp. 304-306.

2. Główny Urząd Statystyczny (Central Statistical Office) *Statistical Yearbook of Agriculture and Agricultural Economy 1982* (in Polish) (Warsaw 1983), p. 326.

3. Zbigniew M. Fallenbuchl, "The Economic Crisis in Poland and Prospects for Recovery," in *East European Economies: Slow Growth in the 1980s* (Washington, D.C., 1986), pp. 359-398; and Ibid.

4. Edward Cook, "Prospects for Polish Agriculture in the 1980s," in *East European Economies: Slow Growth in the 1980s.* volume 3, *Country Studies on Eastern Europe and Yugoslavia; Papers Submitted to the Joint Economic Committee, Congress of the United States* (Washington, D.C, 1986), pp. 471-472.

5

Political and Ideological Factors in Agricultural Policy

Nicholas Andrews

Since World War II, political and ideological factors have played a key role in the formation of Polish agricultural policy. In times of political crisis, pressures on agriculture in the private sector eased, and private farmers benefited. This was certainly true in 1956, when party leader Gomułka, consolidating his leadership, permitted private farmers to withdraw from the collectives.

The foundations of agricultural policy, as formulated after 1956 by the Polish United Workers Party (PUWP) and its coalition partner, the United Peasants' Party, were directed toward the rapid growth of production, the gradual transformation of the social structure in favor of the socialized sector, and a rise in the standard of living of farmers to the level prevailing outside agriculture.

Relieved of the immediate threat of collectivization, private farmers were still subject to the state's legislation and its administrative decisions. Their behavior was strongly influenced by the state's attitude toward agriculture in general and the private sector in particular. Furthermore, they watched carefully how the state manipulated the price structure for agricultural and industrial goods and reacted accordingly.

In the crisis of 1970-71, after Gomułka was replaced by Gierek, private farmers welcomed the new leader's decision to discontinue compulsory deliveries of agricultural goods and the increase in the state's purchase prices for those goods. In April 1971, the PUWP and the United Peasants' Party reaffirmed the principles of their post-1956 policy.[1] In June 1971, the prime minister told the PUWP Central Committee's Tenth Plenum that everything possible would be done to increase the output of all agricultural sectors. The Central Committee's guidelines for the Sixth Congress in December 1971 followed the same line.[2]

Whereas the Gierek regime in the 1970s gave rhetorical support to agriculture, it allocated the lion's share of investments to the industrial sectors, setting aside only between 13 and 17 percent for agriculture. In fact, the proportion of total investments allocated to agriculture declined gradually between 1970 and 1976, and increased somewhat in 1977.[3]

The authorities also pursued a discriminatory policy in favor of the socialized sector, disregarding economic criteria. Although the private sector in 1970 owned over four-fifths of the arable land and accounted for nearly 80 percent of the country's agricultural output, the ratio of investments in socialized to nonsocialized agriculture was five to three in 1971; it grew to more than three to one by 1976 and was still more than five to three in 1980.[4] Large subsidies were paid to inefficient state farms, of which there were many, and the state provided substantial support for the socialized sector in other ways. The private-farming sector received only limited credits, materials, inputs, and assistance. The authorities thereby hoped to demonstrate that the socialized sector, principally the state farms, could become the efficient standard-bearer of Polish agriculture.

The authorities encouraged the transfer of land from the private to the socialized sector by various means. For example, the State Land Fund acquired land from private farmers and readily sold or leased it to the socialized sector. During the first half of the 1970s, it was reluctant to sell or lease land to private farmers, even if the land stood fallow. Later, it was noted that "the expropriation and cultivation by the state farms of land from the State Land Fund is extremely costly."[5]

After three good harvests (1971-1973), the socialization of agriculture was accelerated. At the Central Committee's Thirteenth Plenum in February 1974, Gierek spoke of expanding and deepening the party's influence among farmers, "linking them ever more strongly—economically, socially, and politically—to socialism, modernizing agriculture, and showing the way to the socialist transformation of the Polish countryside." At the Fifteenth Plenum in November of that year, the Politburo's programmatic report, although stating that the party's agricultural policy would continue to ensure the development of all sectors of agriculture, emphatically favored the growth of the socialized sector.[6] In the same year, the prime minister told the Seventh Congress that private farms were to be "permanently linked" to the socialist economy through the state's supply of their inputs, its control of credits, the system of multi-year contracts between private farmers and the socialized sector, and the state's purchase of the private sector's output. The land holdings of the socialized sector should increase by 1980, the prime minister said, from 20 to 30 percent of total arable land.[7]

During the second half of the 1970s, reacting to negative economic symptoms, the authorities resorted to increased state interference in agriculture, turning to directives and controls.[8] In an article published in 1978 in the United Peasants Party's monthly journal, this change of policy was criticized:

> Now we can say that sticking to those foundations [of post-1956 policy] produced good economic and political results and diverging from them caused unfavorable results not only in the countryside and in agriculture but in the entire socioeconomic life of the country....Lack of consistent application of these principles was the source of difficulties in 1975-76, the effects of which we feel today."[9]

The change in the PUWP leadership's policy toward the agricultural sector also caused the resignation (in protest) in 1977 of the communist Minister of Agriculture, Kazimierz Barcikowski. He did not dispute the objective of building up the socialized sector and bringing about the gradual transformation of agriculture. He believed, however, that the government was not meeting the necessary conditions for an increase in efficient agricultural production, i.e., the development of agriculturally oriented industry. He later explained:

> When I saw that my influence in agriculture (because at that time I was in charge of it) was suddenly diminishing, that I was losing the freedom to act in that field, that I received orders inconsistent with the agricultural policy we had worked out after 1970, I resigned from the post of minister. . . . One of the key factors then in agriculture . . . was the implementation of the resolutions of the Fifteenth Plenum of the Central Committee. This was, without doubt, an innovative plenum. In fact, since that time no one has thought up anything new. . . . We agricultural activists had prepared that plenum as an important step toward implementation, but in practice it turned out that the resolutions of that plenum were suspended in mid-air for lack of implementation of the tasks, among others, in industry, which was to be built to increase the means of production for agriculture. The chemical and machine industries mattered most. A whole series of resolutions from that plenum was not carried out. Hence it was no secret to us that the situation in agriculture would grow ever more difficult.[10]

In the aftermath of the workers' strikes of 1980, which resulted in the formation of the independent Solidarity trade union, private farmers also agitated to have their own union and went on strike. The climax of their efforts came in early 1981, just after they obtained the unqualified support of the Primate of Poland, Stefan Cardinal Wyszyński.

In an agreement signed on February 18, the authorities agreed to sponsor a law that would guarantee "the inviolability of peasants' private property, especially land, and the right to inherit it, as well as recognition of private farming as a lasting and equal element in our national economy." In addition, prohibitive restrictions on the sale and purchase of private farmland were to be lifted. Investments in agriculture were to be expanded, prices for agricultural products raised, and the output of fertilizers, agricultural tools, and machinery increased.[11] As First Secretary Stanisław Kania summed up in the report he delivered to the PUWP's Ninth Extraordinary Congress in July, "We must radically break with the anti-agrarian character of the industrialization of the 1970s. . . ."[12]

After the imposition of martial law in December 1981, the Military Council of National Salvation issued an appeal to farmers to bring their produce to market instead of holding it back, reassuring them that the principles of agricultural policy would not change.[13] Later, in order to allay some of the persistent uncertainty plaguing the private farmer about the security of his land tenure, the Code of Civil Law, passed in 1982, included a guarantee of the private ownership of farmland. In addition, the private sector was to be accorded equality of treatment with the socialized sector in the procurement of goods and the allocation of inputs. On July 20, 1983, the parliament passed a constitutional amendment guaranteeing the permanence of private agriculture.[14] Beginning in 1982, productive investments in nonsocialized agriculture have slightly exceeded those in socialized agriculture, in contrast to the situation prevailing in the 1970s.

Concerned about providing a consistent level of food supply to the population, the authorities have steadily raised purchase prices for agricultural goods. Although prices have not kept up with those that private farmers have had to pay for industrial goods, the difference has not been large enough to antagonize private farmers.

Since the decisions of 1981, the authorities have emphasized that the state's policy toward the private-farming sector has not changed. But substantial difficulties impede further improvement in agricultural output:

—The process of mechanizing private farms is very slow. The service industry for agriculture is in an abysmally poor state. The maintenance of farm machinery is inefficient, expensive, and tardy. State-operated service facilities for the repair of farm machinery are grossly inadequate. Polish industry is not manufacturing sufficient spare parts to keep the machinery in operation.[15] In addition, there is a constant shortage of small, useful tools for the private farmer.

—The State Land Fund still holds too much undistributed farmland.

—The state does not produce a sufficient quantity of mineral fertilizers, and the share obtained by the private farming sector of what is produced is too small. Similarly, private farms do not get enough herbicides and pesticides.

—The structure of farms in the private sector is changing very slowly. Between 1970 and 1984, the percentage of farms of less than 5 hectares dropped only one-half of one percentage point, to 58.4 percent of the total number of farms. Farms between 5 and 10 hectares amounted to 25.3 percent of the total, down 3.2 percent between 1970 and 1984. Farms with over 10 hectares reached 16.3 percent of the total, a gain of 3.7 percent during the same period. All those concerned about the efficiency of agriculture and the welfare of private farming in Poland agree that a key goal is the expansion and strengthening of private farms over 10 hectares.[16]

—In September 1986, the church gave up its attempt to establish a private foundation to channel foreign funds and resources into the private farming sector. The authorities seemed unwilling to agree to such a practice unless they controlled the foundation, apparently fearing that it might "become an attempt to create specialized farming enclaves that would . . . give rise to socially harmful comparisons" with the socialized sector.[17]

Under the circumstances, it is not surprising that during the second half of the 1970s, Poland became a net importer of agricultural products, as documented in the previous chapter. At the same time, since 1982 agriculture has recovered more quickly from the mistakes of the Gierek period than other segments of the economy. Favorable weather and the authorities' recognition of the importance of the private farming sector have encouraged private farmers' efforts to increase agricultural production. The results have greatly contributed to the partial economic recovery that has unfolded since 1982.

Nevertheless, much needs to be done. Foreign trade in agricultural and food-industry products is not yet in balance. The Polish standard of living is reckoned to be equivalent only to that achieved in 1977 or 1978. The authorities have not yet made realistic plans to provide the needed farm inputs and economic incentives for the state and private sectors to maximize production.

Numerous questions remain about the degree of flexibility in the Polish system of planning and in its management of economic problems, including those in agriculture. One important step for improving Poland's creditworthiness would be the long-term willingness of the authorities to deal with the agricultural sector, including the private farmers, from economic and pragmatic rather than political or ideological points of view.

Notes

1. Andrzej Korbonski, "Victim or Villain: Polish Agriculture Since 1970," in Maurice D. Simon and Roger E. Kanet, eds., *Background to Crisis: Policy and Politics in Gierek's Poland* (Boulder, Colo., 1981), pp. 282-83.

2. See Prime Minister Jaroszewicz's speech in *Nowe Drogi*, July 1971, pp. 14-17. For the Central Committee's guidelines for the Sixth Congress, see *Nowe Drogi*, October 1971, pp. 45-49.

3. Korbonski, "Victim or Villain," p. 287.

4. Ibid. See also *1983 Statistical Yearbook* (in Polish), p. 156.

5. The Politburo report to the PUWP's Seventh Congress in December 1975 noted that private farms had lost 750,000 hectares and the socialized sector had acquired 800,000 hectares of arable land since the Congress of 1971. The socialized sector now had 20 percent of the arable land, compared to 16 percent in 1971. See "Report of the Central Committee of the PUWP for the Period Between the 6th and 7th Party Congresses," (in Polish) *Nowe Drogi*, January 1976, p. 24; and Jack Bielasiak, *Poland Today: The State of the Republic* (Armonk, N.Y., 1981), p. 52.

6. See "Speeches of the First Secretary of the Central Committee of the PUWP, Comrade Edward Gierek," (in Polish) *Nowe Drogi*, March 1974, p. 15; and "On the Further Improvement in Feeding the Nation and the Development of Agriculture," (in Polish) *Nowe Drogi*, November 1974, pp. 19-54.

7. "The Foundation of the Socio-economic Development of the Country in the Years 1976-80," (in Polish) *Nowe Drogi*, January 1976, pp. 96-97.

8. Józef S. Zegar, "Problems of Polish Agriculture in the 1970s and Expected Developments in the First Half of the 1980s," in Karl-Eugen Waedekin, ed., *Current Trends in the Soviet and East European Food Economy* (Berlin: Duncker & Humbolt, 1982), pp. 101-02.

9. "One More Time on the Basics of Agro-politics," (in Polish) *Wieś Współczesna*, September 1978, p. 3.

10. "On the Crisis, the Party, and Myself: A Journalist of *Głos Szczeciński*, Kazimierz Barcikowski, Speaks," (in Polish) *Głos Szczeciński*, May 19, 1981, pp. 1 and 3.

11. "Signing of the Accord Between the Governmental Commission and the Rzeszów Strike Committee," (in Polish) *Trybuna Ludu*, February 20, 1981, pp. 1-2.

12. "A Paper of the Central Committee read by Stanisław Kania," (in Polish) *Trybuna Ludu*, July 15, 1981, p. 5.

13. "To the Polish Farmers," (in Polish) *Trybuna Ludu*, December 21, 1981, p. 1. See also the appeal of the Secretariat of the United Peasants' Party's Main Committee, "We Fulfill a Specific Aspect of the Ideal of the Union of Worker and Peasant," *Trybuna Ludu*, December 18, 1981, p. 2. The martial law period is discussed in Andrzej Korbonski's "Agriculture and the Polish Renewal," in Jack Bielasiak and Maurice D. Simon, eds., *Polish Politics: Edge of the Abyss* (New York, 1984), pp. 88-92.

14. "Changes in the Constitution of the Polish People's Republic—A Two-day Session of the Sejm," (in Polish) *Trybuna Ludu*, July 21, 1983, p. 1; and "Report of the Rules Commission on the Delegates' Proposal for an Amendment to Change the Constitution of the Polish People's Republic," (in Polish) p. 3.

15. *Report to the Rockefeller Foundation and Rockefeller Brothers Fund by the Agricultural Mission to Poland*, December 1982, pp. 146-50.

16. Dr. Jan Steczkowski, "The Future of the Agricultural Sector in Poland," a paper prepared for the conference "The Polish Economy in the Year 2000: A Critical Appraisal," at the University of Pittsburgh on February 5-6, 1987, pp. 8-9, 12-14, 35, and 40.

17. "Why Won't There Be a Foundation?" (in Polish) *Tygodnik Mazowsze* 180, September 10, 1986, p. 4.

6

The Competitiveness of Polish Industry and Indebtedness

Kazimierz Poznański

The purpose of this chapter is to quantify the changes in the competitive strength of Polish industry during 1970-85 and to discuss Poland's prospective export capability on the world market.[1] The point of reference is the rest of Eastern Europe and, in some cases, the economies of certain other countries. This chapter should help us understand the reasons for the huge debt that Poland accumulated and its prospects for servicing it.

It is argued that the large-scale imports of Western machinery and licenses during the first part of the 1970s may not have been directed and absorbed with full effectiveness. Nevertheless, such imports had a strong, positive impact on Poland's competitiveness. The abrupt reduction in those imports since 1979 has, in turn, caused a severe loss of competitiveness which, if not reversed, promises to lead to a further decline in competitiveness during the next decade.

Given the loss of vital supplies of Western technology and other inputs and the perceived failure of the Polish authorities to significantly improve economic efficiency through economic reforms (see Fallenbuchl's chapter), Poland is becoming less able to service, at a reasonable and socially acceptable cost, its substantial foreign debt.

45

General Level of Competitiveness

Market Share in Western Europe.   Market shares are commonly used as direct indicators of competitiveness.[2] They do not simply reflect the technological strength of the exporting country or its marketing abilities, but also indicate factors not related to trade competitiveness. These factors include: exporters' trade preferences with respect to particular markets, differences in income elasticities of demand, and the degree of discrimination by specific importers; and changes in the supply of exportable goods.

During most of the 1970s, East European exports more than kept pace with the expansion of imports by Western countries, a fact reflected in their slightly increasing market shares.[3] During 1970-78, the share of Eastern Europe in total OECD imports increased from 1.56 percent to 1.63 percent; its share increased in all manufactures groups, except for the chemical industry, which showed a rather substantial drop.[4]

The best export performance, measured by market shares, was that of the two most aggressive importers of Western technology: Hungary and Poland, followed by a modest importer, Romania.[5] These three were the only countries that increased their market shares in total OECD imports, as well as the only ones to show increases in market shares for most manufactures. It follows that the shares of the other East European countries, those pursuing a conservative import policy, had already declined before 1978.

A comparison of Poland and Czechoslovakia—one of the least and one of the most conservative importers of technology—is instructive. During 1970-78, Poland's share in total OECD imports grew slightly, from 0.46 to 0.49 percent, whereas the share of Czechoslovakia declined from 0.33 to 0.20 percent. In machinery trade, Poland increased its share in the OECD market from 0.10 to 0.29 percent, whereas Czechoslovakia's share declined from 0.23 to 0.14 percent.

Poland had achieved a stronger export progress during 1970-78 than did Hungary. This is most striking in the export of machinery and transport equipment (SITC-7), in which Poland tripled its share, whereas the share of Hungary only doubled (from 0.05 to 0.10 percent), and Romania's share increased only moderately.

The year 1979 was a turning point in the evolution of market shares. Since that year the East European share of the total OECD market has been declining: by 1982 it declined to 1.13 percent; in 1983 it fell to 1.17, returning to 1.21 in 1984, 42 points below the level of 1978 and 35 points below that of 1970. This downward trend occurred in all major groups of manufactures (except for chemicals), especially in machinery (from 0.79 percent in 1978 to 0.46 percent in 1984).

The case of Poland is the worst; its share in the OECD market declined during 1978-84 from 0.49 percent to 0.29 percent. This decline explains less than half of the full reduction in Eastern Europe's market share of the OECD imports since 1978; the balance is the result of the declining shares of the other economies in the region (except those of Bulgaria and East Germany).

Market shares measured in dollars are distorted by currency fluctuations. The fact that the dollar appreciated during the first half of the 1980s caused a downward bias in dollar-denominated market shares for the countries that sell mostly for the depreciating West European currencies. This is the case of East European exporters, as opposed to Brazil or South Korea, which sell greater shares to the United States for dollars.

To avoid this distortion, I have calculated market shares in European Currency Units (ECU) for the West European market. But in this case, too, the share of Eastern Europe in the total ECU-denominated imports from Western Europe declined (although by less than was calculated in the case of total OECD imports) from 1.76 percent in 1978 to 1.39 in 1983, and back to 1.55 percent in 1984. Again, machinery and transport equipment showed a sharp decline (from 1.01 percent in 1978 to 0.61 in 1983, and up to 0.64 percent in 1984).

Mirror statistics reported by Western Europe also show that Poland's share in total imports declined sharply during the period 1978-84, from 0.62 to 0.36 percent. This accounts for more than four-fifths of the East European decline, with Czechoslovakia, Hungary and Romania contributing the balance. Bulgaria showed no change; East Germany was the only country that improved its market share.

It is not easy to interpret the trends presented here. Perhaps the superior records of both Hungary and Poland during 1970-78 were due to their aggressive imports of Western technology, although this cannot be the reason for the above-average trade performance of Romania. But the strong performance of Poland may have been due to their above average rates of growth in production. However, the rate for Hungary was about average for Eastern Europe.

It is not a simple coincidence that since 1979 all the previously aggressive importers of technology have performed more poorly than such conservatives as Bulgaria and East Germany (but not Czechoslovakia, which has continued to suffer market share losses). This pattern seems to reflect the fact that the aggressive importers have accumulated bigger debts, therefore they have had to cut more imports from the West, causing more bottlenecks in production.

Technological Content of Exports. The competitive position of Poland is also reflected in the product structure of its exports. The simplest common structural indicator is the share of machinery and transport equipment—containing, on the average, the most technologically advanced goods—in total exports. A more sophisticated measure should also include some complex chemicals and a few instruments classified in SITC group 8.

While all the countries of Eastern Europe, except Czechoslovakia, raised their share of machinery and transport equipment in total sales to the OECD during 1970-78, the most spectacular improvement was that of Poland. The share of Eastern Europe increased by less than half; it almost tripled in the case of Poland (5.8 percent in 1970 to 14.8 percent in 1978, approximating some of the Western economies' share of machinery and transport equipment in their total exports).

Beginning with the adjustment of 1979, Eastern Europe lost much of its earlier gains; all countries followed a similar path, at least until 1983. The share of machinery and transport equipment for the region declined to 10.4 percent in 1983 and 1984. In Poland the respective share dropped from 14.8 percent in 1978 to 11.0 percent in 1983, a level which held in 1984. It is interesting to note that this drop compares rather favorably with that of the economically more tranquil Bulgaria, where the respective shares were 8.1 percent in 1978 and 3.6 percent in 1984.

The initial rapid increase in the share of machinery and transport equipment in Polish exports to the West could be interpreted as further evidence of the positive impact of its more aggressive import policy of technological modernization. But to strengthen this interpretation, one has to consider other important factors.[6]

Export Unit Values for Manufactures. Export unit values are prices that are calculated per weight or unit of the particular product. If one assumes that higher unit values reflect superior levels of technology, then they could be used to measure the technological level of exported goods. This approach is subject to several methodological problems.[7] Nevertheless the indicator supplements the two discussed above.

The statement that more advanced goods receive higher prices per-kilogram or unit does not imply that technological progress always leads to increases of prices in a particular product group. The more general argument is that whatever the direction of price changes, the exporters of less advanced (often heavier) models will have to accept lower prices than suppliers of the more attractive newer models; as a consequence the former will show lower unit values.

To be sure, unit values also reflect conditions of demand. Therefore, exporters that supply booming markets will receive higher prices than those that sell identical goods elsewhere. However, demand by itself, regardless of market conditions, is influenced strongly by technology, i.e., by the degree of modernity, novelty, etc. This makes it difficult to distinguish the technological variables from the variables of demand. Unit values also reflect pure movements of price—inflation or deflation—in the importing countries. However, if unit values of few exporters are compared in a given importing country and in a given year, then one can obtain results free of inflationary (or deflationary) distortions.[8]

With Gierek's emphasis on imports, Poland achieved a remarkable (by East European standards) improvement in the prices that were recorded for its total exports of machinery and transport equipment on the OECD market. In 1970, Poland was the lowest ranked among the East European countries, but by 1978 its unit-value level was second only to Hungary, the permanent leader in that period. Furthermore, Poland was able to somewhat reduce its unit-value disadvantage vis-à-vis many Western countries. In 1970, Polish unit values represented 42 percent of the West European average, but by 1978 they rose to 60 percent of the Western average.[9]

Once again, the improvements did not last beyond 1979. The unit value for Poland declined through 1982, putting the country right above Czechoslovakia, which receives the lowest prices in the region. However, even with this decline, in 1982 Poland remained closer to the top of the East European range than it did in 1970; the same was true in the case of West European prices.

The initial improvements in Poland's relative unit values vis-à-vis Western competitors may be partly attributed to the weakening of import restrictions in the West and, one would presume, to its improved marketing abilities. However, these two factors probably cannot explain Poland's improved price performance relative to the other East European countries, since there are no grounds to believe that Poland was offered greater concessions by the West or that it had dramatically overtaken the other CMEA countries in marketing skills.

A more plausible explanation is that the trends noted reflect the more rapidly improving competitiveness of Poland's exports relative to that of many other East European countries. It is more probable that Poland achieved this edge through the aggressive replacement of traditional, low value-added goods with higher priced ones. This was achieved with the help of license agreements and imports of technology from the West.

It is also possible, however,[10] that some or all of the differences between Polish unit values and those of the other CMEA countries reflect the fact that Poland encountered more favorable price trends for its products sold in the West, either because of the specific product mix of Polish exports or because of the geographical orientation of its trade.

To respond, I deflated the unit values that were already calculated by indexes of export prices paid to the CMEA countries in order to make the unit values better reflect changes in the competitive—or technological—strength of the particular economies.

According to the data released by the Polish statistical office, prices for machinery and transport equipment traded in the West almost doubled during the period 1970-78. Since Poland's unit values tripled during the same period, it looks as if there had been something like a 50 percent real improvement in Polish unit values. This is the magnitude of the competitive improvement, assuming that the official price index is purged of quality changes.[11]

If we assume that all the CMEA countries were facing the same trend in prices for machinery and transport equipment that was sold in the West, then those countries that showed a unit-value index for 1978 below 200 (as compared to that of 1970)—seem to have experienced a technological retardation. This appears to have been the case for the Soviet Union (163), East Germany (180), and even Hungary (189).

To summarize, prior to the crisis of 1979, Poland showed marked improvement in its trade competitiveness in the West, particularly in terms of refocusing its trade on high value-added (relatively more technologically advanced) types of manufactures. (For a different perspective see Brada and Montias.[12]) Even with the losses in competitiveness after 1979, Poland did show some relative improvement in competitiveness in comparison with both the other East European and with Western economies.

Thus, the imports of Western machinery by Poland should not be regarded as a monolithically negative element in the financial situation of the economy. These imports also contributed to the expansion of its export capacities for Western markets, which are critical for Poland's ability to service its credits. Consequently, one has to look at factors other than machinery imports to determine the reasons for the current financial crisis in Poland.

Competitiveness of Selected Manufactures.   In this section, I turn to an analysis of the competitiveness of manufactured products that Poland exported to the West in 1978, 1982, and 1984. All items belong to the category that we will call machinery and transport equipment. Although these products have not been a major source of hard currency, it is precisely the group that the Gierek regime designated to penetrate Western markets.

The sample involves eighteen product groups (further disaggregation, which would improve the analysis, is possible with the Eurostat series,[13] but such an analysis goes beyond the scope of this study) which, in terms of revenues, account for more than two-thirds of Poland's earnings from the export of machinery and transport equipment to Western Europe. The assessment of competitiveness is based on two indicators: market shares in Western Europe and respective unit values.

I begin with an examination of data for 1978, the last year before the crisis. One finds ten products for which Poland's market share exceeded its average share in West European imports of machinery and transport equipment (i.e., 0.43 percent). These products include: household refrigerators, machine tools, ball bearings, electric motors, vacuum cleaners, television sets, radio receivers, tractors, bicycles, and ships.

This information is not, by itself, definitive for an assessment of which Polish products are the most competitive in the West, because the higher-than-average shares may reflect not only technological strength but also the specialization pattern of Poland's total trade with Western countries. Therefore it is necessary to confront market-share data with production statistics, which is also outside the scope of this study.

Additional information on the precrisis competitiveness comes from the cross-product comparison of relative unit values. A number of products were among those with unit values closer to Western levels than those of aggregate unit values of machinery and transport equipment: excavating machines, data processing, and radio receivers.

Next I look at the post-1978 period to find out which products have been the most resistant to both Western recession and the severe import restrictions that have hit Polish industry during the most recent period. "Most resistant" refers to products with the most stable market share and unit values during 1978-84, as opposed to those experiencing a decline in one or both of the indicators.

Such a comparison suggests that among the most resistant products were combustion engines, passenger cars, excavating machines, ball bearings, and vacuum cleaners. Most vulnerable to economic stress were television sets, data processing equipment, washing machines, and type-writers (the latter two products practically disappeared from Western markets by 1984, in part due to pressing domestic needs).

Only in a more detailed case study type would one find the reason for the above-average performance of some of the sample products during the recent period of economic stress. Factors such as the relative technological level, import sensitivity, degree of cooperation with Western companies, policy choices by planners, and demand conditions abroad must be considered in such a case study.

At first glance it appears that the least resistant products, for the most part, employ imported Western technology. There are also good indications that in the cases of television sets, typewriters, radio receivers, and data processing equipment, it was precisely the insufficient scope of technological modernization that made them uncompetitive on the world market.

A comparison of the latest trends in Poland with those in Czechoslovakia and Hungary also implies that internal economic conditions, including reductions of imports, have played a more significant role in determining the market-share unit-value pattern for specific products than external market conditions. This inference is based on the observation that for most Polish products that incurred losses in market shares during the early 1980s, Western demand was sufficient to permit gains by the two other countries. The exceptions are ball bearings, tractors, and electric motors.

Improved Competitiveness or Trade Reorientation. Montias hypothesizes that in the 1970s,[14] trends in Poland's indicators of export performance do not necessarily reflect an increased technological strength, as I have claimed earlier, but rather a shift from the CMEA countries to the West of products of above average quality. This supposedly explains the reported increases in market shares in the West or in relative unit-values.

On the surface this seems plausible, since Poland under Gierek did reorient its trade from the CMEA to the West, particularly in manufacturers[15]. One must question, however, whether the shift toward Western markets could have been possible without some technological improvements—mostly related to the import of technology that were occurring during 1970-78.

It is rather unlikely that Poland could have managed to redirect its industrial exports without a substantial modernization of its products. Western importers generally demand higher quality than their Soviet and East European counterparts. The fact that technical standards are often different in the West is also a problem. This suggests the difficulty of reorienting Polish manufactured exports from regional partners to the West.

To determine the validity of Montias's hypothesis, I calculated the shares of CMEA and Western markets for two groups of Polish exports: those that were heavily injected with Western technology during 1970-78 and those in which imports of technology were less important. The inclusion of exported products in these categories was based on data concerning license-related technology transfers[16].

The analysis of eleven manufactures reveals that the shift to the West took place in the five product lines that were major recipients of Western technology. By contrast, in those product areas where the inflows were small or nil, the respective exports remained geared mainly to the East European and Soviet markets, with the short-lived exception of machine tools (62.5 percent to Western markets in 1979 against 24.7 percent in 1970).

Thus, it seems clear that the redirection of trade was made possible by the import of Western technology. Although Montias is correct to stress the positive impact of trade reorientation to the West on the market share of Polish exports in the West during 1970-78, the claim of the positive role of technology imports in opening Western markets to Polish goods is still valid.

To sum up, the analysis of market shares and unit values reveals that Polish products differ substantially in their competitiveness on Western markets. Apparently, sizable gains in shares of Western markets occurred only among the very few products that have been recently upgraded with the help of Western technology, which showed in their above-average performance during the first half of the 1980s. At the same time, many of the newer exports that have not reached the optimum scale and level of technology proved unable to survive the stress.

Future Competitiveness

Poland's leadership hopes that, under stress, Poland would make an adjustment and that an improved allocation of resources and increased innovation would allow an improvement in export competitiveness, generate a sizable export surplus, arrest the growth of debt, and eventually resume a normal growth path.

The following analysis attempts to determine whether the current economic adjustment is in fact preparing Poland for large payments on its Western debt, which are rescheduled to begin around 1990.[17] Several factors will determine Poland's future competitiveness. The following remarks are limited to technological factors, specifically the role of Western technology imports in the modernization of Polish exports.

Imports of Western Machinery. After several years of rapid annual increases in imports of Western machinery, starting with the dramatic growth of 1970,[18] Poland entered another phase in 1976, one of declining purchases (Table 5). The most dramatic cuts have taken place since 1980, bringing the level of imports in 1984 to about one-third of the precrisis value. This is one of the deepest cuts among all the heavily indebted countries.

By 1984, Poland's index (1979 = 100) of imports of machinery and transport equipment from the OECD (denominated in dollars) was 42.4 (36.4 if 1978 is taken as a base). Only Romania went further in import

Table 5. Poland's Imports of Industrial Machinery[1]
from the OECD and Replacement Needs, 1970-83
(Millions of U.S. Dollars)

Year	Actual Imports (1)	Replacement Needs[2] (2)	Difference (1)-(2)
1970	151	15	136
1971	167	32	135
1972	408	75	333
1973	768	156	612
1974	1024	270	754
1975	1339	424	915
1976	1322	586	736
1977	1257	732	525
1978	1289	906	383
1979	1259	1081	178
1980	1020	1246	− 226
1981	552	1370	− 818
1982	402	1486	− 1084
1983	396	1608	− 1212
1984	418	1350	− 932

[1] SITC groups 7-2, 7-3 and 7-4.
[2] Assuming a 10 year depreciation and five percent average inflation rate for imports.
Source: Import data from Trade by Commodities (Paris: OECD)

cuts (17.0 index) among East Europeans. In Latin America, only Argentina instituted import austerity similar to that of Poland.

Mirror statistics for Western Europe (demominated in ECUs) show Polish imports declined to 78 percent. In Eastern Europe only East Germany (down to 72 percent but as low as 53.4 percent if 1981, the peak year, is taken as a base) and Romania (24 percent) went deeper. In Latin America the deepest cut was made by Argentina (an index of fifty-seven with 1981 as a peak year); the reduction in Brazil was far less severe (index of 93.5 for 1983 with the peak year 1980 as a base). Mexico went through cuts comparable in magnitude to that of Poland (an index of 62.0 with the peak year 1981 as a base).[19]

Nevertheless, while many of the debtors among the developing nations had by 1984 resumed imports of Western machinery, Poland had not. For instance, imports from Western Europe by Brazil reached, in 1984, a level 30 percent above the pre-adjustment one. In the case of Poland, imports since 1984 have, more or less, stabilized at low levels. There are no signs that Poland will markedly increase its purchases during the next few years, given the severity of the financial strains with the West that it faces.

The radical reduction in Poland's imports of Western industrial machinery has probably had some negative impact on the production potential of the new capacities built with the help of Western technology during the Gierek expansion of the 1970s. Given the size of the cuts, it is likely that in many cases the equipment has not even been fully maintained, much less modernized.[20]

To determine the adverse impact of the recent import squeeze on the replacement of Western capital goods, the hypothetical replacement needs of the equipment installed since 1970 are calculated and compared with the actual value of imported machinery. Differences between the two indicate the accumulation or decumulation of capital.

The calculation is based on the following assumptions: that imported capital goods are restricted to the three categories of products (SITC-7.2, 7.3, and 7.4); that all machinery is depreciated over a ten-year period, with one-tenth of the initial capital value depreciated each year; and that the price of imported equipment increased five percent each year.

In addition, it is assumed that there is no import substitution of domestic for Western capital. It is unrealistic to think that Poland has not used some of the imported equipment to modernize its production of import-competing machinery in the three categories mentioned above. This substitution effect should not be exaggerated, however, given that such an important segment of the machinery sector—machine tools— was not given a priority in the import of technology under Gierek's regime.

The calculations suggest that, since 1980, imports of industrial machinery have not been sufficient to meet the replacement needs of capital investment in Western equipment made since 1969. If, prior to 1980, the appropriate share of imports was being assigned for replacement, the new capacity, beginning in 1980, has been subject to decumulation. The loss equals $4.3 billion in the value of capital stock during 1980-84.

The estimate suggests that if all machinery imported in 1983 was devoted to replacement, the one-year (not cumulative) deficit in supplies for the needed replacement would amount to about two-thirds of the total need. Since it is rather unlikely that all 1984 imports were devoted to replacement—some equipment for new installations was certainly imported also—the actual deficit is probably even higher.

Has the decumulation in the import-based capital stock been as bad as implied above, given that much of the plant and equipment imported during the 1970s was never installed or remained underutilized? One may argue that the drastic cuts in imports simply forced a reduction of earlier waste. In other words, if earlier, for example, only one-half of the machinery imported was actually installed, then a reduction of imports by one-half, now fully installed, would leave the economy with a continued growth in production capacities. However, given the existing systemic deficiencies, the degree of capital waste probably was not substantially reduced.

If the process of negative capital accumulation continues, Poland will lose some of its most competitive lines of production. This would not necessarily mean a full shutdown of those lines, since the regime can extend the lifespan of imported machinery beyond the assumed ten years. However, allowing this capital to age beyond the ten years will cause the quality of the resultant products to suffer and their costs to rise.

What has almost certainly deepened the recent decline in the import of industrial machinery is the regime's priority on the importation of materials and components to protect current production at the expense of the modernization of existing capacities. This choice can be explained in terms of the typically short-time horizon of the planners, alluded to in Chapter 2 by Crane and Chapter 11 by Bielasiak. Under current political circumstances, the horizon seems to be even shorter than usual. Trying to prove to society that the imposition of military rule in 1981 was justifiable, the regime presses the economy for indicators of a strong recovery, thus neglecting the long-run consequences of its actions.

Western License Imports. Disembodied technology in the form of license imports grew dramatically during the first years of the 1970s. During 1971-76, Poland was buying an average of 60 licenses a year. Due to the initial expansion of purchases, the number of license agreements in force increased from 142 in 1970 to 385 in 1976. But Gierek's economic policies of 1976, and those pursued since 1980, have had a devastating impact.

Since 1976 the number of licenses began to decline, and between 1981 and 1986 no new licenses have been purchased.[21] This withdrawal has resulted in a rapid reduction of the number of agreements still in force to 181 in 1983. By 1987 the number of active licenses had probably fallen well below the level of 1970.

Poland is not the only East European country to experience a decline in license purchases.[22] The sharp decline in license payments by Eastern Europe is in contrast to imports by most other economies. In the majority of Western countries, license payments to the United States have been increasing during the first half of the 1980s, although the newly industrializing countries, as a group, have reported a modest decline during this period.

But even the newly industrializing countries that in 1980 were forced to make a painful economic adjustment, involving substantial reductions in machinery imports, have not gone as far as Poland in saving on licenses. For instance, in Mexico, where imports of machinery measured in dollars declined by more than one-third during the years 1980-83, payments for licenses have not changed much.[23]

The scale of the recent license squeeze in Poland cannot be explained simply in terms of the general trend in the import of Western machinery. Even though capital purchases are needed for most licenses, the cuts have not been large enough to justify the complete severing of license contracts with the West. Therefore, one has to seek some noneconomic explanation.

Discontinuing the purchase of licenses seems to be a reflection of both the regime's excessive concern with short-run output improvements and its lack of clear developmental priorities. This seems to be the only explanation, for instance, for the government's total neglect of many industries that have good prospects for export but are in desperate need of Western technology to survive on the world market.[24]

Another contributing factor is the fact that the issue of license imports has become overpoliticized since the fall of Gierek. The current crisis is blamed by the Jaruzelski regime and by the social opposition on Gierek. High on the indictment list are his allegedly irresponsible choices of licenses.

Summarizing this section, Poland's manufacturing industry is rapidly aging. The decapitalization of the capacities established during the 1970s is proceeding rapidly and technological deterioration is accelerating. This is due to the dramatic reduction in the absolute level of investment activity and an even sharper curtailing of Western imports; therefore, no license or large Western-equipped plant has been negotiated lately.

Conclusions

Until the end of the 1970s, Poland significantly improved its export competitiveness on Western markets for manufactured goods. This was based on a dynamic restructuring of its product offer, made possible in part by Western technology. Even with the recent damage to Polish trade that was caused by the severe cuts in imports, industry still enjoys some of the benefits of improvement in relative competitive strength. Whereas the imports of Western technology and its ineffective employment have shared in the responsibility for the accumulation of the debt, they were also helping Poland to service it.

The export products in Poland's machinery and transport-equipment sector vary greatly in terms of competitiveness. Many products for which Poland purchased Western licenses showed remarkable achievements prior to 1979 and an above-average performance in the years since then. At the same time, many other licensed goods have not reached the optimum technological level or production scale, and they have shown low resistance to domestic economic disturbances and demand constraints abroad.

Poland's current adjustment is focused primarily on an investment squeeze and the protection of current production. This imposes excessively high costs on the technological level of export production, as a result of both minuscule imports of Western machinery and a moratorium on the purchase of new licenses. Economic adjustment has so far failed to produce export results comparable to the majority of other heavily indebted countries around the world. Particularly striking is the absence of a single case of a manufactured product making substantial recent progress on Western markets, in contrast to the experiences of such indebted nations as Brazil, Mexico, and South Korea.

Though many economic factors make Poland's adjustment to the foreign debt crisis more difficult than that of other East European economies, the role of political factors is especially significant. Examples include the overpoliticization of the license issue and the politically motivated emphasis on imports of industrial supplies, based on the need to show short-term improvements in output.

Poland is becoming less able to generate a significant supply of competitive goods to be sold in the West, and the Soviet pressure on balancing trade and on redirecting highquality products to the Soviet Union is leaving fewer of those goods for the Western markets. Since only Western markets can serve as major sources of hard-currency revenues, Poland very likely will arrive at the second wave of debt payments around 1990 with greatly weakened export potential in manufactured goods.

Notes

1. This paper benefited from the research project with Joanna Poznańska, Jan Svejnar, and Kathy Terrel for the National Council for Soviet and East

European Research [J. Poznańska, K. Poznański, J. Svejnar and K. Terrell, "The Impact of Western Technology on Poland's Economy: 1970-1984," Final Report for the National Council for Soviet and East European Research, Cornell University, July 1985 (mimeo)]. Michael Montias provided several very insightful comments during the Smithsonian Conference on the Polish Economy and Debt, and gave permission to incorporate them into the final version of the paper.

2. On the methodology of market shares see: K. Poznański, "Competitiveness of the Soviet Bloc: A Global Perspective," Institute of International Studies, University of California-Berkeley, 1987.

3. G. Fink, et al. *Commodity Composition of East-West Trade*, Wiener Institut für Internationale Wirtschaftvergleiche, Reprint Series, no. 48, (August) 1980.

4. Tabulation showing changes in Eastern Europe's, Poland's, and Czechoslovakia's market shares in the OECD during the years 1970-84 by main groups of manufactures is available from the author.

5. Evidence based on statistics on volumes of machinery trade in Smolik, Donald P., 1986, p. 57.

6. For example, there is a possibility that Poland was simply expanding its production of machinery and transport equipment faster compared to its counterparts in Eastern Europe, without necessarily making better progress in the industrial technology used, thereby making it possible to expand its supplies of exportable machinery and transport equipment more rapidly.

Also, it could be that while Poland was modernizing its machinery and transport equipment sector more rapidly than the rest of Eastern Europe, the latter was making better progress in technology for other sectors of industry (e.g., chemicals, food processing), so that they would be better prepared to expand exports in other sectors.

7. K. Poznański, "Competitiveness of the Soviet Bloc: A Global Perspective," Institute of International Studies, University of California-Berkeley, 1987.

8. Averaging unit values over two or three years could prove to be more accurate because it smoothes seasonal fluctuations. However, sample coumputations for a few commodities showed no significant differences in results based on annual vs. average multiyear data.

9. K. Poznański, "The Impact of Western Technology on Importing Economies," paper for the workshop *Technological Trends in the Communist World*, Hoover Institution, July 20-21, 1985.

10. J. M. Montias, Written comments on the early version of this paper presented at the Smithsonian Conference on The Polish Economy and the Debt, Washington, D.C., October, 1985.

11. Ibid.

12. J. Brada and J.M. Montias, "Industrial Policy in Eastern Europe: A Three Country Comparison," *Journal of Comparative Economics*, no. 8, 1984, pp. 377-419; and Ibid.

13. Eurostat—NIMEXE is a highly detailed and disaggregated reporting of the foreign trade of the EEC members. It is all computerized and is done by the Statistical Office of the European Communities, located in Luxembourg.

14. Montias, 1985.

15. Z. Fallenbuchl, *East-West Technology Transfer, Study of Poland, 1971-1980* (Paris, 1983).

16. Poznańska, et. al.

17. K. Crane, *The Creditworthiness of Eastern Europe in the 1980s*, Rand Corporation, R-3201-USDP, January 1985.

18. S. Gomulka, "Growth and Import of Technology: Poland 1971-1980," *Cambridge Journal of Economics*, no. 2, 1978, pp. 1-16.

19. Poznańska, et. al.

20. B. Wojciechowski, "Structural Changes and Poland's Import Difficulties," (in Polish) *Gospodarka Planowa*, no. 9, 1984.

21. Except for the latest deal with Italian Fiat for the "restyling" of an obsolete, small two-cylinder model with only minor hard-currency investment and largely comestic changes (e.g., new starter, additional doors), the motor car industry has been supplied with very little Western machinery and no licenses in recent years. This has happened even though the industry brought in millions in hard-currency revenues before the crisis, and even now shows considerable export potential.

22. F. Levcik and J. Skolka, *East-West Technology Transfer: Study of Czechoslovakia*, (Paris, 1984); and P. Marer, *East-West Technology Transfer: Hungary 1968-1984* (Paris, 1986).

23. In 1982 Mexico paid to the U.S. $154 million in royalties; in 1984, $146 million. Source: Survey of Current Business, June 1985.

24. K. Poznański, "Economic Adjustment and Political Forces: Poland Since 1970," *Industrial Organization*, Vol. 40, no. 2, Spring 1986.

References

Brada, J., and J.M. Montias, "Industrial Policy in Eastern Europe: A Three Country Comparison." *Journal of Comparative Economics*, 1984, no. 8, pp. 377-419.

Crane, K., *The Creditworthiness of Eastern Europe in the 1980s*. Rand Corporation, R-3201-USDP, January 1985.

Fallenbuchl, Z., *East-West Technology Transfer, Study of Poland, 1971-1980*. Paris: OECD, 1983.

Fink, G., et al. *Commodity Composition of East-West Trade*. Wiener Institut für Internationale Wirtschaftvergleiche, Reprint Series, (August 1980) no. 48.

Gomulka, S., "Growth and Import of Technology: Poland 1971-1980." *Cambridge Journal of Economics*, 1978, no. 2, pp. 1-16.

Levcik, F. and J. Skolka, *East-West Technology Transfer: Study of Czechoslovakia*. Paris: OECD, 1984.

Marer, P., *East-West Technology Transfer: Hungary 1968-1984*. Paris: OECD, 1986.

Montias, J. M., "Poland: Roots of the Economic Crisis." *The ACES Bulletin*, Vol. 34, no. 3 (Fall 1982), pp. 1-19.

Montias, J. M., Written comments on the early version of this paper presented at the Smithsonian Conference on The Polish Economy and the Debt, Washington, D.C., October, 1985.

Poznańska, J., K. Poznański, J. Svejnar and K. Terrell, "The Impact of Western Technology on Poland's Economy: 1970-1984." Final Report for the National Council for Soviet and East European Research, Cornell University, July 1985 (mimeo).

Poznański, K., "The Impact of Western Technology on Importing Economies." paper for the workshop *Technological Trends in the Communist World*, Hoover Institution, July 20-21, 1985.

Poznański, K., "Economic Adjustment and Political Forces: Poland Since 1970." *Industrial Organization* (Spring 1986) Vol. 40, no. 2.

Poznański, K., "Competitiveness of the Soviet Bloc: A Global Perspective." Institute of International Studies, University of California-Berkeley, 1987.

Wojciechowski, B., "Structural Changes and Poland's Import Difficulties." (in Polish) *Gospodarka Planowa*, 1984, no. 9.

7

The Current State of the Economy

Zbigniew Kamecki

The economic situation in Poland is still difficult, although there are certain elements of improvement, which is cause for optimism for the future. I would like to call attention to some positive developments that have taken place since 1982.

First, the decline of national income, which began in 1979 during the Gierek administration, was reversed in 1983. Since then national income has increased yearly—about 6 percent during 1983-84 and about 3-3.5 percent in 1985. These rates would probably be considered impressive even in capitalist countries. The cause of the increase in national income during the last three years is largely an increase in labor productivity and a decrease in the energy and material intensity of national income. This is a positive sign.

Second, the domestic market has improved considerably during the last several years, although there are still many bottlenecks. To evaluate the situation properly, it is necessary to compare it with that of 1981 or 1982. Unbelievable as this may sound, in the early fall of 1981, vinegar was the only commodity readily available in the shops. Despite rationing, many products were not available. All Poles had coupons, but there was still not enough meat to satisfy even the limited quantities that individuals had the right to purchase. This is no longer a problem. The fact that the rationing of dairy products and cereals has been eliminated shows an improvement (currently, only meat and chocolate are ra-

tioned). There is also a significant improvement in the supply of manufactured products.

Third, an important change took place in foreign trade, especially
in the area of convertible currency. The balance of hard-currency trade
was negative during the 1970s, as well as in 1980 and 1981 (the deficit
reached about $3 billion in 1975-76 and about $2 billion annually in 1977-
79). Since 1982, Poland has achieved a surplus in this trade for the first
time since 1970. It is true that this improvement has resulted primarily
from cuts of imports. However, the fact that the Polish economy did
not break down in spite of these cuts and is actually improving testifies
to its strength and ability to adjust to difficult conditions.

Fourth, a visible weakening of inflation took place between 1982
and 1985. The rate of inflation has dropped from 101 percent in 1982 to
15 percent in 1984 and 1985 (Table 1). These noteworthy achievements
were attained at a time when Poland faced commercial and credit restrictions imposed by the NATO countries. There were also two internal
factors, namely, the five-day work week, agreed to in 1981 as a result
of social conflicts, and the right to early retirement, introduced in 1982.
These measures have contributed to a shortage of labor—of skilled labor
in particular—which currently constitutes a barrier, in many areas, to
the growth of output.

In conclusion, I think that the image of the Polish economy should
not be presented in a one-sided manner, as is often done in the West.
This does not mean, of course, that I underestimate the country's economic difficulties; indeed, the situation is still very complex. Due to the
balance-of-payments difficulties (caused mainly by indebtedness), Poland has to limit the growth of imports; this in turn causes less than full
utilization of production capacities and the decapitalization of portions
of the economy's fixed assets. At the same time, Poland confronts difficulties in restructuring its industry. The standard of living has dropped
sharply in comparison to the precrisis period. However, the improvement in the economic situation since 1982 gives us hope to overcome
these difficulties during the next several years. National income will
return to an annual rate of 3 to 3.5 percent for 1986-90, and significant
improvement is expected in the supplies available on the domestic market. The rate of inflation will be slowed to below 10 percent by 1990.
Labor productivity will increase considerably, and the energy- and ma-
terial-intensity of national income (that is, the excessively high amount
of energy and raw materials used because of the structure of industrial
production and the wasteful use of inputs) will decrease, easing the
problem of decapitalization (mentioned in Chapter 6 by Poznański) as
well as environmental degradation.

PART II.

THE POLITICAL ECONOMY OF REFORM IN POLAND

8

The Political Economy of Reforms

Włodzimierz Brus

The terms "reform" and "economic reform" in the context of communist countries have become ambiguous from journalistic overuse.[1] Therefore, I must begin by stating that I understand "reform" as a meaningful change in the operating *principles* of an economic system and not *any* modification within the old framework. In this sense, Poland, along with most other communist countries (but unlike Hungary or, outside the bloc, Yugoslavia), has thus far not succeeded in carrying out economic reform; the command or centralist model of obligatory output targets and the physical allocation of resources has shown remarkable resistance to change. The actual subject of this chapter is the political economy of the failed reforms in Poland. In plain language, why have they failed? This may also throw some light on the prospects of current attempts at reform.

As stated above, the Polish experience of failed reform is shared by most communist countries. This might point to the advisability of a general examination that would concentrate on common elements. On the other hand, however, the Polish case stands out; reform ideas were posed and developed there at an early stage and remained a public issue for over thirty years, never actually being repudiated by the party. (As a matter of fact, each party congress since the "Polish October" in 1956 has had to assert a commitment to reform.) Several more or less comprehensive attempts at reforming the economic system were made in 1956, 1964, 1970 and 1973. Therefore, a separate analysis of Polish developments may well be revealing not for that country alone but in a wider context as well. There are, of course, numerous publications on this subject in Poland and several in the West; a critical survey of them would certainly provide a useful way of discussing our topic. But that is not what I propose to do in this chapter, which is conceived as a personal presentation based on direct experience of the struggles for reform at one stage and continuous observation of the process in Poland (and elsewhere) later. I adopt a historical approach, with special emphasis on the period of 1956 which, in my view, brought into focus all the major issues of the Polish (and perhaps other countries') economic reforms.

Polish October: the First Attempt

The main feature of the reform attempt of 1956 was that it became a part of the entire sociopolitical fabric of the "Polish October." Its significance was similar to that of the Czechoslovak reform in 1968, when the interaction between political and economic factors emerged so strongly. This feature has been acquired gradually by economic reform; at the outset, from 1953 to 1955, the reform proposals were somehow separated from the political context. The rising wave of open criticism of all facets of public life under Stalinism, the revelations of the twentieth congress of the CPSU, and, above all, the Poznań workers' revolt and its aftermath, changed the situation profoundly. Friends and foes alike began to look at economic reform from an increasingly political point of view. For the proponents of reform, decentralization of economic decision making necessarily combined with some kind of market mechanism within the planning and management system was not only an instrument for raising economic efficiency, but at the same time an indispensable condition and factor of political change of a pluralistic nature (democratization, as popular language had it at the time). The feedback effect of political changes on the economic scene was perhaps not fully elaborated, but it was clearly perceived both on a micro and on a macro level. On the microeconomic level the main link went through workers' self-management (some impact of freshly "rehabilitated" Yugoslav concepts was discernible, but spontaneous pressures reflecting traditional endogenous tendencies were, in my opinion, stronger), which was expected to improve what has since become known as x-efficiency. On the latter level, the removal of the suffocating hold of the center on all details of the operation of the economy was expected to rationalize the criteria of allocation, to unblock the channels of information, and to bring the idea of *social* cost-benefit calculation closer to reality. The interconnection between both sides led some to advocate the extension of the function of workers' councils beyond the enterprises by creating vertical representation up to the national level. The economic reformers of 1956 were aware of the reverse relationship (political changes *conditioning* the implementation of economic reform), but on the whole they failed to make it explicit; the trend of democratization was taken too much for granted.

By the same token, economic reforms engendered political resistance. Particularly hostile was the attitude toward institutional changes with a greater political connotation, such as the workers' councils. I remember well that one of the party stalwarts said to me, during an interval in a meeting of the Economic Council early in 1957, that self-management representation above the enterprises is tantamount to the creation of a dual power system, aimed at challenging the leading role of the party. The vehement opposition of the official trade union apparatus to the workers' councils was clearly in its own interests. The same was obviously true of the vast economic administration that was threatened by a loss of power and jobs. Opposition to the strictly economic aspects of the reform, on openly political grounds, fluctuated over time under the influence of a number of factors, including tactical ones; the periods in which conservative forces were on the defensive, ideological purity (the "undermining of socialism") usually gave way to welfare arguments (especially stressed was the supposition that an economic reform would pose a threat to job security).

The link of the 1956 economic reform with the entire fabric of the "Polish October" was the source of both its strength and its weakness. The reform movement was strong for a period of three to four months, riding the crest of a political surge. In early September 1956, "in order to stem the spontaneous process and to steer it in the right direction," a special governmental commission was charged with the task of "helping the workforce in the proper development of their management initiatives," as the drive from below to establish new rules for the enterprises and to freely elect workers' councils was euphemistically called. In the almost revolutionary atomsphere three important documents were drafted in just a few weeks, published in the press for public comments, and put on the statute books. Regulation No. 704 (10 November 1956) provided the state industrial enterprises with substantial autonomy; the Workers' Councils Act established them as managing bodies of socialized enterprises on behalf of the work force, and the Enterprise Fund Act established the principles and rules of profit-sharing (both acts adopted by the Sejm on November 19, 1956).

After October 1956, the political content of the economic reform turned from an asset into a liability. Contrary to the illusions cherished by numerous party intellectuals (including myself) about Gomułka's own reformist intentions in the political sphere, he threw his then enormous political weight fully behind the "leading role of the party," i.e., behind the one-party system. As at the same time the return of Gomułka and his associates to power was hailed as the victory of "socialist renewal," and a number of very popular steps were taken in particular areas (de-collectivization in agriculture, accommodation with the church, an apparently more independent stance toward the USSR, the release of Polish prisoners and exiles, repatriation, compensation for underpriced coal deliveries, the regulation of the status of Soviet military units stationed in Poland, etc.), the appetite for change, prevalent among young party secretaries, as well as pressure from society in general, gradually subsided. This made it possible to attack, very soon after October 1956, the directly political aspects of the economic reforms; worker's councils were subjected to all kinds of manipulation by the local party apparatus, which quickly re-established its control over the personal composition of the councils. In 1958 the authorities changed the law and created the so-called conferences of workers' self-management, in which the workers' councils became fully subordinated to the party and trade union committees of enterprises. Attempts to change the structure of the central state organs, including those of economic administration, failed completely. The Central Committee apparatus, briefly reduced in numbers, deprived of its supervisory role, and charged instead with the task of servicing specialized commissions (composed of party members working full time outside the apparatus), returned to its previous functions and size; the policy running of more candidates than the number of seats in national and local elections soon became an empty formality. The central economic administration remained basically in place (as a rule with somewhat changed names), and by 1959 even the number of ministries and coordinating vice-premiers began to grow again. The degree of freedom of expression reached in 1956 was determinately curtailed (closure of the weekly *Po Prostu* in 1957, a forced change of editors of many papers, e.g., *Zycie Gospodarcze*, and the immunity of economic decisions to public opinion was gradually restored.

With the balance of forces virtually reversed after October 1956, the case for economic reform had to rest entirely on its economic merits as perceived by the party leadership. The party was obviously concerned with improving economic performance and raising the standard of living—a politically sensitive issue, for the memory of Poznań was still fresh. However, Gomułka did not find an economic reform the only or even the most promising road to success, particularly in the short term, for the following reasons: the new stimuli for agriculture engendered by stopping the collectivization drive; the delayed effects of past investment projects which were coming on stream against relatively small additional outlays; the cancellation of liabilities to the Soviet Union (compensation for coal); and the post-Suez boom in the export of coal which, along with American credits, improved the external position. As a result, from 1956 to 1958 national income and real wages reportedly grew by 7.5-8 percent annually, which considerably reduced the pressure for systemic changes to enhance the capacity to "deliver the goods." Under the circumstances the party leadership saw the economic reform with increasing mistrust. After all, the only familiar type of planned economy was that of command and physical allocation, and, although an excessive degree of centralization and mistakes in policies were officially acknowledged, they seemed amenable to correction, without the risks—sociopolitical as well as economic—involved in designing and operating a substantially reformed system. Gomułka voiced this sentiment as early as the eighth plenary meeting of the Central Committee on October 20, 1956: "The question of the change in the management of industry is profoundly structural in character. . . . To put the whole machinery upon new tracks without having throughly tested the efficiency of the functioning of the new mechanism which we want to create is a dangerous thing. . . . One should greet with great appreciation the initiative of the working class concerning the improvement of industrial management, concerning the participation of workers in the management of their work establishment. . . . But one should make haste slowly insofar as broad-scale practice is concerned."[2] Before long, this and similar statements were interpreted as a decision for the status quo; despite the rather moderate character of the proposals adopted in May 1957 by the Economic Council, and some gradualism in their intended implementation (basically until the end of 1958), actual changes went away from the position reached at the end of 1956, thanks to the three new statutes mentioned above.

To what extent did external political factors contribute to the erosion of the drive to reform in Poland? This question is most difficult to answer without archival evidence. Drawing again on my personal recollections, some degree of displeasure from Moscow could certainly be detected, although it was much less direct than in the cases of decollectivization, greater openness to the West, or the relative outspokenness of the Polish press. For instance, direct attacks against myself and other Polish economists accused of market-oriented revisionism came from East Germany (where our ideas were quite popular up until the beginning of 1957, when a couple of Polish articles published in *Wirtschaftswissenschaft* triggered off a wave of criticsm and the infamous campaign against Fritz Behrens and Arne Benary). Soviet criticism took the form of a summary of the East German attacks. Similarly, Oskar Lange was attacked by an East German author, whereas in Moscow he was named as a target in an oral presentation at an anti-revisionist conference at the end of 1957. All this, however, had clear ideological connotations which should not automatically be identified with a real and effective veto. Despite the obvious displeasure with decollectivization, Gomułka got away with it. Why could the same not have happened with an economic reform in industry, particularly in 1957-58 when the threat to communist power in Poland and to the cohesion of the bloc was already over? I stand by my assessment, made a few years ago, that the conservative tendencies of the Soviets notwithstanding, the attitude of the local power elite is decisive for narrowly defined economic reform.[3]

The question frequently discussed is whether the very character of the reform proposals, particularly the acceptace of a gradual change from the old to the new system, had not itself been a factor that acted against the implementation of the reform. The main exposition of the reform program, the "Theses of the Economic Council on Certain Directions of Change in the Economic Model," was indeed a compromise between the radical and the more conservative wings in the Council (even more radical and more conservative positions were not represented on the Council). The indication that the advocated change was to be from a command to a regulated market system of planning was clear enough. Similarly, there was no insistence on immediate implementation of the recommendations as a package, although the new system was scheduled to be in place by the end of 1958. The "Theses," to be sure, did not contain any direct political demands, but they stressed the importance of the democratization of management of the national economy (an active role for workers' councils, local authorities and the Sejm in the process of planning), which in turn required "openness in economic life and such presentation of problems which would make fully clear the real alternatives of choice taken into consideration in the plan"; this elaborate formulation was meant to convey the Council's conviction that public scrutiny of economic decisions taken at the center is indispensable.[4] There is some slight confusion about the formal attitude of the government to the "Theses"; the editor of Kalecki's collected works[5] refers to Bobrowski's (then acting vice chairman of the Council) conversation with the prime minister, who said that the document was neither approved nor rejected. In my own recollection the "Theses" were approved "in principle," but there is no discrepancy in the fact that they were never put into practice. Hence, the otherwise correct observations about the logic of the reassertion of the old system over partially introduced elements of the new one[6] and about the ease of retreat at the first hurdle when the old institutional structure remains basically intact do not seem to apply to the fate of the Polish reforms in the 1950s. This was, in my opinion, not a case of a rejected transplant but a refusal to carry out the operation.

Economic Conservatism and Political Crisis

The fallacy of incoherent partial changes could have played a greater role in the failure of later attempts, starting from 1964-65 when Poland hesitantly joined what I call "the second wave" of reforms in European communist countries. By then, the Hungarian-Polish type of threat to the political system had passed and the "reserve of past mistakes" was largely exhausted; economists singled out systemic inefficiencies as a course of substantial set backs in economic performance (particularly in Czechoslovakia and the GDR ahead even in the USSR), and an economic reform was seen as the likely remedy.

The changes announced at the fourth congress of the PUWP (1964) and at the Fourth Plenum meeting of the Central Committee (1965) showed no aspirations to produce a grand design (like the "new model" of 1956-57, or like the "New Economic System," as the parallel East German measures were called). Changes were modestly presented as "improvements in the methods of planning and management" and restricted to a reduction in the number of success indicators, an increase in the relative weight of profitability as one of such (planned) indicators, another attempt to transform industrial associations from purely administrative organs of the ministries into more economically oriented units, and an introduction of special incentives for export. The party leadership avoided all political implications and sought to repair its flagging "renewalist" image and to stop the economic downturn (the most ominous sign was the sharp fall in the growth rate of real wages, which was reported officially as 5.1 percent annually in the second half of the 1950s and only 1.5 percent in the first half of the 1960s).

This half-hearted response to mounting economic difficulties not only failed to bring relief but was short-lived: scattered and superficial measures were simply absorbed by the traditional system, which was impervious to efforts devoid of any political muscle. Later, a leading academic close to the Gierek regime stated that "this attempt remained on paper. The inertia of the apparatus of economic administration and the activity of interest groups engendered by the existing system of planning and management simply did not allow deeper changes to be introduced."[7] This evaluation of effects is certainly correct, but inertia and the vested interests of the apparatus must have interacted with a lack of conviction and political will at the center as well as with the incoherence of the new measures that were set to work against the existing system.

The conflicting factors of political-ideological allegiances of the party leadership on the one hand, and of the growing pressure of economic realities on the other, surfaced with particular clarity toward the end of the decade. One of the ideological sticks used to beat the students' and intellectuals' protest movement in March 1968 was the accusation of "market deviation." This charge was accompanied by pseudo-populist attacks on widening income, purportedly directed at "marketeers." The fear of a spread of the "Prague Spring" added ferocity and urgency to these attacks. Nevertheless, having achieved the immediate political objectives of the witch hunt, the party leadership had no choice but the resumption and even the intensification of the systemic changes. The economy proved continuously incapable of securing increases in the standard of living, the main foundation of the regime's legitimacy after the frustration of the hopes for the "likeable socialism" of October 1956. The official data on the dynamics of real wages over the period 1960-70 showed Poland worse off than any other East European country. Small wonder, therefore, that the fifth congress of the PUWP (November 1968) called for a "transition to the stage of selective and intensive development," which implied expediting technological modernization as a factor for increased labor and capital productivity, economy in the use of material inputs, and competitiveness in foreign markets. The conservative leadership could not cope with these tasks, particularly with regard to the premise that the importation of Western technology and know-how for the modernization of selected industries should be paid for mainly from the country's own resources, i.e., without major, longer-term foreign credits. This meant, at least in the short term, a further squeeze on incomes. In this respect an economic reform seemed doubly suitable; first, it might have contributed to a genuinely faster growth of productivity than of earnings, and second, it could have provided a convenient cover for an otherwise brutal assault on incomes. Thus, the two pillars of the modified system of planning and management to be introduced from the beginning of 1971 were reforms in pricing and incentives (apart from changes in the mechanism of foreign trade). The price reform was designed to encompass both producer goods prices (a new formula linking part of the mark-up with the amount of capital employed and new rules of price determination providing some flexibility) and retail prices in which huge increases in the price of food (especially meat) were only thinly disguised by "compensating" reductions in the prices of industrial consumer goods of secondary importance. As for incentives, the scheme intended to link the wage fund of an enterprise with progress achieved over the preceding year as measured by two types of indicators: synthetic (financial) and specific (four selected indicators of output, productivity, use of materials, etc.). Each indicator was given a relative weight in order to make them additive. An overall ceiling of 16 percent for five years was placed on the increase in earnings according to the scheme, and the deferment of payments until the first quarter of 1972 meant an effective two years' freeze on wages. The incentive scheme was ritually presented as a joint decision of the "Council of Ministers and Central Council of Trade Unions," but no one believed that genuine representatives of the employees had agreed on it; the increase in food prices was kept secret until it was announced. New price lists had already been distributed to the shops ten days before Christmas 1970. The news of the price increases triggered the workers' revolt on the Baltic coast, which was drowned in blood. The Gomułka leadership was swept away. The events of 1970 marked a new powerful dimension in the political economy of Polish reforms: the articulated interests and attitudes of the industrial working class.

The Polish revolt of 1970 had some repercussions throughout the communist bloc; it was, after all, the first eruption on this scale not directed against post-Stalinist leadership. However, the measures taken in most communist countries were not of the reformist kind; a revision of the 1971-75 plans providing a somewhat better deal for the consumer was the predominant response. Poland itself was another matter; here the workers' revolt opened a new cycle of reform attempts, in conditions resembling to some extent the situation after 1956, but with a number of specific features of its own.

The most important difference compared with the crisis of 1956 was that in 1970 the new leadership had no political charisma on which it could rely in "normalizing" the situation; much more depended on tangible economic results. On the other hand, the political demands of the Baltic strikers were less explicit than during the "Polish October" (one of the effects of the isolation of the workers from the intelligentsia, which was beaten in 1968), and open outbursts were restricted to one region of the country (with Warsaw quiet.) The duration of pressure from below was shorter (the peak passed after Gierek's successful appearance in Szczecin and Gdańsk in January 1971, and certainly after the rescision of the food price increases under pressure from women textile workers at the end of February). As in 1956 the new leadership soon found non-reformist means to improve its economic image (this time mainly of external provenance). Finally, the room for maneuvering in matters concerning real personal incomes, particularly in the field of prices, became most restricted in the shadow of the successful workers' protest.

The impact of these factors on the reform of the economic mechanism was complex, but the overall tendency of the old system to reassert itself again came to the fore. In the initial period of relative weakness, in the very aftermath of December events, and still without external resources, the Gierek leadership displayed a greater zeal to reform, emphasizing the need not only for economic but also for political reform (the modernization of the system of functioning of the economy and of the *state*—this was the official brief for the so-called "Szydlak Commission"). By the time of the commission's report in April 1972, the political element had practically disappeared, as had the concessions granted to trade union autonomy in early 1971. Even the full text of the proposals for an economic reform was not made public (this document allegedly envisaged a far-reaching restructuralization of the central organs of planning and management, as well as a comprehensive price reform). What was left was the increase in autonomy of industrial units (this was not a complete abolition of the command system but a substantial reduction of the number of targets, not on the enterprise level but on the level of conglomerates called large economic organizations, or WOG in Polish, hence the name "WOG reform"), a new incentive scheme with the wage fund linked to value added, a greater flexibility in price formation, and a more direct connection between domestic and foreign trade operations.

The WOG reform was to be introduced gradually, and for some time the growing number of WOGs transferring to the new system was one of the subjects of triumphant press reports.

The first WOG operating under the new rules appeared in 1973, but by 1975, despite the increase in the number of "pilot units," the reform was, for all practical purposes, over, with most of the decentralizing measures cancelled, suspended, or curbed. Even by past standards, the hastiness of this retreat was extraordinary; the new rules were not given a serious chance to prove themselves, nor were they properly introduced. More ironic is that one of the overriding areas of reform was to replace the short-term scramble over indicators and resources by longer-term normatives and incentives as necessary components of a planning system with a broader perspective.

To a considerable degree the WOG reform was undermined by the overexpansionary policy of the Gierek leadership, which had to yield to the pressure for higher incomes while simultaneously starting an unprecedented investment drive and stepping up the roundabout policies for the socialization of agriculture. The very fact that imbalances and shortages occurred shows how low a successful economic reform was placed on the party's list of priorities. Evidently, at no time was there an option to use at least part of Poland's large supply of foreign credits to reduce tensions in the economy and to prop up market equilibrium. The overall growth policy, the sectoral allocations reproducing old structural proportions, and the chaotic "open-plan" formula that allowed a disregard of elementary requirements of coordination even for major projects undertaken ad hoc was decided on by the center without considering the consequences for economic reform. On the contrary, as Waldemar Kuczyński plausibly suggests,[8] the grandiose expansionary programs themselves made the party leaders and the local barons even more reluctant to relinquish direct control in order not to forfeit the personal glory of building the "second Poland" and promoting all the prestigious projects for which they successfully lobbied without due attention to cost-benefit calculations.

Sources of Resistance to Change

Our brief survey of Polish reform attempts before 1980 brings out a general thread in the attitudes of the party leadership toward changes in the economic system. This thread seems particularly clear in the context of the developments after the "Polish October" as well as in the 1970s. The dominant element was one of resistance to change. Under economic and political pressure, resistance would periodically turn into reluctant acceptance of reform, after which the following sequence would appear: (1) the elimination of directly political aspects of reform; (2) the limitation of the actual scope of changes in the economic mechanism;

(3) a gradual implementation, with particular attention to preservation of the institutional set-up in the center and of the *nomenklatura* principle in appointments; and (4) the utilization of all avenues promising to overcome economic difficulties without reform, while the preserved institutional structure provided the framework for a return to the old system.

The problem is not with the attempt to subvert the reform but with the motivation behind this subversion. Needless to say, there is little definitive evidence in this area, but the history of aborted reforms in Poland provides the basis to form an opinion. In my view, four interconnected and often overlapping groups of motives for resistance or reluctance toward decentralizing and market-oriented economic reforms can be discerned:

—first, the fact that certain individuals and groups benefit from the command system in terms of power, social position, and material advantage. It may well be that this factor has played a greater role in the apparatus (including part of the managerial stratum) than in the very top political elite, but its direct and indirect impact seems to me important and least controversial.

—second, lack of confidence in the pragmatic value of the reformist solutions. This is now seldom discussed in the context of reform failures, although it should be, despite the enormous complications. Doubts in the efficacy of reform could derive from the realization of genuine difficulties in combining meaningful planning and public ownership with market mechanisms (which has been, after all, the gist of Polish reform proposals rejecting the pure logic of both the market and the command planning).

—third, ideological considerations: a market-oriented economic reform in a direction opposite that of the traditional image of communism, which is supposed to do away with commodity exchange and money, individual incentives and competition, income and wealth differentials. It is of course impossible even to guess how widespread and influential among the Polish ruling elite *genuine* ideological concerns of this kind were (popular opinion regards them as rapidly diminishing over time and by now almost extinct), but they cannot be totally discarded, particularly if one takes into account that an economic reform might acquire a momentum of its own. Such a development would not necessarily stop short of tackling such fundamental concepts and institututions as property rights, entrepreneurship, etc.

—fourth, political motives, however difficult it is to distinguish them from other factors. Conservatives strive to maintain and to strengthen the monolithic, single-party system, or "monarchy." I have tried to show, among other things, that the "marketization" of the economy is by no means such a straightforward factor in the "pluralization" of the polity (transformation of a monoarchy into polyarchy) as is often assumed; Yugoslavia and Hungary can serve as examples of reformed economies without fundamental change in the political system. Nevertheless, a link certainly does exist in the actual processes (more market influence means less economic power for the state and better conditions for maintaining elements of pluralism won in direct political struggle), as well as in the perception of them both by the ruling elite and by mass movements fighting for political rights. Thus, the phenomenon of the economic reform became a hot political issue in the "Polish October" and in the "Solidarity" period.

I am convinced that the political factor, in a strict sense, has played a paramount role in the history of Polish reform attempts; the ultimate criterion for choosing a course of action by the communist policy makers is, after all, the preservation and strengthening of their power (the principle of the "leading role of the party"). But as abundantly shown by the experience of Poland and other countries, this criterion can lead, under certain conditions, to contradictory choices—reform is bad because it curtails the power of the state and may directly facilitate political developments adverse to the monolithic system, but at the same time reform may prop up the system if no other avenues for averting the political danger of economic setbacks are in sight. Hence, the peculiar stop-go process, or as one Polish political sociologist puts it, generalizing on the experience of the 1970s: "the destiny of the changes is a resultant of two conflicting tendencies—to preserve the continuity of the political system and to enhance the efficiency of the economic system. In effect, the shape of the reform becomes inconsistent, reflecting the contradictions in the interactions between politics and economies.[10] In the light of these contradictions the sequence of moves presented at the outset of this section acquires its own peculiar logic, which leads nowhere. The vicious circle is particularly visible in the persistent striving to eliminate any political connotations of an economic reform, thus depriving it of the popular support that is necessary not only for fighting inertia and vested interests but also for reducing the social risks involved in systemic changes aimed at increasing efficiency. Such changes may bear eventual fruit but require some immediate, unpleasant steps. Politically sterile economic reforms seems, on the one hand, the most attractive and possibly the only acceptable proposition for the communist rulers, but, on the other hand, it becomes the most dubious choice because a purely "technocratic" reform is less likely to cure the ills of an economy and to avert social discontent. An additional push for a U-turn comes from the fear that this discontent will be used as a weapon in a factional struggle for power.

The Prospects at Present

It seems to me that the interactions present in the aborted reforms of the past are at play in the post-1980 period as well, although the dimensions of the problems involved are much greater. I would like to trace the general pattern of this newest reform attempt in terms of the political economy.

Poland's economic disaster was on an unprecedented scale, as was the challenge to the existing political system. Under the circumstances, an economic reform soon appeared as the main feasible institutional contribution for dealing with the crisis. The reform did not happen immediately after August 1980, for the very restricted first version of the official proposals was announced in January 1981. Both the government and Solidarity came to share the position that the horrendous imbalances in the economy were not to be treated as an insurmountable obstacle to the speedy introduction of a market-oriented reform, despite obvious indications to the contrary. I think this policy was correct in the extraordinary circumstances, which rendered the old system simply unworkable. The differences in respect to the degree of radicalism in the strictly economic aspects of the reform plan (in particular, the question of enterprise autonomy and of new methods of central planning) were actually narrowing in the autumn of 1981. The true area of contention was *control* over the process of reform and over the institutional structure that would emerge as its outcome: a public control inseparable from pluralism (the most explicit form of which was the very existence and role of Solidarity itself) versus authoritarianism under the catchword "the leading role of the party." The sharp conflict around the issue of the appointment of managers was perhaps in part symbolic, nonetheless it reflected well the real preoccupation of both sides with genuine lines of dependence.

Thus the communist rulers were faced once again with the task of depriving the economic reform of its political edge, which is how economic reform reemerged in the security of martial law at the beginning of 1982, and how it is supposed to have operated since. No matter how much effort is devoted by the party-military establishment to present the approved unions, self-management institutions, front organizations like PRON,[11] modifications of electoral law, etc., as evidence of democratic progress cleared only of Solidarity extremism, there can be no doubt that the monolithic system has been restored, and the prospects of narrowly defined economic reform must be considered within this framework.

I am prepared to accept that at this time, the Polish rulers are more deeply committed to changes in the economic system than ever before, for reasons which have already been mentioned (no hope of getting out of the crisis with the old compromised system). The likely goal is some imitation of "kádárism" There is little use in discussing here the similarities and differences between post-1956 Hungary and the present Polish situation; I have tried to do this elsewhere.[12] What seems necessary is to assess briefly the impact of the existing political environment on the actual course of economic reform introduced in January 1982.

In my opinion, the negative impact is visible. I see it not so much in the retention of large numbers of direct targets and physical allocation orders for producer goods (this may be, to some extent at least, justified for a time by the omnipresent deep disequilibria), but in keeping almost intact the institutional structure of, in Janos Kornai's terminology, the economic "control sphere," particularly at the center, where the link with political control is closest. I also believe that the evident lack of success in fighting strong inflationary pressures can be traced to the failure in gaining political support for government policies. Time and again, measures designed to reduce the yawning gap between the purchasing power of the population and the value of goods and services have been thwarted by the need to buy off the potential sources of sacrifice for the sake of overcoming the crisis. The predominant mood seems to be one of suspicion and frustration, and in some circles, of outright hostility to the state's policies, including the economic reform. The political stalemate is thus being transplanted into an economic stalemate that cannot but strengthen those who, for one reason or another, press for return to the old system. The familiar sequence of retreat has not yet appeared, and the official line is still that of going ahead. It is, however, difficult to imagine how such a retreat can be ultimately avoided without a political breakthrough.

The role of the political factor may be seen even more clearly in the notorious story of the church fund for the development of private agriculture. The attitudes toward the private or quasi-private sector form an important element in changes in the economic mechanisms in all communist countries (Hungary is the best known case in point), but nowhere is it as important as in Poland, where, in my view, the whole issue of reform should actually revolve around agriculture and agriculture-related industries. The church fund cannot in itself solve the problem, but it offers a country starved of foreign currency a unique opportunity to start the ball rolling. Nevertheless, the matter drags on, and the only explanation must be that the Jaruzelski regime fears a weakening of its control. In different forms, attitudes of this kind make themselves felt in other actual or potential areas of private economic activity, including those with foreign capital participation.

Needless to say, political factors are not the only ones that affect the destinies of economic reforms that attempt to combine meaningful planning with market mechanism on the basis of public ownership. Substantive difficulties of such a combination are evident, and require separate examination. Nevertheless, the political factors acquire an importance that can hardly be overestimated—as the long and painful history of Polish reforms abundantly shows.

The overriding objective of the preservation of the monolithic system was and still is in conflict with the economic interests of the country. This is the simple lesson of the political economy of Polish reform.

Notes

1. Reprinted, with minor alterations by the author and with the permission of the publisher, from *Praxis International*, Volume 5 (July 1985).

2. Paul E. Zinner, ed., *National Communism and Popular Revolt in Eastern Europe* (New York, 1956), pp. 212-213.

3. In a brief note published in Karen Dawisha and Philip Hanson, ed., *Soviet-East European Dilemmas* (London, 1981).

4. Large excerpts from the "Theses" have been published in English by Nicholas Spulber in *Organizational Alternatives in Soviet-type Economies* (Cambridge, 1979).

5. *Kalecki's Collected Works* Volume 3 (in Polish), Warsaw: 1982.

6. See, *inter alia*, the late J. G. Zielinski's *Economic Reforms in Polish Industry* (Oxford, 1973).

7. Jan Szczepański, (in Polish) *Changes in Polish Society in the Process of Industrialization* (Warsaw, 1973), p. 264.

8. Waldemar Kuczyński, (in Polish) *After the Great Leap* (Warsaw, 1979).

9. "Political Pluralism and Markets in Communist Systems," in Susan S. Salomon, *Pluralism in the Soviet Union* (London, 1983).

10. A. Rychard, (in Polish) *Economic Reform: A Sociological Analysis of the Links between Politics and Economics* (Wrocław, 1980), p. 70.

11. Polski Ruch Odrodzenia Narodowego (Polish Movement of National Rebirth): a front organization, similar to the "national fronts" or "patriotic fronts" of other communist countries, pretending to represent a broad spectrum of non-party members cooperating with the authorities.

12. W. Brus, P. Kende, Z. Młynar, *"Normalization" Processes in Soviet-dominated Central Europe* (Cologne, 1982).

9

Reform Cycles in Poland, the USSR, the GDR, and Czechoslovakia

Władysław W. Jermakowicz

This chapter describes and interprets the direction and intensity of changes in Poland's macro-management system in the postwar period and then compares Poland's experience with those of the USSR, the German Democratic Republic (GDR), and Czechoslovakia.[1] In all cases the focus is on the industrial sector.

Macro-Management System Defined

A country's macro-management system (MMS) is defined as the set of arrangements by which the center determines what is to be produced, how the goods shall be produced, and how the resulting income shall be distributed. MMSs may be characterized by:

— the *organizational structure*, composed of institutions responsible for the production and distribution of goods and services as well as the administrative arrangements, such as the ministries and associations that plan or supervise the activities of enterprises;

— *direct regulation*, which includes all administrative instruments— such as commands, instructions, rationing decisions—used by the center to manage the economy;

— *indirect regulation*, which includes all the financial regulators (parameters), such as price regulation, relied on by the center to accomplish its goals. The difference between direct and indirect regulation is found only in the way in which the instructions are delivered. Under direct regulation, instructions take the form of specified plan targets that are addressed to specific units. Under indirect regulation, the center influences fields of activity, such as the influence of agriculture on the production of medical equipment.

There are two pure models of MMS. One is the *autocratic model*, a fully hierarchical organization of management, relying exclusively on direct, command regulation by the center. The other is the *parametric model*, a fully functional organizational structure that manages economic activity using only indirect financial regulation. In addition to these two pure MMS models, which can exist only if the central authorities play a dominant role in the economy, there is also a third economic system model: *laissez-faire*.[2]

The relationship between the three models is presented in Chart 3. On the A-P line lie all combinations of centrally-managed economies (CMEs). On the P-L line lie all models of market-directed economies (MDEs), systems that combine a competitive market with fiscal and monetary "dirigism" to achieve certain public policy goals. On the A-L line lie models that combine competitive markets with direct, centrally-controlled sectors of the economy. Such systems can often be found

Chart 3. Graphic Typology of Basic Economic Systems

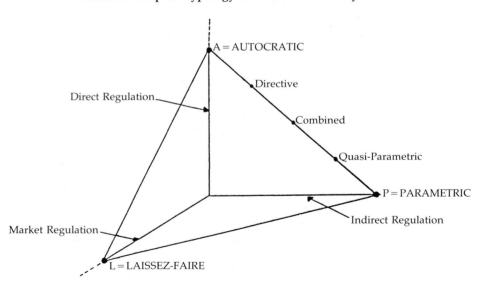

during wartime—in Germany during the world wars and in Soviet Russia during its New Economic Policy in the early 1920s.

Methodology for Identifying Any Economic System

I have developed a technique to locate any economic system along the three-dimensional model shown in Chart 3. For the purpose of measuring the evolution of the economic systems of selected East European countries, only combinations of direct and indirect regulation will be discussed. I will focus on the industrial sector. I am assuming that the third dimension—market regulation—can be neglected because in the industrial sector it plays only a marginal role.

An unlimited number of MMSs can be located between the pure autocratic and the pure parametric systems outside these poles as combinations of the two types. For the sake of simplification, I have identified and characterized five MMS models that may have existed or might exist in CPEs:

—the *autocratic model*, which is a pure command economy. It closely parallels a system of military management. It is characterized by the perfect congruence of party, economic management, and administrative structures. For example, the same person often wears different "command" hats—that of party secretary, enterprise director, and boss of the trade unions within the organization. The closest approximation of such a system was the period of war communism in Soviet Russia.

—the *directive model*, which resembles a Soviet-type CPE. The command system dominates; financial regulation mainly monitors implementation. Industrial branch ministries have a great deal of power; the Ministry of Finance plays the role of the accountant for the whole economy. This system was dominant in the East European countries during the 1950s, and essentially still prevails in the USSR, Romania, and Albania.

—the *combined model*, which is characterized by the coexistence of specific targets with financial motivation. This type of MMS appeared after the reforms in several East European countries in the 1960s.

—the *quasi-parametric model*, in which the central authority regulates the economy by centrally-set prices and other financial "regulators," such as taxes, exchange rates, tariffs, and wage rates. The center, however, has the right, through the Ministry of Industry, to directly set certain compulsory plan targets and exercise ownership functions over enterprises. This system has been closely approximated in Hungary since the reform of 1980.

—the *parametric model*, in which central authority simulates what the market would do if it existed. That is, the center adjusts prices to try to equate supply and demand. It does not have any right to regulate directly. This MMS is sometimes called the "regulated market model."[3] As a theoretical construct it was described by Oscar Lange.[4]

I have developed a system of indicators that can measure the directions and intensity of systemic changes. Each of the five MMS models is identified by a set of twelve parallel descriptors, identified and discussed briefly in the Appendix. Each descriptor of the autocratic model is assigned zero points on a scale. Thus, if a system is purely autocratic, the sum total of its "system points" will be zero, each of the twelve descriptors of the parametric model. At the other end of the spectrum, four points are given. Thus, if a system is purely parametric, the total number of points will be 48. As the system moves from autocratic to parametric through the three intermediate stages, the point value of each descriptor increases (1 point each under the directive, 2 each under the combined, and 3 under the quasi-parametric system). The summary indicator, i.e., the total number of points, is thus called "degree of parametrization" (DoP).

In real life no pure MMS exists; each actual MMS is a mixture, identified by a certain combination of descriptors that correspond to various models. "Snapshots" of a given country's MMS at various points in time can be taken. Changes in the total number of system points over time will thus indicate the direction and intensity of systemic change, which can then be charted.

The Reform Cycles in Poland

The evolution of Poland's MMS from 1944 to 1985, as measured by the DoP indicator, is shown in Chart 4.[5] Chart 4 graphically depicts what Brus indicated in the previous chapter, namely, that after a period of the introduction and consolidation of the Soviet-type economic model during the first postwar decade, six reform attempts have occurred to "parametrize" Poland's economy: the New Course reform of 1953; the Polish reform of October 1956; the Rentability Index reform of 1964-65; the Jaszczuk reform of 1969-70; the WOG reform of 1973; and the Polish reform of August 1982. Some of these reform packages represented real changes in the economy, that is, serious attempts to parametrize the MMS; others can be called pseudo-reforms, because there was little real change in the MMS.

The real reforms were those of 1956, 1970, and 1982. The beginning of each was marked by a political crisis. The strikes in Poznań marked the crisis of 1956; in 1970, there were strikes in the major port cities of Gdańsk, Gdynia, and Szczecin; and in 1982, a wave of unrest brought agreements in Gdańsk, Szczecin, and Jastrzębie, as well as the birth of Solidarity. Each crisis was followed by a change in leadership and the

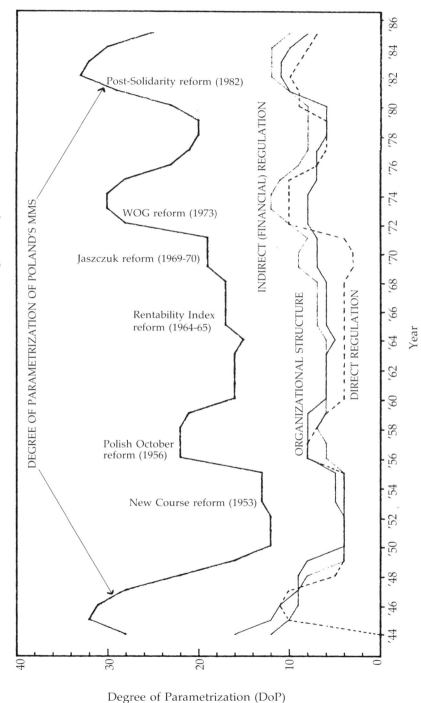

Chart 4. The Evolution of Poland's Macro-Management System, 1944-85

introduction of a more or less comprehensive reform program. The authorities eventually retrenched, an act best characterized not as recentralization but as redirectivization—that is, the reintroduction of greater direct control by the center.

One fundamental conclusion that emerges from my more detailed analysis (not presented here) is the gradual decomposition over time of Poland's MMS.[6] The system has moved gradually away from what can be called a "clean" or internally consistent system, one that embodies a more or less complete set of variables belonging to one of the theoretical models presented in the Appendix. Poland's MMS was clean only twice— in 1948, and from 1951 to 1953. As the MMS evolved, internal breakdowns occurred more frequently. This is especially evident at the end of each reform cycle, when various modifications, taken from different models, were combined into increasingly hybrid systems. For example, beginning in 1966 liberal profitability indices coexisted with strictly specified plan targets that were given to enterprises by the Planning Commission. Enterprises thus sat between liberal financial regulation and very strict planning regulations.

Central control by financial regulators is more flexible than by rigid directive planning. But these two methods of control, and their respective instruments, are generally in disagreement with one another. Thus, a system that combines them in certain ways may become inconsistent, hindering economic performance. One typical inconsistency is the introduction of indirect regulation without any significant change in the organizational structure. Such a situation is not unique to Poland; to a lesser degree it can be found also in the reforms introduced, for example, in the USSR in 1973 and 1979.

A further conclusion concerns the long-term evolution of Poland's MMS. Despite fluctuations, Poland's MMS has gradually evolved from a directive system in the early 1950s into a quasi-parametric model by the mid-1980s, although the road traveled was far from straightforward. Actually, the MMS has evolved in a somewhat circular fashion, from a quasi-parametric system in the immediate postwar period back to a quasi-parametric system by the early 1980s (Chart 4).

A third conclusion concerns the method of "learning" within the system. We often find that a specific idea introduced into a reform blueprint during the formulation of a new system will be implemented later, during one of the next reform phases. For example, limited financial independence for enterprises was first postulated in 1958 but was realized only during the WOG reforms of 1972-75. The idea of separating central planning from the internal plans of individual enterprises was first proposed during the 1970s but was realized only in the 1980s. The proposal for sweeping labor democracy was originally proposed in 1956 and partially implemented only in 1981.

This experience suggests that the articulation of certain proposals for systemic change during a given reform cycle may well be realized only with delays, during one of the next reform phases. This allows us to forecast some of the changes that are likely to occur in subsequent reforms. For example, during the next reform cycle, in the 1990s, I predict that an entire, multilevel structure of self-governing bodies will be introduced at both the enterprise level, through workers' councils, and at the level of the entire economy, through the second workers' chamber in the Sejm. It is also likely that in the next reform cycle only one industrial ministry will survive at the governmental level and that the idea of privatizing certain segments of the state economy will probably be implemented for the first time. A more comprehensive privatization of the economy, however, will probably have to wait until the twenty-first century.

The last reform, that of 1982, interests us especially for two reasons. First, will the introduction of the reform blueprints of 1981 really improve the performance of the economy? Second, will Poland generate the political will to continue and implement those reforms fully? I have rather pessimistic answers for both questions. Although the Polish management system is spiraling toward its roots of the 1940s, i.e. toward the quasi-parametric system, the effectiveness of the management system will not necessarily improve (for a complex set of reasons discussed in several other chapters).

Next, the political will, as discussed by Brus, goes through a cycle that starts with political support for a comprehensive reform blueprint and ends with retreat from the advocation and implementation of the reform. For Poland, such a course of action can already be observed in case of the last reform cycle. To be sure, many hope that domestic and external economic and political pressure and the sudden burst of reform in the USSR will also have a positive impact on countries like Poland. Validating this hope, however, requires more detailed analysis. This leads us to the question of the relationship between reform cycles in the member countries of the CMEA.

Influence of the Other CMEA Countries on Reforms in Poland

Will the current reforms in the USSR have an impact on the evolution of the reforms in Poland? Analyzing the presumed impact of previous Soviet reforms on Poland can provide useful insights. I have attempted to measure the evolution of the MMSs of the Soviet Union, the GDR, and Czechoslovakia using the same methodology that I used to measure the MMS of Poland. The results of the comparisons are presented in Chart 5.

Chart 5 shows that 1945-52 was a period of forceful centralization and "directivization" of the MMSs of the GDR, Czechoslovakia, and Poland to conform to a very high degree with that already in place in the USSR. The most striking information revealed by Chart 5 is the

Creditworthiness and Reform in Poland

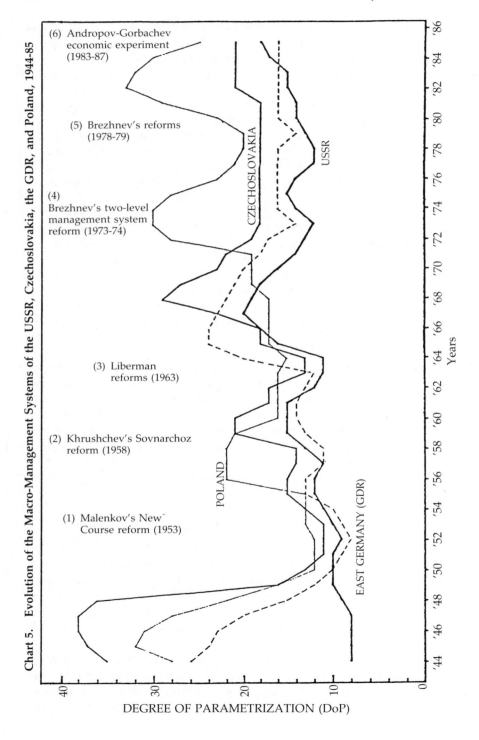

Chart 5. Evolution of the Macro-Management Systems of the USSR, Czechoslovakia, the GDR, and Poland, 1944-85

(6) Andropov-Gorbachev economic experiment (1983-87)

(5) Brezhnev's reforms (1978-79)

(4) Brezhnev's two-level management system reform (1973-74)

(3) Liberman reforms (1963)

(2) Khrushchev's Sovnarchoz reform (1958)

(1) Malenkov's New Course reform (1953)

CZECHOSLOVAKIA

USSR

POLAND

EAST GERMANY (GDR)

DEGREE OF PARAMETRIZATION (DoP)

Years

pattern of reform cycles since 1953, when the first wave of reforms began in the USSR. We find that whereas the reform cycles of the GDR and Czechoslovakia closely match those of the USSR, the case of Poland is different; neither the timing nor the amplitude of its reform cycles have matched closely those of the USSR.

The first reforms were started by G. Malenkov in 1953, and were known as the *new course reform*. His measures were copied in Czechoslovakia and the GDR but not in Poland. The second wave, known as the *sovnarchoz reforms*, was announced by Khrushchev in 1957. His reforms were marked by the abolition of the industrial ministries in the GDR and by similar reforms in Czechoslovakia. The third wave of reforms, also proclaimed by Khrushchev, began in 1962 with the publication of the ideas of *Liberman*. This reform began with discussions about new economic indicators, which tied the premium fund to the "rentability" of enterprises. The Soviet authorities reduced the number of indicators of enterprise performance and introduced new methods of their calculation, at first experimentally and then in a comprehensive fashion. New types of material incentives were introduced. The GDR introduced similar reforms in 1963, as did Czechoslovakia and Hungary in 1965.

The fourth wave of reforms started in 1973-74 and can be called Brezhnev's *two-level management system reform*. In the organizational sphere, the union-republican ministries were purposely transformed into all-union ministries in order to reduce the number of organizational levels from three to two. The instrumental changes concerned the introduction of an indicator of the normative planning of enterprises, based on a predetermined ratio of total wages to output. These changes were reflected in the GDR where, in 1974, 11,000 private industrial plants were nationalized and integrated with the combines. Experiments with new performance indicators were initiated, a change that was copied in Czechoslovakia.

The fifth wave of reforms started in 1978-79 when, in the USSR, compulsory five-year contracts had to be signed between producing and buying enterprises, specifying the assortment and quality of product transfers. At the same time, a series of new financial indicators were introduced for ministries and enterprises. In the GDR, a special decree (1978) declared "a unity of plan and contracts"; in Czechoslovakia the "Comprehensive Package of [New] Measures" was published in March 1980. Andropov's economic experiment in 1983 started the sixth wave of reforms, continuing at the present time under Gorbachev.

A comparison of the evolutions of the MMSs in different countries in Chart 5 reveals that certain countries have imitated the changes in the USSR fairly closely, while others (or the same countries at different times), showed less conformity. Of the Eastern bloc countries, the GDR traditionally followed Soviet schemes the closest. For example, it was the only country to follow the Soviet lead in abolishing industrial ministries in 1958, creating the German version of *Gosekonomkommissiya*. The only exception to the apparently servile imitation by the GDR was its "New Economic System" reform of 1963. It was based on Liberman's paper, which, surprisingly, was published in the GDR two weeks after it appeared in the Soviet Union (September 23 and September 9, 1962, respectively). There are reasons to suspect that in this reform the GDR preceded the USSR, because Khrushchev used East Germany as a "guinea pig", so to speak, to test the solutions that he intended to implement one or two years later in the USSR. It is interesting to note that East Germany was the only East European country which discontinued this reform, as did the USSR after the invasion of Czechoslovakia in August 1968.

The evolution of the Czechoslovak system shows a higher degree of independence from that of the USSR, especially during the former's autonomous wave of 1965-69, although those reforms began, or at least were encouraged, by the Liberman reforms in the USSR. According to stories circulating in Prague in 1964, Novotný decided to discuss the final draft of the proposed reforms at the Central Committee Plenum in January 1965, because Khrushchev, during his last visit to Czechoslovakia prior to his ouster in October 1964, expressed considerable interest and support for them. During the 1970s and early 1980s Czechoslovakia had no reforms, and remained more "orthodox" than even the USSR, although the conformity of their systems was quite close, as shown by Chart 5. In brief, the author is convinced that the rhythm of changes in the GDR and Czechoslovakia was influenced significantly, if not actually determined, by systemic changes in the USSR.

Surprisingly, the evolution of Poland's MMS shows a much more independent pattern. Poland's "real" reforms were either too early, as in 1956, or too late, as in 1973 or 1981. They have never followed the sequence of the general system cycles in the CMEA. This lack of congruence had a negative impact on the success of the reforms in Poland, because they were introduced in a hostile ideological environment.

At the same time, the introduction of Soviet reforms did have a slight influence on the introduction of pseudo-reforms in Poland. The party elite usually copied the main ideas of change from the Soviet experiments and officially accepted them during party congresses, but then there was little movement to implement them.

Lack of close past correlation between real Polish reforms and reforms elsewhere in the CMEA suggest that we have no reason to expect that *"glasnost"* or any type of modest reforms in the USSR will generate a big momentum for real reforms in Poland. That could happen only if the reforms in the USSR were much more progressive, more "parametric," than the system already in place in Poland. Rather, as long as the Soviet MMS is less "liberal" than the Polish system (which is the case today, as shown in Chart 5), conservatives in Poland can use that as an excuse to push for the centralization of the system.

What, then, is really needed for a positive introduction of reforms in Poland? The answer is clear: the country's leadership must strongly support the continuation of reforms. The lack of sustained political support in the postwar history of Poland has been closely related to the lack of security of the leading power elite. The past shows that "real" reforms required a real political shake-up—the turnover of a minimum of 60 percent of the *party's* elite. If large personnel changes happened exclusively in the state apparatus, then it led only to the announcement of pseudo-reforms. From this point of view, the continued implementation of the post-Solidarity reforms depends first of all on the strength of the political opposition in Poland as well as on the strength of the political opposition against the leading faction in the party apparatus. Based on past experience, the stabilization of the ruling nucleus within the party apparatus after 1982, coupled with increased turnover within the Council of Ministers in recent years, will, in spite of very loud pro-reform rhetoric, halt real efforts to reform the economy and lead only to pseudo-reforms in the near future.

Notes

1. This chapter summarizes a portion of a large research project on system reforms in centrally-planned economies, underwritten by the Volkswagen Foundation, whose support is acknowledged. The author is grateful for the comments and suggestions made by the co-editor of this volume, Paul Marer.

2. This classification of economic systems was first presented by the author in "Eine Typologie der Wirtschaftssysteme. Der dreidimensionale Ansatz," *Wirtschaft und Gesellschaft*, Vol. 4.

3. This terminology is used, for instance, by Paul Marer in "Economic Reform in Hungary: From Central Planning to Regulated Market," in *East European Economies: Slow Growth in the 1980's*, Vol. 3, Joint Economic Committee, Congress of the United States, (Washington, D.C., 1986).

4. O. Lange, "On the Economic Theory of Socialism," in B. E. Lipincott, ed., *On the Economic Theory of Socialism* (Minneapolis, 1938).

5. The evolution of Poland's MMS is discussed and quantified in the author's *Das Wirtschaftliche Lenkungssystem Polens* (Marburg/Lahn, 1985).

6. J. Liberman, "Plan-Profit-Premium" (in Russian), *Pravda* September 1962.

The appendix to this chapter is on page 345.

10

A Sociologist Looks at Public Opinion, Politics, and Reform

Witold Morawski

The Setting

For the first two or three decades after the war, a majority of Poles was of the opinion that their political system was deficient but that socialism was a workable idea. They criticized the system because it failed to meet their aspirations and because it tended to disregard the nation's traditions. Simultaneously, they were in favor of the system of social welfare, new educational opportunities, free health services, moderate egalitarianism, and the possibilities for social advancement. Society was convinced that, although the system itself was not by the people, it was at least for the people.

The erosion of the positive feeling began in the mid-1960s and has accelerated rapidly since the events of 1980-81. Poles have concluded that the system is not living up to the promises it made. It has also become obvious to a large segment of society that leading party and government bureaucrats—the "center," for short—do not have the ability to deal with the demands of various interest groups throughout the country. The experience of martial law has led some to see the system as one of naked power.

Public Opinion and the Political System

Public opinion in Poland changes constantly with alternations of times of social and political tensions, during which public opinion is highly critical, and times of stabilization, when public opinion becomes more moderate. Based on scientific surveys of public opinion (conducted during 1983-85), we found that the population may be divided into three groups: those who consider themselves supporters of the system (25 percent), those who reject it (25 percent), and those who have mixed feelings about many of its features and about the controversial issues (50 percent).[1] Recent trends show that the third group is gaining ground.

I will summarize the representative set of beliefs held by each group. Supporters of the system often base their views on the fact that the system was able to transform a relatively backward country into an industrial one. Many in this group support the theory and practice of the leading role of the communist party and, more generally, the strategy of revolution and reform from above. Persons in this category also emphasize geopolitical factors.

Opponents of the system reject it mainly because it does not give people the possibility to articulate and effectively promote their values and interests. They argue that revolution and reform from above cannot be successful, that any attempt to reform the economy or to change governmental institutions has to fail either because the system is based on false premises or because the attempts to change it are improperly implemented. They do not agree that the best yardstick for measuring the performance of the system is prewar Poland; they would rather choose West European countries such as Austria, Italy, or Spain. Many people in this group no longer consider the socialist pattern of socio-economic development an optimal one; to some, even non-socialist paths, such as those followed by South Korea or Taiwan, appear attractive.

Those in the third category—with mixed attitudes and views—are concerned primarily with bread-and-butter issues, although they also have more general convictions. Most of them hold the inefficiency of the economic system responsible for its failures to realize society's justified aspirations in such areas as housing and food. They would also prefer a polycentric rather than monocratic government system. Two further important sets of beliefs characterize this group. Its members are rather passive now (though not long ago they took part in social protests), and they are still in favor of retaining such features of the system as state-controlled prices (preferring them to uncontrolled market forces which would endanger their standard of living, at least in the short term), private agriculture, the expanding role of the Church, the degree of intellectual freedom, and the freedom to travel abroad. To be sure, many are confused by the realities they are experiencing, are full of anxieties, and do not know how to interpret events. Many in this category are ready to agree with the arguments of both the center and the opposition.

Public Opinion and Political Behavior

Popular attitudes toward the system are not the same as actual behavior, which in Poland has always been some mix of principle and compromise. Behavior is much more complex than the verbalization of views.

In any system, the link between attitudes and behavior is indirect. In Poland, the link is even less discernible than in other countries, because of various circumstances: the relative weakness of the nation-state concept due to the long-term absence of national sovereignty; the war-time revolutionary genesis of the system, which explains why the advocates of the system form a minority of the people; and the postwar experience with political cycles that convince the people to expect permanent systemic changes. The most important question is who wants to change what and how.

To try to answer this question, we conducted a survey during 1983-85 of industrial enterprises which, in Poland, are the main arenas of social and political activity (the places where Solidarity was formed).[2] The industrial enterprise is the most important political and social institution for the Polish people, the "base" from which people have been able to achieve changes in political leadership every 10 to 15 years. In the socialist system the industrial enterprise plays a much more important political role than in liberal democracies, because of the absence of alternative outlets for political expression. This is illustrated by Solidarity: a trade union movement was transformed into a social movement. Instead of the politicization of the industrial enterprise from above, a spontaneous politicization took place from below, through Solidarity and bodies such as elected workers' councils. To be sure, one may doubt the support of such a political group for meaningful economic reform because, in theory, the essence of economic reform should be an increase in the autonomy of enterprises and of the entire economic system by giving greater scope for market mechanisms.

The empirical results of our study are not conclusive and can support "optimistic," "fatalistic," and "pessimistic" interpretations of the political attitudes of the people regarding the possibility of desirable socio-political and economic reforms. Next, I discuss the reasoning of each set of views, with interpretations that indicate personal preferences.

Optimistic Attitudes and Scenarios

The arguments in favor of an optimistic scenario concerning system change are the following. First, regardless of the many serious social, economic, and political differences and conflicts in Poland, society's unifying forces—tradition, religion, and patriotism—are stronger than the divisive ones. Only one out of five persons stated that more divides than unites us.

Second, although the majority of Poles consider the conflict between center and society great, the state is still seen as a necessary vehicle for the resolution of the crisis as well as for other purposes. Many emphasize the virtues of the benevolent, paternalistic state. This is especially true of relatively poor people, who are afraid of the vagaries of a market system with uncontrolled prices and unemployment. Paradoxically, the most powerful lobbies, such as the steel, the coal, and the heavy-metal industries, also prefer the bureaucratic state machinery to market solutions because the former allows them to keep the status quo in the behind-the-scenes tug-of-war bargaining process. Although not all forms of support for the center are conducive to meaningful political and economic reform, the fact that the center has what may be called "tolerant understanding" can, under the right circumstances, be mobilized to make substantive changes. Even on such thorny issues as the responsibility for martial law and the introduction of various restrictions on civil liberties, society's attitude toward the center shows understanding. To illustrate this point, five times as many persons placed the responsibility for the conflicts and tensions leading to martial law on the government than on Solidarity; however, three-fourths of the respondents assigned partial responsibility to Solidarity as well. Regarding the restriction of civil liberties, the majority believes that in exceptional circumstances, when a vital interest of the state is involved, temporary restrictions could be allowed. The point is that conflict between society and the center is not necessarily something that is preordained.

Third, a significant segment of society is inclined, under the appropriate circumstances, to enter into some kind of compromise with the center. To be sure, there is a growing tendency to blame the authorities for many things. Society's doubts are reinforced by previous failures to reform the economy, and by the constant changes in policies toward private agriculture, artisans, the church, and so on. The decreasing trust of society toward the authorities, in evidence since the mid-1960s, had led many, by the early 1980s, to advocate the necessity of steady pressure on the authorities from below. That this "reform-from-below" movement was stopped by martial law has led many people to a fatalistic perspective about the situation. But in a growing number of others, it has led to a renewed search for appropriate new strategies. By "others," I mean those followers of Solidarity who are still active, as well as the reformist elements within the center. Many in the first group are developing a so-called "alternative society" strategy: a long-run strategy of reconstructing the civil society through small, issue-oriented, independent, and self-defense institutions that could keep people united against the alien center and prepare them to act when the opportunity comes.[3] Although this may represent the abandonment of the strategy of immediate political action, it does advocate a steady pressure on the authorities. It gets people involved, although the horizon for their activities may be in the distant future. Despite the hostility of this group toward the center, it wants to achieve incremental change. This conditional strategy, which assumes that the center will at times be ready to make concessions and compromises, is prepared to seize any opportunity. To sum up, without steady pressure from below, party-state bureaucracies are unwilling to mobilize themselves to act. However, if they are pushed too much, they strike back and conservative forces gain the upper hand.

This leads me to the conclusion that there is no other alternative than a compromise between the rebellious society and the party-state bureaucracy. But a real compromise can be made only if the political system is reformed. To be precise, a political reform is needed not only because the center is ineffective (owing to such factors as its lack of innovativeness, poor work methods of the apparatus, negative selection of key persons and inertia), but more important, because it is unable to assess accurately and to deal politically with various social interests. Therefore, no agreement can be reached on a reconciliation of the interests of different social groups and the center. Political reform is thus a precondition for economic reform as well as a real commitment from society to support a comprehensive social change.

My own personal conviction, tempered by experience against excessive optimism, is that there are persuasive arguments for being optimistic about the possibility, if not of comprehensive and quick reforms, of at least a protracted reform process. But this urgently requires the building of a coalition of reform-minded forces from society and the center. This is not easy, as we have seen in recent years in Poland, where a conservative backlash has become visible, putting reform forces on the defensive. Conservative forces exist not only in the party-state-industrial bureaucracies but also in society among those "educated" by years of experience with a command economy, centralized decision-making structures, and bureaucratic habits in which conformist behavior is often rewarded while innovative behavior tends to be punished.

Fatalistic Attitudes and Scenarios

The empirical data from our study could also be interpreted in more pessimistic ways than under the scenario just discussed. According to the fatalistic scenario, society exerts pressure from below, but there is no positive response from the center which, rejecting the idea of a real compromise, will again try "to do the same but in a better way"—in the official rhetoric, "perfecting the system"—using traditional, bureaucratic methods. If the pressure from society grows, coercive methods would be used to control it. Since the punishment would be greater than the reward, many view social pressure and experimentation as futile; the only course of action is to remain passive.

This scenario assumes that the "vicious circle" cannot be broken and that crises will continue. It is difficult to say how many people adhere to this view. But the percentage of those who are of the opinion, for example, that economic reform can never be successfully instituted in Poland represents about 25 percent of the population and is higher among persons with university diplomas.[4] For some members of the fatalist group, as for those of the active opposition, gradual democratization and a real change in the system are like "fried snowballs": impossible to achieve. In my personal view, this attitude conveys the message that society would prefer to stagnate or decline—muddle through at best—rather than advance. Hence, such an attitude represents a step backward, not forward.

People who tend to fatalism form a large group and are part of Poland's long tradition of defeatism, a tradition that nourishes them and prompts them to advance a justification for the nation's catastrophes that borders on the philosophical. In their perspective, Solidarity's demise is just another example of the eternal return to classic insurrectionist struggle for national independence—this time from the USSR—and for democracy—this time against the communist regime. To them, Solidarity's struggle is a new version of the many failed struggles Poland has experienced in the past. According to this view, Poles live out their contemporary destiny as part of a history of failure to a degree unparalleled elsewhere in Europe.[5]

Many foreign observers help reinforce this fatalistic view. For example, to the American historian M. Malia, Poland is "less a place than a moral community, an idea or act of faith lived almost compulsively by a people oriented less toward the here and now than toward the idealized past, in order to redeem an intolerable present and to bring forth a more glorious future."[6] In this perspective, the Solidarity movement was more "the eternal return of a total national idea" than a mere trade union organization. The battle was lost as we have lost many battles in the past. That is why some call us eternal losers. But perhaps Malia is right that, in Poland, not to lose absolutely is itself a victory, which reminds us of the saying of B. Pascal: "It is not necessary to hope in order to undertake, nor to succeed in order to persevere."

In my opinion, those who emphasize the role of Poland's historical tradition and culture undoubtedly have a point. Nevertheless, there are other important factors. Society's contemporary interests and values are also formed by the institutional arrangements of contemporary socialism. They cannot be excluded from the picture; they are a part of the everyday life-experiences of all Poles. This is why our history should be treated as an asset that can help us understand how to cope with emerging problems.

Pessimistic Attitudes and Scenarios

The normal strategy for an individual who encounters obstacles on the path to his goals should strive to remove the barriers. Since in Poland such an attempt on a mass scale has failed repeatedly, only a small number of Poles today consider such a strategy optimal. Hence, only a minority is pursuing vigorously the goal of social change and reform. A much larger segment practices passivity and retreat.

Passivity and retreat are manifested in several ways.[7] One is the strategy of avoiding or bypassing obstacles to the achievement of goals— for example, by escaping into the private sector, finding jobs in foreign firms in Poland, looking for temporary jobs abroad, and so on. Another manifestation is to drastically alter one's goals in life—for example, a famous journalist becomes the owner of a used bookstore, another a taxi driver, and so on. Still others are unable to cope with reality, and their anxiety causes them to develop deviant behaviors, such as alcoholism, drug abuse, and suicide.

In my view, while a pessimistic attitude is not unwarranted, it does not take into account the accumulated experience of society. For instance, while it certainly remains doubtful that all of Solidarity's ideals can be realized, we should remember that some of Solidarity's recommendations have now become a part of social practice. Pessimists should come around to the view that there is hope for change and join the cautious optimists who work for gradual and incremental reform in the system.

Feasible Reforms in the Politico-Economic System

What kind of bridge could link the present monocratic system with proposals voiced by society in recent years? For the most part, Solidarity represented more of a negative reaction to the system than a positive suggestion to it. However, from the spring of 1981 on, Solidarity did voice certain substantive proposals which revolved around the idea of a self-governing society, with the self-governing enterprise serving as its nucleus.[8] The idea—a proposal for the socialization of nationalized industries—was then transplanted to territorial units. There were also other proposals, such as the reform of the planning and management system, the creation of a truly democratically-elected second chamber of Parliament, and so on. These proposals had a concrete, structural character. They indicated a wish for more than just another change of political leadership and policy or of the grafting of another kind of new consultative body onto the existing system.

Actually, Solidarity's recommendations have meant different things for different segments of society. In my interpretation, they could be considered proposals for a system of shared power, namely, a system that would give different interest groups in society legally guaranteed prerogatives as well as responsibilities. One problem is that the proposals were treated by certain radical Solidarity leaders as tactical rather than strategic; they could have had strategic character only for its moderate elements.

The proposals were not entirely rejected by the center. On the contrary, they became the basis of two laws passed by Parliament on September 25, 1981: the law on industrial enterprises, and the law on workers' councils. They were accepted by the center when it decided to go forward with the idea of economic reform. Those very ideas are still alive among the workers. On the question, "What form of ownership should predominate?", the majority of workers rejected both the existing form of centrally managed state ownership and private ownership. The largest group of articulate workers prefer state ownership entrusted to self-managing bodies. It is not clear that this would ensure economic efficiency,[9] because of the poor performance of the Yugoslav system, which is organized on the same lines.[10] The Yugoslav example should not mean that a self-managed enterprise could not be more efficient than the one totally controlled by the state bureaucracy. Self-management activists are a driving force for making enterprises more autonomous, that is, they are, in most cases, a pro-reform force.

In 1984, only 15 to 25 percent of self-managed enterprises had workers' councils with real influence on the most important decisions.[11] Most other firms in which self-management has supposedly remained have either been co-opted into the power system of the enterprise or, in fact, remain completely on the margin, with the managerial staff retaining the greatest influence in decision making (see Chapter 14 by Holland).

Worthy of note is the appearance of a new idea: that workers' self-governing bodies should have a role in deciding matters of national importance, such as the division of the national income (to ensure a just division of income and burdens between the classes), the drawing up of socioeconomic plans for the economy, or the establishment of a second chamber in Parliament for the representatives of workers' self-management bodies. This vision of workers' self-management expresses the popular opinion that workers themselves should keep an eye on the welfare of the nation as a whole. In our survey, self-managing bodies took second place, just behind the church and ahead of Parliament and the government as institutions the public considers worthy of trust.

To sum up, industrial democracy is a potentially acceptable compromise proposal through which both sides can seek modifications of the system. It is envisaged as a slow process rather than immediate radical change, that is, a process through which society would gain gradual influence in selective areas of the economic system. Admittedly, technocrats could treat this strategy as a method for achieving *de facto*, indirect centralization (in Poland this is sometimes called decentralization) rather than real democratization. Nevertheless, it is a step forward.

The same readiness to compromise is visible in the area of territorial government, though a faster pace of implementation would be highly desirable.

Implementation of the proposals sketched above would bring about a qualitative change of the system, but it would not mean the transplantation of a Western-type pluralistic democracy. This is because such an attempt would not be realistic and because society does not seem to be interested in copying Western patterns, even as people consider them appropriate institutions for societies in the West. To be sure, a growing number of Poles would like to see some elements of Western economic-political systems introduced in Poland. At the moment, however Polish society prefers to seek its own road, using step-by-step methods rather than fundamental and radical strategies, even though the latter was recently considered the most desirable.

The creation of a new social order could be achieved through, on the one hand, increased social participation in decision making and, on the other, through honest work of individual citizens in their workplaces. Both tasks are difficult. Many people are not very interested in committing themselves to public service, which is a symptom of general frustration and apathy. Moreover, aspects of the economic system—incentives, promotion, management—are in a pathetic shambles, making sloppy work a natural behavior. But Poles should and must realize that there is no chance of seeing meaningful systemic change without taking part of the responsibility on their own shoulders.

Empirical data suggest that society is, once again, becoming engaged in a search for an alternative system. The vision of the new system is not yet clearly drawn, but it is already more than the negation of the existing system. The contours of a positive program are emerging. The rejection of the old bureaucratic socialism, in which all of society was treated as one big factory and ruled from above by decree, is automatically an option for some kind of a new system, in which society's role would be enhanced. The fact that so far the groups actively engaged in the search process constitute a minority—if we count real commitment and not surface acceptance of the reform—necessitates intensifying the struggle against conservative tendencies. Such a fight should be treated as a national imperative, realizing that Poland is falling further behind in meeting the challenges of becoming a highly developed nation. Ultimately, the process of transformation of society's attitudes and dilemmas into a fruitful game for a better future is, of course, tied with other changes. The interruption of the existing "vicious-circle" demands, in the Polish case, simultaneous changes in all spheres of our life: political, economic and social.

Notes

1. See, for example, results from the two empirical studies: "Poles 1984," carried out by a team in the larger project headed by Franciszek Ryszka, Warsaw University, Warsaw, the results of which are in *Poles 84: Dynamics of Conflict and Consensus* (in Polish), edited by Władysław Adamski, Krzysztof Jasiewicz, and Andrzej Rychard, (Warsaw, 1987); and "Social Groups and Institutions in Carrying out Socioeconomic Tasks—Dynamics of Values and Interests," carried out by a team comprised of Witold Morawski, head, Jolanta Babiuch, Bogdan Cichomski, Kazimierz Frieske, Alina Kosmider, Wiesława Kozek, Paweł Kuczyński, Jadwiga Staniszkis, and Wojciech Widera. The results are reported in W. Morawski, ed., *Economy and Society: Values and Interests of Industrial Crews* (in Polish) (Warsaw, 1986).

2. The study was carried out in four Warsaw industrial enterprises. Four socio-occupational groups were studied: blue-collar workers (307 persons), activists of social and political organizations (192), managers (219), and professionals, mostly engineers (151). The data was collected by means of questionnaires and interviews (a total of 869 interviews were conducted for 3-4 hours each).

3. For example, Timothy Garton Ash, "Does Central Europe Exist?" *New York Review of Books* (October 9, 1986).

4. Witold Morawski and Wiesława Kozek, "Society Towards the Reform," (in Polish) *Życie Gospodarcze*, no. 27 (July 7, 1985). It is a short report on the representative poll of the Polish population.

5. Martin Malia, "Poland's Eternal Return," *The New York Review of Books*, (September 29, 1983).

6. Ibid.

7. For example, Stefan Nowak, "Dilemmas of Social Consciousness in the Second Half of the 1980s," (in Polish) in J.J. Wiatr, ed., *Fulfillment of Needs in the Conditions of Crisis* (Warsaw, 1986); and studies by Antoni Sułek at the Warsaw University Institute of Sociology.

8. W. Morawski, "Employees' Self-Management and Economic Reforms," *The Polish Sociological Bulletin*, no. 1-4 (Wrocław, 1982), pp. 47-60.

9. H. A. Simon, "What is Industrial Democracy?" *Economic Impact*, Vol. 43, no.3, 1983.

10. Harold Lydall, *Yugoslav Socialism: Theory and Practice* (Oxford, 1984); and Paul Marer, "Economic Policies and Systems in Eastern Europe and Yugoslavia: Commonalities and Differences," *East European Economies: Slow Growth in the 1980s*, Joint Economic Committee, U.S. Congress, Vol. 3 (Washington, 1986).

11. "Employees' Self-Management in Industrial Enterprises" (in Polish), *CBOS—Center for Opinion Polling* (Warsaw, 1984).

11

Economic Reform Versus Political Normalization

Jack Bielasiak

An obvious tension exists between an economic recovery program based on decentralization and a political program of "normalization" aimed at the consolidation of power and hegemony over society. Although it is theoretically possible to separate economics from political power in a centrally planned economy (CPE), the historical record of Poland and the other socialist states demonstrates the failure to achieve economic decentralization while maintaining political centralization. The latest Polish reform seeks the devolution of decision making in the economy while reestablishing monopolistic authority in the polity.

Reform and the Sociopolitical Environment

The blueprint for economic change, adopted in July 1981 by the Ninth Extraordinary Congress of the PUWP, was one of the few "renewal" programs retained by the regime of General Jaruzelski in the wake of the imposition of martial law on December 13, 1981. In fact, martial law had the effect of accelerating the implementation of the reform on January 1, 1982, which to a large extent was a reflection of the dire economic situation in the country. It enabled the Jaruzelski leadership to claim that military intervention was essential to prevent further economic erosion and to foster a plan of economic recovery.[1] Rapid introduction of the reform was to serve as a visible sign of the government's commitment to the national welfare. This emphasis on

economic action, however, should not be confused with the entire program of the state of war. General Jaruzelski did not reach for power
primarily to introduce economic reform, but to normalize the domestic
political situation as well. Economic recovery was but one component
of a complex process of political, social, and economic policies designed
to stabilize the country by means of control over society by the state.

In the context of the normalization effected after 1981, a central
issue is the relationship between economic performance and political
stability. The question is whether economic reform can enhance the well-
being of the country and thus serve as a vehicle for political stabilization
and social reconciliation. In other words, the question is whether economic reform can succeed only after a compromise has been reached
between the authorities and society, rendering social and political stability a precondition for economic reform. There is no doubt that since
the formulation of the reform proposal, the Polish authorities have sought
to use the prospects of economic change to gain popular support and
achieve social tranquility. Such a strategy had considerable merit in the
political environment of the renewal of 1980-81, when the existence of
Solidarity and other autonomous groups could be employed as social
backing for the implementation of the *Directions of Economic Reform* approved in July 1981.[2] The military action of December 13, 1981 drastically
altered the possibilities. The suppression of social autonomy, through
the dissolution of Solidarity and other independent organizations, made
it difficult to channel the popular will in support of any governmental
action (even that of economic recovery). In effect, the alienation of the
population relegated the blueprint of the reform to the official sphere,
stripping it of legitimacy.

The Jaruzelski government did seek to restore credibility to the
reform plan by identifying it with the renewal ideas that prevailed in
1980-81. This approach was characterized by proclamations of a continuity in policy and verbal commitments to important reforms inaugu-
rated during the Solidarity period.[3] In particular, the promise of economic
reform and improved material performance played a central role. However, the authorities' rhetoric was careful to distinguish between the
substantive merits of the reform policies and the methods of the determination and implementation of the policy. Under the conditions of
normalization, social forces were no longer to inhibit the preferences of
the ruling elite. On the contrary, the aim was to eliminate this practice
of the Solidarity period and restore centralist, monopolistic norms in the
exercise of power. Here again one encounters a direct contradiction
between the political *raison d'être* of normalization—that is, the establishment of state hegemony over society, and the principle of economic
reform, namely, decentralization and market exchange. The latter per-
petuates a condition that tends to accentuate the autonomy of socioeconomic forces in Polish society, which is contrary to the prevailing notions

of political normalization. The success of the reform depends on the possibility of relegating the autonomous, decentralizing features of the new reforms exclusively to the economic sphere while continuing political consolidation. I would argue, however, that such a separation between the program of economic reform and the larger social and political issues of stabilization is extremely difficult under any circumstances in socialist systems. This is usually so in conditions of normalization, in which political instruments of control are the prevailing foundation for the stability of the regime.

Systemic Obstacles to Reform

There are *systemic* impediments to the disengagement of economic choices from the political process. This is due to the "fused" nature of Soviet-type systems, wherein the political and the economic realms are closely interdependent, characterized by one-party rule and central allocation of resources.[4] This fusion, derived from several ideological premises, including state ownership of the means of production and the party's role as vanguard in the construction of socialism, is responsible for the most significant, defining features of communist systems. Most visible is the formation of a complex bureaucratic-administrative structure that is responsible for the distribution of economic resources and political privileges. The tasks of this administration, including the coordination of material allocation and the reconciliation of conflicting interests, serve simultaneously as economic and political integrators for the entire system. Political authority is dependent on this network of hierarchical decisions and controls, signifying the concentration of political and economic power at the top of the structure and the interlocking of political and economic policy making.

The unitary logic of the system infers the coalescence of the polity and the economy in the form of the single-party, centrally planned state. The party-state's power is henceforth defined in terms of the maintenance of a monopoly of decision making over political and economic issues. Precisely for that reason, economic reform becomes a problem not only of management (in the economy) but also of governance (in the polity). This problem, in turn, explains the timidity of experimental reform in Soviet-type systems.

As documented in the chapter by Brus, the history of economic reforms in postwar Poland demonstrates clearly the leadership's ambivalence, which is based on economic exigencies and political fears. The primary concern has been the limitation of change in the economic sector without endangering the institutional and procedural status quo in the political arena. Due to the fear of a spillover from the material sector to the political one, the Polish regimes were reluctant to tinker with the structure of the system, often preferring inertia in policy to alterations in the operation of the economy. The result was a growing stagnation in economic performance, leading the nation toward major economic and political crises.[5] When finally faced with challenges to the country's stability, as in 1956, 1970, or 1980, the political leaders responded by accepting the idea of economic reform. But even at such times, the concern with the potential crossover from economic to political reform was paramount and was reflected in blueprints for change that sought to limit innovations to the economic sector without touching the political arena.

In such an environment, the dynamics of reform culminate in failure, among other reasons, because of the difficulty of insulating, for both substantive and procedural reasons, economic decision making from the political process. The *Directions of Economic Reform* (1981) is a case in point. The very concept of the reform, captured by the "three S's" (*samodzielność, samofinansowanie, samorządność*) of enterprise autonomy, self-finance, and self-management, was aimed at the separation of economic decision making from political-administrative dependence. The goal was to create an autonomous economic sector in which operational characteristics would not infringe on the political and social dynamics of the country. The fused integration of the economic and political systems in socialism, however, prevents the creation of a fully autonomous economy subject to its own operational laws.[6] At best, only some degree of partial autonomy is possible, such as the replacement of political-administrative targets and criteria by economic parameters.

The shift to such a goal in the reform venture carries another danger to the successful completion of economic change. In this case, the authorities fear that the connection between economic and political processes may result in a diffusion of political power from the regime to autonomous social forces. The attempt to reform the economy therefore endangers the stability of the polity and the leading role of the party in society. This perceived threat leads to a backlash, as was elaborated and documented by Brus in Chapter 8. The options for the central leadership are either the institution of political as well as economic changes, or the accommodation of the opposition by withdrawing full support for the new economic system. The reality of state socialism often precludes the implementation of the first option because the top leadership is too dependent on the support of the incumbent administrative personnel. The second alternative—a procedural deemphasis on the implementation of the reform—is thus preferred. The political timidity of the regime prevails over risk-taking, and the changeover process is stalled.

The interlocking nature of the socialist state is, under the best of circumstances, a severe impediment to successful reform. In those instances when the implementation of economic change is able to overcome political resistance, as in Hungary's New Economic Mechanism of 1968 or China's Four Modernizations of 1979, the relative success of the reform process is associated with prior cataclysmic events that force the hand of the top leadership. The Hungarian revolution of 1956 thus led to the destruction of the prevailing political structures and created a power vacuum, enabling the Kádár leadership to proceed to the fulfillment of a major reform platform. Similarly the cultural revolution in China severely attacked the existing political institutions and personnel, opening up the road for a subsequent program of reform.[7] In Poland, despite major crises, no such extensive and overall political breakdown has occurred.[8] Nonetheless, the period of renewal (1980-81), represented a major challenge to the political power on the part of autonomous social groups. For that reason, economic reform was most likely to succeed during the circumscription by society of administrative and managerial authority. However, the opportunity for economic reform passed with the declaration of martial law in December 1981. The political and social circumstances were altered to such an overwhelming extent that the successful implementation of the "three-S" experiment was precluded, despite the regime's continuing advocacy of reform within the economic realm.

Strategic Impediments to Reform

The events of December 1981 introduced a new obstacle to the successful implementation of the economic blueprint for change. In addition to the systemic problem of fusion, a strategic impediment to reform was the divergence between policy orientations in the economic and political spheres. While the fused nature of socialism is a constant obstacle to economic change, specific policies can either aid or hinder the process of reform. During the Solidarity period, the pressures for autonomy, decentralization, and democratization encompassed both the economic and political arenas. The conditions necessary for the transformation of the system's features were being created in both sectors simultaneously. That pattern of change drastically altered the military intervention of December 13, 1981, when the policy of renewal was replaced by the policy of normalization. The thrust of the official economic policy and the political course of normalization went in opposite directions. The coexistence of the two strategies was most precarious. Ultimately, the conflict had to be resolved either through the pursuit of a more conciliatory political course or through the erosion of the commitment to economic change.

The tensions between the distinct strategic policies pursued on the political and economic fronts quickly became apparent both in terms of the goals and the means of implementation. The first and primary task of normalization was the demobilization of those social groups that had achieved organizational autonomy during the renewal period. Next, by the establishment of new political controls, the normalization program sought to reintegrate into government-sponsored institutions the social forces previously represented by the autonomous organizations.

In contrast to the sharp reversal of Poland's political course, the economic transformation from the pre- to post-December phase was much less marked, largely as a result of the disastrous economic conditions in the productive and consumer sectors, which required improvements in economic performance. To attain that goal, the government announced innovative steps in mid-1981, which it hoped was the best path to increased efficiency. Efficiency was to lead to an improved material situation, in turn eliciting popular acceptance of the new regime and culminating in social reconciliation. The successful implementation of this strategy was predicated on obtaining the cooperation of the planning and administrative bureaucracy in order to improve the flexibility and self-regulation of the economy.

An evaluation of the methods of governance and management initiated by the martial-law regime demonstrates the incompatibility of the two programs. Normalization depended on the presence of social and political institutions that subscribe to the authority of the party state. The building of institutions, through the re-creation of public organizations and their incorporation into the official political process, became a predominant state activity after 1981. The formation and activity of the new organizations was circumscribed by a variety of limitations, including recognition of "the leading role of the party" in the construction of the "normalized" society and deliberate fragmentation of social groups.[9] The aim was the inhibition of collective-group identity by structural barriers, as in the case of the new trade unions, whose organization was restricted to a federation based on discrete industrial branches. The effort of these policies was to replace the former social self-organization and solidarity with a system based on the corporate technique of integration through social atomization and vertical linkages.[10]

The political strategy of societal integration did not form a conducive political environment for an implementation of the adopted blueprint or reform. The thinking embodied in the reform proposals was a combination of economic decentralization, as in Hungary's New Economic Mechanism, and social participation in economic management, as in Yugoslavia's system of associated labor. Both aspects emphasized self-motivating features that went against the grain of political normalization. The administrative alteration envisaged a devolution of decision-making prerogatives away from the central planning office and the central ministries toward the basic economic units—the enterprises (as elaborated in a subsequent chapter by Fallenbuchl). The command character of the economy was to be replaced by relations among direct producers, free of the pervasive interference of the state.

Furthermore, these administrative and procedural changes were to be matched by managerial developments that substantially enhanced the influence of the workforce in economic choices at the factory level. The self-management provision of the reform package opened up the process of decision making to self-governing bodies empowered with the rights of management, as detailed in the chapter by Holland. From an economic standpoint, this feature was an important component of the reform because it sought to improve productivity by the direct involvement of workers in economic decisions and activities. From a sociopolitical perspective, however, the self-management mechanism was the most sensitive aspect of the reform blueprint, because during periods of economic and social crises in Poland, enterprises have become the most politicized institutions. The process of normalization was the authorities' response to this phenomenon during the interlude of 1980-81, and was directed specifically at the elimination of self-organization in the workforce. The advocacy of enterprise autonomy and self-management, therefore, operates counter to the predominant political interests of the regime by re-creating a condition which fosters the independence of social groups vis-à-vis the government.

The tension between the political and economic implications of self-management embodies the essence of the conflict between the "governance" and "management" aspects of normalization. The difference centers on the locus of power in the post-1981 era. The thrust of the economic reform is decentralization: the granting of substantial decision-making authority to individual enterprises by means of autonomy, quasi-market operations, and self-government. The essence of political normalization is the consolidation of power at the center through the demobilization of social autonomy and the imposition of controlling instruments of rule over society. The impasse between the decentralization and centralization strategies was resolved by the restriction of the self-management feature. Organs of self-governance in enterprises were thus suspended entirely for the duration of martial law and reactivated in a new, more circumscribed form at the time of the lifting of the state of war on July 22, 1983. As Fallenbuchl explains in his chapter, the legislative modification of the laws on state enterprises and self-management resulted in a major alteration of the economic blueprint. Most significantly, the changeover restricted the autonomy of enterprises and their self-government, turning the latter from organs of management to consultative bodies to factory administrators. The process was strikingly reminiscent of previous attempts at self-management, most notably the incorporation of the workers' councils of 1956 into the existing administrative structure in 1957. This time, too, the result was a lack of confidence and a loss of interest among the workforce, rendering the formation of post-1983 self-management bodies slow and ineffective. The apparent perception on the part of the workers is that there is little point in participating in institutions that have few powers and are under the control of the enterprise's top management.[11]

The experience of self-management exemplifies the compromises made in the name of political expediency. Although the de-emphasis of the self-governing institutions does not theoretically mean an end to reform, for all practical purposes the abandonment of social participation in the restructuring of the economy spells an effective end to many provisions of the blueprint. The constraints imposed on the implementation of the reform in the past four years are well documented by Fallenbuchl.

The absence of social participation in the reform process has significant consequences. The self-management device was the last vestige of a policy that incorporated social groups as pressure points for the implementation of meaningful economic reform. The de-legalization of autonomous social organizations left a vacuum that could be partially filled by enterprise self-government councils. These could function as relatively independent forces counteracting the interests of the political and administrative elite for centralized and bureaucratic controls over the polity and the economy. The eradication of the self-management bodies thus removed a substantial potential force for the realization of the new economic system.[12] Without the institutional mechanism of self-governance, the ability to mobilize societal interests diminished considerably, and the reform process gradually eroded.

Tactical Obstacles to Reform

In addition to the systemic and strategic obstacles to reform, the approach of the government to the implementation of policy is also at fault because it prevents the fruitful incorporation of the new blueprint into the Polish economy. The *tactical* conception of the Jaruzelski leadership in the martial-law period was the abandonment of the political context of the reform, thereby cutting off the social base of support for the economic innovations. Without the support of autonomous social groups, either in the form of independent trade unions or self-management councils, the economic conception degenerated from a broad social transformation into a narrow tactical reform. Rather than the promotion of societal interests in favor of change in the economy, the government preferred to stress the potential dangers of social autonomy and therefore acted to curb all manifestations of institutional independence. For political reasons, demobilization of the population was much more important than the invigoration of social interests that favored reform. The problem with such a policy of depoliticization, besides the withdrawal of channels for popular influence, was the deliberate encouragement of political apathy and social anomie. The resulting passivity, however, had an impact beyond the political arena to include mass withdrawal from greater economic efforts. The tactical policy of demobilization thus has had a negative impact on productivity and has involved substantial economic costs.

A second aspect of the operational maneuvering in Poland after 1981 is the government's reliance on the prospects of improved economic performance as a vehicle for societal stability. While such an approach seems to reinforce the authorities' commitment to economic innovation, the policy actually subsumes reform under the overarching goal of normalization. The regime's primary concern remains the legitimization of the current political situation. In case legitimization conflicts with reforms, the choice of the authorities has been to limit economic changes. The most recent interpretation places economic reform as a component of the current stage in socialist construction; in other words, as subservient to the process of normalization.[13] This assessment in turn reflects the tactical error of the separation of the reform program from a mobilized, supportive social base. The restriction of the implementation of the reform to the official, administrative sector places the latest economic experiment alongside the last attempt at economic innovation—programs designed and instituted without consultation with social groups whose support is essential to the successful conclusion of economic transformation. Without the mantle of popular backing, the "three S's" are but another reform from above, bound to flounder due to bureaucratic inertia.

Conclusions

The combination of systemic, strategic, and tactical pressures gradually relegated the reform idea into the background of the course of normalization. Since the highest priority was given to the reconstruction of a monolithic polity, it precluded the utilization of social groups as a support for the economic innovations that were outlined first in the open political atmosphere of the Solidarity period. Normalization signified, above all, an official environment of political hegemony in which changes were viewed with suspicion. In such conditions, economic reform could not thrive. This does not mean that the traditional CPE system was not altered but that the hopes for the institution and maintenance of major changes in the operation of the economy succumbed to the more pressing expediency of politics. Successful reform of the economy is dependent upon a receptive political milieu—a condition that is still absent in the "normalizing" Poland of today.[14]

The present situation continues to be defined by the regime's attempts to pacify the country. Five years after the end of the Solidarity experiment, the authorities remain concerned with the aspirations of society for self-organization and autonomy. Official policy aims primarily at the interdiction of these societal hopes in order to prevent their emergence once again into an "open" arena of politics. The consequence is best defined as a case of arrested normalization, in which the imposition of the regime's political will on society continues to be dependent primarily on power and control without sufficient attention to the necessary positive aspects of the long-term program of stabilization: economic recovery and social reconciliation.

Evidence shows that, since the dominant concern of the leadership is the maintenance of political hegemony over society, the resolution of economic problems is relegated into the background. Lack of a dialogue with representatives of society, the apparent stalling of progress in church-state relations, and the increasing ideologization of the political and economic sectors testify to the dominant concerns of the ruling elite. As long as concern with the maintenance of political power is the prevailing perspective in the polity, there is little hope of resolution of the larger issues of national stabilization. Arrested normalization relegates economic reform and relations between the state and society to second place, behind the need to safeguard the political gains of the state of war.

Notes

1. Wojciech Jaruzelski, Speeches of December 13, 1981 and January 25, 1982, in *Selected Speeches* (Oxford, 1985).

2. *Trybuna Ludu*, July 1981.

3. Jack Bielasiak, "The 'Normalization' of State Socialism: The Reorganization of Political Power in Poland," paper presented at the APSA Annual Meeting, September 1985.

4. Alec Nove, "Socialism, Centralized Planning and the One-Party State," in T.H. Rigby, Archie Brown, and Peter Reddeway, eds., *Authority Power and Policy in the USSR* (New York, 1980); and Valerie Bunce, "The Political Economy of the Brezhnev Era: The Rise and Fall of Corporatism," *British Journal of Political Science* Vol. 13, no.2, April 1983, pp. 129-158.

5. Jack Bielasiak, "The Evolution of Crises in Poland," in Jack Bielasiak and Maurice Simon, eds. *Polish Politics: Edge of the Abyss* (New York, 1984).

6. Witold Morawski, "Economic Reform in Poland," (in Polish) *Studia Socjologiczne* Vol. 2 (73), 1984.

7. William Robinson, *The Pattern of Reform in Hungary* (New York, 1973); Elizabeth Perry and Christine Wong, eds., *The Political Economy of Reform in Post-Mao China* (Cambridge, Mass., 1985).

8. The crucial distinction here concerns the penetration of the crisis into the political apparatus and economic bureaucracy. In the Hungarian and Chinese cases, the crises led to a breakdown of stability within the bureaucracy. In Poland, the *apparat* itself remained insulated from the changes occurring in society and continued to demonstrate—and ultimately to act—against any reforms of the system.

9. Bielasiak, "The 'Normalization' of State Socialism," pp. 10-19.

10. Valerie Bunce and John Echols, "Soviet Politics in the Brezhnev Era: "Pluralism" or "Corporatism?" in Donald R. Kelley, ed. *Soviet Politics in the Brezhnev Era* (New York, 1980), pp. 1-26.

11. Morawski, "Economic Reform in Poland."

12. Morawski, "Economic Reform in Poland," pp. 8-9, 26.

13. Władysław Baka "The Shape of Reform in the Years to Come," (in Polish) *Rzeczpospolita*, July 30, 1985; T. Jeziorański, "Three Years After," (in Polish) *Życie Gospodarcze*, no. 8, 1985.

14. Ryszard Bugaj, "Why does the Crisis Continue?" (in Polish) *Tygodnik Powszechny*, January 5, 1986.

12

Present State of the Economic Reform

Zbigniew Fallenbuchl

The Program of the Reform

The program of a comprehensive economic reform in Poland was adopted by the Ninth Extraordinary Party Congress in July 1981.[1] Its official document, "The Directions of Economic Reform," stresses that a rapidly implemented economic reform is necessary for three reasons:

a) the clearly visible weakness and decomposition of the old system of planning and management (the command-allocative system);

b) the appearance of a very serious socioeconomic crisis on a scale unknown before in the People's Republic of Poland, with consequences which cannot be overcome under the command-allocative system; and

c) the deep sociopolitical changes that are taking place in Poland to which the functioning of the national economy must be adjusted.[2]

The reform was to be introduced immediately in all sectors, although it was recognized that it would take up to 3 years before the new economic system became fully operational.[3] The main purpose of the reform was to improve the overall efficiency of the economy. This, according to the program, required major modifications in the institutional structure and significant changes in the mechanism of planning and management.

The institutional modifications envisaged included a changed role of the central economic administration (the Council of Ministers, the Planning Commission, and the economic ministries); the increased role of the Sejm (Parliament) and of regional authorities; the abolition of the middle administrative units, that is, the associations of enterprises, regarded as representatives of the branch ministries that controlled in great detail the day-to-day operations of the enterprises; and, above all, changing the status of enterprises to make them fully autonomous, self-financing and self-governing units (the "three S's," from the first letters of these terms in Polish, see preceding chapter by Bielasiak).[4]

The operation of the economic mechanisms was to be based on "three pillars:" (1) social participation in planning at all levels of the economy; (2) the objective function of enterprises should be the maximization of their financial results (profit or value added), except in some special cases; and (3) the use of economic "regulators," such as prices, interest rates, taxes and exchange rates, rather than administrative commands by the center to "steer" the economy, with a gradual increase in the role of economic instruments and a decline in the role of commands.[5] The program states that "the proposed system rejects both the idea that the market is the only regulator of the economy or that enterprises should be dominated by the central authorities, such as in the old system." For this reason "the economy will function on the basis of central planning with the use of the market mechanism."[6] It is generally accepted that under the prevailing political system the economic system will always have to be a mixed one: central planning with the self-regulatory market system.[7]

At the time the program was adopted by the party, the proposed new system was described as being somewhere between the Hungarian and the Yugoslav models, as it would involve the use of market forces as well as worker participation in enterprise management. In reality, however, the following recent evaluation of the program tells more accurately what really happened:

> ...while the envisaged changes in the social and political sphere had some original features, in the economic sphere the program did not represent anything that could be regarded as a real innovation. In the main outline it was a repetition of the proposals that had been advanced in Poland at the end of the 1950s and in its specific solutions it did not move beyond the Hungarian "New Economic Mechanism."[8]

Whereas in 1981 Poles put forth a claim of uniqueness for their reform, it is presented differently today. For example, General Jaruzelski has recently pointed out that the reform is in conformity with the requirements of the present stage in the building of socialism; the fact that all socialist countries are now modifying their economic systems points to its necessity.[9]

The Sejm followed the adoption of the program with two principal laws that were to serve as a basis for the reform: "On State Enterprises" and "On Workers' Self-Government in State Enterprises."[10]

Implementation: General Conditions

The reform was introduced on January 1, 1982, under a markedly changed domestic political situation from that which existed when the program was prepared. The imposition of martial law interrupted international, interregional, and intercity communications and transport. The situation can best be described as administrative chaos, and the economy was paralyzed during the first months of the year. The specific instructions, regulations, and decisions concerning the working of the new system were issued with considerable delay, and enterprises were thus left in a vacuum.[11]

The legislation on self-government and several provisions of the code on state enterprises were suspended, although self-government was later gradually reintroduced on a firm-by-firm basis. Nevertheless, only since the termination of martial law on July 22, 1983 have the two legislative acts become operational in a restricted version, modified by special legal regulations enacted on July 21, "for the period of overcoming the crisis."[12] The two legislative acts passed in September 1981 were to provide the legal basis for the functioning of the "three-S" formula and were intended to make a withdrawal from the reform impossible without breaking the law or a formal revision of it by the Sejm. However, because the laws had not become fully operational, the old personnel continued to make many decisions operating within the old structures and using the old methods. This has led to "the breach of some provisions of the law of the reform by the creation of *fait accompli*." In this way "the circumstances that existed at the starting point of the reform still influence its present state."[13]

A specific characteristic nature of the Polish economic reform has thus emerged, and it makes the assessment of the reform difficult. There is a dual discrepancy here: that between the original program (to which the authorities continuously declare their full commitment) and the specific legal provisions enacted by the Sejm; and that between the various legislative acts and the changes that have actually been introduced.[14]

The official position is that "although not all details of the reform are final," a new system has been introduced and "no retreat is possible without losses and social complications."[15] In the words of General Jaruzelski, "the reform is a vital need and the only chance to overcome difficulties and to stimulate development. Without it there would be economic deterioration and the pauperization of the population."[16] This was the official position presented by the Sejm when it declared in July 1985 that the implementation of the economic reform takes place in accordance with the program adopted by the Ninth Extraordinary Party Congress.[17]

Not everyone, however, agrees with this assessment. For example, at a joint conference of experts and members of the Sejm, held in the Parliament building a few weeks before Jaruzelski's declaration was made, a view was expressed that "after three years of gradually increasing limitations of enterprise autonomy in all possible fields, with the financial field in the lead, practically nothing has been left of the reform."[18] Some managers of the state enterprises apparently agree with this conclusion, stating that "we are departing from the principles of the reform and this happens in every sphere ... from the point of view of the operation of the enterprise."[19]

The erosion of the reform can be discerned clearly. The Sejm has enacted one law after another, so that there are now about 320 legislative acts that regulate the reform. Various levels of the central administration have been issuing supplementary regulations, instructions, and interpretations of the newly enacted laws that seriously restrict the operation of the legislation. The total number of these interpretations is now about 12,000, including approximately 8,000 issued by the Minister of Finance. This whole mass of documents is not internally consistent and not oriented toward increasing efficiency; it actually destroys the reform.[20] To some extent this is the result of a lack of precision in the legislative acts, which leave the interpretation of certain specific provisions to the administration. For example, the legislative act on the finances of the state enterprises has 46 articles and includes 36 such authorizations.[21]

A group of experts from a subcommittee of the Committee on Economic Reform recently evaluated the reform, noting: (1) delays in the legislative process in some areas that are vital for the reform (including, for example, the regulation of the functioning of central economic authorities and the control of monopolistic practices); (2) a clear tendency in the new legal acts and administrative regulations and interpretations to restrict the basic "three-S" formula; (3) the existence of various administrative decrees inconsistent with the two basic legislative acts of the reform; and (4) a considerable degree of uncertainty in the formal legal basis of the financial operations of the enterprises, in part caused by the practice of introducing regulations with retroactive validity.[22]

Several economists point out that the system that has emerged is "overregulated"[23] and that the reform has not created the self-regulatory mechanism on which its success depends.[24] This is no longer the traditional command-allocative system; in the opinion of some economists, it is better than the system that was in operation during the 1970s or 1960s.[25] However, it is not the system that was envisaged in 1981. It has not resulted in improved economic efficiency or in better quality products, and it does not stimulate innovations.[26]

To what extent can this situation be explained by the persistence of the economic crisis? Some economists in Poland stress that the authors of the original program could not have foreseen the full extent of the economic breakdown. The changed situation had to influence the pace and form in which the reform could be implemented.[27] Others argue, more convincingly, that "various instruments of the original program were introduced with full awareness of the conditions in which they would have to work," that "they were accepted because they were regarded as necessary to cope with the situation," and that "perhaps the departure from the original solutions under the pressure of the economic situation was a mistake."[28] Dr. Sołdaczuk pointed to the paradox that, with gradual improvement in the economic situation, the drift away from the original vision of the reform continues.[29]

The authorities have now decided to slow down the pace of the implementation of the reform. This is clearly seen from two recently published documents: "The Report on the Implementation of Reform in 1984" and "Some Conclusions Concerning the System of the Functioning of the National Economy in the Years 1986-90."[30] This decision is defended by those who stress the need for stability and believe that the transitional system should be retained unchanged in its present form in order not to further destabilize the economy.[31] It is criticized by others who see in it another departure from the original program which stipulated comprehensive and prompt implementation, with a transitional period that should not exceed about three years.[32]

There are also some critical voices concerning the original program of the reform. To some extent it was not an internally consistent document, especially in the field of foreign trade.[33] Critics claim that the program was not quite clear on the nature of the final systemic model. "The Directions" did not indicate "whether the state would continue to perform the function of the director of the multi-plant enterprise and would be criticized for all economic failures, or should become the sovereign master of the whole economy, one who controls it but is not responsible for every change in prices or wages."[34]

So far, very few have claimed that the decision to introduce the reform was a mistake and that there should be a full return to "the well proven and reliable command-allocative system."[35] Allegations are often made, however, that there are members of the central administration who are not happy with the process of reform and create various obstacles for it.[36]

This overview of the official pronouncements, the legislative acts, the implementing regulations, and divergent voices concerning the reform experience demonstrates that the overall picture is far from consistent; the most likely reason for this is the political one, as stressed in the chapters by Brus and Bielasiak.

Modifications in the Institutional Structure

The "branch structure" of the economy, with the "branch ministries" at the top of the hierarchical organization of sectors that exercise effective control over enterprises in their respective sectors, is an important and typical feature of the centrally planned command system. The ministries represent enormous concentrations of power, operate in a typically bureaucratic manner, and represent centers of vested interests that often tend to ignore the interests of the economy as a whole and are thus largely responsible for the ossification of the industrial structure. They direct their sectors like monopolies and eliminate competition between individual producers in the name of "rationalization." They manage enterprises in a rigid way, restricting their initiative and making horizontal links between firms reporting to different ministries difficult, since such transactions are typically subject to lengthy delays caused by the need for inter-ministerial coordination.

The proposal for an economic reform that the Polish Economic Association put forth in October 1980 demanded the reduction in the number if industrial branch ministries to one or, at most, two. This was regarded as an essential condition for decentralization, the working of a self-regulatory mechanism, and increased efficiency.[37] The official program, adopted by the Ninth Congress, repeated that the number of industrial ministries should be reduced to one or two, except during a brief transitional period when three ministries could be allowed (for mining and power, metallurgical and engineering, and other manufacturing industries). It stressed the enhanced role of the functional ministries, such as the Ministry of Finance, Ministry of Foreign Trade, Ministry of Labor, and the State Price Commission. These agencies would create and use economic instruments to "steer" the activities of economic units, in consultation with the branch ministries. They would not supervise the enterprises and would be allowed to intervene directly only if the latter broke the law. They would not allocate production targets but would cooperate with the Planning Commission in the preparation of the central economic plans that have an indicative and not compulsory nature.[38]

The legislative act on state enterprises says that firms conduct their activities on the basis of their own plan, which is adopted by the general meeting of workers in the case of multi-year plans and by the workers' council in the case of annual plans (Article 46). The ministry (called the establishing organization, responsible for setting up the autonomous, self-governing and self-financing enterprises) has the right to order the fulfillment of a compulsory target only when such an action is necessary for the purposes of national defense, because of a natural disaster, or in order to meet international agreements. In such cases the ministry must provide the necessary means for the enterprises to fulfill these special targets (Article 54). The act makes a special provision for public utilities, which "have to satisfy current needs of the population without interruption." It authorizes the Council of Ministers to regulate their activities administratively and, if necessary, provide subsidies (Article

9).[39] This provision has created the possibility for the government to exempt some enterprises from the reform legislation by declaring them to be public utilities.

As a result of the use of this provision and of other legislation, certain industries have been exempted entirely from the operation of the reform. They include the coal, power, cement, sugar, and meat industries.[40]

The reform also envisaged a changed role for the Planning Commission. Its duties were to be limited to analytical, methodological, and forecasting studies, the organization of planning activities in the national economy, and the preparation of variants of the central plans for the government and the Sejm. "The Directions" explicitly mentions that the commission would not make any operational decisions.[41] It was also expected to be reorganized along functional lines to replace its organization according to branch principles.[42]

The authors of the reform regarded (1) the limitation of the branch structure, (2) the widespread elimination of administrative commands and allocations, and (3) the increased role of functional ministries and the banks, as essential to the autonomy, self-government, and self-financing of enterprises as well as to the operation of the new economic mechanism.[43]

In the middle of 1981 a reorganization of the branch ministries was undertaken. Four new ministries were formed from the previous nine and one ministry was split in two in order to separate the Office of Maritime Economy (which became a branch office) from the Ministry of Foreign Trade (a functional ministry). The reduction did not, therefore, go as far as was envisaged in the reform program. As a result of this reorganization, between 1980 and 1983 employment in the branch ministries declined by more than 1,500 persons and in the Planning Commission by 500 persons. At the same time, employment in the functional ministries increased by more than 11,000, and total employment in central state administration increased by more than 8,000.[44]

These changes in employment suggest a reduction in the role of the branch ministries and an increase in the role of the functional ministries, indicating that the program of the reform is at least partly being implemented. On the other hand, however, the substantial increase in employment in the functional ministries (except in the ministry of Foreign Trade, in which employment declined by more than 500 persons) indicates that they have assumed new bureaucratic duties to a much greater extent than was originally envisaged. The new controls have little to do with the operation of the self-regulatory market mechanism that was planned in the original program of the reform.

At the same time, despite the reduction in the number of branch ministries and in the total number of persons employed by them, their grip over the enterprises has not loosened. Since the introduction of the reform, these ministries have increased their range of non-financial instruments of direct administrative control and indirect organizational control.[45] The first group of measures includes: (1) the imposition of the obligatory orders by the government for the delivery of some specific products and the obligatory fulfillment of the so-called "operational programs," both clearly inconsistent with the provisions of the law on state enterprises; (2) the allocation of foreign exchange among enterprises in order to secure the fulfillment of the obligatory orders and operational programs, which means that enterprises that need imports in order to utilize their productive capacities are forced to request these orders or their inclusion in the operational programs; (3) the acceptance of certain centrally planned investment projects which are given priority; and (4) the approval of the plans of enterprises classified as public utilities, as well as the enlargement of the list of such enterprises.

The instruments of the organizational type include: (1) the creation and liquidation of the enterprises; (2) dividing larger enterprises into several smaller ones or combining a number of smaller enterprises into larger ones; (3) the granting of permits for the enterprises to join or to leave the associations or joint companies; (4) the authorization of enterprises to start activities other than those which were originally designated; (5) the confiscation of some of the enterprises' capital assets as the result of an enforced reorganization or sale of unutilized productive resources; (6) a stringent control over the activities of the enterprises and their managers; (7) the appointing and firing of managers of those enterprises deemed as "of special importance for defense or the national economy," as well as of public utilities (at present about 1,400 enterprises—about 20 percent of the total number—have been so classified), and the right to veto the decisions of the workers' councils on the appointment of managers; and (8) the establishment of a temporary management when this action is regarded as necessary.[46]

In addition, the ministers have been given the power to grant enterprise-specific exemptions or reductions in taxes, including the new tax on employment (PFAZ), and to provide various privileges, such as help in obtaining credit from banks. Such attempts affect the financial positions of enterprises independently from considerations of efficiency.[47]

General financial instruments are thus converted into branch- or enterprise-specific "regulators." This leads to the retention of centralized management which, however, uses different instruments than those applied in the past.[48]

In July 1984, legislation concerning the Planning Commission was enacted by the Sejm. The intention of the reform was to insure that the commission would not exercise the same power that it did before the reform. Most notably, it would not be involved in the day-to-day operations of enterprises. However, it was discovered that until 1984, the commission operated on the basis of the legislation of 1959, which formally gave it a similar role to that which was now envisaged. On the basis of the Council of Ministers' administrative regulations, the commission has acquired all those powers that it exercised during the 1960s and 1970s. Therefore, few legislative changes were necessary. The practice of the commission apparently is at the discretion of the Council of Ministers, which, as in the past,[49] can easily change this practice. However, the commission retains its role as a decision-making body placed above the branch and functional ministries. Its actual role is suggested by the fact that various formulations of the legislation restrict the autonomy of enterprises in the preparation of plans.[50] More recently, all matters connected with the reform have been transferred to the commission, with one of its vice-chairmen acting as chairman of the Committee on Reform.

In accordance with the reform, the old associations of enterprises (*zjednoczenia*), which represented the middle level of the ministerial administration and had effective control over enterprises, were liquidated in 1982. According to the reform, the enterprises may form voluntary groupings (*zrzeszenia*), which would not be a part of the state administration. They were expected to be involved in joint market research, the coordination of export activities and investments, the stimulation of technological progress, the training of skilled personnel, and the organization of supplies for member enterprises when they need joint efforts. They were to be subject to anti-monopoly legislation and the market mechanism and guided by the rules of profitability.

The associations were liquidated under martial law, when scarce resources, including foreign exchange, were allocated according to priorities established for the "operational plans" and, later, in connection with the government's obligatory purchases. Many enterprises operated under the control of military commissioners. The government required the formation of some new associations (about one-quarter of all new associations are in this category), primarily in the coal-mining, power-generation, metallurgic, engineering, and food-processing industries. They form a typical, middle-level state administration and do not differ much from the old associations. Other associations were often voluntary in name only. Their formation was a precondition for an operational program that provided access to the allocation of resources, favorable terms of credit, subsidies, or exemptions from taxation. According to the law, the decision to join the association required approval by the workers' councils. As workers' self-management was, however, suspended during martial law, the decisions were approved "ex-post." At present, about 90 percent of all enterprises have joined the new associations. The form that was to be an exception has become the rule. Although the staff of the offices of the associations has been reduced by about 70 percent, most of those remaining are the previous employees of these organizations, and their methods of operation have changed little.[51]

The following conclusion concerning modifications in the institutional structure seems valid:

> The organization, methods of operation and status of the central authorities have not been changed to any significant extent. Dominant still arethose features that are typical for centralized management. One of these features is a *de facto* branch structure which plays a more important role than the functional organizations. The most important decisions originate in the former, and the decisions of the latter adjust to them rather passively.[52]

Changes in the Economic Mechanism

The use of the price mechanism was accepted as the most important feature of the new economic mechanism that was projected in the official reform program. In this field, actual changes have been particularly disappointing. After three years of the reform, the price mechanism does not operate better than before the reform began. The situation in 1985 even shows some regression relative to the first year of the reform.

A major revision of the process of producers' goods was effected at the beginning of 1982 in a typically bureaucratic fashion. Average prices more than doubled. With some lag, retail prices almost doubled, and the price of foodstuffs increased more than those of non-alimentary goods. The population received partial compensation, which did not, however, prevent a drastic decline in real income. Unfortunately, because of the time required for the simultaneous revision of hundreds of thousands of interrelated prices, cost of producers' goods was not calculated on the basis of the rate of exchange that was determined at the time. Distortions appeared, and the authorities' attempt to coordinate domestic prices and world prices failed.

In 1982 the domestic prices of only two out of twenty-one selected raw materials and intermediate goods exceeded their transaction prices, i.e. those prices that actually were received or paid in foreign trade with convertible-currency countries (Table 5); in some cases the gap was substantial. There was an improvement in the overall situation in 1983, but in 1984 the gap widened again in several cases.

The traditional mechanism of periodic, comprehensive revisions of prices was retained, and several revisions have occurred in recent years. A modification in the old price system was introduced in 1982. The new system included officially fixed prices (determined by the central authorities), regulated prices (based on the formula determined by the central authorities), and so-called contractual prices, which originally were expected to become prices determined freely by the forces of supply and demand. In 1983 the share of this third group of prices declined (in comparison with the level of 1981); in the retail market, on the producers' goods market, and on the agricultural-produce market.

In 1982 and 1983 all transactions in the retail and agricultural produce markets, whatever the type of prices, were based on costs plus a profit margin. In the producers' goods market, 80 percent of transactions in 1982 and 68 percent in 1983 were based on prices using this formula, and only 20 percent and 32 percent, respectively, were calculated as transaction prices.[53] Since the middle of 1983 the government has been authorized to freeze prices for designated periods. Moreover, since the end of 1983, all contractual prices have to be calculated on the basis of "justified costs," the determination of which involves a bureaucratic control of enterprise price formation and more or less arbitrary decisions by the central authorities.[54] Thus, even contractual prices have lost, for all practical purposes, the character of free prices that was sought at the early stage of the implementation of the economic reform.[55]

Under these conditions, it is futile to discuss the operation of a self-regulated price mechanism. Prices are not flexible. They do not help to reduce the domestic and external disequilibria. They continue to misinform buyers and sellers and make all financial results of an enterprise and its economic calculations meaningless or even misleading.[56] As has been pointed out by the Consultative Economic Council

> "enterprises do not have to watch costs and their various elements, such as the absolute or relative levels of the prices of raw materials, the level of the rate of exchange, interest on credits, the rates of those taxes that are included in costs—because any changes in these parameters are automatically transformed, through the mechanism of "justified costs," into the increases in the prices of the goods which they produce.... The economy continues to be insensitive to both market signals and the preferences of the central authorities that are expressed with the help of financial instruments because the latter operate through changes on the level of costs and are automatically passed on to the buyer."[57]

The lack of reasonable prices encourages the wide use of the turnover tax and similar deductions and subsidies to eliminate distortions in the financial result of enterprises, which are caused by price distortions. The ratio of the turnover tax and similar deductions to the total revenues from sales by all socialist enterprises in the national economy increased from 5.8 percent in 1982 to 6.7 percent in 1983 and 6.8 percent in 1984. Subsidies as percentage of the total revenues from sales declined from 5.7 percent in 1982 to 5 percent in 1983 but increased to 5.3 percent in 1984.[58] For all socialist enterprises combined, as well as in many individual sectors, net losses would have been registered during these three years without subsidies. The absolute amount of subsidies for all socialist enterprises combined increased from 1982 to 1983 and again in 1984. In most sectors they increased in 1984 in comparison with 1983.

The amount of subsidies given to socialist enterprises in total expenditures from the central state budget have been declining slowly and still represent a vary large proportion of budgetary expenditures: 47 percent in 1982, 41 percent in 1983, 40 percent in 1984 and 38 percent in the budget for 1985.[59]

If the ratio of the sum of the turnover taxes, other deductions, plus subsidies to total revenues from sales is taken as an indicator of the degree of price distortions, then the situation deteriorated during 1982-84; the ratio increased from 11.5 percent in 1982 to 11.8 percent in 1983 and to 12.1 percent in 1984.

With distorted prices it is impossible to judge whether an enterprise that shows profits is really profitable and if the one that has to be subsidized is really making losses. In this situation, it would have been surprising if any enterprise had been liquidated since the beginning of the reform.[60] Clearly, the ability of enterprises to guard their autonomy, manage themselves, and provide their own finance is threatened by a situation in which no one can discern if a firm is actually profitable. Enterprises must depend on the authorities in so many ways.

Similarly, the expected changes in employment policy have not materialized. There are no signs of improved labor allocation, in spite of the introduction of a new tax payable on the size of the work force in the enterprise (the so-called PFAZ deduction). On the contrary, increased shortages of labor, while the economy's total output has declined, suggest that the labor force is now allocated even less efficiently.[61] Changes in the regulation of wages can be described as "small and unimportant" and "completely insufficient from the point of view of the three principles of the reform: the autonomy, self-government and self-financing of enterprises."[62]

With the malfunction of the price mechanism, the allocation of resources must depend on the use of administrative measures. In order to provide sufficient labor for the priority enterprises, the authorities introduced the obligatory use of labor exchanges, at first in 15 and later in 19 of 50 districts.[63] In 1982 direct allocation applied to 16 groups of materials, 10 groups of machines and transport equipment, and 97 percent of the foreign exchange available to finance imports. According to the legislation enacted in February 1982, the direct administrative allocation of the means of production and foreign exchange was to be terminated at the end of 1983. In December 1983 it was extended without any time limit, with a provision that every year the government must present to the Sejm its program for the limitation of direct administrative allocation (a completely useless device).

To cope with the shortages of goods in 1982, 14 "operational programs" were introduced to fulfill governmental priorities. Almost all enterprises participated in at least one such program in order to secure for themselves the supply of scarce materials. The number of programs was reduced to 6 in 1983 and to 4 in 1984. They were, however, replaced by the government's "purchase orders," which in 1983 covered about 30 percent of materials and final products and 10 investment projects. In 1984 the number of these "purchase orders" increased to 111. Together with other priority production, such as defense production and cooperatives employing the handicaped, about 40 percent of total production is based on the administratively guaranteed supply of materials and goods. Moreover, "informal pressure on the enterprises to accept governmental purchase orders has been increasing."[64]

Another form of governmental control over the allocation of materials and final goods is the compulsory designation of suppliers. In the supply of materials to producers this function is performed by more than 20 wholesale organizations; in the field of consumption goods (involving 42 groups of products), by 4 organizations. They all have monopolistic positions and strengthen the role of the branch ministries in the allocation of resources among enterprises.[65]

The reform has achieved very little progress in the allocation of foreign exchange. In 1982 enterprises were authorized to retain for their own use or that of their suppliers a small proportion of their export earnings in foreign currencies that were on deposit in special bank accounts. About 3 percent of imports in 1982 and 9 percent in 1983 were financed this way. However, foreign exchange deposited with the bank is subject to administrative control, whereas the size of the retention quotas is at the discretion of the central authorities. Neither the sale of foreign exchange by auction nor the use of foreign-exchange credits has assumed any practical importance.[66]

The following observations by Polish economists on the nature of the new allocative mechanism and its efficiency should be noted. One states:

> ... the range of the direct administrative allocation of the means of production and foreign exchange has not been reduced to any significant extent. Moreover, the new form of administrative allocation, in the form of the obligatory use of intermediaries in transactions, has not proved to be any better than the old, inefficient direct allocation.... It has a demoralizing effect on the personnel of the distribution organizations. It induces the appearance of the branch and local vested interests which fight among themselves for the share of the allocation of scarce goods. Often it leads to corruption as a way to win in this competition. This type of competition, unlike the market competition, does not harmonize economic processes but, on the contrary, it disintegrates them. For this reason the administrative allocation is not a road which can lead to economic equilibrium.[67]

Another economist notes:

> Administrative allocation creates a special type of interrelations which is contrary to the basic rules of the economic mechanism and efficiency criteria. Autonomy, self-financing, and self-management do not mean much when production, the level of the employees' wages and the development of the enterprise depend on the allocation of raw materials, intermediate goods, power, fuels, etc.[68]

The reform has not resulted in the establishment of a self-regulatory economic mechanism. The old centrally planned system has been modified as the result of a mass of legislation, administrative regulations, and discretionary decisions by the central authorities. This has not, however, resulted in the change in the direction of an increased use of market instruments that was envisaged in the officially adopted program.

Poland's "new" economic system is not the traditional command system, nor is it a socialist market system. It is a system in which the authorities try to manipulate the decisions of formally autonomous enterprises with the help of financial and direct administrative measures. On their part, enterprises try to manipulate the decisions of the authorities by bargaining for exemptions, favorable treatment, and the allocation of scarce resources. It is doubtful, however, that the outcome of this "manipulative system" is an improvement in economic efficiency.

Notes

1. For the discussion of the preparation of this document by the Committee on Economic Reform (established in October 1980), other proposals that were presented by various groups, and the circumstances under which the debate on economic reform was conducted, see Z.M. Fallenbuchl, "Poland's Economic Crisis," *Problems of Communism*, Vol. 31, no. 2, 1982, pp. 1-21; Z.M. Fallenbuchl, " The Origins of the Present Economic Crisis in Poland and the Issue of Economic Reform," in A. Jain (ed.), *Solidarity: The Origins and Implications of Polish Trade Unions*, (Baton Rouge, 1983), pp. 149-166; and Z.M. Fallenbuchl, "The Polish Economy Since August 1980," *Canadian Slavonic Papers*, Vol. 25, no. 3, 1983, pp. 361-379.

2. "The Directions of Economic Reform," (in Polish) *Trybuna Ludu*, 1981, p.6.

3. Ibid., pp. 52-63.

4. Ibid., pp. 9-19.

5. Ibid., pp. 19-22.

6. Ibid., p. 21.

7. "The Reform," (in Polish) *Życie Gospodarcze*, no. 13 (1985), p. 4.

8. C. Józefiak, "Prices, Administrative Allocation, Wages," (in Polish) *Życie Gospodarcze*, no. 14 (1985), p. 4.

9. As quoted in "The Three S's After Three Years," (in Polish) *Życie Gospodarcze*, no. 23 (1985), p. 4.

10. *Legislative Acts: On the State Enterprises and on Workers' Self-government in the State Enterprise* (in Polish), (Warsaw,1981).

11. Z. M. Fallenbuchl, "The Polish Economy under Martial Law," *Soviet Studies*, Vol. 36, no. 4, 1984, pp. 513-527.

12. I. Dryll, "The Three S's in Legislation and in Life," (in Polish) *Życie Gospodarcze*, no. 14 (1985), p. 2.

13. L. Stępniak at a meeting of the subcommittee on self-government and legal foundations of the functioning of the economy (Sub-Committee X) of the Committee on Economic Reform, as quoted by Dryll, Ibid.

14. J. Rymarczyk, "The Reform in Foreign Trade: An Attempt at Diagnosis," (in Polish) *Życie Gospodarcze*, no. 33 (1985), p. 8.

15. K. Barcikowski (member of the Politbureau and secretary of the Central Committee at the economic conference of the party delegates in Poznań in June 1985) "Three S's After Three Years," p. 1.

16. W. Jaruzelski at the Poznań conference, Ibid.

17. I. Dryll, "An Evaluation of the Reform," (in Polish) *Życie Gospodarcze*, no. 32 (1985), p. 1.

18. T. Jeziorański, "The Jungle," (in Polish) *Życie Gospodarcze*, no. 29 (1985), p. 2.

19. K. Grześkiewicz in the debate published in "The Reform," (in Polish) *Życie Gospodarcze*, no. 13 (1985), p. 10.

20. Jeziorański, p.2.

21. Ibid.

22. As reported by Dryll, "Three S ...," p. 2.

23. See, for example, L. Gluck's statement at a meeting of the Commission on Economic Reform, as reported by T. Jeziorański, "A Meeting of the Committee on Economic Reform," (in Polish) *Życie Gospodarcze*, no. 21 (1985), p. 4; and C. Bobrowski in "The Reform," p 6.

24. Z. J. Mikołajczyk in "The Reform," p. 4.

25. J. Mujżel, Ibid., p. 7.

26. M. Nasiłowski, " The Reform in the Straight-Jacket of Constraints," (in Polish) *Życie Gospodarcze*, no. 20 (1985), p. 1.

27. W. Rydygier in "The Reform," pp. 4-5.

28. L. Gluck at a meeting of the Committee on Economic Reform as reported by Jeziorański, "A Meeting of the Committee on ...," p. 4.

29. T. Jeziorański, "Three Years After," (in Polish) *Życie Gospodarcze*, no. 8 (1985), p. 6.

30. Jeziorański, "A meeting of the Committee ...," p. 1; W. Baka, "The Shape of the Reform in the Next Few Years," (in Polish) *Rzeczpospolita*, July 30, 1985.

31. C. Bobrowski in "The Reform," p. 13.

32. Mujżel and K. Chmielewski, Ibid., p. 7.

33. See. W. Trzeciakowski, "Problems of Efficiency and Equilibrium," (in Polish) *Handel Zagraniczny*, no. 10, 1983, pp. 8-11.

34. W. Wilczyński in "The Reform," p. 6.

35. These isolated views are held by some engineers rather than economists. A. Kopeć, for example, in Jeziorański "A Meeting of the ...," p. 4, and in Jeziorański's "Three Years After," p. 6.

36. For example, A. Łukasiewicz's statement as reported by Jeziorański, "Three Year's After," p. 1.

37. *A Proposal for Fundamental Solutions to Economic Reform in Poland* (in Polish), (Warsaw, 1980).

38. *Directions of Economic Reform*, pp. 17-18.

39. *Legislative Acts:*, pp. 26, 29.

40. C. Józefiak, "The Structure and Functioning of Central Administration," (in Polish) *Życie Gospodarcze*, no. 5 (1985), p. 5.

41. *Directions* .... pp. 65-66.

42. Józefiak, "The Structure and Functioning ...," p. 5.

43. Ibid.

44. *Statistical Yearbook 1981*, pp. 605-6; 1983, pp. 465-6; 1984. p. 502.

45. Józefiak, p.5.

46. Ibid.

47. "The Consultative Economic Council on the System of Functioning, Part 2," (in Polish) *Życie Gospodarcze*, no. 46 (1984), p. 5.

48. Józefiak, p. 5.

49. J. Szymańczyk, "The Legal Status of the Planning Commission at the Council of Ministers," (in Polish) *Gospodarka Planowa*, no. 2, 1985, pp. 74-76.

50. Józefiak, p. 5.

51. Ibid.

52. Ibid.

53. Z. Zdyb, "Conditions of Efficiency of the Financial System" (in Polish), *Finanse*, no. 3., 1985, p. 14.

54. Józefiak, "Prices, Administrative Allocations, Wages," p. 5.

55. P. Dziewulski, "Prices," (in Polish) *Życie Gospodarcze*, no. 21 (1985), p. 12.

56. Józefiak, "Prices ..., " p. 5.

57. "The Consultative Economic Council on the System of Functioning," (in Polish) *Życie Gospodarcze*, no. 45 (1984), p. 11.

58. *Życie Gospodarcze*, no. 10, 1984, p. 9; no. 9, 1985, p. 15.

59. Zdyb, p. 18.

60. Ibid.

61. For more details see Z.M. Fallenbuchl, a chapter on "Employment Policies in Poland," in J. Adam (ed.), *Employment Policies in the Soviet Union and Eastern Europe*, (London, revised edition forthcoming).

62. Józefiak, "Prices ...," p. 5.

63. "The Consultative Economic Council ...," Part 1, p. 10.

64. Ibid.

65. Józefiak, "Prices ...," p. 5.

66. Ibid. For more details, see Z. M. Fallenbuchl, "Foreign Trade Reform in Poland," paper presented at the annual meeting of the American Association for the Advancement of Slavic Studies in New Orleans, November 1986.

67. Ibid.

68. Nasiłowski, p. 10.

13

The Difficulties of Implementing Economic Reforms

Zbigniew Kamecki

The implementation of the economic reform began in January 1982, within two weeks of the imposition of martial law. The government's decision was an act of political courage because the economy was badly unbalanced, and the reaction of Polish society to the imposition of martial law was uncertain. The gradual political stabilization that followed did not imply that economic equilibrium had been regained. On the contrary, neither domestic nor external equilibrium had been fully restored. As a result, it is fruitless to compare the present state of the Polish economic reform to that of Hungary, for the Hungarian reforms were introduced under different conditions. Hungary had no foreign debt, the domestic market was relatively balanced, and the political situation was stable.

Although political factors played an important role in the initial stage of the implementation of the reform, they became less important as the political situation returned to normal. It is the economic factors that have constrained the scope of reform. For instance, the shortages of many raw materials and imported goods have forced the continuation of the central allocation system, which is completely inconsistent with the reform. The Polish authorities can abolish the system of allocation only through a gradual restoration of market equilibrium, not by decrees.

The second factor that restricts the implementation of the reform is the fear of its negative impact on the standard of living. One of the basic preconditions of economic reform is a rational system of prices. Given the constraints on the increase of production, a rise in prices to market-clearing levels would mean a further deterioration of the standard of living. This would, perhaps, be unacceptable to Polish society. Therefore, equilibrium prices have to be reached gradually; in the meantime, the prices of numerous products have to be maintained at artificially low levels.

Although I consider these factors the main practical obstacles to the implementation of economic reform in Poland, I also consider the more subjective constraints. The reform is being introduced by the very people who worked for decades under a highly centralized system. Some of them were accustomed to giving or receiving directives or, even worse, waiting for them. These are habits that hamper the reform, and they are present at all levels of management.

Some enterprises take advantage of existing market shortages, exerting monopolistic practices that further constrain the implementation of the reform. The autonomy granted to enterprises within the framework of the reform facilitates these practices. Poland is the only socialist country that has introduced antitrust legislation, although its role will be small as long as the domestic market remains unbalanced.

Is there a chance that the current economic reform will be fully implemented despite these difficulties, or will it share the fate of the earlier, unsuccessful attempts to reform the economy? I am convinced that the success of the present reform is quite possible. First, the impact of the constraints discussed earlier will grow weaker as the economy improves. Second, a great majority of Poles is convinced that there is no alternative to a consistent implementation of the reform. The previous centralized system proved to be completely ineffective. Third, the implementation of the economic reform remains a political commitment of the present leadership. In light of the vociferous public opinion in Poland, the authorities cannot afford to face the complaint that they did not fulfill their promises. Fourth, the economic reform has proved its value even after its limited implementation. This strengthens support for the reform and weakens the position of those who oppose it.

14

Workers' Self-Management Before and After 1981

David C. Holland

Historical Perspective

Three times in the postwar history of Poland (in 1945, 1956, and 1981), programs of workers' selfmanagement have been advanced.[1] On each occasion they have been associated with a deep-seated political, social and economic crisis. The idea has been consistently associated with decentralizing, market-oriented economic measures. Workers' self-management has simultaneously represented an attempt at broadening the political base of the regime and a programmatic alternative to the Stalinist methods of a centralized command economy.

In 1944-45 workers' councils were spontaneously established to maintain production and defend plants in the situation of a political vacuum, in which the owners or administrators of the German occupation had fled the approaching Red Army. The provisional communist authorities were eager to grasp at a source of legitimation for an extremely shaky new regime. The councils operated in the undoctrinaire framework of the first Three Year Plan, which guided reconstruction without excessive centralization and encouraged decentralized and private initiatives. It could be regarded as a forerunner of "market socialism." The councils did not survive the period of economic andpolitical pluralism of 1945-47, and, with the onset of the Cold War and the imposition of Stalinist political and economic methods, they were integrated into the centralized trade union structures.

In 1956 the renewed emergence of workers' councils played a key role in the crisis of the transition to post-Stalinist conditions. The authorities discussed a program of economic reform, centering upon the introduction of a market mechanism, parametric planning, and the delegation of much decision making to the enterprises. The plan included the participation of workers in planning at the plant level.

The opportunity to introduce this major reform, when the authorities enjoyed a level of popular support unequaled before or since, was wasted. The recommendations of the Economic Reform Council (of which Brus, a distinguished contributor to this volume, was a member) were ignored and the workers' councils were integrated into the Conferences of Workers' Self-Management. These included various social and political organizations under Party control; their role was one of a transmission belt. By 1980 there were, reportedly, only five workers' councils in Poland.

In the face of the political and economic crisis of 1980-81, workers' self-management again appeared on the agenda. New workers' councils were spontaneously elected (usually excluding Party-influenced professional, social and political organizations in the workplace),[2] a development which the Party encouraged, hoping to outflank Solidarity. The Solidarity leadership, however, outflanked the Party by placing self-management at the center of its program by the summer of 1981.

Once more workers' councils were to become a part of economic reforms that were aimed at decentralization, enterprise autonomy and market conditions. The government and Solidarity differed over the retention of powers of central intervention and over the demand that enterprise directors should be elected by workers' councils, which threatened the system of *nomenklatura*.

Solidarity's conception of self-management was reflected in the draft bill on the "social enterprise," developed by the "Network of Leading Solidarity Enterprises." The authorities' conception was embodied in two draft bills, one on state enterprises and one on self-management. The clash between the two concepts was resolved in September 1981 after arduous negotiations and an unprecedented defiance of party instructions in the Sejm.

This compromise legislation was not entirely satisfactory to either side. Solidarity, in fact, demanded a referendum to amend the law in the direction of group ownership based on the Yugoslav model. However, it did not rest upon a "basic unit of labor," as in Yugoslavia, but delegated authority to a council at the enterprise level. The government's concept favored worker participation rather than worker control.

In purely formal terms, the legislation placed the councils in a comparatively strong legal position, with powers to take binding decisions on all important enterprise affairs, including the plan, investments, wage systems, division of profit, and social spending. The director is responsible to the council, and the council may block any decision by the director running contrary to its wishes. The director has, however, a countervailing power of veto. Councils in enterprises judged (by the government) not to be of "basic national importance" can select and dismiss their directors. Most important, the councils are directly elected by the whole workforce.[3] No screening process exists to control those who may become candidates.

These powers provide for a much higher level of worker participation than the proposed EEC directive that requires employee consultation, or than exists for German worker directors, or in recent self-management measures adopted in Hungary, although these last include the right of some workforces to participate, in a qualified way, in the selection of directors.[4]

Self-management bodies, like Solidarity, were "suspended" by the martial-law regulations introduced on December 13, 1981. All their powers were transferred to enterprise directors or to the military commissars. The authorities removed the legal immunities, such as those from dismissal, enjoyed by members of workers' councils. Self-management activists generally escaped internment, but many faced other difficulties.

The self-management project has remained a programmatic idea of the opposition as well as a central strut in the authorities' program of "normalization" and economic reform. It is one of the "three S's" detailed in the chapter in this volume by Fallenbuchl.

Thus, even though conditions have greatly changed, both the economic reform of 1981 and the role of self-management within it have, in some sense, remained on the agenda since martial law. How far the authorities' pledge to continue with these programs has been realized and how the constituency of Solidarity has responded are issues discussed in the next section.

Government and Opposition Policies

Senior official spokesmen from Jaruzelski downward have repeatedly and categorically reaffirmed the government's commitment to the economic reform and to workers' self-management, asserting that there was to be "no turning back." However, the "long history of the short reform" in Poland provides strong grounds for doubt of the most categorically phrased commitment. What Józef Pajestka has described as the characteristic "softness" of the Polish legal order has to be taken into account.[5] That is, laws in Poland can easily be bent, fudged, and forgotten, although they remain on the statute book.

The government has cautiously sought to reactivate the selfmanagement bodies, suspending—under various special provisions emanating from the martial law period through 1985—several of the councils' more important powers. Demands voiced in the Central Committee for the amendment of the law to extend these restrictions were not acted upon.

Theoretically, then, the councils are now in full possession of the powers provided for in the legislation of 1981. Information submitted to the Sejm at the end of 1984 indicated that self-management existed in 87 percent of the plants that were empowered to have them (a total of 6,403 enterprises, embracing 5.5 million workers and involving 133,000 people in their activity, 55 percent of whom were manual workers).[6] What is the reality of the situation?

First, many of these councils exist formally, with little independence or vitality. A minority of perhaps 10 percent are independent-minded and active, often where there has been a direct continuity from 1981. Many councils that were active in 1981 have, however, never resumed activity. In some important plants (Ursus, WSK Okęcie and ZK Polcolor in Warsaw and the refinery in Gdańsk, for example), the political situation was regarded as too unsafe in 1985 to permit resumption of the councils' activities.

Second, the right of the councils to select directors has been sharply restricted. In late 1981 the government prepared a list of 200 enterprises of "basic national importance" as part of a compromise with Solidarity, in which the right to nominate the director was retained by the authorities. The list has now been enlarged to 1,371 firms, some of which are categories of enterprises. Given the high level of concentration of Polish industry, this "reserve list" must cover all major areas.

Third, although Article 35 of the self-management law provides for councils to cooperate with one another, regional or national activity has been kept to a minimum and carefully controlled. The 25 spontaneously formed (in 1981) regional coordinating committees have only regional caucuses of Sejm deputies or commissions established alongside the Voivodship People's Councils to replace them. Nothing has been heard of the proposal, floated by a government commission in 1981, to establish a new chamber of the Sejm to represent workers' councils. Attempts at grass-roots organization have been prevented (as at Elana in Toruń in April 1984). National rallies with Party leaders take place, but these are carefully orchestrated. Politically "awkward" workers' councils may not be invited.

The authorities appear to be bent on confining the "democratic" element of the councils to the enterprise level. A return to the narrow "mobilizing" or "transmission-belt" role of the pre-1980 Conferences for Workers' Self Management cannot be excluded. The trend of official policy is clearly illustrated by two examples.

First, the role of the official trade unions is being expanded at the expense of the workers' councils. One of the successes of the councils has been to disrupt the prevailing patterns of patronage in the allocation of enterprise housing, vacation-home placements, and other social spending. The trade unions acquired a right of veto in these areas in amendments to the law in 1985. Similarly, in wage bargaining, the trade unions acquired the right in the wage law of 1984 to conclude agreements with management regardless of how many (or how few) workers they represent.

Second, developments at the end of 1985 indicated a major shift in policy toward the creation of giant new industrial combines. This disregarded the provisions of the law on enterprise autonomy and threatened to wipe out any room for self-management on the enterprise level. The East German model, apparently favored by the new Soviet leadership, is possibly gaining ground. However, the first of these combines, embracing the entire metallurgy sector, was blocked by an outcry of economists and workers' councils. This incident reflects the continuing vitality of the pro-reform forces as well as the difficulties they face.

Information on whether pressure has been applied in the elections of 1985 to the councils to weed out troublesome activists is not available at the time of writing. In 40 percent of the elections that had been completed by the end of May 1985, however, there was a turnover of 60 percent. This is a disruptively high drop-out rate.

The attitude of the political opposition to self-management has undergone a marked change since martial law. Initial accusations that work in self-management institutions was tantamount to collaboration with the authorities have given way to more frequent and explicit calls to make maximum use of this opportunity for legal activity in the public sphere. This process has stemmed from the realization that it is possible to use the councils as trade unions. In several instances Solidarity has successfully stood its own slates in elections to workers' councils. A number of strongholds of workers' self-management exist (Huta Warszawa, the FSO car factory, Elana in Toruń) in which the blessing of the opposition is a significant factor in the continuing vigor and independence of the councils.

What Can the Post-Martial-Law Councils Do?

The answer, stated briefly, is very little. This is largely a function of the modest progress of the economic reform. If decisions on important areas such as pricing, investment allocation, or distribution of raw materials remain in the hands of the center, there is very little room for enterprise autonomy. The extent of the reform's progress will be discussed by other contributors to this volume.

The main role of the councils in economic reform is to provide a counterweight to the economic bureaucracy and to mobilize pressure to defend enterprise autonomy and expand autonomous local initiative. It would seem that there *are* cases in which councils have been able, for example, to defend a director under pressure from above or to resist the imposition of decisions from above. The councils have displayed an ability to act independently in the division of the enterprises' profits, the establishment of new wage structures, and the supervision of social and welfare funds.

In 1984 the authorities exerted strong pressure from above to introduce new incentive-type wage systems, and many councils appear to have taken advantage of this opportunity. It seems possible to construct a new wage system with common sense and with the benefit of experience. To intervene in the plan, however, requires current data, not only about the enterprise but about the general economic environment. Even if information is available, the difficulty is compounded when plan-bargaining continues until the very last minute or well into the plan period itself.

The councils are represented at the level of industrial associations, but it is the exception rather than the rule that their representatives are able to caucus separately (e.g. in Unitra) and make efforts to intervene at a level which necessarily determines many enterprise options.

In management's personnel policy, the influence of the councils is generally weak. In 1983 they lost the right to determine the pay and job description of enterprise directors. There are cases in which councils have competitively selected directors—in 1984 about 200 in the whole country.

There are also examples of the intervention of councils in every-day production arrangements: the reorganization of repair facilities; attempts to reduce administrative staffing; the sale of unused reserves and the purchase of new ones; and the undertaking of minor investments and innovations. But these remain activities of little importance.

Following martial law, the reassertion of traditional patterns of authority in the workplace has naturally imposed constraints on the councils. The party has also exerted itself to win representation in the councils, a fact which is likely to affect their independence. At a party seminar on the subject in May 1985, the party secretary from the Gdańsk shipyards boasted that 14 out of the 21 members of the council were party members. Party representation in the councils is triple its presence in the work force as a whole. About one-half of the presidents of the workers' councils are party members.

The councils, then, are not able to exercise anything like the full powers envisaged in the 1981 legislation. A significant minority, however, retain independence and vitality. They are imbued with a perceptible trade-unionist character, in the absence of any other legal and democratic workers' representation. Their contribution to the reform is modest, but could be developed, if official commitments to pressing ahead with the reform were to be honored. Widespread skepticism on this score and the general instability of the economic rules are the principal factors that work against such a development.

Do the Workers Support Self-Management?

Evidence from 1980, 1981, 1983, 1984, and 1985 demonstrates conclusively that a large majority of Polish workers support the concept of "authentic" self-management.[7] At the same time, levels of dissatisfaction with or disinterest in the existing self-management institutions indicate that self-management is not yet credible.

A significant minority supports work within the existing structure. Research from the first half of 1983 showed that 20 to 25 percent of the workers voiced support for the self-management organizations. Research in 1984 revealed that 41 percent of the employees wanted to influence enterprise decisions through the workers' council, as opposed to 7.4 percent who wanted influence through the trade unions and 6.1 percent through "political organizations." However, among young workers (under 25 years of age), support for self-management has fallen to negligible levels, even in such a citadel of self-management as the Warsaw Steel Works; support has risen in the older age groups. Overall, 61 percent of the workers asserted that self-management had no influence and 33 percent thought it had not much influence.[8]

Conclusion

Since the introduction of martial law, the far-reaching debates of 1981 on the character of ownership in the economy, social control, and economic democracy, together with radical economic reform, have receded into the past. The scope both for the reform and for workers' self-management within it are now much more limited. Achieving "Kádárization" in Poland—the combination of decentralizing economic reforms and a relatively liberal regime founded on a firmly managed political stability—also looks increasingly implausible. Political repression appears to be gradually increasing rather than (as in Hungary) gradually stopped.

What, then, are possible scenarios for the future role of the workers' councils in Poland?

First, there is a distinct possibility that they will have no future. A return to a full-fledged, centralized, economic management would leave no role for the workers' councils. If this were to happen, their remaining independence would be crushed and their organizational structures neglected and allowed to fall into disrepair, as happened in the 1970s with the Conferences for Workers' Self-Management. Such an event would contradict the professed intentions of the central authorities. However, given the pronounced distrust of the middle levels of the economic and party apparatus toward the councils and the past record of co-option and bureaucratization of such bodies, the decadence of the councils is not an entirely improbable scenario.

Second, there is the possibility that a limited but genuine degree of autonomy will be conceded to the enterprises, albeit one that will remain quite circumscribed, preserving the pattern of lobbying and pressure-group politics. In this scenario self-management will probably become an instrument in bargaining between the levels of the economic apparatus. Such a system would aim to recruit the most active workers to the structure of authority. Technicians, specialists and low-level foremen would be able to use the self-management structures to promote their own interests. Management would use the legitimating stamp of the workers' council to justify its decisions to the workers. This scenario is more probable than the first one but might also serve as a stage in transition to the first alternative.

Third, there is a slim possibility that the dominance of economic liberals in the central administration may hold open the field for the growth of activity by workers' councils, which supposes that the economic reform, as advertised by the authorities would actually be progressively implemented. The continuation of the reform would make possible the return to social activity of the many skilled workers who were mobilized by the self-management movement in 1981. Their desire to rid the workplaces of the waste and nonsense of the relations of bureaucratic production could be harnessed as a powerful engine to promote the reform. The support of the new leadership in the Kremlin for economic reform and the strengthening of the Jaruzelski leadership against some of its "hard-line" critics bodes well for this possibility. Recent policy moves do not, however, seem to be going in this direction.

Finally, I should reiterate that support for the *idea* of self-management has become well established in the Polish working class. The story of this movement is unlikely to end. Even the modest activity of the workers' councils, with the limited support they enjoy today, constitutes a force on the side of economic reform, which the Polish authorities would be reckless to squander.

Notes

1. Research for this paper was conducted as part of a Ph.D. degree for the Center for Russian and East European Studies, University of Birmingham. Research was carried out in 1984 at the Department of Economics, Warsaw University and has also been supported by the European University Institute, Florence, Italy.

2. These "new" workers' councils originated spontaneously in a highly heterogeneous manner. Probably the first was initiated by 1956 activists at *Unimor* in Gdańsk, where a new directly elected council was in place by the end of September 1980.

3. Translations of the two laws on state enterprise and self-management have been published in Peter Raina, *Poland 1981: Towards Social Renewal* (London, 1985).

4. For the EEC proposal, cf. Bulletin of the European Communities, Supplement 3/80. Employee Information & Consultation Procedures. The Hungarian system introduced on 1/1/85 is detailed in Paul Marer, "Economic Reform in Hungary: From Central Planning to Regulated Market," in Selected Papers of the Joint Economic Committee of the U.S. Congress, *East European Economics Slow Growth in the 1980s*, vol. 3, *Country Studies in Eastern Europe and Yugoslavia*, Washington, D.C., 1986.

5. Józef Pajestka, "About the Reform after Three Years," (in Polish), *Życie Gospodarcze*, no. 37, August 15, 1985.

6. Irena Dryll, "A Portrait of Self-governance" (in Polish), *Życie Gospodarcze*, August 18, 1985.

7. For a fuller treatment of opposition attitudes see the author's "Self-Management Without Solidarity" in *Labour Focus on Eastern Europe*, Winter 1984, and "Self Management in Poland," *Labour Focus on Eastern Europe*, May 1986.

8. There is a large body of such survey literature available in Polish. I have quoted selectively from various sources.

15

Foreign Trade Reforms Since 1981

Benjamin Slay

Overview of the Economic Reform Implementation

This chapter reviews the state of the post-1981 attempt at economic reform in Poland, focusing on changes in the foreign-trade mechanism. General background on Poland's economic crisis can be found in the contributions included in Part I of this volume; the reform blueprint and implementation are discussed by Fallenbuchl.[1]

The reform introduced on January 1, 1982 was thrust into an environment hostile to its implementation because of falling real income and wages as well as deep internal and external disequilibria. The difficulties were compounded by the imposition of martial law three weeks before the reform's implementation, which produced a deep public hostility toward the Jaruzelski regime and further disrupted economic activity.[2] It is worth noting that such conditions are unprecedented in the history of economic reform attempts in socialist countries.

The reform blueprint contained, in addition to the "three S's"—enterprise self-reliance, enterprise self-financing, and workers' self-management—a redefinition of the scope and instruments of central planning. Direct-planning instruments were to be replaced by financial instruments (e.g. prices, taxes, subsidies). Only 25 percent of investments would be controlled and financed from the center; enterprises were supposed to plan the remaining 75 percent. These changes would facilitate a reduction in the scope of central planning, permitting the center to concentrate on strategic and macro-issues.

A reorganization of the planning bureaucracy was also envisioned to facilitate the application of the new "regulators," in order to guarantee enterprise autonomy. The number of branch ministries was reduced from nine to six, and the intermediate level in the branch hierarchy, the associations (*zjednoczenia*), were abolished. It was believed that further structural reform would be carried out at a later date.

A thorough analysis of the checkered history of the reform's implementation has been provided elsewhere in this volume (see Chapter 12 by Fallenbuchl and Chapter 28 by Gomulka), so I highlight only a few facts as background for a discussion of the foreign trade aspects of the reform.

Inflationary Pressures. The first half of the 1980s witnessed a tripling in the quantity of cash balances held by enterprises and households. At the end of 1985, these holdings were estimated in the range of 700 billion zloty.[3] This monetary expansion produced both high rates of *overt* inflation (retail prices tripled in 1982 and remained at double-digit levels from 1983 through 1986) and supressed inflation in the form of the 700 billion zloty inflationary gap (1985 data). These pressures have made the authorities reluctant to let prices rise to equilibrium levels, thus reducing the viability of the reform's financial instruments.

Insufficient Structural Reform. The reduction in the number of branch ministries from nine to six was a reorganization, unaccompanied by major reductions in budgets and personnel (see Chapter 12 by Fallenbuchl). The *zjednoczenia* were replaced by *zrzeszenia*, a new intermediate link which, contrary to the reform's intentions, continue to perform that layer's traditional functions.[4] Structural reform of the banking system has been largely dormant also. Thus, the predominantly branch structure of the traditional planning hierarchy has remained essentially intact.

Monopolistic Practices and Market Structures. The planning bureaucracy's branch orientation and the high levels of industrial concentration have created monopolistic market structures. In the absence of competitive pressures, enterprise price and output decisions often become exercises in price fixing and output restriction (especially when coordinated by their *zrzeszenie*!). No significant anti-monopoly legislation has been passed since the reform was conceived in 1981, although a draft bill which would establish an anti-monopoly commission was submitted to the Sejm in early 1986.

Cost-plus Pricing. The administrative character of the pricing system was further strengthened by a Council of Ministers' ruling in 1984, according to which only factors "internal" to the firm (i.e. costs, not demand conditions) may be price-determining. Costs must, in turn, be "justifiable" to the central authorities.

Old Habits Die Hard. The central authorities have reacted to difficulties by taking steps contrary to the spirit, if not the letter, of the reform. These include diluting enterprise autonomy with regard to price formation (reducing the share of "free" prices relative to regulated and administered prices); authorizing "operational programs" and "government orders" in which physical planning directives supersede enterprise autonomy; and designating 1300 of the largest (and best-connected) enterprises as objects of prime importance for the national economy, for which different rules of the game apply (e.g., reductions in workers' council authority, first priority on the central supply lists, direct control of managerial personnel by the relevant branch ministry).[5]

Foreign Trade Aspects of the Reform Blueprint

Based on official statements of the reform's principles, the following propositions constitute the key elements of the reform blueprint in foreign trade:[6]

1) The zloty-dollar exchange rate should be a single, unified rate, supplanting the multiplicity of exchange rates typical of the traditional foreign trade planning mechanism.
2) The zloty-dollar exchange rate should approach the marginal rate ("submarginal" in the official parlance), that is, it should be a rate at which 75 to 85 percent of the planned export volume is profitable, to facilitate the attainment of external equilibrium (for details, see the next chapter).
3) The zloty-dollar exchange rate should be flexible, changing in response to a five-percent (or more) fluctuation in the cost of obtaining hard currency through exports.
4) There should be a close link between world-market prices and domestic prices, via the uniform zloty-dollar exchange rate, to rationalize the domestic price structure and to improve the export-orientation of enterprises.
5) The eventual convertibility of the zloty is an objective to be realized when Poland's external situation improves sufficiently.

The reform blueprint also sanctioned two financial innovations, in effect, steps toward creating a (legal) domestic market for foreign exchange:

6) So-called "RODs" (*rachunki odpisów dewizowych*), or foreign exchange accounts, were established. Under this scheme enterprises earning hard currency through exports are entitled to retain a certain portion (usually between 5 and 20 percent) and use it freely to finance hard-currency imports.
7) Exporters would eventually be able to auction off the foreign exchange obtained to the highest bidder, either directly or through the Foreign Trade Ministry. Additional hard-currency funds would be available through the banking system, allocated by some type of bidding process or on the basis of the bank's assessment of the requesting enterprise's creditworthiness, profitability, etc.

Implementation and Effects of Foreign Trade Reforms

Achievements and problems in this area reflect progress in other areas of the reform. The implementation of the foreign trade aspects has been hindered by the following factors:

Inflationary Pressures. Poland's external disequilibrium has made the authorities unwilling to establish the zloty-dollar exchange rate at an equilibrium level. Fear of importing inflation has resulted in the significant overvaluation of the zloty, with all its pro-import, anti-export implications.

The extent of the overvaluation is not certain. But according to a 1985 study, exchange-rate policy from 1982 to 1984 guaranteed the profitability of only 60-65 percent of Poland's hard-currency exports. This figure falls to approximately 50 percent if hard-currency receipts from coal are subtracted, since the price of coal is kept artificially low by the Price Bureau, well below its social costs of production. It may also be noteworthy that, throughout 1983-86, the black-market exchange rate in Warsaw was consistently higher (i.e. more zloty per dollar) than the official exchange rate, by a factor of four. These disparities raise the question of whether the ostensibly submarginal zloty-dollar commercial exchange rate, which, on average, is set at the same level as the tourist rate (170 zloty per dollar as of March 1986), actually guarantees the profitability of 75 percent of Polish exports. The zloty's overvaluation also precludes the use of world prices to rationalize the domestic price structure.

Inflationary pressures create disincentives to export. Pent-up demand on the domestic market makes export sales, especially to hard-currency markets, relatively unattractive for Polish enterprises. Why redesign products, retool factories, and invest in marketing campaigns— steps that must be taken to compete on world markets—when virtually everything produced can be "disposed of " domestically, owing to shortages and artificially low prices? In this situation, export promotion through financial instruments (subsidies, tax deductions and the like) cannot be very effective.

Hard-Currency Shortage. This is a consequence of Poland's external position, which has complicated the attempt to create an internal market for hard currency. In the face of this shortage, the authorities have preferred to retain central control over much of hard-currency receipts in order to finance the central acquisition of certain imports, primarily raw materials and semi-finished products not produced in sufficient quantities domestically. Consequently, only 15 percent of hard-currency imports were financed by RODs in 1983 and 1984, while only 3 percent were financed by RODs in 1982.[7] Further, according to Polish law, RODs are not the property of exporting enterprises, but that of Bank Handlowy (the Foreign Trade Bank). Bank Handlowy may in turn legally deny enterprises access to these accounts in times of (perceived) insufficient central-bank liquidity. This seems to have been occurring on a large scale since March 1985. According to one report, the value of backlogged ROD requests that Bank Handlowy had yet to honor as of April 1986 had reached $400 million, a sum which accounted for approximately half of the total value of requests filed.[8] While such maneuvers may, in the short run, increase the ability of Bank Handlowy to meet Poland's external debt obligations, their impact on the ROD's effectiveness as an export-promotion instrument is likely to have the opposite effect in the long run. Hard-currency bank loans are rare; only 25 such loans, totaling $44 million, were granted through 1984. For the most part, the recipients were a handful of well-connected enterprises with strong bargaining power.[9] Attempts by importers or manufacturing enterprises to legally acquire hard currency from exports are virtually unheard of. Instead, enterprises look to their associations (*zrzeszenia*) or ministry to secure foreign-exchange allocations, even though the lack of enterprise willingness to export to hard-currency areas seems to have kept the demand for foreign exchange at lower-than-anticipated levels.

Insufficient Structural Reform. Although some progress has been made in increasing enterprise influence in the foreign-trade distribution system (see next chapter) retention of the economy's traditional institutional structure and the absence of an equilibrium zloty-dollar exchange rate have given rise to a whole series of "exceptions," contrary to the spirit if not the letter of the reform. To remedy the anti-export bias of the zloty's overvaluation, exporting enterprises receive a gamut of direct and indirect subsidies. These include product-specific subsidies, exemptions from or reductions in income- and turnover-taxes, and reductions in the "PFAZ" levy, i.e., the wage-fund tax. Importers routinely pay product-specific "price-equalization" charges, designed to reduce whatever cost disadvantages domestic producers of import substitutes might face, as well as a variety of other import duties. Thus, the "reformed" foreign-trade planning mechanism bears a striking resemblance to its unreformed predecessor, both in terms of its structure and the instruments employed.

As for the impact of these partial reforms, one may observe what have been referred to as "mutations" in the behavior of some of the reform instruments. For example, whereas RODs were intended to be an export-promotion device by making the acquisition of hard currency through export more attractive to enterprises, the lack of a secondary market for hard currency has altered the way in which the RODs influence exporters' behavior. Since firms cannot (legally) sell such earnings to the highest bidder, the second-best solution is often that of spending them on hard-currency imports that would not otherwise be purchased. Thus, the theoretically pro-export RODs have partially "mutated"[10] into a pro-import device, contrary to the rationale which led to its creation.

This is not to say that the prevailing foreign-trade mechanism is without incentives to export. On the contrary, the subsidies and "pressure from above" have created an environment in which enterprises feel obliged to export at almost all costs:

> The system decisively promotes the quantitative growth of exports at any price but, on the other hand, it has no impact on producers in terms of the efficiency of their export activities.[11]

This implies that the improvement in Poland's hard-currency export performance since 1983 and 1984 was realized at a higher cost to the domestic economy than would have been the case if the foreign-trade reforms had been implemented more fully. The underfulfilling of the hard-currency export plan in 1985 confirms this hypothesis.

Implications for the Future

Although fundamental changes in the structure and instruments of foreign-trade planning alone may improve foreign-trade performance significantly, it is difficult to conclude that isolated reform efforts are likely to lead to such an outcome. In the prevailing environment, for example, the exchange-rate elasticities on both the supply and demand sides are likely to be low. This fact, as well as the persisting domestic and external disequilibria, reduce the effectiveness of the reform's financial instruments, in foreign trade as throughout the rest of the economy.

It should also be noted that a large percentage of Poland's foreign trade will continue to take place with CMEA partners. This means that bilateral trade agreements, expressed essentially in physical terms and concluded at the level of the Ministry of Foreign Trade (or higher), will continue to play a major role in foreign-trade planning; no reform can change this.

Nevertheless, the road back to external creditworthiness and an improved economic performance lies in the introduction of further and more comprehensive reforms. These should include a sustained commitment to establish an equilibrium exchange rate and removing the legal and financial restraints that discourage direct investments by transnational corporations (as the Yugoslavs have done recently). The passage of legislation in 1986, creating more incentives for direct foreign investment, as well as the establishment of an export bank in that same year, are hopeful developments in this area.[12] But most important would be reforms of the administrative/market structure of the domestic economy to remove its branch-monopolistic orientation (as the Hungarians are currently undertaking) and to introduce a genuinely functioning market mechanism, at least to the extent envisioned by the 1981 reform blueprint.

Notes

1. Research for this chapter was made possible by a fellowship arranged by Indiana University's Polish Studies Center and Warsaw University's American Studies Center during the academic year 1983-84, as well as by a joint IREX-Fulbright grant for the academic year 1985-86, enabling the author to spend more than a year in Poland.

2. Zbigniew Fallenbuchl, "The Polish Economy under Martial Law," *Soviet Studies*, October, 1984, pp. 513-27.

3. Kołodko, "Our Inflationary Sentence," (in Polish), and Misiak, "Sick Money," (in Polish), both in *Życie Gospodarcze*, August 18, 1985, pp. 4-5.

4. Wiesław Caban, ed. *An Evaluation of the Logic of the Economic Reform's Implementation: Economic and Social Aspects* (in Polish), (Łódź, 1985); and Kopycińska, "The Association as a Representative of Organized Interest Groups," (in Polish) (Warsaw, 1984).

5. Ibid.

6. Witkowska, "The Instruments Steering Foreign Trade," (in Polish) in Caban.

7. Rymarczyk, "The Reform in Foreign Trade: An Attempted Diagnosis," (in Polish) *Życie Gospodarcze*, August 18, 1985, p.8.

8. Edward Lipiński, "In the Crooked Wheel of Hard Currency," (in Polish) *Życie Gospodarcze*, April 16, 1986, p. 1.

9. Ibid.

10. Zieliński, "On System Remodeling in Poland: A Pragmatic Approach," *Soviet Studies*, Vol. 30, no. 1, pp. 3-37.

11. Witkowska, "The Instruments Steering Foreign Trade."

12. Szczepan Baczyński, "Lonely Little Banker," (in Polish), *Polityka*, May 17, 1986, p. 15.

References

Albinowski, Stanisław. "The Bermuda Triangle of Inlflation." (in Polish) *Przegląd Tygodniowy*, 1984, no. 12, pp. 4-5.

Baczyński, Szczepan. "Lonely Little Banker." (in Polish) *Polityka*, Import-Eksport section, no. 20 (May 1986), p. 15.

Baka, Władysław. *The Polish Economic Reform.* (in Polish) Warsaw: 1981.

Brumberg, Abraham. (ed.). *Poland: Genesis of a Revolution.* New York: 1983.

Caban, Wiesław (ed). *An Evaluation of the Logic of the Economic Reform's Implementation: Economic and Social Aspects* (in Polish), Łódź, 1985.

Dryll, Irena. "A Portrait of Self-management (in Polish)." *Życie Gospodarcze*, no. 33 (August 1985), p.2.

Fallenbuchl, Zbigniew. "Poland's Economic Crisis." *Problems of Communism*, Vol. 31, no. 2 (March-April 1982), pp. 1-21.

Fallenbuchl, Zbigniew. "The Polish Economy under Martial Law." *Soviet Studies*, (October 1984), pp. 513-27.

Gomulka, Stanisław and Jan Rostowski. "The Reformed Polish Economic System 1982-83." *Soviet Studies*, Vol. 36, no. 3 (July 1984), pp. 386-405.

Gotz-Kozierkiewicz. "Exchange Rate Unity—Abstraction or Reality?" (in Polish) *Handel Zagraniczny*, 1983, no. 4, pp, 16-17.

Humisz. "Exchange Rate Problems during the Implementation of the Economic Reform." (in Polish) *Handel Zagraniczny*, 1983, no. 5, p. 14.

Instytut Koniunktur i Cen (IKC). "Fundamental Problems of Industrial Cooperation with the Capitalist Countries." (in Polish) conference paper, Warsaw: November, 1985.

Foundations of Economic Reform. (in Polish), Warsaw: 1984.

Kołodko. "The Inflationary Alternative." (in Polish) *Życie Gospodarcze*, 1984, no. 9, pp. 13.

Kołodko. "Our Inflationary Sentence." (in Polish) *Życie Gospodarcze*, no. 33, 1985, pp. 1, 4-5.

Kopycińska. "The Association as a Representative of Organized Interest Groups." (in Polish) Warsaw: 1984.

Lipiński, Edward. "In the Crooked Wheel of Hard Currency." (in Polish) *Życie Gospodarcze*, no. 14 (April 1986), p. 1.

Mieszczańkowski, Mieczysław. "Finance in the Process of the Reform." (in Polish) *Życie Gospodarcze*, 1985, no. 38, pp. 1, 6.

Misiak, Władysław. "Sick Money." (in Polish) *Życie Gospodarcze*, no. 33 (August 1985), p. 4.

Parkola and Rapacki. "Today and Tomorrow for the Reform in Foreign Trade." (in Polish) *Przegląd Techniczny*, 1982, no. 24, pp. 24-26.

Płowiec, Urszula. "Economic Reform and the Economy's Pro-Export Orientation." (in Polish) *Gospodarka Planowa*, 1983, no. 1.

Rymarczyk, Jan. "The Reform in Foreign Trade: An Attempted Diagnosis." (in Polish) *Życie Gospodarcze*, 1985, no. 33, p.8.

Witkowska. "The Instruments Steering Foreign Trade." (in Polish), in Caban, above.

Wojciechowski, Bronisław. "The Exchange Rate." (in Polish) *Handel Zagraniczny*, 1983, no. 102, pp. 6-7.

Zieliński. "On System Remodelling in Poland: A Pragmatic Approach." *Soviet Studies*, Vol. 30, no. 1.

16

Reforms and Export Promotion

Carlo Boffito

Introduction

The purpose of the economic reform adopted by Poland in 1981 has been the creation of an economic system in which the management of the national economy is based on parametric instruments and not on direct administrative interventions.[1] Changes introduced in the foreign-trade system since the beginning of 1982 have been an attempt to bring the export and import activity of enterprises closer to that model by implementing, in this field, the ruling principle of the economic reform: the autonomy and self-finance of enterprises.

This program is being implemented in a difficult economic situation and unfavorable political atmosphere. The economic difficulties can be summarized by the need to compel (badly supplied) enterprises to move from a domestic sellers market to a foreign buyers market. Moreover, the staff of the economic ministries and enterprises has remained essentially the same as that before the reform, that is, mainly those who had earlier shown their loyalty to the government by resisting the radical transformation demanded by the political opposition between August 1980 and December 1981.

The new economic system has been forced upon the officials and staff of the ministries and enterprises without a period of preparation and institutional adaptation. The outcome has been a system which in many respects still retains aspects of the old one, in spite of the frequent and often substantial formal changes in the rules of its workings. Economic difficulties have often been used to justify a slowing down of real changes and to reestablish the old principles of management.

The following sections deal with the various aspects of foreign trade reforms and their impact on export promotion: organization, planning, direct administrative intervention, the foreign-exchange allocation system, retention quotas, prices and exchange rates, taxes and credit policy, foreign capital, and the promotion and steering of exports. The final section offers some concluding remarks.

Foreign Trade Organization

The main innovation introduced by law in 1982 in the organization of Poland's foreign trade was the transformation of certain foreign-trade enterprises (FTEs) into foreign-trade joint stock companies (hereafter called Foreign Trade Corporations, or FTCs) and the issuing of permits (*koncesja*), which allows producers, or even individual craftsmen and farmers, to carry on foreign transactions independently. Therefore, three types of organizations can now import and export: old FTEs, new FTEs, and licensed units (*jednostki koncesjonowane*).

A permit to engage in foreign trade must not be confused (as it often is) with the licensing or authorization (*licencja*) to undertake specific import or export transactions, which is one of the means of central control of foreign trade. The Ministry of Foreign Trade (MFT) gives FTEs and FTCs general or specific (i.e., confined to certain goods and/or markets) rights to import and export, in agreement with the central plans and the State protocols signed with socialist countries. Scarcity of hard currency is the official reason for the central control of imports, which can be paid for only from funds obtained as retention quotas (see below) or as central allocation of foreign exchange.

Permits to trade are provided only to economic units that show themselves able to carry on foreign transactions independently; they must have already exported 1 billion zloty or be exporting 25 percent of their current production. By the end of 1984 almost 300 permits had been issued, more than half to small producers. In 1984 their share of total Polish exports was about 3.5 percent.

The bulk of Polish foreign trade (60 percent) is carried out by the new FTCs; at the end of 1984 twenty-five FTCs were operating. The surviving FTEs, responsible for the remaining share of Polish foreign trade, deal with the import and export of primary goods.

The FTCs take the form of joint stock companies, with at least 51 percent of the capital belonging to the Ministry of Finance, which is represented on the boards of the FTCs by the MFT. At the end of 1984 the remaining shares were scattered among 1360 industrial enterprises producing the goods sold or using the inputs bought abroad by the FTCs (excluding machinery, the import of which is concentrated in a specialized FTE in order to strengthen central control at home and bargaining power on foreign markets).

A significant change in the old system is the ability of industrial enterprises to choose FTCs other than "their own" to deal with the external world. However, up to now, this right has been "exercised only rarely." In the new system, central control is preserved, but on a different basis than earlier; formally, the MFT should no longer impose its will on FTCs by giving orders; rather, it should participate in their management, confining itself, in spite of its majority position, to influencing their activity by using economic arguments and levers.

The aim of the new system is to link production and commercial activities. But several of its aspects are widely criticized. First, many argue that the change from the FTE to the FTC format is not significant; there is suspicion that it may even have been suggested by the FTEs themselves, who were afraid of losing their monopoly position and clients. In fact, exporters have practically never changed the organization through which they conduct foreign trade.

Furthermore, the legal framework is not considered suitable for efficiently carrying on the activity of the FTCs. The management of these joint stock companies is not a settled practice and is based on the commercial code of 1934, which has been out of use for a long time, at least as far as joint stock companies are concerned.

Finally, the financial situation of the FTCs has worsened in comparison to that of the FTEs. Although their profitability is about the same as before the reorganization, their income tax is higher than in the other sectors (75 percent of new profits versus 65 percent in industry). In addition, their shareholders must now be paid dividends out of profits, reducing the FTC's income and the incentives for its staff. This represents a disincentive for the entrance of new partners. Bank credit is more advantageous than equity capital (which can be used by the FTCs only as working capital) because the interest paid is a cost while profits are taxed. Moreover, there is some imbalance in the position of the Ministry of Finance, which receives a double revenue from FTCs. Having allocated funds to the FTCs out of its budget, the Ministry collects taxes and takes the greater part of the dividends.

Short-Term Planning

According to the law, central plans should establish only general targets and macroeconomic proportions, leaving the task of influencing enterprise activity to parametric and economic policy instruments. Major limitations to the autonomy of enterprises are brought about by the trade agreements signed by the state with other socialist countries and by the "operational programs" and "government orders" that imply direct central allocation of scarce resources, including foreign exchange. The planning of trade with CMEA countries has not changed, as imports from and exports to them are compulsory for the FTEs and FTCs, which, in order to comply with the state's export obligations, have to sign agreements with industrial enterprises. To be sure, deliveries to CMEA countries are formally not compulsory for the industrial enterprises.

The planning process of trade with the convertible-currency area follows the traditional methods, with the exceptions noted below. In the first stage, that of plan formation, the Planning Commission, in collaboration with the branch ministries and the network of trade offices abroad (the latter thus providing, respectively, information on domestic export capacity and demand conditions and trade regulations on foreign markets), determines the annual targets for exports, both overall and those decomposed by domestic branches and foreign markets. There is nothing new in all this. In practice, the MFT provides enterprises with information about the outline of the annual central plan, about the central physical allocations of inputs, and of import finance; at the same time, enterprises inform the MFT about their export possibilities.

Innovations appear in the second stage of planning, when the central targets and the export targets, freely set by enterprises, are compared. If there is a mismatch (usually three-fourths of enterprise targets are lower than planned), negotiations begin between the enterprises and the branch and functional ministries. In this stage, given the weak influence of economic incentives to increase exports, direct pressure by ministries often plays an important role. If agreement is not reached and the government wants to assure a certain level of exports, "government orders" can be imposed on enterprises. But in this case, the central authorities have to guarantee the inputs necessary for their fulfillment.

Does Poland Have an Export Strategy?

The process of the medium- and long-term planning of foreign trade, i.e., foreign-trade strategy, is still vague. Recent decisions on the restoration of frozen projects in energy, infrastructure, and fuels and raw materials have reduced to about nil the scope for investment in the restructuring of industry. On the basis of agreements already signed or about to be concluded, in the next five-year plan Poland is expecting to get more supplies of gas and electricity from the Soviet Union and to substitute for Western deliveries imports from Hungary and the GDR, primarily in chemicals, biochemicals, electronics, and equipment for the construction of infrastructure.

As for exports to the convertible-currency area, one can find only two partially elaborated ideas. One is that, in the next five years, Poland should concentrate on the export of mature industrial goods and agricultural products to offset the upcoming stagnation in exports of raw materials and fuels mentioned in the chapter by Soldaczuk. At the same time, it should make an effort to modernize industry, to prepare it for generating more ·technologically advanced exports in the 1990s. The rejuvenation of industrial cooperation agreements, negotiated directly by enterprises with Western firms, should play a major role in such an effort of modernization. However, Poland's current performance in the export of manufactures does not appear to support the feasibility of these programs.

Although the possibility of a sizable influx of foreign capital is unlikely, Poland should try to attract direct investment into joint ventures in Poland. Foreign capital is expected to make only a marginal contribution to the solution of the economy's problems. It will eliminate minor bottlenecks (as Polonia firms are already doing on a small scale) and improving the quality of Polish labor and management. However, in this case, foreign investment is not going to have significant effects in the short run. In the meantime, Polish industry, waiting for the reestablishment of industrial cooperation with Western firms, is deepening its integration with partners in the other CMEA countries, thereby laying the foundations for an increase of future investments to shift production from Eastern to Western markets.

Direct Administrative Intervention

Central allocations—limiting the autonomy of enterprises and strengthening the role of central authorities—involve both scarce products and hard currency. Physical allocation is implemented through the material balances system, giving priorities to certain sectors and enterprises. Such a system is maintained for energy, fuels, raw and other materials. (There are currently more than 150 of these balances.) About 80 percent of Poland's imports are centrally allocated. According to the authorities' rather political point of view, material balances are justified because of scarcity and inadequate workings of the price and exchange rate system. Be that as it may, it is certain that they strengthen the branch ministries, whose survival is assured by the key supply role they still play. Furthermore, it is also clear that central allocation puts additional constraints on restructuring exports. A project exists, though apparently not fully developed as yet, to move from central allocations to an assured supply of inputs for exporting enterprises.

The Foreign-Exchange System of Allocation

Certain Polish officials have, after signing the framework agreement with the Paris Club in 1985, conveyed the impression that the central authorities will compute the amount they wish to make available for debt service; they will put aside foreign exchange allocated for the so-called retention quota of enterprises, to which they will add an amount needed to finance the country's minimum import requirements. The funds available for foreign debt service will be the residual. Since this residual will be insufficient for such a purpose, the remaining amount required to meet Poland's debt-service obligations will be sought as new credits from Western governments and the IMF.

In 1984, the center played an overwhelming role in allocating foreign exchange. More than 80 percent of the foreign exchange that Poland earned was distributed through central allocations based on the tasks specified in the annual plan. Less than 20 percent was reserved for use as retention quotas. A negligible share (less than 0.3 percent) was devoted to foreign currency tenders and credits. Foreign exchange is distributed according to rules established every quarter by an ad hoc ministerial committee. Allowances to enterprises are influenced strongly by the recommendations of branch ministries.

Foreign Currency Retention Quotas

Polish economists and officials seem to agree that, in the present situation, the most effective incentive to export is the possibility that enterprises have to retain a quota of the foreign exchange earned through exports. Retention quotas (OD, *odpisy dewizowe*) were introduced in 1982. By the end of that year, 402 accounts had been opened (377 of which were still operating in 1985) for 1322 industrial enterprises; by the end of 1984 their number had increased to 662 (643 still operating), owned by 2188 enterprises. Thus, almost all Polish exporting firms have such accounts. In addition to the retention quotas of industrial enterprises (ROD), about 120 accounts were opened for retention quotas of transportation enterprises (TROD) and cooperatives. In 1984 about 2 billion dollars were paid for imports of goods and services drawing on OD accounts. Retention quotas should assure greater flexibility and quicker deliveries of inputs. However, their present level is far from being considered satisfactory by enterprises.

OD coefficients are fixed according to the current import requirements of exporters, and differ sharply from one enterprise to another, although it is difficult to establish general rules for their determination. In 1984 enterprises supposedly had the opportunity to increase their retention quota by 0.7 percent for every percentage point of increase in export, but this principle found only negligible application in practice.

Retention quotas also have a distorting effect on foreign trade. It seems that central controls and the way Poland uses foreign exchange do not allow the legal transfer of retention quotas to those who need foreign currency the most. There is no market for foreign exchange, as there is, for example, in Yugoslavia and China. Enterprises that earn foreign currencies try to use them as much as possible to import goods that are less expensive in domestic currency (computed at prevailing exchange rates) than inputs from domestic or CMEA sources. Thus, to some extent, the system is possibly more pro-import than pro-export, as mentioned in the preceding chapter. Moreover, final exporters are in a stronger position to negotiate OD coefficients than enterprises delivering intermediate goods to them. Therefore, enterprises strive to become direct exporters regardless of the percent stage of the production process. The structure of exports and the supply for the domestic market is thus aggravated.

In addition to central allocations and retention quotas, enterprises may obtain free convertible currency through tenders and credits. But these alternative forms of import financing, at present, play—and for some time are expected to play—a negligible role. They were introduced in order to establish their practice and to show the direction of possible future developments.

Prices and Exchange Rates

Two laws, adopted at the end of 1981 and at the beginning of 1982, established new relations between prices and exchange rates. As in other socialist countries striving to reform their economy, global market prices have begun to determine prices in Poland, as a substitute for prices that could be determined on the real markets—if they existed—in the domestic economy. The starting point was to fix the official domestic prices (*krajowe ceny zbytu*) of basic raw materials at the level of average prices earned or paid in foreign trade (converted to zloty at the prevailing exchange rate [*ceny transakcyjne*]). Free-currency, international prices, being equilibrium prices, were preferred to prices in intra-CMEA trade that are negotiated on the basis of some moving average of international prices in previous years.

In 1981 the exchange rates of the zloty to the dollar and the transferable ruble were calculated on a "submarginal" basis, as is noted in the preceding chapter. This means that the exchange rates were set so that at least three-quarters of exported goods to both currency areas should be at least marginally profitable. More precisely, according to the law, exchange rates should be pegged at levels assuring the profitability of not less than 75 percent and no more than 85 percent of Polish exports. The calculation took into account the shadow international prices of raw materials that was embodied in exports.

The story of setting the submarginal exchange rate according to the three-quarters rule is an old one. At the Foreign Trade Research Institute (of the Ministry of Foreign Trade) in Warsaw, work on an efficiency curve of exports was begun in 1962. In 1971 the rule mentioned was adopted to calculate the foreign trade multiplier, precursor of the commercial exchange (for details, see Marer 1985). The rule is based on the finding that a quarter of exports is made up by occasional sales of highly subsidized goods, mainly foodstuffs, which are expected to remain subsidized in the future.

The exchange rate calculated according to the price level prevailing in 1981 was 50 zloty per dollar. However, at the beginning of 1982, when the foreign exchange zloty (*złoty dewizowy*, worth 0.3 dollars on the average in 1981) was abolished and the new system of exchange rates was introduced, the 50 zloty per dollar rate was no longer consistent with the new, higher level of domestic prices. Therefore, the basic rate was fixed at 80 zloty per dollar (and 68 zloty per ruble), even if at that level the zloty was still undervalued.

Between the beginning of 1982 and February 1, 1987, a series of successive devaluations brought the rate of exchange of the dollar from 80 to 240 zloty. These devaluations always attempted to catch up with rising domestic prices. Between one devaluation and the other, the current zloty value of the dollar has changed (as has been the practice in the foreign exchange zloty system since 1978) on the basis of the weighted basket of convertible currencies that account for no less than 1 percent of Poland's current-account transaction in the balance of payments. However, the devaluations of the zloty were not sufficient to reach an exchange rate consistent with the domestic price level. For example, in 1984 the cost in zloty of earning one dollar by means of exports was still higher (11,372 zloty per dollar) than the average exchange rate for the year. Moreover, the ratio of the average dollar cost of exports and the exchange rate increased in comparison to that of 1983. Thus, the share of exports whose costs were not covered by the prevailing exchange rate increased and required growing subsidies.

In 1984 the exchange rates encouraged imports and discouraged exports, and since the changes in the ratios between export costs and the exchange rate were more favorable in trade with the ruble area than with the dollar area, they induced exporters to prefer Eastern to Western markets. It appears that the devaluations in 1985, 1986, and early 1987 brought the exchange rates closer to their average export costs.

The rate at which the zloty is devalued is a matter of negotiation and compromise between different ministries and enterprises. Of course, the MFT and exporting enterprises always favor a greater devaluation, to boost exports and because MFT's management of Polish foreign trade is evaluated according to the size of the subsidies or profits required to balance the so-called Foreign Trade Price Equalization Fund. This is calculated as the difference between the fixed domestic prices and the equivalent in zloty of the actual export and import prices. Branch ministries tend to resist devaluation, fearing a rise in costs. But the strongest opposition to a faster devaluation is from government agencies concerned about inflation, even though calculations by Polish economists show that the foreign component of inflation is quite small. To the extent that the foreign sector does contribute to inflation, the impact is mainly due (according to those studies) to the often indiscriminate transfer of resources abroad, not to changes in the exchange rate.

Establishing a link between the domestic and external prices of raw materials is also an unfulfilled target of economic policy. According to the law of February 1982, the ratio of the free-currency transaction price (*wolnodewizowa cena transakcyjna*) and the domestic selling price (*krajowa cena zbytu*) should not be lower than 0.9 or higher than 1.1 for any basic material. However, in 1984 Poland complied with that rule in almost none of the cases of imported and exported raw materials, and in 1984 the ratio increased for most such goods. It does not seem that increases in prices of most raw materials, which took place at the beginning of 1985, have brought selling prices significantly closer to transaction prices.

Taxes and Credit Policy

Indirect taxes and duties paid at any stage of the production process of exported goods are reimbursed to the exporting enterprises, as is the practice in most countries. In addition, exporters may obtain relief from the taxation of profits and wages. Income tax rebates add 3 to 6 percent of the value of exported goods computed at transaction prices; the rates differ according to product or market and rise as a function of increases in exports. Income-tax relief is supposedly provided to exporters to the convertible-currency area if the value of their exports in transaction prices is not lower than in the previous year; but it is quite doubtful that in 1985 this rule found full application.

For enterprises investing in export projects, there is a new policy that offers them tax relief. This scheme should be developed further. In mid-1985, 20 percent of investments in export projects could be financed by tax reductions. In the view of some experts, it will soon be possible to finance such projects by a higher percentage of tax rebates and the remaining parts by the retention of depreciation (20 percent), bank credits, enterprise internal funds (10 percent), and allowances from the MFT's Fund for Structural Reconstruction (better known as the Fund for Small Restructuring, given its still limited scope), which can provide either interest-free credits or grants, based on the expected performance of the project. Given the constraints on new investments already mentioned, the stimulation of investments in exporting sectors through tax reductions is likely to have only minor effects during the next two years but could play a wider role afterwards.

Wage taxes are peculiar: they are fixed at different levels for domestic and exported production. The famous PFAZ system, aimed at checking wage increases and inflation, is a serious hindrance to export because production for foreign markets, especially Western ones, is much more labor-intensive than production for the domestic market, even within the same enterprise. This surprising tax rule makes it difficult to construct a system that could efficiently stimulate exports. Discussions of the way to tax inflationary wage increases while recognizing the labor-intensity of export activities are underway. At present, PFAZ rebates equal one-fifth of the percentage reduction of income tax due to export performance. In 1986 the system will become more complicated. It will reduce taxes directly in proportion to the increasing labor of exports. In particular, PFAZ-exemption quotas will be graduated as a function of the total amount of the PFAZ itself in the different enterprises, and, according to the production problems encountered in different sectors, so that there will be a subjective element, strengthening "bargaining" between enterprises and the authorities. Moreover, PFAZ rates will decrease as the ratio of the value of exports to the value of total production declines.

There is no specific allocation of domestic credit to exporting enterprises. Total domestic credit is determined by the Annual Credit Plan adopted by the Sejm, and is allocated by the banks. Within the amount of credit allocated to them, banks have discretionary power to finance individual enterprises. In principle, there is no priority between credits for production for the domestic market and for foreign markets. However, *de facto* priority is given to production for export; one form of this is slightly preferential interest rates.

Attracting Foreign Capital

According to a law adopted in 1982, foreign capital can be invested in Poland only in small-scale enterprises, the so-called Polonia firms. In 1984, 633 Polonia firms were operating, producing mainly clothes, textiles, leather articles, wood products, metal products, and electronics. They have no obligation to export; their production is sold almost entirely on the domestic market. In 1984 Polonia firms exported less than 5 percent of their output and accounted for about 0.3 percent of total Polish exports.

One of the first tasks of the new Sejm, elected on October 13, 1985, was to approve a law on joint ventures, which, unlike the Polonia firms, would have to be export-oriented. Such a law was passed in 1986. The main disputed points were the retention-quota coefficients for joint ventures and the share of capital to be invested by foreign partners. The share of foreign capital was set to not exceed 49 percent, in order to allow Polish enterprises and the government to retain control. In Poland, joint ventures are not going to operate in free-trade zones, as they may in some other socialist countries. However, in the opinion of potential investors, it does not seem that even giving majority control to the foreign investor would suffice as a precondition to establish joint ventures in Poland. Even a satisfactory retention quota will not be enough to attract foreign capital. The most important factor, rather, would be the granting of sufficient incentives to enterprises to look for foreign partners. The main obstacles to capital inflow will be the level of the exchange rate and, given the general situation of the economy, the risk of not being able to obtain continuous supplies of the right kinds of inputs.

Conclusions

With the exception of the law on joint ventures that was introduced in 1986, no big changes are expected to take place in the foreign-trade system in the coming years. Minor changes are likely in the organization of foreign trade. For example, the Ministry of Finance and the MFT could give up direct control of the FTCs; the role of FTEs and FTCs could be reduced, allowing more industrial enterprises, or maybe their associations, to go directly to the foreign market and permitting commercial importing enterprises to establish direct links with domestic customers, which is already beginning to take place.

Much still remains to be done in making effective the parametric framework that is supposed to influence the activity of enterprises, inducing them to boost exports and seek out the effective substitution of imports. The new domestic prices and exchange rates that replaced the *złoty-dewizowy* exchange rate have not yet been able to enhance enterprise efficiency or to restructure their supply consistently with external demand. Regulations of imports have precluded any international competition on the domestic market.

It is difficult to say to what extent Poland's general economic difficulties, the domestic political situation, or bureaucratic resistance to change are responsible for the limited impact of the new system. Certainly the role of administrative intervention is still very wide and plays a central role in managing every aspect of the foreign-trade system. Cumbersome as it is, the reforms have increased the autonomy of enterprises, mostly by giving them stronger bargaining power with the authorities. A statement that is often repeated is, "It is very difficult to make enterprises do something they do not want to do." The pressure to increase exports and the inability of the central authorities to improve foreign-trade performance, together with the limited possibilities to rely on CMEA supplies, could induce the government to enlarge the autonomy of enterprises and to speed up the process of linking Poland's economy with that of the external world. For this to be done effectively, however, a well-functioning mechanism on the domestic market must be created. Perhaps the IMF and the World Bank can play a useful role in this process.

Note

1. To conduct research for this chapter, I visited the Foreign Trade Research Institute of Warsaw in September 1985. I am deeply grateful to its director and staff for organizing meetings. Any responsibility for errors and misinterpretations is, however, entirely that of the author.

References

Białecki, K., "The Marketing Aspects of Foreign Turnover Organization as Reflected by the Law on Licensing Foreign Trade Activity." *International Trade in the Eighties*, Warsaw: 1984.

Calus, A., "Company as a Legal Form of Polish Foreign Trade Enterprise." in *International Trade in the Eighties*.

Derbin, K. and C.A. Stańczyk, " A Proexport Tendency in the Economy: Concept and Methodology." (in Polish) *Życie Gospodarcze*, 1985, no. 18.

Gomulka, S. and J. Rostowski, "Polish Economic System, 1982-1983." *Soviet Studies*, Volume 36, no. 3, July 1984.

Instytut Nauk Ekonomicznych PAN, "The Economy in the Process of Reform, 1982-83." (in Polish) *Studia Ekonomiczne*, 1984, no. 8.

Konsultacyjna Rada Gospodarcza, (in Polish) *On the Manner in which the Economy Functions in the Polish People's Republic*. Warsaw: 1985.

Ledworowski, D., R. Michalski, and Z. Piotrowski, "The Zloty Exchange Rate and Domestic Costs and Prices." (in Polish) *Handel Zagraniczny*, 1984, no. 3.

Ledworowski, D., "The Economic Mechanism of the CMEA and Economic Reform in Poland." (in Polish) *Handel Zagraniczny*, 1984, no. 2.

Marer, P. *Dollar GNP of the USSR and Eastern Europe*. Baltimore: 1985.

Narodowy Bank Polski, *Information Bulletin*. 1983, 1984, and 1985.

Government Representative for Economic Reform, "Report on the Process, Implementation, and Results of the Economic Reform in 1983." (in Polish) *Rzeczpospolita*, (August 1984).

"Report on the Implementation of the Economic Reform in 1984." (in Polish) *Rzeczpospolita*, August 1985.

Rosati, D., "Comments on the Economic Strategy for 1985-95." (in Polish) *Handel Zagraniczny*, 1985, no. 2.

Rymarczyk, I. "The Reform in Foreign Trade: An Attempted Diagnosis." (in Polish) *Życie Gospodarcze*, 1985, no. 33.

Sołdaczuk, J., *Implementation of the Economic Reform in Foreign Trade in Poland*. Warsaw: 1984.

PART III.

BALANCE OF PAYMENTS AND DEBT SCENARIOS BY EXPERTS IN POLAND

17

Factors Influencing Creditworthiness

Stanisław Rączkowski

Why Are New Credits Needed?

Poland always declared its willingness to repay the debt incurred during the 1970s.[1] All kinds of economic and financial efforts are being made to fulfill this obligation.

During 1982-1985, Poland paid, in installments on principal and interest on its outstanding debt, about $9 billion ($6.5 billion interest and $2.5 billion capital installments). During the same period the new credits which could be utilized by Poland amounted to only $3.5 billion. This means that during this period, there was a net outflow of capital from Poland toward the creditor countries of $5.5 billion. It was a tremendous economic effort to realize such an outflow of capital from Poland.

Incidentally, quite the opposite situation has prevailed in Poland's relations with the CMEA countries, where there was actually an inflow. During 1982-85 Poland obtained, mostly from the Soviet Union, new credits in the amount of about 2.8 billion transferable rubles. After repaying current interest, we had a net inflow of capital from the CMEA member countries of about 2.2 billion transferable rubles. To some extent it offset the net transfer of capital to the West. Our total indebtedness in the East at the end of 1985 reached 5.6 billion transferable rubles. This figure is expected to grow for some time, but at a declining rate, and will be gradually repaid after 1990 by increased exports to the CMEA countries. Because of imports made possible by the credits granted by the Soviet Union, Poland was able to increase production and exports to the West, thus facilitating the repayment of its debts.

It is obvious that any heavily indebted country, aiming at restoring its debt-servicing capacity, should implement a stabilization program, assuring a durable surplus on the current account of the balance of payments. But what this means for such a country is a radical change in its economic situation. As I noted elsewhere,[2] at the time of heavy borrowing, national income distributed exceeded income produced in the debtor countries. This enabled Poland to increase capital investments and to raise the level of domestic consumption over the level that could be attained on the basis of their own domestic possibilities. In Poland, for instance, during 1972-81, national income distributed exceeded income produced by 2.5-2.7 percent a year. But the excess of national income distributed is bound to disappear as soon as the debtor country's current account is balanced. And if a surplus on this account appears and is used for debt repayment, national income distributed is bound to be less than that produced. If, in such circumstances, the level of national income produced remains constant, it is necessary to curtail capital investment or lower consumption. Even if the national income produced shows a modest growth, it is necessary to conduct a policy of "belt tightening." There are, however, limits to such a policy. It could provoke social tensions, harmful to the functioning of the national economy, and retard restoration of the ability to service foreign debts. Moreover, curtailment of investments might impede the modernization of the economy and thus hamper the increase of exports needed for financing debt service. Therefore, it is in the best interests of both debtors and creditors to facilitate the debtor's transition from a surplus of national income distributed to a surplus of that produced. This is only possible by speeding up the rate of growth of national income produced—recognized by the plan proposed by U.S. Secretary of the Treasury Baker. This, in turn, requires a temporary inflow of additional finance from abroad for financing indispensable imports.

Admittedly, the partial suspension of debt repayment during the grace period allows the debtor country to use the foreign exchange saved for additional imports. But the amount involved may be insufficient for the imports required to make the indispensable economic adjustments involved in the stabilization program. That is why, for a certain time, rescheduling of foreign debts should be accompanied by additional new credits. Their size and distribution in time would depend on the requirements of the stabilization program. Rescheduling operations effected in the past were linked, as a rule, with the grant of additional credits, sometimes involving quite considerable amounts. This has recently been the case for certain Latin American countries faced with the imminent danger of default. For them, a combination of loans from the

IMF from some governments, and from some commercial banks has been arranged. In some cases, creditors granted new credits to a heavily indebted country which was unable even to pay current interest on its debts, because they realized that the strain on the debtor would otherwise be too great. Such additional credits might amount, for instance, to about 50 percent of the interest due.

At first glance, the grant of new credits to an indebted country at the time of rescheduling seems paradoxical. Notwithstanding the fact that the country is already in difficulties because of excessive foreign indebtedness, its debt is increased further. But, in fact, the granting of new credits is in the interest of both debtor and creditor. It immediately helps the debtor to carry through its stabilization program and later enables the debtor to resume normal debt servicing at the lowest possible social cost. The creditor, at the expense of an immediate increase in the amount of credits granted, gains a greater certainty of obtaining the repayment in the future of all credits granted, including the additional one.

Access to new Western credits for the East European countries was considerably curtailed after the Polish rescheduling agreement of 1981. Among the socialist countries, Poland found itself in a particularly difficult situation. As early as 1981, it obtained fewer new credits from the West than before; after the beginning of 1982, a total blockade on credits was imposed by most Western countries, for obvious political reasons. It was initiated by the United States and, under their pressure, was applied by nearly all Western creditors. Until 1980, Poland was absorbing about $7 to $8 billion in foreign credits per year; this amount fell to about $5 billion in 1981 and to only $1.5 billion in 1982 (mostly representing use of credits granted previously). In 1983, it was $0.6 billion, in 1984 $218 million, and in 1985 a similar small amount. Few countries have ever undergone so rapid a fall in the influx of funds from abroad. Only Western commercial banks, when concluding the rescheduling agreements with Poland, granted new credits, in the amount of 50 to 65 percent of the interest paid (medium-term credits to the Bank Handlowy w Warszawie SA, for financing imports of goods from the West). They took the technical form of short-term revolving credits, continued over several years. The fact that in this difficult and dangerous situation the Polish national economy did not break down completely, but has started to expand again since 1983, is due mainly to the introduction of severe austerity measures in the whole economy and partly to the replacement of certain imports from the West by imports from the USSR and other socialist countries. It is noteworthy that, in 1982, Poland achieved, for the first time in 11 years, a surplus in the balance of trade with the West (of $0.4 billion). In 1983, 1984, and 1985 the trade surplus was even larger, exceeding $1.0 billion in each year (Table 2). This is the best evidence of Poland's extraordinary efforts to restore balance-of-payments equilibrium with the West. It is sometimes claimed that Poland obtained new credits in the form of rescheduling the old ones. That is true, but there is a great difference between a new credit that a country can use to increase imports, and rescheduling credits which are purely bookkeeping entries. No new imports can be paid by such credits. When on July 15, 1985 the agreement with the Paris Club was signed, rescheduling about $10 billion, no new money came to Poland. Hence, rescheduling cannot substitute for new credits. The two should be treated as complementary financing.

I have strongly stressed the necessity of new credits for Poland as a precondition for the increase of exports because I do not see any possibility of further cuts in imports, which are considered unavoidable (Chapter 21 by Fink and Gabrisch). In 1984, Polish imports were 44 percent lower than in 1980 (Table 1). Per-capita imports, amounting to $288, were the lowest in Europe. They were even 30 percent lower than in Romania. It is astonishing that at such a low level of imports the Polish economy is running at all. This is, to some extent, due to better crops and to the substitution of some Western imports by those from the CMEA countries.

External Market Conditions And Export Expansion

The ability to increase exports is a crucial factor that determines the creditworthiness of Poland. When concluding a rescheduling agreement, Poland, as any other debtor country, takes upon itself an unconditional obligation to repay the capital installments, after the expiration of the grace period, and to pay currently the interest due. For this purpose, it must secure, in due time, the necessary amounts of foreign exchange. In practice, only merchandise exports can provide it. As I mentioned elsewhere,[3] the debtor's obligation to pay is not reciprocated by any corresponding obligation of the creditor to enable its partner to earn the necessary export revenue. The debtor country must make its own efforts to earn the revenue. It is frequently assumed that a rapid rate of economic growth in the creditor countries will increase the demand for the debtor's exports and automatically bring sufficient foreign exchange for servicing their debts. It is hard to believe, however, that this will in fact happen automatically, in view of the general slowing down of economic growth in the world and stagnating international trade. Moreover, the debtor countries' export revenues from agricultural products and mineral raw materials run the risk of price fluctuations on international markets. If prices fall—as they have dramatically between 1980 and 1986—they earn much less foreign exchange for the same volume of exports. It should be added that many developed creditor countries, in view of their own payment difficulties, were themselves striving to achieve export surpluses and were reluctant to let their debtors earn such surpluses. They even introduced various impediments on trade.

In these circumstances, it seems desirable to create some mechanism to enable the debtor country to earn the necessary export proceeds and pay in due time the rescheduled capital installments. The most efficient solution probably lies in the acceptance of a rule providing that, in concluding a rescheduling agreement, the creditor country should take upon itself the obligation of creating the necessary conditions for the debtor country to place on the creditor's market an adequate amount of export goods. This would not, perhaps, be fully compatible with the principles of multilateral free trade, and in some instances would not be feasible; the creditor country might not need all the goods produced by the debtor that are required for the debt repayment. But in some cases, such a rule might be seriously considered during rescheduling negotiations. So far, however, no such mechanism—facilitating the earnings of foreign exchange for the repayment of rescheduled debts—has in fact been introduced.

In business with the indebted socialist countries, additional impediments were introduced by the creditor countries. And once more Poland found itself in the worst situation. Under the so-called sanctions, the U.S. in defiance of the rules of GATT, unilaterally suspended the most favored nation treatment that was granted to Poland in 1960. Consequently, Polish exports to the U.S. became less profitable and, for certain products, quite impossible. The ensuing losses are estimated at about $80 million a year. Further losses of foreign exchange were caused when the U.S. broke the fishery and air-traffic agreements with Poland. The European creditor countries did not follow this example and did not suspend MFN treatment, but they did not facilitate the growth of Polish exports. Moreover, they created a new impediment. Many Western commercial banks introduced the practice of asking for an advance transfer of foreign exchange to cover letters of credit that are opened in connection with Polish imports of goods. Other socialist countries are also faced with various difficulties in their trade with creditor countries. All this aggravates their payment situations.

Due to the sanctions, cooperative ties between Polish and Western enterprises were also interrupted. One consequence is that many enterprises lack certain raw materials, components, and intermediate goods necessary for the increase of production and of exports.

Floating Interest Rates, World Inflation, and the Debt Burden

There are further reasons why Polish efforts alone are not sufficient to solve the external-debt problem. These relate to adverse external financial developments for the debtor countries. One possible form of assistance would be some relief in interest payments. During 1982-83 the rate of interest was at a historical high. When Poland entered the financial markets as a borrower in the mid-1970s, the rate of interest was much lower. The debtor has no influence on the level of the rate of interest on foreign credits. This rate is formed on the international credit markets and, in practice, on the domestic markets of the creditor countries. The interest rate in the United States and on the Eurodollar market is particularly significant because about half of the foreign indebtedness in the world is denominated in dollars. The rate of interest largely depends on the international monetary and financial policies of the creditor countries. In the U.S. this policy was, after 1980, aimed at checking inflation (caused mainly by the persistent Federal budget deficits connected with high expenditures on armaments and, in part, with various social programs). The prime rate—that asked from the best customers—then reached the unprecedented level of 21.5 percent. In 1981, it dropped to about 16 percent; later, it gradually fell. The rise in American interest rates was followed by a general increase as other creditor countries tried to check the flight of capital to more profitable investments in the U.S. Because a large part of foreign credits was subject to a variable-market rate of interest, the total amount of interest paid increased considerably. As a result, some countries were compelled to incur new foreign credits, thus increasing the general level of their foreign indebtedness. Poland, among other countries, found itself in such a situation.

It is to be stressed that the domestic monetary policies of the creditor countries, primarily those of the U.S. although aimed at desirable changes in the U.S. domestic structure of prices and costs, had a strong negative impact on the balance of payments and on the domestic economic situation in the debtor countries, including those in Eastern Europe. These countries were thus burdened, quite undeservedly, with part of the costs of the domestic economic policy of a far-away creditor country. This fact should certainly be taken into account in considering the general problems of foreign indebtedness.

In the past, a debtor country obtained foreign credits either at the rate of interest established for the whole credit period, or at the variable market rate. It is to the debtor's advantage to stabilize, during the rescheduling negotiations, the original interest rate if it is lower than the current market rate. The creditor's interests are, however, diametrically the opposite, and as a rule, he demands an increase of the old rate to the market level. For credits granted or guaranteed by governments, particularly those granted in the past at a privileged rate of interest, the creditor can in some cases consent to the demands of the debtor. By contrast, commercial banks never make such concessions and claim the application of the variable-market rate for the rescheduled obligations. It is true, of course, that it is very difficult to foresee future movements of the interest rate, and for that reason the application of the variable-market rate may seem justified. Both sides bear the risk of market rate changes. But, after all, the situation of the debtor is worse. Although he certainly profits when the market rate falls, he incurs losses when it increases; he has to pay a higher rate and does not receive any compensation from any source. On the other hand, the creditor bank makes a profit when the rate increases and, when it falls, compensates for losses by paying a lower interest to depositors (since the interest rates on credits and on deposits always move in the same direction). So far, the commercial banks always applied a variable rate of interest in their rescheduling agreements with the East European countries.

When granting a foreign credit, commercial banks normally apply a market rate of interest augmented by a margin—a "spread"—differentiated according to their assessment of the balance-of-payments situation of the debtor country. During rescheduling, generally at a time when this situation is worse than usual, the spread is customarily very large, exceeding 1.5 percent and frequently reaching 2 or more percent. This increases the cost of the whole transaction for the debtor country. When the whole—usually long—period of rescheduling is taken into account, the aggregate additional cost caused by the spread may exceed 15 percent of the capital borrowed. This represents an additional strain on the balance of payments of the debtor country just when it is making great efforts to improve its balance of payments. It is thus in the interest of the debtor to lower the spread. Banks justify the spread by the need to reduce the risks connected with rescheduling. But by worsening in this way the debtor's situation, they increase the risk and get the opposite result. That is why, when searching for the solution of the global problem of foreign indebtedness, it is very important to take into serious consideration the claims of the debtors and to keep down the spread applied to the market rate. The same could be said about the so-called front fee, that is, the commission collected by banks on the conclusion of a rescheduling agreement. This commission is usually 1 percent of the whole amount of the rescheduled obligations and is paid in full at the time of signing the agreement.

For Poland (and for Romania also), the creditor commercial banks augmented the market rate of interest by a very large spread (1.75 percent) and also required a 1 percent commission. These charges constitute a serious strain on the payments situation of both countries.

In a rescheduling agreement, the nominal rate of interest is always established, but vitally important for both debtors and creditors is the *real* rate of interest. Its level depends on the relative movements of the index of prices and of the nominal rate of interest. In the second half of the 1970s, the real rate of interest was much lower than the nominal rate and was sometimes even negative. Consequently, in real terms, the creditors sustained a loss and the debtors made a profit. But after the considerable reduction of inflation in the West, the real rate of interest went up; in 1983 it reached about 7 percent in the U.S. and 3 percent in West Germany and Great Britain. This, in turn, worsened the situation of the debtors, improving at the same time the real situation of the creditors. Bearing in mind that the rate of inflation in the creditor countries depends, to a large extent, on their domestic monetary and financial policies, it can be said that the domestic policies of creditor countries now exert, through the real rate of interest, a negative influence on the economic situation of the debtors.

The rate of inflation in the world is important to the debtor countries because of the real burden of interest payments as well as the real burden of repaying the principal in installments. Repayments are always established in nominal terms and their real burden diminishes with the increase of the rate of inflation. In this sense, it could be said that the anti-inflationary policies of industrial creditor countries do not seem to be in the interest of the debtor countries.

Domestic Conditions and Prospects

I would like to make only one statement on this complex problem, namely, that Poland has domestic reserves that it can—and is—mobilizing. However, the extent to which these reserves will yield good results is not independent of developments in the external environment. The problem of inadequate supplies of imported inputs is of crucial importance to the Polish economy.

Nevertheless, there are some potential sources to increase production and exports. I see six such sources. The first is the increase of the productive capacity, resulting from the projects that were started in the 1970s and have not yet been finished but are expected to be completed during 1985-87. The second source is the elimination of certain bottlenecks that have appeared in the last few years. The third is the possible increase of the utilization of manpower in Poland's industry. The shift coefficient (average number of shifts of the maximum possible of 3) dropped from 1.43 in 1978 to 1.29 in 1985. There is a possibility of increasing it again due to the economic reform. Apparent labor shortages can be overcome by simply closing some inefficient firms and shifting labor to more efficient enterprises. The fourth source of increased production is the research and development program. In 1984, about 1.5 percent of Poland's national income was allocated to research and development. According to the plan, by 1990 about 3 percent of national income will be so spent. A strong effort is under way to coordinate Poland's research and development with similar programs of other socialist countries. The fifth source that may be tapped is the increase in the efficiency of the national economy due to the economic reform. Economic reform is a process, and certainly, during the next years, the effects should be more visible than they have been up to now. The sixth source is to restructure the Polish economy to enable it to improve its export potential.

Moreover, we are expecting the positive effects of the joint ventures between Polish and foreign enterprises. The necessary legal framework for such joint ventures has been approved by our Parliament in 1986.

As a first step toward the improvement of the Polish balance of payments in convertible currencies, it is necessary to increase exports to the West to a level that will allow Poland to repay all interests currently due. At present, Poland is able to pay those interests only partially, because it cannot lower the imports from the West below the present level of slightly over $4 billion (Table 2) without considerable damage to the national economy and the standard of living. A second step should be a further increase in exports to assure "future debt sustainability." Exports should grow at a rate at least equal to the interest rate, but for the moment Poland is unable to achieve such a rate. The level of exports should be sufficient for the full service of the foreign debt, that is, for the repayment of interests and capital installments.

Some people have referred to the Polish "twenty-billion-dollar misunderstanding" or to the "squandering billions of dollars" by Poland. I can agree that using foreign credits for financing imports of 7 or 8 million tons of grain annually in order to improve the diet of the population might be considered as economically unsound, although it contributed to the better health of the people. I can also agree that some of the investment projects chosen were not the best, particularly those not assuring sufficient exports for the repayment of credits. However, I would like to stress that most credits utilized contributed to the modernization of the Polish economy and to the creation or development of whole new branches of industry. The newly created copper industry, one of the most modern in Europe, may be mentioned. The Fiat automobile factory, the whole chain of meat-packing plants, several artificial fertilizer plants, the modernization of the textile, machine building, electrical, and electronics industries are further examples. Everyone who visits Poland can acknowledge that perhaps the Polish economy might have been better conducted, but one can certainly not claim that billions of dollars borrowed from Western countries have been "squandered."

Notes

1. Portions of this chapter are based on the author's "Debt Rescheduling: Benefits and Costs for Debtors and Creditors," in C.T. Saunders (ed.), *East-West Trade and Finance in the World Economy* (New York, 1985).

2. Ibid.

3. Ibid.

18

Poland's Indebtedness

Zbigniew Kamecki

Poland has always acknowledged its obligations to creditors. The rescheduling agreements that have been concluded and the continuous servicing of the debt—however constrained we are by our current payment capabilities—support this statement. In 1985, for example, Poland paid nearly $2 billion to service its debt, which was an enormous burden for the economy. The extent of this burden is illustrated by a comparison of this payment to Poland's convertible currency imports, which in 1985 were about $4.2 billion (Table 2). It has been suggested that Poland should increase its exports to and cut its imports from the West in order to be able to service its debt fully. Let us consider what would happen if Poland followed such advice.

In 1981, Poland's exports decreased dramatically; volume, compared to 1980, dropped by 22 percent. After 1982, exports increased considerably; by 1984 they reached the pre-crisis level of 1979 (Chart 2). Such a rapid recovery of Poland's exports should be considered an important achievement. It required, however, a considerable effort. This increase was achieved in spite of a sharp decline in domestic output. Although production has started to grow, in 1985 it was still lower than in 1979 (Chart 1).

A further increase in exports could have been attained only at the expense of deliveries to the domestic market. This in turn would restrict domestic market deliveries and, ultimately, exports. Production for export requires certain machines, raw materials, components, etc. that are produced at home. At the same time, the drainage of the domestic market would make the existing shortage of numerous consumer goods even more acute and strengthen inflationary pressures. This, in turn, would cause the labor force to be less motivated and would exert a negative impact on productivity, further decreasing the output for both the domestic and export markets. Closing the circle, export earnings would decline. Because further cuts in imports would not be possible, Poland would have even fewer means of servicing the debt.

Let us consider imports. Their present level is very low. Their volume in 1985 was about 40 percent lower than in 1979 (Chart 2) and more than 50 percent lower than in 1976, when imports were the highest. Such a dramatic decrease of imports has resulted in a significant underutilization of production capacities and constitutes one of the main barriers to the growth of output for the domestic market and for exports. Output depends considerably on imported inputs. A further decrease of imports would only decrease Poland's capability to service its debt. Therefore, either additional increases of exports through a forced drainage of the domestic market or further cuts in imports would be counterproductive. Either solution would be detrimental to the interests of Poland and its creditors.

Poland should, therefore, seek other solutions. I am convinced that only one is acceptable: an upward spiral that would simultaneously enable a cumulative increase of imports, output, and exports, leading to an eventual increase of the current capacity to service the debt. A precondition of such a solution is an open-minded compromise between the need to assure the means for financing a gradually increasing volume of imports and the expenditures for servicing the debt.

The extent of this spiral will depend not only on Poland but also on its creditors. Poland is the only country among the major debtor nations that has been deprived of new credits. Furthermore, it has even been hindered by credit embargoes and trade restrictions. We expect that the sooner this policy changes, the sooner it will be possible for Poland to increase imports—and, indirectly, exports. Poland would thus expedite its full economic recovery and increase its capacity to pay its debts. This, I believe, is not only in Poland's interest but also in the interest of its creditors.

19

The Polish Economy and New Credits

Michał Dobroczyński

Introduction

The difficult state of the Polish economy is an undeniable fact. National income fell during 1979-82 by more than one quarter, and per capita consumption fell by nearly one-third. The latter is due, among other factors, to the relatively high growth rate of the population. Poland's economic crisis was also strongly connected with political and social tensions. As a result, recent events in Poland have contributed to one of the deepest and longest economic crises in the postwar economic history of the world, and to a nationwide sense of disappointment, frustration, and pessimism.

The recent turn of events is relatively well known to the Western public. The contributions of Western experts to this volume also discuss in detail the barriers to a Polish economic recovery, including the acute problem of indebtedness. Still there is a need to present a more complex and balanced picture of the Polish reality and its links with the external world, stressing some broader, more positive assessments of the Polish state of affairs, much of which is not readily available to the majority of Western readers.

It should be stressed at the outset that any analysis of the Polish economic situation that is separated from political and social aspects of the problem cannot lead to a proper understanding of the past, the present, or the future prospects of the country.

Poland and East-West Relations

The present socioeconomic and political position of Poland is largely determined by the events of World War II and the postwar international situation. This includes, above all, the division of Europe into two parts. This division was accepted in practice by all the Western powers, including the United States. Any realistic spectrum of behavior on the part of the Poles—whether prosocialist, neutral, or antisocialist—has always been bound by the framework created by the real consequences of World War II. An expectation of a radical alteration of the established order lacks any practical importance and sense.

Political, economic, and social developments in Poland were certainly induced by internal as well as external factors. It is important to stress in this respect that the periods of détente in East-West relations (e.g., the mid-1950s and the early to mid-1970s) contributed to the expansion of Polish economic, cultural, and political contacts with Western partners. Détente also helped to introduce some positive changes in Poland, including the modernization of technology and management and the democratization of political relations. Conversely, periods of international tension (e.g., at the end of the 1940s, at the end of the 1970s, and the beginning of the 1980s) were accompanied logically by restrictions imposed from the outside and by defensive measures introduced from the inside.

Despite the fluctuations in global sociopolitical and economic developments, Poland has consistently advocated, especially since 1956, a policy of cooperation with the West. Poland has also steadfastly belonged to the group of pioneers that helped shape an understanding between the two major political camps of the contemporary world. Polish achievements in this field deserve particular international attention, since a considerable number of other countries often followed—either tacitly or openly—Polish initiatives. Poland contributed, during the difficult postwar period, to the creation and extension of the UN Economic Commission for Europe, which for many years has been the sole standing forum for East-West economic contacts. Due to the Polish initiative of December 1964, the Conference on Security and Cooperation in Europe was convened. Poland started a new period of East-West economic contacts when, as first among the CMEA countries, it joined the GATT. The Polish experience in bilateral relations (including credit arrangements) was closely analyzed and not infrequently followed by the other CMEA countries. Although these facts are unimportant from the perspective of private traders or bankers, they should not be forgotten by politicians who are interested in improving East-West relations.

Another argument of general significance is the relationship between Polish economic cooperation with Western partners and the extent of Polish contacts—cultural, scientific, and social—with Western civilization. The larger the volume of commercial turnover, the more numerous are the links that contribute to a closer cooperation and better understanding of nations in this politically divided world. While this fact holds not only for Poland, in the case of this country it is of particular importance to stress the unusually deep traditions of interdependence with Western culture and civilization.

During the postwar period all external attempts to radically change the political system in Poland through sanctions, economic pressures, and restrictions have invariably failed and lack any realistic chance of success when one takes into account the international balance of power. On the contrary, such attempts lead to a reduction of contacts with the West and to a strengthening of cooperation with other socialist countries, especially with the Soviet Union, as has been the case since 1981.

In spite of the detrimental consequences of its socioeconomic crises, in the present world Poland remains an important factor in the global political situation. Poland, as a country, is the Soviet Union's biggest and most populous ally. Its geopolitical position at the center of Europe usually draws international attention to internal developments. The character of Polish cultural life, the reforms in its political system, the democratization of its political process, and the directions of changes in its economic mechanisms were, on many occasions, cited in other socialist countries as examples to be followed.

Poland's economic crisis, combined with the dramatic reduction of its trade with foreign partners, caused a serious deterioration of the country's position in international economic relations. Nevertheless, Poland remains among the seventeen biggest industrial producers in the world. Taking into account the size of its population (nearly 38 million) and its rising demand, the Polish market should not be neglected by any far seeing foreign partner interested in long-term cooperation with a promising and important national economy, despite its present difficult situation. The experience of history proves that, as a rule, economies recover after periods of stagnation. Why should Poland be the only exception to the overall economic regularity confirmed by centuries?

Domestic Reserves for Improvement

Poland's economic crisis was indeed without precedent in the postwar world. This phenomenon should not, however, overshadow the fact that during 1945-78 Poland's economy was one of the most dynamic in the world. From 1960 to 1978 alone, Polish national income more than tripled.

Since 1983, the Polish economy has been recovering in a rather consistent way. I will not repeat the facts stated in the contributions by my colleagues Sołdaczuk (Chapter 20), Rączkowski (Chapter 17), and Kamecki (Chapters 7, 13, and 18), but I want to call attention only to the strategic position of uncompleted investment projects as a reserve that can be tapped for economic recovery.

A large number of investment projects were started before the crisis and then abruptly halted, often at advanced levels of construction. There is probably no single case in the present world economy which could be compared in this respect with Poland. More than 1,500 major investment projects and a large number of smaller ones await completion—quite often a step away from full-stage production. This sort of economic waste, which is also a reserve, deserves special investigation. In numerous cases relatively minor capital expenses could generate substantial output.

Even more important is the strategic role of the human factor. Too often neglected in narrow economic investigations is the professional quality of Polish manpower, both skilled and unskilled. True, these resources have been far from properly used in the period of socioeconomic and moral crises. But under improved conditions, that manpower certainly represents a reserve to help solve the economy's difficult economic and technological tasks, thus strengthening the international competitiveness of the Polish economy.

Whether and when Poland will be able to mobilize these reserves depends on several factors, among which the progress of the economic reform should be mentioned as most important. Although the reform dates from the beginning of 1982, the unfavorable economic situation has so far not allowed its full implementation, for the reasons outlined by Kamecki (Chapter 13). I would add only that the prevailing economic mechanism cannot be compared with that of the 1970s. Polish enterprises today are much more independent, and the planning system is less rigid. In many instances, economic instruments have replaced former administrative measures. Progress in implementing the principles of the economic reform is indeed Poland's biggest chance for radical improvement. The Polish authorities understand better than ever that there are a great many unexploited possibilities and reserves in nearly all fields of the Polish economy and that only a radically better system of economic management can mobilize them.

Another important new element in Polish economic policy is the unprecedented emphasis on export orientation. Never in the last forty years has the necessity of higher export performance been better understood than it is now. Although the importance of foreign trade was often listed as one among many targets, only recently has the growth of exports been recognized as the national economic task of highest priority.

Poland faces the difficult task of restructuring its export composition because several important traditional items—such as coal, some foodstuffs, timber, and various semi-processed goods—have to be increasingly supplemented by goods of more technological sophistication. This requires both capital and new technology and certainly cannot be completed in a relatively short period of time. Although the scope and time it will take to implement the radical structural changes are not cause for optimism, one should expect that, within the next fifteen to twenty years, the Polish economy will be able to achieve a new place in the international industrial division of labor. And those foreign partners— Eastern and Western—that will be more integrally involved in the restructuring of Poland's economy are the most likely to become the biggest beneficiaries of the newly created economic opportunities.

Aside from industry, there are still many unexploited possibilities for the expansion of Polish agriculture, which has been predominantly private since 1956. The uncertain political future of the sector, for a quarter of a century, has hampered the natural propensity of the farmers' road to economically rational expansion. Only during the last several years have the authorities given Polish farmers long-term legal guarantees of political stability. Moreover, special governmental assistance has now been offered to agriculture, with a view to enabling this sector to fulfill a program of food self-sufficiency and at least a partial reconstruction of the country's former export achievements. Indeed, within a relatively short period of time, one can observe in the Polish countryside an unprecedented postwar boom in investments, modernization, and initiatives, all of which contribute to a significant rise of output. If this trend continues, an important part of the ambitious agricultural program can be achieved in a few years. And since the approach in Poland to agricultural affairs is nowadays more pragmatic than at any time since 1948, optimistic expectations are more than justified, at least in comparison with experiences of the past quarter of a century.

Poland also has potential in the field of invisibles. Services which Poland can offer to foreign contractors are numerous and diversified, including transport and transit, tourism, and construction. For various reasons many possibilities of generating foreign exchange through such activities have not been well exploited in the past. In contrast, the present leadership is less dogmatic (for example, construction is less attached to heavy industrial development). One should also note that Poland's relatively liberal policy on worker migration creates another source of foreign exchange, as income remittances from the West and South are becoming more important. From this angle, too, Poland deserves special attention as a country opening new vistas of foreign contracts among the centrally planned economies.

Further important reserves exist in the sphere of East-West industrial cooperation, especially with regard to direct foreign investments in Poland. Today, the largest number of foreign enterprises in Eastern Europe operate on Polish soil, but these so-called Polonia firms are small and do not contribute very much to capital and technology inflow. A new law (1986) on foreign investments is, however, supposed to improve the situation and to fill at least to a certain extent the gap which had existed in the Polish legal system for half a century. This change should be assessed as another proof of the flexibility of the present economic policy.

The same could be said about Poland's ability to join the IMF and World Bank and to follow the rules of these organizations. Although Poland received a large amount of foreign loans in the 1970s, the decision concerning cooperation with the IMF and World Bank reveals a qualitatively new attitude toward the external world—just as the decision to join GATT pioneered a quarter of a century ago signaled the intention to expand rapidly with Western partners.

The Polish economy is seriously indebted to foreign creditors. At the end of 1985, the convertible-currency part of the debt was about $30 billion. The value of Polish exports to the West in 1985 was $5.3 billion. Based on accrued obligations, more than four-fifths of Polish export earnings are supposed to be transferred abroad for debt service (Table 2). But such a situation leads to a vicious circle because it makes it impossible to import equipment, spare parts, materials, fuel, etc., which are urgently needed for normal production and for increasing the exports required for debt service. Therefore, aside from rescheduling, new foreign credits are necessary to create the preconditions for a return to relative payment equilibrium. Although members of the Paris Club, representing seventeen creditor states, appeared to understand that despite the fact that in recent years more than $5 billion worth of resources flowed, on a net basis, from Poland to the West, practically no new credits have been offered since 1983.

A large part of Polish industrial capacity—about 25-30 percent—is standing idle because of a lack of imported goods. At the same time, industrial equipment is still quite modern—more than 50 percent is less than 10 years old. Therefore, the present waste (this includes also the uncompleted investment projects) could be reduced considerably with the help of new credits.

Polish economic targets and trends, for both the next five- and fifteen-year periods, are realistic. Although they are not excessively ambitious, they are rather dynamic in comparison with the average rate of growth of the industrial Western countries. The attitude of Western partners, particularly regarding credits, will influence actual outcome in the coming years.

We hope that decisions by our Western partners will not be based exclusively on narrow and short-term economic considerations. The development of Polish culture, and the strengthening or loosening of its ties with Western civilization, will depend on, among other factors, the willingness or unwillingness of the West to understand the specific, difficult, and complex problems of the Polish economic situation. In conclusion, the Polish economy, indeed the whole Polish nation, should certainly be considered creditworthy.

20

Economic Performance, Reform, and Debt-Servicing Capability Through 1995

Józef Sołdaczuk

Economic Crisis and the Road to Recovery, 1978-85

After the very deep and prolonged economic crisis of 1979-82, when national income declined by about 25 percent compared to the level achieved in 1978, the Polish economy is again moving up. National income produced increased in 1983 by 6.0 percent and in 1984 by 5.6 percent. Industrial production grew during that period 6.4 percent and 5.1 percent respectively. Due to favorable weather conditions, both years also registered relatively good results in agriculture, with total production increasing by 3.3 and 5.7 percent in the two years. These results were reached with unchanged employment in the economy in 1983 and with only a small increase in employment (by 0.4 percent) in 1984; employment in industry declined by 1 percent in 1983 and by 0.5 percent in 1984. Thus, the productivity of labor—measured as an increase of

---

Editors' Note: Convertible currency trade and debt statistics presented by Sołdaczuk differ somewhat from those cited by the IMF (Chapter 1), also based on data provided by the Polish authorities. Reasons for this discrepancy may include the treatment of convertible-currency transactions with other CPEs, the reclassification of transactions by the IMF to conform to its standard reporting format, and the fluctuation in exchange rates between convertible currencies, which can alter current-dollar values.

output per employee—grew by more than 6 percent in 1983 and 5.2 percent in 1984; in industry it grew by 7.4 and 5.6 percent respectively.

As the average nominal wage rate increased by 27 percent in 1983 and by 21 percent in 1984, the rate of "cost inflation," measured as a difference between the rate of wages increases in productivity, declined significantly, from 48 percent in 1982 to about 21 percent in 1983 and 16 percent in 1984.

It must be stressed, however, that the "demand-inflation" rate was higher, since the total expenditure of the population grew by 31 percent in 1983 and by 24 percent in 1984, while the deliveries of consumer goods to the market increased in "real terms" by 8 percent and 5.4 percent respectively. Thus, the "inflationary gap" may be calculated as 23 percent in 1983 and 18.6 percent in 1984. However, in 1982, that rate was about 90 percent.

Despite the positive results registered during 1983-84, the level of national product was still lower by 14 percent at the end of 1984 than in 1978. Since the total population increased during these six years by more than two million—approximately 1 percent per year, per-capita national income produced was about 20 percent lower in 1984 than in 1978. At the end of 1984 national income distributed was lower by 18 percent, on a per capita basis by 23 percent, than in 1978.

In 1985 the economy improved further. Industrial production grew by 3.8 percent, and manufacturing production increased by 4.2 percent. With relatively fair results in agriculture (total production increased by 0.9 percent, while animal production grew by 4.6 percent) and in construction (3.1 percent increase), national income produced in 1985 was 3 percent higher than in 1984.

The data for 1985-86 point to a slowdown in the overall rate of growth in comparison with the period 1983-84, after which the readily available reserves of the economy had been exhausted. Nevertheless, the three-year plan for 1983-85 was overfulfilled, with national income higher by 15 percent (instead of the 10-12 percent planned), industrial production grew by 16 percent (in comparison with the 14-16 percent target), and agricultural production rose by 10 percent, i.e., more than 8.5 - 9.1 percent beyond that planned for the period.

To be sure, in 1986 national income was still lower than in 1978. One must remember, however, that the income level in 1978 was produced with the help of a more than $2 billion trade deficit with the West, whereas during 1982-86 the Polish economy achieved balance-of-trade surpluses of more than $1 billion each year with convertible-currency countries. Today the country is, after all, living "within its means."

Foreign Trade and the Balance of Payments

In foreign trade, Poland also achieved comparatively fair results in 1983 and 1984, despite unfavorable external conditions. Prolonged recession or stagnation in the West European countries in 1982 and 1983, with growing protectionist tendencies in the West in general, also affected Poland's trade results. Furthermore, through 1986, Poland was, for political reasons, subject to specific restrictions on the part of Western countries. The suspension of the MFN treatment by the United States, the embargo on official credits and on our entrance to the IMF were among the most painful. In addition, most industrial cooperation arrangements and contracts between Polish and Western companies were disrupted during 1981-82 because of the problems of the Polish economy and the political uncertainties in East-West relations. This adversely affected Poland's industrial production and exports of manufacturers not only in 1982 but also during 1983-86.

Nonetheless, Poland's total exports started to grow in 1982 after the sharp decline in volume of 25 percent during 1979-81. In 1982 the volume of total exports increased by 5.8 percent. In 1983 and in 1984 the growth trend of our exports continued by 10 and 9 percent, which was the result of the restoration of coal exports (43 million tons in 1984, surpassing the pre-crisis level) and increases in the production and export of copper, sulphur, and other industrial raw materials and semi-finished products. Timber and agricultural exports (after good crops of 1984) also contributed substantially to our total export results and partly compensated for declines in the export of machinery and other manufactures, such as textiles.

Because of Poland's large trade and payment deficits and its rapidly growing indebtedness to foreign countries—particularly to the West—imports were severely restricted. By the end of 1982 import volume amounted to only 69 percent of the level of 1978. In trade with convertible currency countries the decline was much larger; the level of 1982 was only 46 percent of that achieved in 1978. The dramatic decrease in imports adversely affected the level of industrial production, so that in 1982, 40 to 50 percent of the productive capacity in many branches and production lines were idle. Under the circumstances, this was the only way to achieve the balance-of-trade surplus.

In 1985 there was a substantial slowdown—to 1.7 percent—in the rate of growth of export volume, which is attributed entirely to the decline of 3.8 percent in the export volume to the convertible-currency countries. This is in contrast to the situation in 1983 and 1984, when the rates of growth of export volume to the convertible-currency countries were significantly higher than the rate of growth of total export volume (amounting to 14.3 and 12.4 percent respectively).

The decline in 1985 of the volume of exports to market-economy countries was mainly the result of a drop of coal exports (by 5 million tons), after the all-time record registered in 1984. The unusually heavy winter months in January and February were responsible for that drop. Problems with exporting transport equipment—mainly ships—connected with adverse world market conditions for that type of product, also contributed to the unfavorable export performance in 1985.

Despite the less-than-satisfactory results of 1985, the trade data for 1983-85 were slightly better than planned. The volume of total exports increased during the period by 23.8 percent (versus the 17.5 percent planned). Exports to convertible-currency countries rose by 24.2 instead of 21.9 percent. On the import side, the volume of total imports increased by 21.8 percent (with 11.9 percent planned) and imports from convertible currency countries grew by 31.4 percent instead of 17.2 percent. The growth of imports during 1982-85 (after the substantial declines during 1978-82) was an important factor in allowing the recovery of industrial production since 1982.

The value of total exports reached $11.8 billion by the end of 1984 and nearly $12.0 billion in 1985, but it was still $2 billion lower than in 1978. The value of export to convertible currency countries reached $6.3 billion in 1984 and dropped to $6.1 billion in 1985. The value of total imports amounted to about $11.3 billion in 1985, i.e., $4 billion less than in 1978. In trade with convertible-currency countries the value of imports reached about $5 billlion, i.e., $2.5 billion less than in 1978.

During the period 1982-85 Poland registered surpluses on the trade account with convertible-currency countries of $1.1 billion in 1982, $1.5 each in 1983 and 1984, and $1.1 billion in 1985. However, even those substantial surpluses were unable to service the total indebtedness of Poland to the West, which at the end of 1985 exceeded $29 billion.

In 1982 and in 1983 Poland concluded agreements with Western commercial banks that provided for the refinancing of 90 percent of the principal due in each year. Interest payments were in part (50 percent in 1982 and 65 percent in 1983) loaned again to Poland in the form of six-month revolving credits. In 1984 a more comprehensive agreement was concluded with Western commercial banks, which rescheduled all at once the principal due in four consecutive years, 1984-87, for ten years with a five year grace period. Thus, no payment will have to be made until 1989. Arrangements for the interest payments were similar to those provided for in the previous rescheduling agreements. The agreement of 1984 by and large normalized Poland's relations with commercial banks and created an important "breathing space" for the Polish economy. At the end of 1984 negotiations were resumed with the Paris Club for restructuring Poland's debts that were guaranteed by Western governments. After long negotiations an agreement was signed in July 1985, providing for the rescheduling of about $10 billion of the debt for eleven years, with a five year grace period. At the end of 1984 the U.S. government withdrew its veto against processing Poland's application to the IMF and the World Bank, and Poland resumed membership in these organizations in June 1986.

There are chances, then, that over-all economic relations with Western countries will finally be normalized, with beneficial results for Poland as well as for its Western partners.

Economic Reforms are Being Introduced

Poland is undertaking further serious efforts toward improving its internal and external economic situation. In order to improve the performance of the economy generally, the authorities initiated in 1981 a comprehensive reform of the whole economic system. It was passed by the Sejm and has been in the process of implementation since February 1982. The purpose of the reforms is the transformation of the economy from the "extensive" to an "intensive" growth pattern in order to improve economic efficiency.

The reform abandons the traditional system of directive planning and central management by administrative methods. It strengthens the strategic role of central planning, indispensable for determining the path of economic development. It intends to base the activities of enterprises and their associations on the three principles of enterprise: self-management, self-finance, and employee participation in management. The reform should leave enterprises wide discretion for decision making in production, investment, sales on the domestic market, as well as in exports and imports. The central plan determines the desirable and achievable rate and pattern of economic growth, including the main lines of international specialization.

Industrial, trade, and other enterprises prepare their own production and trade targets. Enterprises base their plans on the production capacities they possess and on their own evaluation of the situation on the domestic and foreign markets, taking the assumptions and targets of the central plan as points of departure. The main principle they have to follow is a maximization of economic results, i.e., of profit. Profits after taxes are divided into a fund for investment—the further development of enterprises; a fund for the increase of wages, remunerations, and bonuses for workers and employees; and a fund for social activities (e.g., housing, health services).

In the field of foreign trade, the economic reform departs from the system of specialized foreign-trade enterprises (FTEs), which in the past were the sole exporters or importers in particular branches and thus isolated industrial and domestic trade organizations from foreign markets. The new system allows industrial, commercial, transport and other enterprises that meet certain legal, financial and personnel requirements to apply for and to receive permits for the direct conduct of foreign trade operations. The reform opens possibilities for the establishment of equity joint ventures between industrial and foreign trade enterprises, with or without the participation of the so-called "state interests" which are represented by the minister of foreign trade.

The specialized FTEs are still acting in their traditional field of foreign-trade activity, but they no longer have sole responsibility for the foreign-trade activities of particular branches. Several FTEs may now operate in the same or in similar lines of activity. This system allows industrial producing enterprises to choose one or another FTE as an intermediary. It must be added that not only state but also cooperative and private enterprises in small business may apply for permits to engage directly in foreign trade activity.

The state influences the decisions of enterprises with economic "regulators," such as the exchange rate, tariffs, taxes and rebates, credits, foreign-currency allocation quotas, the direct allocation of scarce raw materials, subsidies, and the granting or withholding of specific export and import licenses.

The state may set certain compulsory targets for selected firms—on the basis of which government contracts are concluded with enterprises—to assure preferred production and to fulfill state obligations in commercial agreements with other countries. The goal is to achieve conformity of the activities of enterprises with social interests and to assure maximum economic efficiency for the national economy.

After four years of experience with the implementation of economic reform, we can state that Poland is going in the right direction. Despite the extremely difficult conditions under which the reform was and is being implemented, it has begun to yield the first positive results, as shown by the data for 1983-85 presented at the beginning of the chapter.

The experience achieved during the last three years, together with improved domestic and external conditions, should allow us to proceed more vigorously and consistently with implementing the principles of the economic reform during the 1986-90 plan period. Some instruments and parameters will have to be adjusted in accordance with the accumulated experience and observed obstacles and irregularities.

Assumptions and Limits of Debt Service Through 1995

Poland's economic plan for 1986-90 is widely discussed in various economic, social, and political organizations and associations. The plan sets rather cautious targets. It provides for an annual 3.2-3.5 percent growth of 3.2-3.5 percent for national income in real terms and an increase of 3.5-4.0 percent in industrial production. It assumes an increase of 7-8 percent in the value of imports (an increase of 3.5-4.0 percent in volume, and an increase of 3.5-4.0 percent in prices) and similar increases in the value and volume of exports (comprised of 4-5 percent growth in the volume and an increase of 3-4 percent in prices). The assumption is that the terms of trade with Western countries may deteriorate somewhat.

Taking into account our current (1985) balance-of-trade surplus of $1.1 billion, the similar rate of growth of exports and imports in value terms should further enlarge our trade surplus. Should the terms of trade improve as a result of more favorable conditions on the world market or as a consequence of a positive change in the commodity pattern of our exports to the West, a higher export surplus could be achieved, which would create better chances for the higher growth of the national economy and for servicing our foreign debt. By the end of the next five-year plan (by about 1990) Poland should balance its current account with convertible-currency countries. Total foreign debt should then be stabilized at a level of $34-35 billion dollars and during 1991-95 decline relative to the growing level of national income and export. These projections assume the rescheduling of Poland's outstanding debts as well as the availability of some new Western credits.

The problem of Poland's external debt and inability to service it has been aggravated by the rising trend during 1980-84 and very high level of interest rates in developed creditor countries. By the end of the 1970s the average rate of interest on our outstanding debt was about 8 percent; by 1984 it increased to 12 percent. The four percent difference is the equivalent of over $1 billion in interest payments per year. Had the rate of interest been maintained at 8 percent, Poland would already have been able to pay its interest fully in 1984.

The decline in the rate of interest during 1985 and its expected further decline in 1986 (to about 8 or 9 percent) will lower our interest payments and thus smooth the process of debt servicing. Generally, the solution of Poland's indebtedness is possible only in a growing economy. In a stagnant or a declining economy there is no solution to the problem. One must note, however, that even under favorable circumstances, the cost of debt service to society will be high. The problem is further complicated by our rather high rate of population growth (about 0.9 percent a year; in 1985, the population increase was 0.7 percent).

As a consequence, a real rate of growth of approximately 2 percent in national income produced is required to achieve a growth of income per capita of 1.3 percent. And since servicing our foreign debt will require interest payments equal to at least 1.5 percent of the national income produced (also in real terms), a rate growth in income of 3.2-3.5 percent is necessary to achieve a 1.0-1.5 percent growth rate of real income per capita.

These proportions also determine the real limits of our ability to service our foreign debt, and we as well as our foreign creditors must take them into account. If a higher proportion of national income would be devoted to debt service, it would result in a stagnant or declining per-capita national income. In the long-run, that would undoubtedly create social strains, a decline of productivity, and economic stagnation. Our debt-servicing ability would also be impaired. No one would gain in such a situation.

The crucial element of our long-term growth strategy is the reorientation of the whole economy toward the promotion of exports. Such a reorientation must be tied to a radical change in the composition of our exports. Poland is known in the West as an important supplier of coal, sulphur, copper, other metals, basic products of the chemical and light industries, as well as agricultural products. Those exports will be maintained in the future. But we will have to effect gradual changes in our commodity structure of trade with the West. Since the production of our traditional exportable raw materials is growing only moderately, about 2-3 percent a year and much of the increase will be absorbed domestically, a high rate of export growth for these products can hardly be expected.

Agricultural products and processed foodstuffs are—and ought to remain—an important source of hard-currency earnings. The growth of their exports may stay in line with the growth of agricultural production. We have undertaken a comprehensive program for increasing and intensifying agricultural production, seeing in it also a chance to raise our export capability and earnings. In addition to traditional agricultural products, we have developed some new export specialties: fresh, frozen, and processed fruits and vegetables, which offer the promise of further export expansion.

The growing population and the growth of national income will absorb a part of the increases in food production. Our results will therefore be increasingly dependent on our ability to speed up the export of manufactures to the West. In this field Poland has developed a substantial capacity, based partly on Western licenses. But as a result of the crisis and the balance-of-payments constraints, some of our productive capacities are still not used fully, mainly because of insufficient imports of raw materials, semi-finished products, components and parts. The disruption in our former cooperative ties with Western companies has also played a role in this problem. Now, with normalization and the improvements in our economic performance, more and more Western companies are becoming interested in restoring former contracts and ventures or in signing new ones. Together with some additional investments to complete projects in progress and the restructuring of some others, it is reasonable to expect that Poland ought to enlarge the export capability of its industry. Key roles will not only be played by the electrical and engineering industries but also by the chemical, light, and mineral industries. We are fully aware that international competition is growing and that our export performance will depend on the efficiency of our production, ability to enter into industrial cooperation ventures, the technical level and technical progress in those industries, the improvement in the quality of our products, and more effective marketing.

We are also aware that the new pattern of industrial production and export cannot be decreed. It can be realized only if proper conditions and incentives are created within the economic system so that particular enterprises will be compelled by economic factors to become more export oriented. We expect to achieve all those aims as a result of a comprehensive reform of Poland's economic system.

PART IV.

Balance of Payments and Debt Service Scenarios by Experts in the West

21

Hard-Currency Debt Scenarios

Gerhard Fink and Hubert Gabrisch

After the uprising against consumer prices in the summer and fall of 1980, Poland was faced with escalating difficulties. With decreasing export capabilities after the last quarter of 1980, exports to the West were reduced by 33 percent in 1981. Regular debt service was no longer possible and the country had to ask officially for rescheduling in March 1981. While a favorable agreement with Western governments was relatively quickly achieved, negotiations with Western banks took some time. After martial law was imposed in December 1981, Western governments, as a sanction, broke off negotiations about further reschedulings. This proved favorable for Poland, because although neither maturities nor interest on government-guaranteed credits was paid, Western governments did not declare default. Meanwhile Western banks continued to conclude rescheduling agreements with Poland in 1982, 1983, and 1984.

One year after martial law had been rescinded, negotiations with Western governments were resumed and in January 1985 an agreement was reached concerning arrears of maturities and interest from 1981-84 of about $10 billion. For some time Polish authorities made their signing of the agreement dependent on fresh credits from Western governments, but willingness of Western governments to supply fresh money was and still is limited.

The stalemate is characterized by the basic line of argument on both sides. The Polish authorities claim that they would need an additional

$4-5 billion to enable them to step up imports of materials and spare parts from the West. With those imports, domestic production and export capabilities could be raised significantly. That would ease the situation sufficiently to clear the way for economic reform, which would further stimulate economic recovery. Each of the contributors in the four previous chapters essentially voices this argument.

Their Western opposite numbers, however, are mostly reluctant to accept this line of reasoning. Fresh money may be easily wasted if used to step up imports before the reform is fully implemented. So far the Polish authorities are either not willing or not able to discard incomplete and inefficient investment projects. Investment outlays remain higher than planned and contribute to budget deficits and the money overhang in the economy. Until now, no serious and effective steps were taken toward export promotion, the zloty is still significantly overvalued, and so on. The Western attitude is rather to wait until the Polish authorities have fully implemented the economic reform and have turned to a reasonable economic policy which successfully tackles the crucial problems. After decisive steps taken by the Polish authorities, fresh money could be made available.

Developments during 1985 seem to confirm Western objections. Export revenues in convertible currencies decreased while import outlays in convertible currencies rose (Table 2). Import prices have been falling, and real imports have been rising (Chart 2) much faster than output (Table 1), although purchases of cereals and fodder have declined substantially. Gross debt in convertible currencies which stood at about $26 billion at the end of 1982 and also 1983, rose to almost $30 billion by the end of 1985. Current-account deficits have remained substantial (Table 2).

On the basis of all rescheduling agreements from 1981 through 1985 we estimate that:

—thus far, close to 90 percent of all medium- and long-term credits have been rescheduled;

—approximately 60 percent of all credits will be due after 1989.

Disregarding the arrears, annual maturities due during 1986 and 1987 will amount to well over $2 billion each year because credits rescheduled during 1981-1983 will now fall due. If we assume interest obligations on a level of about $2.6 billion to $3 billion yearly (Table 2), Poland will hardly be able to avoid a further rescheduling of already rescheduled amounts. Without drastic and efficient measures Poland's net foreign debt will increase considerably beyond the $30 billion it owed at the end of 1985.

Unless the OECD countries grow rapidly and Poland increases its market shares, Poland's growth external equilibrium can be restored only by restricting imports. It can be shown that Poland could restore external equilibrium before the year 2000 by cutting imports from the

West by another 30 percent; this implies cuts by the same percentage by which Romania has reduced her imports from the West in recent years. After such a sacrifice, imports could resume significant growth.

However, no indication can be found that the Polish authorities do aim at such drastic measures. The draft five-year plan (1986-1990) outlined in the chapter by Soldaczuk has three rather ambitious variants, with 3 percent, 3.5 percent and 4 percent growth of national income produced; the Sejm has declared a preference for the 3.5 percent version.

According to all plan variants, investment shall grow significantly faster than consumption. A major part of investment shall be devoted to finishing projects started in previous years, including many of those regarded as "inefficient" whose completion was stopped during the early 1980s.

There is no indication in the draft plan that equilibrium in the consumer goods market shall be restored. Per capita consumption is planned to grow by 1.5-2 percent per year, but nothing is said on wage and price policy.

National income distributed will grow slower than national income produced. But the planned figures imply that even if the total difference were to be used for improving the hard currency balance of payments, the deficit on current account would *not* be eliminated by 1990. In many respects the economic reform program has remained on paper, as the many contributions in Part II of this volume have documented.

It appears that the prevailing disequilibrium in the consumer goods market is used as an argument against the implementation of the reform (Chapter 13). But the authorities hesitate to apply decisive measures to improve the situation; instead they try to blame the West for not supplying fresh money, which, according to their way of reasoning, would help the economy out of the permanent crisis.

Considering external equilibrium as one of the most important preconditions for a recovery of the Polish economy, we raise the following questions: Can maintaining the status achieved in 1985 lead to restoring equilibrium, or are further adjustments needed? If further adjustments are needed, what can Poland do, and what can the West contribute to achieve it?

To find an answer to these questions, we have drawn up a set of scenarios projecting Poland's trade with the West under various assumptions detailed elsewhere.[1] The basic conclusion of the projections is that only the relatively slower domestic growth variant implies a vary modest, long lasting adjustment process. If Poland could maintain a satisfactory (nominal) export growth of 9 percent and import growth of 7.6 percent through 1993, then the debt service ratio would finally fall to a manageable level of 39 percent in 1999. But the growth projections of the draft 1986-90 plan appear to give little consideration to restoring Poland's external creditworthiness.

In sum, we find that Poland's adjustment is highly sensitive to variations of its NMP growth. At an average NMP growth of 3.5 percent the adjustment period would be significantly longer, and balance on the current account would be achieved only in 1998. At 4 percent NMP growth, the balance on the current account could never be attained.

In our opinion, a satisfactory adjustment would be if Poland put herself in a position to service its debt fully from 1986 on, in what may be called the "Paris Club Solution." This would imply that Poland would have to cut imports by a further 30 percent, to approximately $2.5 billion a year. This would be less than half the nominal imports of 1980. Such a sacrifice would soon enable Poland to resume importing at relatively high growth rates. In 1992 the level of its imports would be the same as under alternative projections that would be "easier" on Poland, but net debt would amount to $17 billion only, compared with the "easier" alternatives that would cause debt levels by then to be in the range of $35 billion.

An additional cut in Poland's imports from the West by 30 percent is widely regarded by the authorities as an unfeasible solution, for the government fears this would lead to renewed unrest. Therefore, we have been searching for alternatives to reduce Poland's payments in the medium term.

If we assume that Western lenders are willing to reschedule 95 percent of the maturities due during 1986-88, at 7 years grace plus 6 equal annual installments beginning with 1996, and that the average rate of interest for the Polish debt will be 7 percent during 1985-90, Poland could service its debt even at nominal export growth of 9 percent and import growth of 7.6 percent. Gross debt would peak in 1988 at $28.2 billion. Such a policy pursued through 1985-90 would sufficiently stabilize Poland's balance of payments; from 1991 on Poland could service the debt even if the interest rate goes up again to 10 percent.

Our basic conclusion is that no solution to the Polish debt crisis is in sight. Apparently the Polish authorities care little about restoring external creditworthiness within the near future and have decided to resume a policy of significant growth, implying recurring reschedulings till the end of the century. A generous rescheduling of the maturities falling due till 1988 and interest reduced to an average rate of 7 percent till 1990 could, however, put Poland in a position of servicing its debts regularly from 1991 on. If the market rate of interest was to remain much above 7 to 10 percent, this "solution" would require a large interest subsidy that would have the equivalent effect as a write-off of one-third of Poland's debt ($10 billion), although it would have less severe consequences for the lenders' books. Western lenders may use an offer to reschedule generously and to reduce the interest burden during 1986-90 as a leverage to induce Poland to fully implement the economic reform and to pursue a more prudent import policy at slower NMP growth. If in the 1990s the market interest rate should fall below 10 percent, Poland could also be made to repay part of the interest subsidy received during 1985-90.

Note

1. Gerhard Fink and Hubert Gabrisch, "Poland's Hard-Currency Debt in Perspective," paper presented at the Conference on the Polish Economy and Debt, Woodrow Wilson Center, The Smithsonian Institution, Washington, D.C., October 21-22, 1985, published as Forschungsberichte no. 110 of the Vienna Institute for Comparative Economic Studies.

22

A Banker's Perspective on Poland's Debt Problem

Gabriel Eichler

This chapter provides a banker's assessment of Poland's debt situation, based on a decade of close involvement in the economic analysis of Poland, in connection with lending money to and rescheduling the debts of that country.[1] I will address questions that I am frequently asked: Why did commercial banks extend large loans to Poland during the 1970s? Did banks exercise conditionality, and if so, what was its substance? What is rescheduling, and does it solve Poland's problems? Can Poland regain creditworthiness? What can and should the West do?

Why Did Banks Lend Large Sums to Poland?

About one-quarter of Poland's $35 billion debt is owed to commercial banks. The lending activity of the banks can be understood only in the context of their political, economic, and business environments.

Four major changes in the global environment occurred during the first half of the 1970s that influenced commercial-bank lending to Poland. First, the banking system was very liquid, due especially to the recycling of petrodollars by the OPEC nations. Second, East-West political relations were relaxed in the early period of "détente."[2] Third, there was a change in the economic strategies of the East European countries, especially that of Poland: they wanted to move from an extensive to an intensive approach to development, which required a major influx of capital and technology from the West. And fourth, Western corporations were desirous and able to satisfy the import needs of borrowers and pressured the banks to lend in order to facilitate their clients' exports. A banker in competition with other bankers for the same client does not want to decline a credit request without a sufficient and obvious reason. Competitive pressures later played a role in the participation of banks in apparently profitable balance-of-payment loans.

During the early 1970s, the question an internationally-oriented bank had to answer was not "Why lend?" but rather "Why not do it?" Why should the bank forgo a profitable stream of earnings and concurrently disappoint its Western corporate customers? In the early 1970s the facts known to bankers were: the payment record of the East Europeans was good; their debt level was low until the mid- to late-1970s; banks had very little East European risk in their portfolios; the natural resources of countries like Poland and the USSR were large; there was central planning and a monopoly of foreign trade and finance, which was then perceived by bankers as assuring good control of trade (especially import) levels; East European financial officials were known to be conservative; and if all else failed, the Soviet Union was thought to be a lender of last resort (the so-called "umbrella theory"), since the USSR had the resources and, bankers presumed, the political interest and will to help out.[3] Therefore, indeed, why not do it? Why not provide the necessary financing to promote exports and add to your earnings?

Eventually, once it becomes clear that the borrower has overextended itself, the nature of lending becomes more strategic and tactical; the desire is to avoid a crisis or default, which could be triggered if many bankers conclude at about the same time that the borrower is overextended. At that point, new money will be provided only if the creditors are convinced that it will be instrumental in getting the debtor to alter its economic policies to help it regain creditworthiness.

As the banks' exposure to Poland grew and Poland's deteriorating economic performance raised concerns about the sustainability of its external debt position, the premise on which banks had been lending to the country had to undergo serious review. At that stage, differentiation occurred among the banks in the actions they preferred to take, depending on their size, sophistication, nationality, international orientation, customer base, and the level of Polish exposure in their portfolios.

In the late 1970s, the larger banks were becoming more cautious in lending to Poland. This was reflected in Poland's difficulty in raising major syndicated credits. In fact, in 1978 it took a year to organize a large syndication, whereas previously it took only weeks to arrange one. A syndicated credit of $550 million was finally arranged because the reasoning of many of the larger banks was that "a sudden withdrawal of credit facilities to any large debtor would collapse any economy, just as it would any corporation."[4] Some banks still joined the syndication because of competitive pressures, or on the urgent request of Polish bank officials. Indeed, one of the reasons that arranging the syndicate took as long as it did was that it required some eight months for me to negotiate the disclosure by Poland (for the first time) of basic information on its external financial situation (debt, balance of payments, etc.), and to write the so-called Placement Memorandum.[5]

While the new large loan was being organized, a considerable net reduction in the exposure of the large banks, at least in the U.S., began to take place. At the same time, some smaller banks were still providing net new loans or maintaining their exposure. They may have been encouraged by the experience of Bulgaria. In 1976-77, there were reports in the Western press about the large debt of Bulgaria. The Bulgarians reacted quickly: within three years they more than halved their debt. That was taken by banks as evidence that the original premises on which their involvement in Eastern Europe was based were valid.[6]

But in the case of Poland, the bankers' situation was complicated by outside forces that did not allow a sufficient reduction of credits. By 1977-78 the predominant portion of its new credits came from Western governments, not banks. During the period of late 1977 to mid-1978, when I was collecting and organizing the statistical and economic report as background material for banks participating in the syndication, Poland's debt was on the order of $15 billion. By 1981, when we actually faced the rescheduling problem, its debt was around $25 billion. Therefore, about $10 billion of new debt came at a time when many large U.S. and other Western banks were not increasing their exposure. The exposure of U.S. banks during that period increased by no more than $200 million, even though the U.S. banking community was the second largest creditor to Poland, after West Germany. I suppose that not more than 25 percent of the $10 billion in net new credits came from the banks; the rest came primarily from governments or government-guaranteed supplier credits.

The governments' decision, at a late stage, to add substantial new credits greatly reduced Poland's ability to service its debts to commercial banks. I believe that Poland could have managed, albeit with some difficulty, a debt of $15 billion, but it could not manage a debt of $25 billion. It is often the last dollar rather than the first one that triggers a debt crisis. Thus, whereas the popular view holds that the irrational behavior of the banks was responsible for their difficulties with Polish assets, the lion's share of the problem was created by "the last dollar" provided in support of the economic mismanagement in Poland.

The Concept of Conditionality and its Application in Poland

Yes, the banks did "impose" conditionality, but one needs to avoid a frequent misunderstanding about the meaning of the word. Conditionality, in a broad sense, exists in every creditor-borrower relationship. Its essence is this: as long as the borrower is perceived to exhibit appropriate behavior leading to the preservation of its credit-worthiness (defined as the ability to service its debts fully), the flow of credit will continue. In this sense, conditionality may be viewed as implicit. But when creditors begin to question the borrower's credit-worthiness, conditionality may become more explicit. Thus, the essence of conditionality is the interplay between the creditor and the borrower, and not just the imposing of specific conditions, as it is frequently understood. Creditors can impose conditions, but that does not mean that the borrower will meet them. Success in conditionality depends on the interplay of relative leverage between the borrower and the creditors. The specific *conditions* that may be involved in conditionality typically refer to a set of rational economic policies, targets, strategies, and structural changes that the creditor would have the debtor implement. But both the borrower and the creditor act within environments that may not be conducive to the concise formulation, or the acceptance and implementation, of specific conditions. An examination of these environments from the points of view of both the lender and the borrower is necessary to understand the problem of conditionality in the context of Poland.

Up to 1977-78, conditionality existed only in the broad meaning of the term. Thereafter, conditionality became more concrete, with specific conditions being articulated. And by 1981, when rescheduling became necessary, conditionality became even more explicit, and a part of the legal rescheduling documents. Let me elaborate briefly on these latter two stages.

As of 1977, some new credits were still being made available to Poland because many banks understood that an inflow of new funds was necessary for Poland to improve the management of its economy. As organizers of the syndicate, we insisted on (and received for the first time) full disclosure of hard-currency balance-of-payments and debt information, as well as plans for the future. Our strong advice, articulated verbally, was that Poland would need to take strong measures to improve its current account by increasing exports or reducing imports. If those measures were taken and the situation improved, then—and only then—would the banks find it justifiable to continue the flow of credits. If improvements failed to take place in the management of the economy or in the direction of change in the current account, then banks would be reluctant to provide new funds. That is precisely what happened. Regrettably, the management of the economy did not improve, policies did not change, and the current account did not move toward a balance. Therefore, banks became increasingly hesitant to provide new credits. During 1979-80, only about half of the sum requested by Poland was made available.[7]

While during 1978-81 bank lending continued at a very reduced rate, and only for relatively short maturities (short-term debt increased from some $600 million to $2 billion in that period), Polish debt increased by nearly $10 billion to $25 billion (with its composition clearly shifting toward Western government credits and guarantees, as was stated). When Polish financial officials finally approached the banks with the request for a comprehensive rescheduling, the banks' portion of Poland's debt was smaller than public estimates, to many participants' surprise. Data show that at the end of 1981, less than one-third of Polish debt was due to banks. Furthermore, several hundred million dollars in short-term deposits by Western banks in Poland were withdrawn shortly after in reaction to the announcement of formal rescheduling.[8]

The banks established a Multinational Task Force (MTF) of some twenty banks from twelve countries; seven banks from six countries then formed a Working Party to work out detailed recommendations and prepare documentation, in cooperation with the lawyers. An eight-member International Economic Committee was established to deal with economic and conditionality issues. (The last two groups continue to exist, while the MTF has since been reduced in number to a Group of National Agents, one bank each from thirteen countries.)

The main issues of contention were the types of credits to be excluded from the rescheduling, the percentage of non-excluded maturities to be rescheduled, choice of the governing law and the law firm to represent the banks, equality of treatment for all creditors (including members of the Paris Club, creditors from Arab and CMEA countries, and non-financial institutions), and the economic aspects—information, conditionality, assessment of stabilization programs, etc. The Paris Club, much less concerned with any of these issues, reached a basic agreement with Poland by April 1981, followed later by bilateral agreements (excluding the U.S.) before the year's end.

Many of the issues listed were resolved in 1981. The discussion about 1982 maturities would have been shorter had it not been for new complications, which introduced considerable uncertainty and a need for the banks to act on their own, without the cooperation of the creditor governments: martial law in Poland and the NATO response (cessation of rescheduling discussions), combined with the failure by Poland to make interest payments and its insistence on new credit facilities.

The issue of seeking to impose specific conditions arose when rescheduling became inevitable. The first difficult hurdle was that the 600 creditor banks from many nations had to reach an agreement among themselves on a negotiation position. A key (but not the only) issue was whether and what kind of economic conditions should be demanded in order to make the rescheduling more successful. Regarding economic conditionality, most non-American banks accepted the Polish view that Poland faced only a short-term liquidity problem that could and should be resolved by "throwing money at it."[9] Furthermore, the representatives of certain banks believed that banks should not "interfere" in the internal affairs of a country like Poland. My view was that it was too late to worry about that since the country, by accepting large credits for its mismanaged economy and by not meeting its obligations, had involved the creditors in its internal affairs and had interfered in the affairs of the banks.

In the early stage of the rescheduling process, the banks' MTF established the International Economic Committee (which I was appointed to set up and to chair), comprised of eight people from seven countries, to deal with economic and conditionality issues and to negotiate the relevant clauses in the rescheduling agreement. Establishing an economic committee to deal with economic and conditionality issues may seem an obvious step now (it has since become routine in all rescheduling exercises), but in March 1981 it required long and acrimonious sessions among bankers to establish it. This is not to say that bankers were not interested in economic issues. However, there was no precedent for an economic committee. In previous cases, such as Turkey, the IMF provided the role, or the bankers (the "line officers") serving on the rescheduling committees received the requested statistical information directly from the borrowers, which was then analyzed by the economic departments of the individual banks. Bankers were used to dealing only with bankers, rather than with policymakers in the debtor countries.

Our wish was to have a wide international representation on the Economic Committeee, to stress its international character and to assure a wide dissemination of information. But it was not easy to attract senior bank economists, even though many desired to participate due to the concern in many banks about "interference in the internal affairs of Poland." Therefore, the decision on whether or not to participate was made at the most senior levels.

There has been no desire at any time on the part of commercial banks or individual committee members to "run" the Polish economy. Nor did we have the capability or the time to do so, not to mention the obvious absurdity of Western bank economists managing a socialist country's economy. To use the proverbial "bringing a horse to water" analogy, we were to focus on the quality of the water and to optimize its proximity to the horse—i.e., we could gather information, perform analysis, and provide advice on the relationship between external finance and economic policy to those who should have influence in Poland, but we could not make them act.

Our first aim was to obtain accurate economic information from Poland. We prepared a document of some fifty pages that was very specific about the nature and timing of information that should be provided to us. The data requirements are included in the legal document of the rescheduling agreement. After initial difficulties, the Polish side became reasonably good about providing this information to us on a quarterly basis. Most of the information was related to external finance, that is, detailed debt and current-account data, sources and uses of foreign-currency funds, and the composition of exports and imports by products, geographic areas, and countries. These data were requested so that we could assess whether Poland's export growth rate plans and import projections were feasible. Cash-flow analysis was also used for the first time.

The primary role of the Committee has been to acquire the information for distribution to all creditor banks. Each bank uses its own specialists and makes its own decisions, both for legal and professional reasons. Thus, the Committee has not served as the official "think tank" for the banking community, even though we are aware of our position as opinion leaders. In addition, we believed that the information should be given not only to us as bank economists but should also be made available inside Poland. Before 1982, we found that not only the general public, but even research institutes which were supposed to analyze and make policy recommendations concerning foreign trade and finance, had little idea about the country's balance of payments. They depended on Western estimates—if and when they could get them. If the authorities in Poland were to depend at all on the analyses prepared by their institutes, then certainly the institutes themselves should be informed. I think we did accomplish both of these purposes. Compared with the situation in the 1970s, when evidently even the top policymakers had very incomplete information or understanding of the implications of the policies they were pursuing (see the next chapter by Terry), information of sufficient quantity and quality is now available to us in the West and in Poland.

The second aim of the Committee was to create formal opportunities to discuss regularly the written information with the authorities in Poland. By discussion, I mean not only to receive oral elaboration of the written information but also a chance to communicate to them relevant developments in the international financial markets, to discuss how economic developments in Poland influence the country's ability to gain access to world financial markets, and to exchange views on how decisions on hard-currency finance influence what may appear to be purely domestic economic issues.

As noted earlier, Western bankers dealt almost exclusively with Polish bankers, that is, officials of Bank Handlowy.[10] They were the sole sources of economic information, including balance-of-payments projections. Yet they have had minimal influence on economic policies and strategies, as documented in the next chapter by Terry. Furthermore, in my discussions with the officials of various government agencies in Poland, it became clear that not only did the balance-of-payments and debt projections bear no relationship to whatever other economic agencies of the Polish government (such as the Planning Commission) were thinking, proposing or projecting, but that top planners were even unaware of any projections that were given to foreign creditors. The Planning Commission, in fact, did not deal with balance-of-payments and debt issues in any meaningful way. And the Sejm (Parliament) approved one- and five-year plans without even discussing the balance-of-payments and debt service!

Therefore, one aim of the Committee was to break the procedural attachment, determined by protocol, of Western banks to Polish bank officials, and to formalize semi-annual meetings with senior representatives of the various ministries and other governmental (as well as nongovernmental) agencies. These meetings were to provide a forum to discuss economic issues with key persons of the institutions that helped shape Poland's economic policies and to make them more fully aware of the relationship between Poland's external financial and domestic economic performance. I believe we succeeded to the extent that we could. Awareness and understanding of balance-of-payments and debt issues among the relevant agencies in the Polish government have improved as compared with the situation as we experienced it in the 1970s.

Although Poland is not near recovery, banks as a creditor group have achieved—within the political, legal, and financial constraints they face—nearly the limit of their abilities to introduce meaningful changes in the management of Poland's economy. By contrast, government creditors (the Paris Club) signed their 1981 rescheduling agreement very quickly, without sufficient consideration of the underlying causes of the crisis, and with only nominal conditions imposed. In fact, we were censured for our insistence on articulated conditionality and for our slowness in reaching agreements. Our offer to share economic information and analyses with the Paris Club was rejected.

Poland is not unique as a country where key decision makers are not methodical, systematic analysts executing only well-conceived plans. In fact, in most countries, leading politicians are arbitrators among numerous and (on the surface) equally valid and competing proposals for solutions to complicated problems. Furthermore, the most brilliant economic blueprint will come to naught if the borrower government is politically unwilling or unable to implement it.[11] Whereas one can assume that governments find a good economic situation desirable, one cannot assume that all governments find it necessary, rational, or desirable to undertake tough measures needed to lead the economy to good performance. A government needs popular support, or at least an understanding by its constituents, to be able to install its economic program so that it would not trigger a mass upheaval. However, since self-preservation tends to be the first priority of governments, internal and external political considerations often subordinate the need for proper economic policies to other considerations.

Creditors can hope, at best, to become one of the pressure groups in the borrower country, alongside the "housewives," industrial lobbies, miners, the church, the big and powerful neighbor, etc. The creditors must be able to articulate their position simply and clearly. More important, the creditor must convince the authorities of the benefits of accepting conditionality and the steps that it requires. But first the banks must reach a consensus and embody in a legal document a set of simple imposable conditions that the borrower's financial authorities are able to sell to the country's political leadership (who are not necessarily the most literate people in financial and economic affairs), conditions that will not be perceived as interference in the country's internal affairs. Thus, creditors represent a lobby striving to promote that faction within the leadership of the debtor country which sees the benefits of economic efficiency and order. To reiterate, conditionality is not a simple presentation of economic conditions.

Can Poland Regain Creditworthiness?

The answer is yes. However, one should not expect short-term miracles. A number of positive factors exist. Others in this volume have analyzed the country's overall economic and political situation and made proposals in the direction of the resolution of crisis. I shall focus on the financial aspects.

Poland has shown a remarkable desire to act positively. It has reached rescheduling agreements with commercial banks and, until June 1987, has been fulfilling its financial obligation under those agreements. It has continued to provide economic information. In return, the banks have provided (during 1982-84) new credits in the form of short-term, revolving trade-related financing facilities totaling about $1 billion. These facilities, which have been fully utilized, are available only to finance imports—that is, to pay for imports directly or as cash-collateral to back letters-of-credit. Poland draws on the funds, pays for its imports, and has six months to repay the funds into the pool, upon which it can draw again. The country has been drawing and repaying as due, without any missed or delayed payments. Recognizing the excellent record, banks have reduced the interest margin in subsequent rescheduling agreements and extended the final maturity of the revolving facilities. Several banks have opened new lines of credit to Poland for import purposes, offered limits for foreign-exchange transactions, provided "daylight" and "overnight" (one-day overdraft) limits to facilitate payment transfers, and in general, have not disrupted payment flows to and from Poland. To retain these essential commercial facilities and to have uninterrupted payment flows in both directions are among the important reasons why Poland continues to meet its interest obligations to the banks. Poland's revealed attitude that the new agreements will be fulfilled is therefore an important display of its desire to normalize its relations with its creditors and ultimately to regain creditworthiness.

Similarly, a number of suppliers have had good experience in providing goods on credit to Poland. Poland has also shown its intentions by rejoining the IMF and the World Bank. However, as available funds in Poland are limited, one major group of creditors, the governments represented in the Paris Club, have not fared well. Here the problems started accumulating upon the introduction of martial law in 1981 and the subsequent imposition of NATO sanctions, including the cessation of rescheduling negotiations. Since then the problem has become very complex and politically delicate, and Poland's debt-servicing requirements have grown much bigger. Herein lies the crux of the problem.

Desire and intention—as displayed by the fulfillment of new financial obligations—are an important step in regaining creditworthiness. Yet they are far from sufficient. The fact that Poland's debt has continued to grow rapidly without any significant improvement in its economic and export potential suggests that major underlying changes have not taken place, as noted in many of the other chapters. Spokesmen from Poland have continued for years to make eloquent pleas for new credits; the four essays in Part III of this book (Chapters 17-20) are representative cases in point. One can accept the argument that credits are needed so that a country can import goods for the production of exports, but doubts remain whether large net new credits will in fact result in Poland overcoming its difficulties.

Our experience leaves several reasons for these doubts. First, as was noted, between 1977-81 Poland received new credits of some $10 billion. Have those resulted in improved export potential sufficient to repay them with interest? No, only its debt has increased. After all, one cannot seriously argue that a few years of social upheaval have destroyed an economic capacity built over 10 years with $25 billion of foreign credits. Since 1981, Poland's debt has increased by another $10 billion. The usual argument is that this debt increase is not a result of new funds but primarily the accumulation of interest arrears. The legal profession may accept this argument, but economically, the non-payment of interest is a financial relief which allows the debtor to use the funds for other purposes.[12] Has the relief been utilized for strengthening Poland's export base? The economic data fail to show it. Second, some new funds (such as the church fund for agriculture) were offered, but the authorities were unwilling to accept them because the providers insisted on preserving control over usage. Third, Poland's economic plans no longer include as a top priority the reduction of the debt level by generating real current-account surpluses. This is a regrettable departure from the priorities expressed during 1981-83.

The common thread in these points of doubt is the absence of evidence that the new funds would be used in an efficient and proper way—that is, to create hard-currency earnings sufficient to repay the borrowed funds, plus interest, plus a surplus which would be specifically earmarked to repay old debt. Indeed, Poland's insatiable import demand for domestic needs suggests the opposite. A creditor will provide new funds as a bridge at the end of which he must be able to see a source of repayment. The source of repayment needs to be specific, or at least one he can prudently rely on. Vague sources of repayment are insufficient to convince a large group of creditors to provide large capital inflows.

Before large new and untied credits can be provided, the creditors need to regain confidence that their funds will be used efficiently. Yet, apparently not much has changed since the 1970s in the process of allocating the hard-currency resources. Funds are borrowed by central authorities through their financial institutions, but these institutions have neither a major influence on economic policy nor a proper set of tools to allocate the borrowed funds to their most productive uses. Since a properly functioning market does not exist in Poland in either the real or the financial sphere, prices (of foreign exchange, of producer goods, and of many retail goods) are not market-determined and therefore are not able to guide the efficient use of hard-currency funds. Central planning is now reduced to indicative planning. Various ministries compete for the scarce hard-currency funds, and it is their coercive potential, not their demonstrated economic efficiency, that determines the allocation of funds. A single ministry, with overall responsibility for the efficient and prudent management of the economy, fails to exist in Poland. Indeed, one could argue without much exaggeration that the Polish economy is not managed; at present, market indicators are not permitted to function, nor do the proper institutions exist to manage it without them.

What Poland and its creditors need is a comprehensive program. Such a program should not be just a plan consisting simply of a set of targets (expressed in the form of indices) for production and consumption by sectors. But, regrettably, that is what is currently practiced by the Central Planning Commission. To achieve the stated aims—a balanced economy and the regaining of creditworthiness with sustained growth—the leadership needs to induce all the relevant groups to cooperate: labor, management, the government bureaucracy, its allies, and the creditors. But all these groups need incentives to co-opt them. The program, therefore, needs to be specific, have the full backing of the leadership, include a timetable for implementation, and be well-articulated and honest so that all the parties can see the ultimate benefit in cooperating. It needs to establish new institutions, as well as economic and political incentives, to efficiently guide and motivate all the relevant players; in other words, Poland needs to introduce a comprehensive economic reform program, not just a haphazard set of new laws, to be modified and rescinded a year later. And the reforms should be introduced quickly, not in marginal steps which have little impact. Small steps will not change the psychology of the nation, which is necessary in order to move forward; they will only introduce more chaos.

Poland is in a good position to introduce such a program. There are no grounds for the usual excuses for inaction. The economy, while improving in some areas, is still in disorder; thus, a new program would not cause chaos much worse than that which exists already. The usual "undesirable" effect of market reforms—the appearance of sizeable inequalities in income and wealth—should not present excessive problems, since large income disparities exist already. The country will not lose its creditors, since it has few new volunteers, and the previous ones are locked in. The Soviets are introducing their own reforms, and a Poland in a prolonged crisis is not to their benefit. Also, the bureaucracy will not lose its power and its privileges, since its "power" is more apparent than real, and in recent years it has already lost much of its previous preferential treatment.[13]

I am strongly of the opinion that as long as there is no efficient mechanism for allocating hard-currency funds, an increase in Poland's debt is *not* in Poland's interest. This is not a banker's excuse. If a country cannot find ways to fully meet all of its obligations with a debt of $35 billion, it certainly will be unable to do it with a debt of $40 billion, unless the additional debt raises its hard-currency earning capability by more than $5 billion, plus interest, and we have little evidence that it would. Poland needs to find ways to reduce its debt, not increase it.

Until a proper economic system and economic policies are in place, smaller credits can be provided for very specific purposes, as long as they are properly evaluated and controlled by the creditors to assure repayment with interest. A number of banks and institutes are investigating such opportunities, as outlined in Chapter 24 by my banking colleague. The World Bank is very capable of investigating and managing such activities. The IMF can be helpful in setting up a standby program but only as an initial step toward the ultimate solution, which will require a much more comprehensive program. As of July 1987, bank creditors are skeptical and most banks have built reserves against possible loan losses in Poland. Several banks have totally written off their Polish assets; others have sold them at a discount, seeing little hope of recovery in the foreseeable future. Nevertheless, as events turn more promising, bank and government creditors can be expected to become more helpful.

New capital can be brought to Poland without an increase in debt, by foreign direct investment. But again, this will not happen if the usual East European approach is adopted: pass a new law permitting joint ventures with minority foreign ownership and then wait for an invasion by Western companies competing to enter the market. Poland competes for direct foreign investment not only with other East European countries with smaller economic problems, but with numerous European, Asian, and Latin American countries and American states, which promote their cause, provide tax and other incentives, with better economic infrastructure, and without limits on percentage of foreign ownership and repatriation of profits. Poland can attract foreign investment, but it needs to take a more active role than just passing laws. In this regard, well-executed conversion of debt to equity schemes may provide an incentive to potential investors by lowering the cost of the investment and concurrently reduce Poland's debt. Commercial-bank rescheduling agreements are in the process of being amended to allow debt-to-equity conversions, but their appeal to potential investors will depend on Poland's officials.

I have been studying and working with Poland for over a decade, during which I have heard many excellent ideas expressed by well-intentioned and presumably influential Poles on what needs to be done and will be done soon. Unfortunately, all of the ideas I hear now are the same ones I heard ten years ago, from many of the same persons. More ideas, excuses, and delays fail to provide fertile ground for utilizing the goodwill which still exists among representatives of creditors, be they affiliated with supranational institutions, governments, or commercial banks. But the representatives have full agendas of issues competing for their attention. Poland's leaders need to act: to start executing a viable socioeconomic program, and to send competent, articulate messengers abroad to champion their country's cause.

Notes

1. This chapter is an edited and updated version of the author's remarks at a conference on Polish debt, held in October 1985 at the Smithsonian Institution in Washington, D.C. The author is grateful to Paul Marer, without whose guidance, persistence, and assistance this chapter would not have been completed.

2. This does not mean that the U.S. Department of State suggested to banks to lend, say, to Poland. It means simply that during the early 1970s, improved East-West relations generally and U.S.-Polish relations specifically were environmental factors that the banks and their corporate customers took into account.

3. Gabriel Eichler, "Country Risk Analysis and Bank Lending" in Joint Economic Committee, U.S. Congress, *East European Economic Assessment, Part 2* (Washington, D.C., 1981).

4. The value of the syndication to Poland went well above $550 million in that the loan was perceived by many creditors as a positive signal and thus additional, not publicized credits were provided.

5. A Placement Memorandum is an information document which is distributed by the agent or syndicate leader to potential participants in the syndication and is used by banks to decide on their participation.

6. Following the first visible signs of the Polish crisis, from early 1981 until 1984, almost all credit to Eastern Europe dried up. Yet East Germany, the USSR, Czechoslovakia, and Bulgaria survived the entire period without resorting to any special assistance or rescheduling and without missing any payments to Western banks. Not many corporate borrowers could withstand without turmoil such a sudden and prolonged withdrawal of credit. This suggests that the orig-

inal premise—the effective central control of foreign trade and finance by the CMEA countries—is indeed not wrong, only that it cannot be indiscriminately applied.

7. A credit of $325 million was provided by non-German banks (plus about DM 1 billion by German banks), and again it took months to complete the syndications. The full subscription (i.e., taking shares in the syndication) could not be arranged without Polish and other East European banks in the West providing some $85 million to complete the deal.

8. For additional details on rescheduling, see G. Eichler, "The Debt Crisis: A Schematic View of Rescheduling in Eastern Europe," in Joint Economic Committee, U.S. Congress, *East European Economies: Slow Growth in the 1980s* (Washington, D.C., 1986).

9. That view was not unusual. A year later Romania supposedly also faced only a "short-term liquidity problem," a view that was supported by the IMF. The same view was held on several Latin American countries when their reschedulings began in the early 1980s.

10. Similarly, until recently IMF teams dealt almost exclusively with the officials of central banks or of finance ministries.

11. See Henry Kissinger's book, *The White House Years*, for a description of the difficulty of serving as an influential outside advisor to a U.S. president.

12. A creditworthy borrower receives new credits which he can use for various purposes, including the payment of interest, the refinancing of its current debt, or for productive purposes. It may increase, maintain, or reduce its debt. However, interest must be accepted as a firm obligation, as a cost of borrowing funds. If interest and/or principal is not paid, the relationship is no longer voluntary. Dismissing this argument assumes that the payment of interest is not a real obligation; this assumption may be acceptable under Islamic law or under a dogmatic version of Marxism, but not in the currently practiced international financial system, where creditors raise funds with associated costs. If a borrower is requesting net new funds and maintains that interest is not a real obligation, he is requesting grants, not credits as we understand them.

13. Today most Poles can travel to the West, there are few special shops for the apparatchiks, and their pay is hardly better than that of Warsaw's private taxi drivers.

23

External Debt and the Polish Leadership

Sarah M. Terry

Among the myths that encouraged Western investments in Poland in the 1970s were, first, a belief that East European financial officials were "conservative" and that, in any event, the Soviet Union could not afford to let one of its frontline allies face bankruptcy; second, that Poland, together with the rest of Eastern Europe, provided a stable, low-cost labor environment; and third, that the hierarchical structure of a CPE, while admittedly inefficient, at least insured coordinated supervision of investments. History has proven all three assumptions wrong in the case of Poland. Until recently we could only speculate about why these assumptions turned out to have been invalid. Now, however, publication of the hitherto secret report, *Protocols of the So-called Grabski Commission*, by the Paris-based Polish emigré press "Kultura," allows us to begin filling in some—though by no means all—of the gaps.[1]

Set up in the spring of 1981 under the chairmanship of then Central Committee Secretary and reputed hardliner Tadeusz Grabski, the Commission's mandate was to probe the causes of Poland's economic crisis—in particular, the "personal responsibility" of members of the leadership—and to report its findings and recommendations to the 9th Party Congress in July. In theory, anyone who had occupied a top-level position in the party or in the government during the 1970s was subject to be called before the Commission or asked to submit a written statement. But, apparently, only twelve witnesses were called, all but two of whom had been removed from office following the strikes of August

215

1980. Despite this, the Grabski report is replete with fascinating and sometimes devastating revelations about the inner workings of the regime. For the purposes of this brief chapter, I will focus on three points: (1) the contrasts between First Secretary Edward Gierek and Prime Minister Piotr Jaroszewicz; (2) the impact of their relative clout in decision making; and (3) the handling of the debt question within the Politburo.

What "Gierek Era"?

The most striking conclusion to be drawn from the Grabski report is that the real strongman in Warsaw during the socalled "Gierek era" was not Gierek, who emerges as a singularly weak and inept leader, but Jaroszewicz. The most charitable appraisal of Gierek came from his closest associate, Franciszek Szlachcic, who noted that Gierek had both "virtues" and "defects": "in Katowice the virtues dominated; in Warsaw the defects began to dominate."[2] The testimony of others provides a more concrete sense of the virtues (primarily his affability and approachability, especially compared with Jaroszewicz) and defects (notably his indecisiveness and tolerance for improprieties among colleagues and subordinates). According to Józef Pińkowski, Gierek "was not a man with whom one feared he could not talk, not at all. He willingly discussed all matters with everyone." At the same time, Pińkowski continues,

> It would seem you'd convinced him, that he understood. He would say, "Yes, you are right, we must get to that." Later there were discussions with others and this whole mechanism would start again. You thought everything was in motion; after a few months you look- and nothing, . . . the situation is, well, just as before. There was simply no consistency in action, in squaring all these programs.[3]

Even by his own testimony, Gierek's lack of attention to (or poor grasp of) important policy questions bordered on irresponsibility, if not outright incompetence. For instance, in response to persistent questioning about the debt, he claims that it was Deputy Prime Minister Jagielski's responsibility, that he personally was not aware of the seriousness of Poland's indebtedness until "sometime at the beginning of 1978." Elsewhere, in an attempt to defend himself on the question of excessive investments, he complains that every deputy prime minister wanted to make his bailiwick the "navel of the world," that each would plead his case as "the most important." Gierek made these statements without any discernible recognition that it is the job of a deputy prime minister to put forward the interests of his domain, and the responsibility of the leadership to set and enforce realistic priorities.[4]

The contrast between the first secretary and the prime minister could not be starker. Even Jaroszewicz's detractors concede that he was "hardworking," while even his supporters admit that he was difficult to work with (others label him arrogant and dictatorial). The more important aspect of his political "persona," however, was that he was universally perceived as Moscow's man. To this fact many ascribe his appointment to the premiership in December 1970, a position for which he was hardly the most logical candidate from a Polish perspective, but for which he was superbly qualified in the eyes of Moscow. In fact, until his promotion he was not even a full member of the Politburo, and had been a candidate member only since the 5th Party Congress in 1968. His primary asset was his decades-long tie to Moscow, dating back to World War II. In the early 1950s, as chief of the "military section" of the Polish Planning Commission, he oversaw the extensive militarization of Polish industry under Soviet supervision. In the 1960s, he was a deputy premier and Poland's permanent representative to the CMEA, a position that kept him in Moscow much of the time. Although none of this demonstrates that Jaroszewicz was "Moscow's agent," the behavior of other members of the Politburo, as reflected in the Grabski Commission's hearings, suggests that they regarded him more or less in this light.[5]

"The Party Leads, the Government Governs"

The consequence of Jaroszewicz's dominant position was an unprecedented perversion of political structures and decision-making processes. By most accounts this became a fait accompli by 1973—four to five years before Western banks and governments began detecting serious problems. Indeed, former members of the leadership cited, with striking consistency, 1973-74 as the point when things began to come unraveled. Although for the most part they were referring to loss of control over investment policy, this was also the point at which control over cadre policy became fragmented and Politburo discussions became less open and substantive. In its official report, the Commission complained that "for all practical purposes,"

> the jurisdictions of the Political Bureau and the government, their interdependence and spheres of responsibility were not regulated, despite the correct (but more theoretical than practical) thesis: the party leads—the government governs. This blurred the picture of relations between the Political Bureau and the government, [limiting] especially the possibility of determining responsibility for decisions taken and implemented at the highest level. . . .
>
> The predominance of representatives of the government in the Political Bureau was highly inappropriate and fraught with consequences. It determined to a significant degree the formulation of many decisions, especially economic. The government presented for political decision few problems of fundamental significance for the country (e.g., the debt and the country's ability to service it, essential socio-economic reforms), while absorbing the attention of the Political Bureau with an excess of detailed matters. . . .

The role of the Prime Minister in the Political Bureau was excessively prominent. Thus the real importance of the Political Bureau and of those members who were not at the same time members of the government was diminished.[6]

Judging from the testimony of Jaroszewicz's erstwhile colleagues, the Politburo virtually ceased to function as a decisionmaking body, except in the most formal sense of ratifying positions presented by the government. The practice adopted in 1971 of holding more or less open Politburo meetings at which any member could "propose something" or "question a comrade"—including one meeting a month with no set agenda—apparently gave way by 1973 to a more rigid format where "it was necessary to submit topics in writing, and already it wasn't the same." The agenda became "cluttered with various trivial matters."[7] Moreover, there was a "principle in the Bureau that no one opened his mouth when decisions of the Presidium of the Government were discussed; [there was] a kind of solidarity."[8] Another "principle" observed was that

> on economic questions essentially all materials were submitted to the Bureau by the Government. Materials submitted directly by responsible departments of the C[entral] C[ommittee], or a CC secretary, were the exception. . . . In practice, during discussions the positions of the government and Jaroszewicz were very strongly defended, and those comrades who sometimes had other opinions were in a very difficult situation, because they were bound by a kind of loyalty with the Presidium of the Government.[9]

The transcript of the hearings is littered with examples of the prime minister's arbitrary style—decisions made without consulting the responsible officials or departments, or despite their opposition. At the time of the June 1976 food price increases, for example, he apparently pushed through the "maximum option" over the opposition of a majority of the leadership. In his testimony before the Commission, Jaroszewicz predictably presented the price increases as a consensus decision, while conveniently misrepresenting some details. Gierek, also predictably, recalled only that no one in the Politburo was against the Government's plan "everyone was for it." Grudzień, however, provided details suggesting extended and heated debate in the weeks preceding the decision, during which the leadership (fearing precisely the outburst of social anger that occurred) was overwhelmingly opposed to increases of the magnitude proposed by Jaroszewicz. Yet, when it came to a vote, no one spoke out against the prime minister.[10]

In the area of agriculture—an increasingly significant contributor to Poland's overall debt burden in the second half of the 1970s[11]—Pińkowski's testimony is particularly revealing. One of his first tasks on becoming CC Secretary with responsibility for that sector in early 1974 was to work out a balanced longterm development program for agriculture. Initially everyone was "for it," and his program was included in the final resolution of the 7th Party Congress in December 1975. "In the meantime," states Pińkowski, "one cannot say that the program totally died out, but there was a struggle (as in so many other matters) how to maneuver out of it, how not to implement it." Pińkowski goes on to talk about the difficulty of working in the agricultural sector: "Comrade [Kazimierz Barcikowski, then Minister of Agriculture] and I were constantly under the gun, . . . whenever agricultural matters came before the Bureau, there was always a row," generally in the form of pressure to accelerate the "socialization of the means of production" by discriminating against the dominant private sector, in turn discouraging production. In this passage, Pińkowski did not single out Jaroszewicz as the "heavy," but a few pages later he noted that the Prime Minister would often discard Barcikowski's position papers and submit his own for Politburo ratification. The latter would then come to Pińkowski and say "Look, I can do no more; you try, maybe you'll succeed."[12]

Another ill-prepared decision—less well-known to Western observers, but with no less serious economic consequences for Poland—was the 1975 administrative reorganization, according to which the country was divided into 49 provinces instead of the previous seventeen. As chairman of the regional planning group within the Planning Commission at the time the reorganization was being prepared, Pińkowski logically should have been a key actor. Yet he testified that, after a preliminary discussion with Jaroszewicz during which he objected to the government's proposal, he was excluded from further participation. Later, when the matter came before the Politburo, he argued—again unsuccessfully— that the administrative division of the country "should be synchronized with the regional economic development plan."[13] Although popular with the party and state bureaucracies—which benefited from greatly expanded patronage opportunities—the reorganization had a devastating impact on an already overloaded investment budget because the boss of each new provincial center demanded its complement of appropriate buildings (party headquarters, local council buildings, militia quarters, special vacation and medical facilities, etc.), the outlays for which came directly out of the local housing and social service investment budgets.[14]

Mismanaging the Debt

Gierek's statements to the Commission were inconsistent on the debt question. At first, especially when he sensed that his role was under attack, he rejected the suggestion that Politburo members were uninformed about the debt or excessive investments: "No decision was taken without the knowledge of the Political Bureau . . . everyone knew."

Then he began to hedge, saying that he could not accept responsibility for the fact that Poland had exceeded reasonable limits of indebtedness—that others, some still in the Politburo, were responsible and did not present the full situation to the leadership.[15] But this statement overlooks the findings of a blue-ribbon advisory panel set up in May 1977 to make recommendations on socio-economic problems. Its first report, submitted at the end of July but never released even in summary form until after August 1980, contained blunt criticisms, often phrased in urgent language, of regime policy. The bulk of the report, which was based on data unavailable to the general public (not to mention Western creditors), was devoted to a graphic description of a runaway economy, including the external debt. Noting the excesses and errors of the regime's economic strategy, the panel warned that "only the most drastic" measures could now turn the situation around. The panel recommended rescheduling negotiations and reapplication to the IMF, as well as a freeze on all new investment projects. None of these was acted upon before August 1980.[16]

Thus, Gierek's claim, cited above, that he was unaware of the seriousness of the debt until the beginning of 1978 lacks credibility. At the same time, Jaroszewicz's counterclaim that the Politburo was kept fully informed (that is, if Gierek did not grasp the severity of the situation, "he probably didn't read" the prepared materials[17]), is equally doubtful. Babiuch directly contradicted him, relating that when he took over as Prime Minister in February 1980, he asked for "precise reports" from the various ministries concerning their foreign obligations and trade balances with nonsocialist countries. He states, "It turned out that we did not possess such data, and the calculations took three weeks before I received them from the departments." Planning chief Wrzaszczyk at first insisted that the leadership was informed, but then made the stunning admission that he himself did not receive the Finance Ministry's secret quarterly (sometimes monthly) reports on "debt service, interest rates, and so forth" until he demanded them—this as late as 1976![18]

The most likely explanation of these inconsistencies is that the same mechanisms that hindered substantive discussion of domestic economic policy governed the Politburo's handling of the debt question. In particular, the information provided by the government to the Politburo appears to have been woefully inadequate to grasp the full implications of the exploding debt crisis. Jaroszewicz himself, while denying that the amount of the debt was a secret, conceded that "of course the documents [concerning the debt] were secret, delivered by hand to each [Politburo member] and later retrieved. There was a tendency not to go out of our way to advertise it, in order not to alarm either the country or our creditors." As on other issues, however, the prime minister's main concern was to play down his own role and establish joint responsibility for decisions (or lack of them).[19]

Others were less charitable. According to Szlachcic, as early as 1973 the debt question could not be raised even in closed meetings of the Council of Ministers or Politburo without fear of retribution.[20] Silesian party chief Grudzień was particularly blunt: "[Our] misfortunes began in 1973 when we misread the [Western] recession, when our economists and advisors assured us it was a temporary phenomenon." Only after 1976 was the debt question posed in an "urgent" way:

> If I remember correctly, comrade Olszowski raised it many times and was told that it was not so bad, that one shouldn't make a tragedy out of it. . . . I had a conversation with comrade Gierek about placing the debt problem before the Bureau. From what I know, other comrades also raised this issue. It seems to me that it's essential to return to the Bureau's [previous style] of work, because it's very difficult for me to say what mechanisms determined that this matter didn't come before the Bureau.[21]

Another revealing perspective is that of Jerzy Łukaszewicz, CC secretary responsible for ideology and propaganda throughout the 1970s (and thus overseer of the regime's image problems and "the propaganda of success"). Complaining that "we never managed" to have a "meritorious discussion" of an issue, he continued:

> We would jump to a problem, then leave it; we were constantly dealing with inconsequential matters. . . . We were divided, especially after 1976. I didn't want to cause further divisions. It wasn't possible to publish the size of the debt in the press until it came from the mouths of official spokesmen. . . . I suggested that the first secretary or prime minister should speak of the debt first, not the press, for how would that look. But no one agreed to this. To tell the truth, despite the fact that the Politburo reviewed our debt status several times, in essence it was never thoroughly discussed. [Such a discussion] was demanded in 1976. . . . In 1977 or 1978, there was a discussion in the CC Secretariat that the Politburo should examine materials worked up by party commissions. But this was never done. Everyone was for it, including the first secretary; but life took another course.[22]

Can We Draw Conclusions?

What conclusions can one draw from this saga of utter irresponsibility and malfeasance? The first and most obvious one is that, despite the wealth of titillating detail contained in the Grabski report about what went wrong in "Gierek's Poland," we never really find out the reasons that explain it. Why, despite more or less predictable consequences, was there such poor coordination of investments?[23] Why, despite serious reservations about the wisdom or feasibility of Jaroszewicz's proposals, didn't other Politburo members challenge him more often? Why, despite his posturing and obvious ambition, was Gierek willing to play the role of an ineffectual "second fiddle" to his prime minister? Most important, why, despite mounting alarm within the top leadership over the size of Poland's hardcurrency debt, was that issue never analyzed or fully discussed either by the Politburo or the Central Committee Secretariat, both supposedly above the Council of Ministers in a Soviet-style political hierarchy?

The Polish rumor mill has typically pointed the finger of blame at the Soviets, as it has done in connection with many other matters.[24] The Grabski report does not directly support those suspicions, but neither does it disprove them. Indeed, one of the striking things about the available transcript of the hearings is the dearth of open references to the Soviet Union; it is the actor whose presence is constantly sensed but rarely seen. A partial explanation may possibly be the numerous and sometimes lengthy gaps in the record.[25] Nevertheless, the fact that, despite grievous errors and failures of judgment, Jaroszewicz got away with it—that the rest went along in a kind of conspiracy of silence for nine years—is an astonishing feat of survival that, I submit, cannot be explained without reference to his real or perceived link to Moscow. Thus, in the final analysis, perhaps the only conclusion one can draw with absolute certainty is that we do not as yet have the full story of why Poland's leadership allowed the external debt to rise to unmanageable levels. That a penchant for secrecy, lack of individual responsibility, and incompetence, pure and simple, played major roles is nearly certain.

Notes

1. *Protokóły tzw. Komisji Grabskiego: tajne dokumenty PZPR*, Grażyna Pomiań, ed., Biblioteka "Kultury," vol. 415 (Paris, 1986). Intended solely for intraparty use (indeed, the report occasionally reveals an almost pathological concern with the need for secrecy), a substantially complete stenographic report of the Commission's hearings circulated in the underground several years before publication by "Kultura." (Cited hereafter as *Protokóły*, with the name of the witness and page reference.)

2. *Protokóły*, p.173. As a longtime protegé in Silesia and then as minister of interior, Szlachcic helped Gierek consolidate his power in 1970-71, for which he was rewarded with promotion to the Central Committee Secretariat and the Politburo. Before his progressive demotions in 1974 and 1975, he was viewed by some as the second most powerful man in the country.

3. *Protokóły*, p.375. Pińkowski was first deputy chairman of the Planning commission from 1971 to 1974, then central committee secretary for agriculture, until serving briefly as prime minister from late August 1980 to February 1981.

4. *Protokóły*, pp. 6465 and 8182. In general, the impression of Gierek that emerges from the hearings is consistent with reports from seasoned political

observers in Warsaw. In sharp contrast to Gomułka, his predecessor as first secretary, who put in long hours and lived in modest, almost spartan, style, Gierek was reputed to be a chronic clock-watcher with a penchant for lavish living. This is reflected in his session before the Commission, where attention focused at length on the propriety of his life-style and his tolerance for abuses and corruption among favored associates and subordinates.

     5. Concerning Jaroszewicz's early career, see Michael Checinski, "Poland's Military Burden," *Problems of Communism*, May/June 1983, p. 34; and Zbigniew A. Pelczynski, "The Downfall of Gomułka," in *Gierek's Poland*, Adam Bromke and John W. Strong, eds. (New York, 1973), pp. 21-22. Jaroszewicz's virtues and faults are a major theme running through the Grabski hearings.

     6. *Protokóły*, pp. 407-408.

     7. Grudzień, in *Protokóły*, p. 231; also Szydlak, pp. 311-12, and Babiuch, pp. 163-64. The last in particular implies that Jaroszewicz packed the agenda with a host of detailed matters, both to avoid a discussion of more fundamental questions and to insure joint responsibility in the event decisions later came under criticism.

     8. Grabski paraphrasing Szydlak, in *Protokóły*, p.366. Enforcement of this "solidarity" applied also at the Central Committee (CC) level. When asked why—given the bitterness in his relations with Jaroszewicz and others—Szlachcic did not speak out in the CC, he replied: "At that time, the obligatory procedure was that a member of the Bureau must get permission to speak. I did not want to break with the Political Bureau. I asked once, and again; the comrades said no. . . . I won't mention their names, but they said: if comrade Szlachcic wants to speak to the plenum of the Central Committee, that will bring about a split in the party which we cannot permit at any price, even at the price of special measures. And you know well what these special measures are. . . ." (p. 184). (In December 1978, Grabski himself, then a provincial party first secretary, was expelled from the CC for criticizing regime economic policy at a CC plenum.)

     9. *Protokóły*, p. 354 (Pińkowski).

     10. *Protokóły*, p. 108 (Jaroszewicz), p. 78 (Gierek), and p. 223 (Grudzień). 11. See Chapters 4 and 5 in this volume by Boyd and Andrews. Jaroszewicz revealed that $12 billion of the total $56 billion hard-currency purchases on credit from 1971 through the end of 1979 were for food products. (Of the rest, $27 billion went for raw materials and semimanufactures and $17 billion for machinery and equipment.) *Protokóły*, p. 113.

     12. *Protokóły*, pp. 351 and 354. Pińkowski was a particularly valuable witness, quite possibly because he was not in the top leadership in the 1970s and therefore did not feel the need to defend decisions. Unfortunately, Barcikowski continued to hold Politburo-level positions after the 1980 crisis and was not required to testify. Nonetheless, Pińkowski's account tends to confirm an anecdote concerning Barcikowski's resignation as Minister of Agriculture in December 1977. According to a well-informed Warsaw source, there was a heated debate in the Politburo during which Jaroszewicz demanded changes in agricultural policy in favor of Soviet-style orthodoxy. Barcikowski reportedly retorted that he would need another high-level administrative slot in his ministry to implement the changes. "Only one?" he was asked. "Yes," he answered, "for God, because it will take a miracle to carry out this policy." He resigned shortly

thereafter, whether in disgust or under pressure is not clear, but possibly both. For further insights, see Chapter 5 in this volume by Andrews.

13. *Protokóły*, p. 348. To the best of Pińkowski's recollection, the preliminary discussion took place sometime in 1973; his objections were based on his view that "everything was beginning to go wrong, and it was a devil of a time for a reorganization. . . ." He suggested fewer rather than more provinces, but apparently the pressure from the local *nomenklatura* for even more than 49 provinces was overwhelming.

14. *Protokóły*, pp. 18 and 165 (Babiuch). The rush to build new nonproductive and restricted-use facilities has been confirmed for me by independent sources, and was reportedly a key source of social discontent in the Solidarity period.

15. *Protokóły*, pp. 64-65.

16. Excerpts of the report were published in *Polityka*, no. 48 (November, 1980), and *Przegląd Techniczny*, no. 23 (June 1981); the latter were translated under the title "Who Knew What?" *Radio Free Europe Research*, RAD Background Report/241 (August 25, 1981).

17. *Protokóły*, p. 113.

18. *Protokóły*, pp. 137 (Babiuch) and pp. 388-90 (Wrzaszczyk).

19. *Protokóły*, pp. 114-15.

20. Szlachcic testified that Finance Minister Stefan Jędrychowski was dismissed for his attempts to raise the debt issue in the Council of Ministers at this early stage. He himself was progressively demoted for his opposition on this, among other, issues. Szydlak confirms that Szlachcic was the first one "to pose openly the issue of debt and credits" in 1973. *Protokóły*, pp. 176 (Szlachcic) and 312 (Szydlak).

21. *Protokóły*, pp. 22526. (At the time, Stefan Olszowski was CC Secretary with responsibility for economic policy. He was dropped from the Secretariat and Politburo at the 8th Congress in February 1980, probably for his opposition to the regime's economic policies, but returned to the leadership after the August 1980 crisis.) Actually, Grudzień is mistaken in suggesting that the regime's economic advisors misled the leadership on the implications for Poland of the global energy crisis and Western stagflation. Other more credible sources indicate that the leadership dismissed warnings from its advisors, assuming that "in conditions of inflation a high rate of indebtedness is not dangerous since inflation cancels out the burden on the economy, with the result that the rate of interest . . . in real terms can be very low or even zero." Criticism of this view "could not see the light of day, because the debt question fell under the state secrets clause." (Mieczysław Mieszczańkowski, "Crisis in the Economy: Causes and the Way Out" (in Polish), *Nowe Drogi*, December 1980, p. 140.) This point is fully confirmed by a recent detailed study of Poland's "debt trap": Wiesław Rydygier, "The Trap of Debt," in *At the Source of the Polish Crisis: Socioeconomic Conditions for Economic Growth in Poland in the 1980s* (in Polish), Aleksander Mueller, ed. (Warsaw, 1985), pp. 230-33.

22. *Protokóły*, pp. 242-43.

23. The largest and best known of these was the "Huta Katowice," the huge Katowice Steelworks, which is still not finished 15 years after the beginning of construction and which forced the postponement of an estimated 150-200 other projects (some of which, like power plants, were essential to the operation of the steelworks). Despite numerous references in the hearings to serious errors

in the planning of this project, we never learn by whom (or even when) the decision to build Huta Katowice was made. In the critical area of energy supplies, Jaroszewicz admitted that Polish planners improperly assessed the country's rising energy needs (*Protokóły*, p. 120). Pińkowski (pp. 347-48) adds details concerning the planners' totally unrealistic projections of Poland's ability to import oil from world markets—later necessitating rapid, unforeseen and uneconomical investments in increased coal production, which further burdened the investment budget. Pińkowski (pp. 351-52) also pointed out that the government would often agree to do things it knew it couldn't do, "just to avoid a row." As an example, he mentions the unrealistic plans for expanded (and urgently needed) production of fertilizer that were written into the Plan; "later [the Government] would blame industry for not realizing [the plan]."

24. For example, whenever something disappeared from the local market (meat, paint, pharmaceuticals, cement, toilet paper) or whenever an investment decision proved misguided or unprofitable (the massive Katowice Steelworks, shipbuilding and ship repairs), Moscow would be singled out as the culprit. For an extreme statement of this view in connection with responsibility for economic policy, see John Van Meer [pseudonym], "Banks, Tanks, and Freedom," *Commentary*, December 1982, pp. 17-24. See also Romuald Spasowski, *The Liberation of One* (New York, 1986).

25. Of the many gaps in the typescript, some involving only a few words to several lines, some a few pages, the longest is a 25-page gap at the end of the session with Gierek. (See notation in *Protokóły*, p. 96.)

24

Poland's Long Road Back to Creditworthiness

Paul I. McCarthy

Overview

Poland defaulted on its debt to Western commercial banks and governments in March 1981. In December of that year, the country was placed in the straitjacket of martial law. The coincidence of these events left the country with a demoralized workforce, seething political and foreign policy troubles, sinking productivity, and doubtful global export competitiveness.

Since 1981, Poland's debt to Western creditors has mounted. Western governments, in turn, have initiated a series of diplomatic and economic sanctions—the U.S. denial of most-favored-nation tariffs and a ban from 1982 to 1984 on Paris Club debt negotiations, which have exacerbated the country's debt problems and prevented access to investment capital for future growth.

In response to these developments, Western banks pursued a strategy based on the negotiation of a series of debt-rescheduling agreements with the Polish government that called for the country to make net payment outflows. During 1981-86, the banks were successful in negotiating six such rescheduling agreements whereby Poland's financial obligations to the banks exceeded the banks' commitments to the country. In other words, no net new credits were made available to Poland over this period.

In essence, the banks got a free ride during this period because the government creditors were not simultaneously negotiating comparable

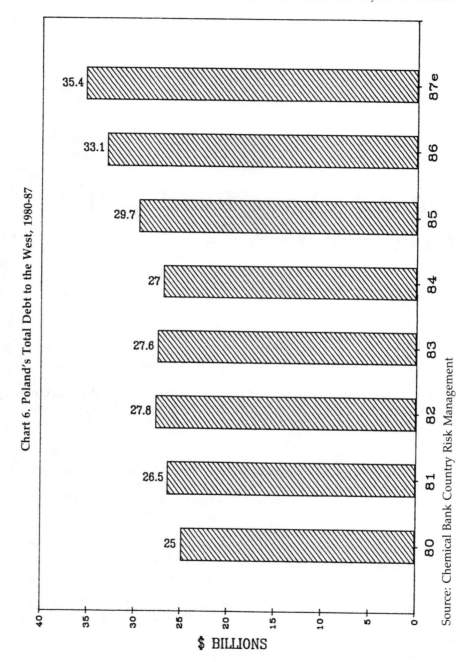

Chart 6. Poland's Total Debt to the West, 1980-87

Source: Chemical Bank Country Risk Management

rescheduling agreements with Poland. As a result, Poland made no significant payments—either interest or principal—to the Paris Club member governments, thereby significantly increasing its debt to them. Western government exposure further increased as commercial banks submitted claims for reimbursement under the various official guarantee programs (i.e., Eximbank, Hermes, COFACE and ECGD).

Another factor contributing to the decline in Western bank exposure has been the ability or (in the case of American banks) the need to write off a substantial portion of the loans. Additionally, many commercial banks have recently been selling Polish loans in the secondary-sales market at a deep discount (i.e., at 45 cents per dollar). Although the Paris Club member governments decided to reopen negotiations in 1985, and in fact have concluded two agreements with Poland covering maturities due during 1982-86, they have almost uniformly (Austria and FRG are exceptions) resisted making available new money. The banks, too, have refused to make new loans a part of the debt rescheduling process. Even the most recent bank agreement, covering obligations due during 1986-87, does not include net new money.

As we list all these negative factors in the Polish debt situation, it is worthwhile to recall that many of the original and productive ideas on debt rescheduling used in other countries were established in the Polish debt negotiations, such as:

—Rescheduling agreements were entered into without IMF involvement in the country.

—Although Western governments own 60 percent of Poland's debt, the banks have negotiated restructuring agreements without comparable arrangements between Poland and the Paris Club.

—The first Multi-Year Rescheduling Agreement (MYRA) was negotiated with Poland.

—Poland was the first country with which the banks agreed to partly capitalize interest payments, by returning a certain percentage of interest payments in the form of short-term trade credits.

—Polish restructuring agreements were the first to require some principal repayments as part of the up-front settlement costs.

Poland is at a critical point with its Western creditors. Its economy requires a major structural reform, for which new investment is desperately needed. Without reform and access to new capital, Poland's chances of regaining competitiveness in finished goods will slip away, perhaps for decades. If the Polish government refuses to undertake a reform program, Western banks and governments will decline to make new loans available and, in the case of banks, continue to write off their current portfolios.

Clearly, the actions of Western lenders in the future are interrelated with Poland's handling of its domestic difficulties, as Eichler indicates in Chapter 22. The granting of new money will be unlikely until the

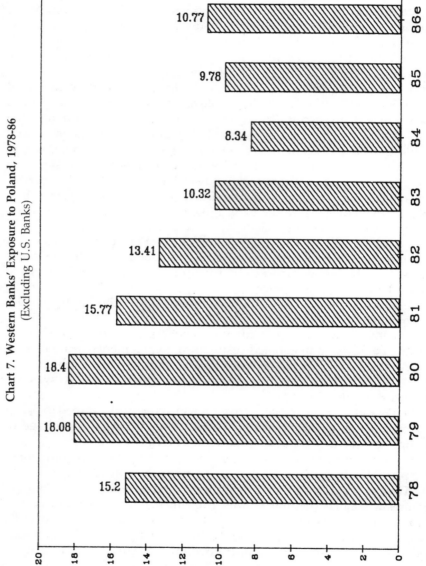

Chart 7. Western Banks' Exposure to Poland, 1978-86
(Excluding U.S. Banks)

Source: BIS—Federal Reserve Bank.

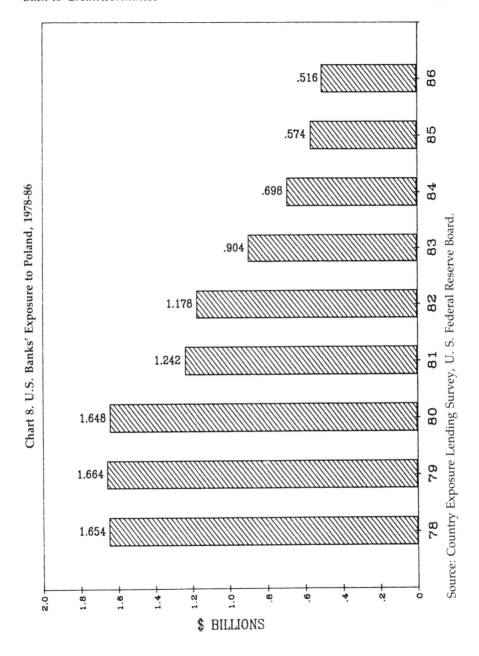

Chart 8. U.S. Banks' Exposure to Poland, 1978-86

Source: Country Exposure Lending Survey, U. S. Federal Reserve Board.

Polish government can assure political stability, which cannot be guaranteed unless the government can fundamentally overhaul the economy and provide the proper environment for long-term dynamism and growth. The economy cannot be structurally reformed without the support of the Polish people and the workforce.

The dilemma facing the Polish government is obvious. Courageous, decisive, and farsighted policies are necessary, without which Poland's aggregate production levels will not recover to those of 1978 until the 1990s. Regaining creditworthiness may take longer. Beyond this need to overcome domestic problems, Jaruzelski must unite the disparate foreign interests into support for his internal policies. European governments and banks seek the establishment of normal commercial and financial relations. American banks, under regulatory pressure, continue to write off Polish loans and are reluctant to increase their exposure. The U.S. government has mixed goals. On the one hand it favors the normalization of diplomatic and commercial relations; on the other, it wants the current Polish government to include the church and the workers in national economic decision making.

The final elements in the complex equation to resolve Poland's economic problems are the IMF and the World Bank. Each of these financial institutions must play a constructive role in developing a growth-oriented approach to the Polish economy. This is contingent on the occurrence of the following four actions within the next two years.

First, the Polish government must become the legitimate representative of the people. In other words, a social compact between the church, labor, and the government must be established. The major domestic constituencies must work collectively in the pursuit of strong economic recovery. Second, the Polish economy must undergo fundamental reform. But any structural change will risk failure if prescribed without the support of the Polish people, a condition which is presently lacking. The third step is for Poland to receive support in its financial and trade policies from Western governments as well as from the IMF and the World Bank. And finally, Poland must be able to refocus the efforts and interests of Western commercial banks on an economic-growth approach instead of the current arrangements under which the only option for the banks is to drain Poland of as much cash as possible.

International Economic Cooperation and the West's Foreign Policy Interest

The first stride in Poland's effort to regain its creditworthiness was taken with its reentry into the IMF and the World Bank in 1986. The efforts of the IMF need to be focused on a quick implementation of a meaningful, short-term program of economic adjustment; developmental support from the World Bank could then follow.

Negotiations with the IMF have already begun. The first step, the Article IV Consultation Report, has already been completed and approved by the IMF Board. This action paves the way for the negotiation of a Standby Program. Although negotiations are likely to be difficult, a Standby Program could be in place by the second half of 1988. The program, geared toward influencing the lending decisions of Western creditors, would seek:

—a significant increase in Poland's current-account surplus (minus interest payments) over the next several years;

—cooperation in devaluing the zloty over the same time period;

—the rationalization of domestic consumer and producer prices (increases in both categories will have to be substantial to better reflect world prices and domestic market considerations);

—the gradual elimination of much of the federal budget subsidies to both consumers and industry;

—guarantees that new credits, from either banks or governments, will receive preferential treatment over the repayment of old obligations.

Admittedly, these conditions are difficult and certainly carry major political and social consequences for Poland. It will not be easy for the authorities to agree to such conditions. However, the IMF has a major bargaining chip in that it controls the single commodity that Poland currently needs the most and is least able to obtain. The Fund can provide substantial credits, ranging to $700 million annually, over a two- to three-year period. If Poland were to agree to the conditions listed, and the economic results were positive, IMF loans could begin attracting new credits from banks and governments. The stage would thus be set for the second level of Polish economic development—long-term growth.

From the point of view of Western lenders, it is crucial to learn the World Bank's intentions in Poland sooner rather than later. As the goal of the IMF is that of economic stabilization and adjustment. The role of the World Bank in today's new policy environment is to create the necessary framework for long-term economic growth, consistent with a sustainable position in the balance of payments. Such a framework would include the following areas of involvement:

—The World Bank can offer assistance in rationalizing Poland's investment policies. Critical major new investments must be based on new product development and future market share opportunities. The World Bank can supply market research and advice.

—Substantial amounts of new equity capital must be attracted. Since Poland's current joint venture laws are inadequate, the World Bank can assist the country in introducing the necessary legal amendments to maximize the possibility of attracting new capital.

—The World Bank can provide assistance on targeting the modernization of specific plants within a given industrial group.

—Since labor will be relocated as a result of new investment and modernization decisions, the World Bank can help design and organize the loan operations necessary to support the new infrastructure, i.e., housing, health care, etc.

—The World Bank can also aid in the development of critically important programs for management and worker retraining.

Under its new leadership, the World Bank must forge a bond between itself and the IMF that will result in the two institutions cooperating more closely than they have in the past. There must be a joint effort in assisting Poland and other debtor countries to open their economies to global market forces in order to establish the foundation for long-term economic growth. To be successful, both institutions must agree that it is in their mutual interests to pool their considerable resources and coordinate their respective goals in debtor countries. Also, member governments must be willing to insist on more integrated efforts between themselves and the IMF and the World Bank in solving individual, sovereign-debtor problems. The most important element of this cooperation is the willingness of member governments to allocate increased funding for joint IMF-World Bank activities that differentiate remedies by country.

The acceptance of differentiation between the debtor countries is the key variable in the problem of Poland's road to economic recovery. Will governments be able to agree, for example, that the problems of Poland are different from those of Mexico? As a result, will they act individually and in concert with the IMF and the World Bank to support new constructive financial programs? More precisely, can the policy of the U.S. government toward Poland be changed?

Although Poland is not as significant a debtor to the U.S. as is Mexico, Poland remains a relatively important country, at least in terms of our East-West interests. Over the past 700 years, Poland has been the fulcrum over which European politics, both East and West, have evolved. It has been this historical fact that has driven American policy during the postwar period until 1981. In fact, the cornerstone of U.S. policy in Eastern Europe has been Poland, which the U.S. has tried to draw away from Moscow. The reality is that the U.S. cannot fully detach Poland from Moscow, although we must continue to encourage Poland to maintain its traditional, vital ties to the West.

Although supportive of U.S. policy toward Poland after 1981, in recent years our allies have begun to disagree with specific American actions. They question why the United States, in the Paris Club forum, has insisted that Poland make certain repayments to Western governments while domestically denying that same country the ability to make other repayments by withholding MFN tariff treatment. In addition, our allies are perplexed to find the motives behind the abstention of the U.S. from the vote to readmit Poland; if the U.S. continued to believe that

Poland did not deserve readmittance to the IMF or the World Bank, a "no" vote should have been cast, since an abstention is the equivalent of a "yes" vote.

Between 1981 and early 1987 when U.S. sanctions were lifted, U.S. policies were designed on the one hand to keep Poland's traditional trading partners (i.e., Western Europe) in agreement on the need for sanctions without insisting that they subrogate their national economic security interests to those of the U.S., and on the other to pressure the regime to reform, to release political prisoners, and to create a workable, representative political coalition.

Many countries in Western Europe insist that their support in Latin America is dependent upon U.S. cooperation on debt problems in Europe. U.S. debt policy, clearly a national security issue, must increasingly merge our interests in Latin America (e.g. Mexico) with those of our European allies close to their turf (e.g. Poland). In other words, if the U.S. expects assistance from Europe with its debt problem in Latin America, our allies expect comparable help from the U.S. on debt problems in Poland. Pressure from the allies probably contributed to the U.S. lifting of economic sanctions on Poland in early 1987.

Concrete Recommendations to Regain Creditworthiness

A serious restructuring effort deals not only with redesigning a country's debt-repayment stream, but also with assisting the debtor in attracting new financial capital needed to fuel economic growth. For Poland, the creditors have thus far been willing only to reorder the sequence of the country's debt-service obligations. The deadlock on the issue of new credits has recently put the banks in the position of having to renegotiate the terms of the rescheduling agreements of 1981 and 1982. The need to amend the original rescheduling agreements (and this will continue to be the case) is an admission that their terms were unrealistic from the outset. Therefore, new alternatives must be explored.

In considering new loans for Poland, banks will insist upon the following conditions:

—An IMF Standby Program must be successfully negotiated.
—Paris Club members must agree to make new loans available.
—New bank loans must be collateralized.
—Banking regulators must be willing to provide regulatory relief on the new loans.
—New loans must be for specific purposes and prove capable of producing net new export revenue streams.

If these conditions are met, banks could be persuaded to arrange new credit packages for Poland over the next two to three years. The key is the ability of Poland to collateralize such loans. At present, Poland would be incapable of providing such security to banks because it is not creditworthy, and its economy is too weak to support substantial new loans, which would only add to the mountain of debt it cannot service. Hence, new loans must be collateralized by creating a new sovereign-debt financial instrument.

New loans to Poland can be collateralized through the use of U.S. Zero-Coupon Treasury Bonds (ZCTs), or their European or Japanese equivalents. Under this scheme, lenders advance monies to the debtor in order to purchase a government security that has a value at maturity equivalent to the original amount of the loan. Below is a chart that illustrates the design of this plan:

Chart 9. Polish Debt Restructuring Via 20-Year, Zero-Coupon Bonds

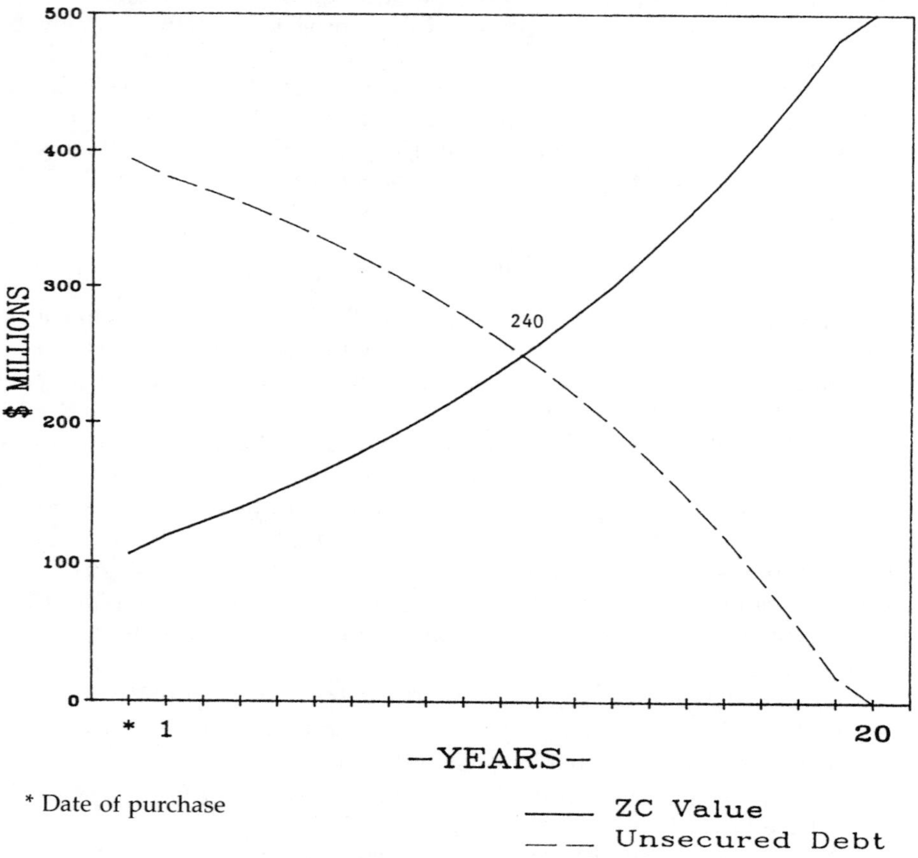

* Date of purchase

———— ZC Value

— — Unsecured Debt

In the example above, the banks would arrange a loan totaling $500 million to Poland. Poland, in turn, would be required to use $106 million of the $500 million to purchase a series of twenty-year maturity ZCTs, having a combined worth of $500 million at maturity, and assign those ZCTs to the banks as collateral for the original loan.

This new instrument would offer the banks and Poland many advantages not provided for in any current sovereign rescheduling agreement. The disadvantages of this approach are clearly overshadowed by the benefits.

Advantages	Disadvantages

Poland:
1. Obtain significant new money more rapidly than would otherwise be possible.
2. Although the debt would increase and interest payments would therefore rise, the relative borrowing costs on the new debt would be lower than the same charges on uncollateralized loans.
3. Source of final repayment is not the debtor. Full principal is repaid at final maturity of the ZCT.

Banks:
1. Collateralized loans are better than unsecured sovereign loans.   1. Polish assets increase.
2. Source of repayment is not Poland.   2. Must rely on Poland for interest payments.
3. Earnings can be realized on what would otherwise be "non-performing" loans.

U.S. Government:
1. Create additional demand for Treasury Bonds.
2. Provide a definition and means for commercial bank involvement in the Baker Plan.

This ZCT approach has undeniable benefits. For the debtor, new funds would be available for a long period at relatively low interest rates. For the lender, the final source of repayment is not the borrower; principal is repaid from the value of the ZCT at maturity. The only risk the banks would have is that of the defaulting by the debtor on interest payments.

The success of this plan depends on whether banking regulators would consider loans backed with ZCTs as collateralized assets, thus allowing them to be carried as "performing" loans on the balance sheets of financial institutions. Banking regulators could have two possible interpretations of the classification of loans backed by ZCTs. First, regulators could regard such loans as collateralized only to the extent that the value of the ZCTs appreciates over time. Thus, as illustrated in Chart 9, the bank loan of $500 million would only be partly collateralized in year one, i.e., for $106 million. In year 10 almost 50 percent of the loan would be collateralized (the exact amount depending on whether interest rates are rising or falling). Alternatively, regulators could take a more liberal approach and decide that, since the ultimate source of repayment is the U.S. Treasury, the new loans could be classified as "performing" from their inception.

The importance of the ZCT scheme is that, as a new financial instrument, it represents the type of creative alternative needed to stimulate economic progress in debtor countries. The banking community must explore such initiatives and be willing to set another precedent in Poland. Since most banks worldwide have written off more than half of their Polish exposure, they should have greater flexibility in participating in longer-term recovery programs.

One reason some banks may resist setting precedents in Poland is the fear that similar actions would be called for in other debt countries of greater consequence: Mexico, Brazil, and Argentina. As long as banks continue to be hesitant about setting precedents, the debt rescheduling process worldwide will continue to be based on uniform approaches, despite the differentiated needs and problems of the debtors.

In the end there remains the most crucial question: What can and will Poland do to help itself? Poland's destiny is in its own hands, but it is not clear whose hands will determine that future. Will it be the Jaruzelski government or the church? Will the sanctioned workers' councils exert a growing influence, as in one of the scenarios mentioned by Holland in Chapter 14? Or is it possible that Solidarity will surface again as a major political force? In answering these questions, the Jaruzelski government has two choices. It can move ahead alone and attempt to apply its will unilaterally on the Polish people, or it can establish a representative political coalition among the major constituencies to work together in support of the government's policies and programs. Since the imposition of martial law, the first approach seems to have been modestly successful. But further improvements are becoming less likely without the authorities convincing the Polish people of the government's ability to return the country to a more productive economic status.

Soviet General Secretary Gorbachev's visit to Warsaw during the summer of 1986 to attend the Polish Party Congress appears to have been a demonstration of Moscow's confidence in General Jaruzelski. Jaruzelski thus may have sufficient room to maneuver to take the steps necessary to deal with his country's economic malaise. However, if Jaruzelski seeks reform without enfranchising the major domestic constituencies, he risks failure. Meaningful reform will require the support of the Polish people, since further substantial, though temporary, cuts in the standard of living would be inevitable. There would also be the risk of introducing unemployment into a society that guarantees economic security. On the other hand, if he finds a way of providing meaningful representation for the workers and the church on matters of economic importance, Jaruzelski stands to become a national and international hero.

In conclusion, the road to restoration of Poland's creditworthiness is a long and difficult one. Creative solutions, policy adaptations, and outright changes on the part of the institutions and governments, both East and West, are necessary for success. The task is not impossible and the time is ripe for bold new initiatives.

Note

The views expressed are the author's and not necessarily those of Chemical Bank. The author wishes to thank Kevin John Windorf for editorial and research assistance and Denise C. Gonzalez for secretarial services.

25

Poland's Debt Situation in Global Perspective

Paul Marer

The purpose of this chapter is to place Poland's debt problems, and the solutions being advocated by experts and policymakers in that country and in the West, into an international perspective. After all, scores of debtor countries throughout the world are in difficult situations that have many apparent similarities with those faced by Poland. This essay attempts to identify the common and the distinctive causes of Poland's debt problem as well as the possible solutions.

Overview of the Debt Situation

By 1987, the combined gross external debts of 130 developing and East European countries exceeded $1 trillion. Twenty-one countries, each with a minimum of $10 billion in gross external debt, accounted for two-thirds of this total. They included seven countries in Latin America (Brazil, Mexico, Argentina, Venezuela, Chile, Peru, and Colombia), six in Asia (South Korea, Indonesia, the Philippines, India, Thailand, and Taiwan), five in Eastern Europe (Poland, the USSR, Yugoslavia, Hungary, and the GDR), and three in Africa (Algeria, Morocco, and Nigeria).

Approximately two-thirds of the total debt is owed to commercial banks, a figure that shows how much the debtors and the commercial banks depend on each other. The average share of U.S. banks in total bank claims is about 25 percent, higher in loans to Latin America and lower in Eastern Europe.

The global debt crisis dates from the early 1980s, when there was an abrupt change in the perceived capacity of certain large borrowers to service their debts. It began in 1981 when Poland was forced to reschedule and hit its stride in 1982 when Mexico and other nations followed suit.

Causes of the Debt Crisis

Although the causes of the debt crisis vary considerably from country to country, they can be attributed to combinations of the following internal and external factors:

Internal Causes

(1) *Excessive borrowing* during the 1970s and early 1980s. During the late 1970s, loans could be obtained at negative real interest rates—that is, the interest rate paid on dollar loans was less than the inflation rate in the U.S. This encouraged excessive borrowing, even though it was not reasonable to expect that the real interest rate would remain negative indefinitely. Much of the borrowing was at floating rather than fixed rates, which caused problems later.

(2) *Poor choice of investment projects*, especially in those countries where the state, rather than private firms, made the decisions, often on political grounds. There were similarities in this regard between Poland and many of the other heavily-indebted countries.

In Poland especially, an "expansion drive" characterized behavior at all levels: a desire to produce as much as possible without worrying about the costs, the quality, or the saleability of the output. At the macro level, the expansion drive stemmed from a commitment of the authorities to rapid growth and industrialization; at the micro level, it was a result of the "soft budget constraint" and the pressure and incentives that stressed the growth of output. The result was a perpetual sellers' market, a desire to increase capacity, and an insatiable demand for inputs, including imports.

(3) *Lax macroeconomic control*. Internal policies produced a rapid expansion of demand, outpacing the economy's supply potential. This caused a fast growth in imports, a diversion of resources to production for the domestic market, and an intensification of inflationary pressures which showed up openly, in rapidly rising prices (as in Latin America), or covertly, in shortages and black markets (as in Poland). Granting wage increases greatly in excess of improvements in productivity was another feature of lax macroeconomic control that Poland shared with certain other debtor countries.[1]

(4) *Misguided trade policies*. Many debtor countries, especially those in Latin America, have pursued extreme versions of import-substitution industrialization, whereas many East Asian countries favored export-

promotion. In Latin America, the initial impetus for extreme import substitution—that is, a high degree of across-the-board protection of industry—came from faulty analysis that underestimated the costs of such a policy and overestimated the obstacles to exports. The result was building high-cost industries that have taken a great deal of imports to establish and to operate, while their output could not compete well on international markets, contributing to severe tensions in the balance of payments.

The import-substitution policies of many Latin American countries have much in common with the foreign-trade strategies pursued by Poland and by the other CPEs, whose policies can also be characterized as highly protectionist. The evidence for this is twofold. First, the authorities do not import anything if demand can be satisfied from domestic or CMEA sources. As a consequence, no domestic producer faces import competition or is forced out of business because imports are cheaper or better. Second, the authorities are continually attempting to replace convertible-currency imports with domestic production or purchases from the CMEA. In Poland, as in the other CPEs, the instruments of protection are not tariffs or quantitative restrictions but the central control over all foreign transactions. The results, however, are similar to the outcomes in Latin America and elsewhere: growing difficulties of competing on the world market with manufactures.

Although Poland's convertible-currency imports had increased rapidly during the 1970s, that does not contradict the statement that its trade policies were protectionist. The main purpose of imports was not to alter production patterns on the basis of the country's comparative advantage or to force domestic producers to become efficient, but to alleviate the many domestic shortages that constrained the planners in achieving their objectives.

(5) *Overvalued exchange rates*, that represented an added incentive to import and disincentive to export. Such exchange rates, combined with too much government intervention and economic and political instability, created incentives for capital flight, worsening the debt-servicing problems of many countries, particularly in Latin America.

If, during the 1970s and early 1980s, Poland had a market economy, its prevailing exchange rate would have been considered overvalued. But it is not clear that in Poland's "modified" CPE system, exchange rates could be relied upon to improve the balance of trade. In any event, Poland and the other CPEs had no need to be concerned with capital flight, which they prevented by full direct controls on all external trade and finance.

External Causes

(1) *Excessive lending by commercial banks and governments* went hand-in-hand with the excessive borrowing by the debtors. Banks were eager

to place surplus funds or accommodate with financing their corporate customers who found new export markets in the developing and the East European countries. Governments were eager to lend to promote exports. All too often, lending decisions by both were imprudent, made without carefully evaluating the borrower's creditworthiness.

(2) *Deteriorating terms of trade* is one of the factors said to be responsible for the payment difficulties of many countries. To be sure, the success or failure of debt-management does not seem to be tied directly to the size of the terms-of-trade shocks. Many nations suffering economic failure, such as Mexico and Venezuela, had improved terms of trade during 1975-83, while many of the successful Asian economies suffered severe declines. South Korea had experienced external shocks that were much larger than those of any of the Latin American countries, while Thailand's shock was virtually as big as the largest in Latin America, that of Chile.[2] Nevertheless, the dramatic declines in energy, raw material, and agricultural prices during the first half of the 1980s have indeed hurt many developing and East European countries, including Poland.

(3) *High interest rates.* The negative real rates of interest of the 1970s changed suddenly into high positive ones during 1981-82, owing partly to a combination of expansionary fiscal and restrictive monetary policies in the U.S., and partly to the sudden realization by lenders of the risks inherent in loaning large sums to the developing countries and to the CPEs.

(4) *Sluggish growth, trade imbalances, and protectionism in the industrial countries.* Since the first oil crisis of 1973-74, economic growth in the industrial countries has remained below potential, which has had an adverse impact on their demand for the products of the debtor countries. Through 1987, the U.S. was the only industrial country running substantial trade deficits, absorbing the surpluses of Japan, Germany, and those other countries that could remain or become competitive on its markets. But the continued large imbalances in the current accounts of Japan, Germany, and the U.S. do not augur well for the debtors because they can lead to even lower growth in the industrial nations, further exchange rate instability, a higher real rate of interest, and new protectionist measures in the U.S.

Managing the Global Debt Problem

The international debt crisis concerns two related problems. One is the threat of massive financial loss facing creditor banks and the resulting instability in the international financial system. The other is the development crisis faced by the debtor countries attempting to cope with the burdens of servicing their debt. I discuss these two aspects briefly.

Global Debt and the International Financial System

It is not entirely clear whether the probability of domino-like defaults by the major debtors has increased or decreased since the early 1980s; there is evidence to support either contention. One sign that tension is growing is that the external payment arrears of members of the IMF have been increasing, reaching about SDR 40 billion by the end of 1986. A total of 57 countries, equivalent to about two-fifth of the Fund's developing country membership, had arrears outstanding at the end of 1986. The number has been rising steadily since 1976, as has the number of countries and the debt amounts being rescheduled.[3]

On the other side of the coin, there have been significant accomplishments also. The system has not collapsed, governments have cut back on excessive borrowing, credit exposure has been maintained with reschedulings to defer debt repayment, and some new credits have been made available (not always voluntarily, to be sure). Many countries continue to have market access, and some debtors have improved their external payment positions.

Further on the plus side is the strengthening of the industrial countries' commercial banking systems. For example, while in 1982 the LDC exposures of U.S. banks as a percentage of their primary capital was at a peak of about 200 percent, by 1986 this ratio declined to about 100 percent, largely as a result of increased capitalization. In 1987, a growing number of U.S. banks began to set aside large loan-loss reserves, following the examples of their competitors in other countries. This has lessened the concern that a default by several major debtors would threaten the stability of the world financial system.

The significance of setting aside loss reserves does not lie in acknowledging explicitly that the value of loans to certain LDCs and CPEs is considerably less than their face value. This fact has already been recognized by the market, where the loans to debtor countries sell at large discounts (see below), and where the stock prices of big American banks have been depressed in direct relation to their loan exposures to countries with debt-servicing difficulties. The real significance of setting aside large loan-loss reserves is that it has made it possible for banks to divest billions of dollars of such loans by selling them to other investors on the secondary market or by swapping them for equity in the debtor countries. This represents the "marketization" of an important aspect of the global debt problem. As long as banks maintained the accounting fiction that the market value of their foreign loans was equal to their face value, they could not undertake such transactions.

If a debtor country pays the interest on its outstanding obligations, buying the loans at a discount can yield a good rate of return for the investor, plus or minus capital appreciation or depreciation (reflecting the debtor's changing policies and prospects). The market for such dis-

counted loans is underpropped by the borrowers themselves: the greater
the discount, the greater the debtor's incentive to use foreign currency
to buy back its own debt and thus, in effect, to repay cheaply. There is
no reason why Poland, whose debts are now selling at less than 50
percent of face value, could not do this.

In mid-1986, the market prices for sovereign debt—cents paid per
dollar of debt—were as follows:[4]

Romania	86-89	S. Africa	60-65
Columbia	86-88	Argentina	59-60
Ivory Coast	76-78	Mexico	58-59
Yugoslavia	74-77	Ecuador	53-56
Venezuela	72-74	Egypt	49-51
Philippines	70-71	POLAND	43-45
Chile	67-69	Nigeria	37-39
Morocco	66-68	Zaire	24-26
Panama	66-68	Peru	13-15
Brazil	64-65	Bolivia	6-8

Debt-claims may be bartered or sold by commercial banks, as each
institution adjusts its loan portfolio to suit its judgment and income-tax
circumstances. Or a foreign investor may purchase a debt paper at a
discount and present it to the debtor country for exchange into national
currency at nominal value. The local-currency equivalent may be used
to repay domestic debt or to finance an equity participation or an investment project. Several countries have established debt-to-equity
schemes; practical details vary by country. For example, debt-equity
swaps may be limited to certain debt papers and certain classes of creditors, and the debtor's central bank may charge a discount when ex-
changing foreign for national currency.[5]

Chile was the first country to establish, in May 1985, a wide-ranging
debt-equity conversion scheme. Its regulations provide for repatriation
of capital after ten years and for the repatriation of returns and dividends
after four years, compared with three years for both in the case of nor-
mally-financed investment. In two years, more than $500 million in debt
has been converted.

Mexico followed suit in April 1986. Its authorities charge a discount
between 0 and 25 percent when changing foreign into national currency,
as a way of channeling foreign investment into particular sectors. Several
other countries have established or are contemplating setting up debt-
to-equity schemes. One purpose is to attract foreign investment that

contributes to the country's export potential. If nationals are allowed to conduct swaps, a repatriation of flight capital may be induced.

In 1986 the main debtor countries, principally Chile, Brazil, and Mexico, swapped some $2 billion of debt into equity. To be sure, not all of this represents an improvement in the debtor's external position because some of the inflow of foreign direct investment would have occurred anyway, and possibly on more favorable terms.

Debt-to-equity conversion could have potential relevance for Poland, assuming that the country will further liberalize its joint-venture laws, improve greatly the efficiency of its domestic economic system (since few joint ventures remain insulated from the rest of the economy), and pursue with much greater vigor, and with the help of foreign investors, policies of export-promotion.

Development Prospects of the Debtor Countries

The other aspect of the debt problem is the development crisis facing many of the heavily-indebted developing and East European countries. Since the early 1980s, the bulk of their adjustment has been undertaken by lowering demand, which has meant, in practice, reducing imports and investment. To be sure, an important reason why the adjustment has mainly taken this form is the difficulties that many countries have faced in increasing their exports, which in turn can be traced, in large measure, to their poor economic policies and systems. But be that as it may, a large number of countries are now facing severe economic difficulties. The volume of imports of the heavily indebted middle-income countries in 1986 was approximately one-third below their 1981 level, about the same as in Poland (Chart 2). In many countries, GDP has stagnated since 1980, and per-capita incomes have declined substantially. The reduction in demand has pushed the collective trade balances of the debtor countries into a large surplus, which has brought their current accounts into approximate balance. (Poland has reduced its current-account deficit, but has not been able to bring it fully to balance, as shown in Chart 2.) Yet at the end of 1986, for many nations, the main debt indicators were close to their previous peaks. Despite painful adjustment efforts, many countries seem to be as far as they ever were from reconciling growth and creditworthiness.

In many developing countries, debt-servicing obligations absorb 5 to 7 percent of GNP; the percentage in Poland—excluding intra-CMEA trade, on which we don't have reliable information—is considerably lower. These debtors especially are desperate for additional credits because their export earnings are not large enough to finance both the full interest payment on the debts outstanding and the volume of imports needed for satisfactory growth.

A consensus is now emerging in the debtor and creditor countries that, after years of decline and stagnation, the debtor nations must have rising levels of real incomes, as much for political as for economic reasons. In the absence of a satisfactory rate of economic growth, the political pressures for unilateral debt repudiation may well become uncontainable. However, sustainable growth cannot be assured simply by the provision of new credits. Growth depends first and foremost on the internal economic policies and improved efficiency of the economic system. This is why industrial restructuring and comprehensive economic reforms must be implemented, in the case of Poland especially, but in many other countries also. This is an indispensable precondition for any country's meaningful participation in managing its portion of the international debt problem. Regardless of what happens on the global scene, only if a country pursues policies that lead clearly to the maintenance or re-establishment of its creditworthiness can it make an effective case for receiving new credits. There must be credible guarantees that the new loans will be invested productively, and that even with an increase in debt, it will decline as a percentage of the debtor's GNP and exports. Who is to provide, new financing, how much, and on what terms, are critically important and controversial issues.

Utopian Versus Realistic Approaches

Calls by certain academics and politicians for explicit forgiveness of debts represent utopian approaches to the debt problem. Debt-servicing is an intensely political process. Outright forgiveness of the debt for any one country would generate irresistible pressures for equal treatment of the other countries. Forgiving the weak would induce repudiation by the strong; if that became widespread, it could still easily undermine the global financial system. Across-the-board debt forgiveness or default would send the wrong signals: it would encourage debtors to seek ways to avoid their obligations. Ultimately, that would hurt the debtor countries by eliminating any prospects that they might resume borrowing from commercial banks, on a regular basis, at any time soon. To be sure, there are countries—in Africa especially—that are likely to be unable to service their debts fully for a long time, so that pressuring them to do so would not be realistic. But such countries account for only a small fraction of the total. Continued good performance by the "reasonably" creditworthy would be enough to assure the financial health of the creditors as a group, which is in the interest of the debtor nations also.

Another utopian suggestion is that the industrial countries arrange something like a Marshall Plan for the heavily-indebted countries. Whatever merit such a proposal may have on moral grounds, politically it is not a feasible one. There is little chance that the U.S. Congress would appropriate large funds for such a purpose, not only because the U.S. itself faces a huge and seemingly intractable budget deficit and a rapidly-growing foreign-debt problem, but also because the Congress would not do anything that might be construed as a bailout of the large commercial banks—institutions that are not exactly popular with the electorate.

It is a fact of life also that for some time, the global economic power of the U.S. has been declining. Thus, not only America's political will but the resources at its disposal have also been shrinking. And the two countries that in recent years have gained so much over the U.S.—Japan and Germany—are not in a good position politically to translate their enormous economic and financial strengths into taking over the global leadership role of the U.S.

Thus, considering that two-thirds of the global debt of the developing and East European countries are held by commercial banks, that these institutions will remain the dominant players in global finance, and that the governments of "rich" countries are not in a position to provide massive new finance, there is no alternative but to continue to hammer out agreements between the commercial banks and the debtor countries. There is no substitute for a case-by-case approach, including reschedulings, as needed. Developing countries need new credits to prime their economies; large commercial banks depend on debt servicing to remain solvent. Rescheduling is a last-resort device that can accommodate the interests of both sides. A debtor country prefers to reschedule rather than to repudiate because it does not wish to have its assets seized and its trade impeded. Lenders prefer rescheduling to default because they retain some probability (given future favorable developments) of recovering some or all of their assets.

Notes

1. Laura D. Tyson, "The Debt Crisis and Adjustment Responses in Eastern Europe: A Comparative Perspective." *International Organization*, Vol. 40, no. 2 (Spring 1986).

2. Jeffrey D. Sachs, "External Debt and Macroeconomic Performance in Latin America and East Asia" and "Comments" by John Williamson. *Brookings Papers on Economic Activity*, February 1985.

3. *IMF Survey*, July 27, 1987, pp. 225, 231.

4. Shearson Lehman Brothers, *International Newsletter*, July 1986.

5. Wolfgang Spieles, "Debt-Equity Swaps and the Heavily Indebted Countries," *Intereconomics*, May/June 1987.

PART V.

POLAND IN THE IMF AND THE WORLD BANK

26

History of Poland's Relations with the IMF and the World Bank

Piotr Mroczkowski

Poland was among the 44 countries that participated in the United Nations' Monetary and Financial Conference held at Bretton Woods in July 1944. During this conference, the International Monetary Fund (IMF) and the International Bank for Reconstruction and Development (World Bank) were founded. On December 27, 1945 the Polish government approved the decision to join both organizations.

The motives that led Poland to sign the Bretton Woods agreement were clearly stated by Leon Grosfeld, the head of the Polish delegation to the Conference: "We could never hope to overcome successfully the mounting tide of difficulties if we could not look forward to the help of the highly developed industrial countries of the world. . . . The adoption at the Bretton Woods Conference of the projects of the International Monetary Fund and the International Bank for Reconstruction and Development constitutes a concrete promise of that cooperation, which nations—ruined by war—so greatly need and so confidently expect."[1] Poland thus joined both organizations, mainly to obtain credits to reconstruct its economy. It also explains why, during the short period of membership in the IMF and the World Bank, Poland's activities concentrated generally on relations with the latter organization.

At the beginning, Poland's relationship with both organizations was good. As a member of the World Bank, it was supposed to pay 2 percent of its total capital subscription in gold or U.S. dollars. But under Article II, Section 8 (a) of the Articles of Agreement, Poland, as a country that had suffered from German occupation, was excused from paying 25 percent of the obligation mentioned above.[2] Poland was also allowed to delay the establishment of the par value of its currency. But soon, relations started to deteriorate steadily, due mainly to political factors. Most important was the fact that Poland, having been liberated by the Russian army, became a member of the Soviet alliance system.

Although Article IV, Section 10 of the World Bank's charter stresses that the organization should neither be influenced in its decisions by the political character of a member country nor interfere in its political affairs,[3] the World Bank's policy in the late 1940s embodied significant political factors. "The Bank," as the third Annual Report admitted, "is fully cognizant of the injunction in its Articles of Agreement that its decisions shall be based only on economic considerations. Political tensions and uncertainties in or among its member countries, however, have a direct effect on economic and financial conditions in those countries and upon their credit position."[4] Such a broad definition enabled the World Bank to include in its decisions political criteria; this actually happened during the first years of the organization in the case of Poland and Czechoslovakia.

Generally, it can be argued that political considerations were and still are playing a decisive role in the entire history of Poland's interactions with the IMF and the World Bank. These considerations were dominant in the Bank's handling of Poland's first request for reconstruction assistance, the country's withdrawal from both organizations in 1950, and its second application for membership in 1981.

In the autumn of 1946, Poland requested a general reconstruction loan of $600 million which, in that period, was far beyond the capabilities of the World Bank's resources. However, officials of the Bank thought that a smaller loan of approximately $125 million, for the reconstruction of the Polish coal industry, would be justifiable and would make good economic sense, not only for Poland's economy but for Western Europe as well. Therefore, the Polish government submitted a revised request for a loan for its coal industry of $128.5 million.[5]

During negotiations, officials of the World Bank were somewhat sympathetic to the Polish request, although they "naturally wondered whether Poland's relations with Russia were such that Poland might find itself unable to devote the necessary resources to repaying a loan from an institution toward which the USSR was hostile."[6] This probably explains the fact that the Bank's fact-finding mission to Poland in June 1947, which generally praised Polish efforts to rebuild its economy, finally recommended only a $45 million short-term loan, with a special provision that part of the coal be exported to Western Europe.[7] The Polish government was clearly disappointed with such a large reduction, and negotiations continued until mid-1948, when the entire procedure was halted.

Private financial investors and organizations had, to some degree, an influence on the Bank's attitude toward the Polish loan. The American Undersecretary of State for Economic Affairs, during his meeting with the Polish minister of trade and industry, admitted that because of the deterioration in Polish-American relations, "the Bank would have great difficulty in selling debentures to the American public for the purpose of obtaining funds with which to make loans to Poland."[8]

The loan for the Polish coal industry fell apart mainly because the U.S. government was not willing to support it. In mid-1948, after Poland's refusal to participate in the Marshall Plan, the U.S. government vetoed the Polish request.[9] J. McCloy, president of the World Bank, was informed that the U.S. government would not grant export licenses for the mining equipment and that the U.S. executive director would vote against the loan. In this situation, the Polish authorities decided that their application would not be presented to the board, and the negotiations were suspended.[10]

From that point on, Poland's relations with the IMF and the World Bank rapidly deteriorated. Polish representatives maintained that the decisions of both organizations were politically motivated and that they were partners in economic warfare against Eastern Europe.[11] On March 14, 1950, Poland voluntarily withdrew from the IMF and the World Bank. The official letter of withdrawal "recited various purposes of the Fund and alleged that the Fund had failed to fulfill its duties, had been a submissive instrument of the policy of the government of the United States, and had cooperated lately with the United States in forcing a number of members to devalue their currencies."[12] Officials of the IMF and the World Bank rejected the Polish accusations. In their opinion, Poland's withdrawal was "tied in with the Kremlin's efforts to control the satellite countries more closely."[13]

The Polish case was a significant example in the history of the IMF and the World Bank, showing that in an intensely political world, it was very difficult to make any decision only on the basis of economic criteria. Successful cooperation between Poland and both organizations required either a major shift in Polish internal and foreign policy or a strict observance by World Bank officials of Article II, Section 8(a). In the late 1940s and early 1950s both alternatives were highly improbable.

In the late 1950s, after significant internal political changes, Poland made informal efforts to renew its membership in the IMF and the World Bank. Unfortunately, according to Polish sources, these efforts failed because of the negative attitude of the U.S. government.[14] Afterwards, relations between Poland and the two organizations were frozen for more than twenty years, although at that time the idea of Poland's membership was still considered (particularly in Poland). In 1976 a group of economic advisers to the first secretary of the Polish United Workers Party suggested the renewal of Poland's membership. At that time, the Polish authorities were hesitant, fearing that the IMF would demand structural changes in the economic system.[15]

The decision to rejoin both organizations was finally made in 1981, after the consecutive economic and political crises in Poland. The rationale for this decision seemed obvious. As Michał Dobroczyński stated in *Życie Warszawy*, membership in the IMF and the World Bank would:

—enable Poland to obtain new credits on favorable conditions which would increase production and exports;

—rationalize the utilization of foreign credits, due to IMF control, thus improving the efficiency of the Polish economy and the country's standing on the international financial markets; and

—stimulate the process of economic reform.[16]

Poland's application was submitted in November 1981. One month later, the procedure was frozen because of informal signals from the U.S. and from the West European Executive Director of the IMF. Because of the imposition of martial law, a positive consensus regarding the Polish application could not be reached.[17] After three years, during which no formal action was taken, the Reagan Administration, in October 1984, dropped its objections to the IMF's and the World Bank's processing of Poland's membership application. The Polish application could again proceed. In June 1986 Poland was admitted, with the U.S. abstaining, reportedly so that the administration would not antagonize certain key members of Congress who opposed membership for Poland.

Notes

1. *Proceeding and Documents of the United Nations Monetary and Financial Conference*, (Washington, D.C., 1948), Vol. II, p. 1233.

2. International Bank for Reconstruction and Development, Articles of Agreement, Article II, Section 8(a).

3. Articles of Agreement, Article IV, Section 10.

4. International Bank for Reconstruction and Development, "Third Annual Report 1947-48," p. 14.

5. E. S. Mason and R. E. Asher "The World Bank Since Bretton Woods," (Washington, D.C., 1973), p. 170.

6. Ibid.

7. Foreign Relations of the United States 1948 (Washington, 1974), Vol. IV, p. 515.

8. Foreign Relations of the United States 1947 (Washington, 1972), Vol. IV, p. 437.

9. In the early years of the IMF and the World Bank it was a custom that every loan application had to get a priori approval from the IMF Executive

Director for the United States. See: J. K. Horsefield and M. G. de Vries, "The International Monetary Fund, 1945-65" (Washington, D.C., 1969), Vol. II, p. 11.

10. Mason and Asher, p. 171.

11. *New York Times*, March 15, 1950.

12. J. Gold, "Membership and Nonmembership in the International Monetary Fund," (Washington, D.C., 1974), p. 342.

13. *New York Times*, March 15, 1950.

14. J. Kranz, "Socialist Nations in the IMF and World Bank," (in Polish) *Sprawy Międzynarodowe* no. 11 (1984), p. 32.

15. Ibid. p. 40.

16. M. Dobroczyński "Relaxation, the Crisis, and the Monetary Fund," (in Polish) *Życie Warszawy*, November 13, 1981.

17. In the IMF decision-making process, formal voting does not play such an important role as in other international organizations. In practice, most of the decisions of the Board of Governors and the Executive Board are taken by consensus. If there is no chance to reach it, the motion is dropped, as in Poland's case. See: H. Aufricht "International Monetary Fund. Legal Bases, Structures, Functions" (London, 1964), p. 43; "The International Monetary Fund. Its Evolution, Organization, and Activities," Pamphlet Series no. 37, International Monetary Fund (Washington, D.C., 1984), p. 19.

27

Romania and Hungary in the IMF and Implications for Poland

Petra Pissulla

The International Monetary Fund (IMF) was founded in 1944 to promote international cooperation in exchange-rate policy, thereby supporting a balanced growth of international trade. Its aim was, and remains, to prevent its members from pursuing restrictive trade policies in case of balance-of-payments disequilibria and to reduce the extent and duration of such imbalances. In principle, membership of the IMF is open to all countries, regardless of their economic and political system. The only stipulation is that the country accept and support the Fund's general objectives and meet the obligations of membership defined under Article VIII of the IMF Agreements.

Membership of Socialist Countries: An Overview

Since the IMF's objectives can be reached only on a worldwide basis, the Fund had always been interested in the cooperation of all countries, including the socialist ones. However, the relationship between the IMF and the countries of the Eastern bloc began with much hesitation after one founding member had left the organization (Poland) and another had been expelled (Czechoslovakia), both in the early 1950s. The Soviet Union never signed the agreements, although the country had played an active part in the formative negotiations in Bretton Woods.[1]

259

Romania, the first European CMEA country in the IMF joined only in December 1972. It took another ten years before a second CMEA country became a member. In 1981 both Hungary and Poland applied. While Hungary became a member in May 1982, Poland's application was not accepted until June 1986. Although until recently the prospects for membership of the other European CMEA countries seemed poor, this negative assessment should be modified, particularly with regard to the Soviet Union, which has been putting out feelers about the IMF, the World Bank, and the GATT. To be sure, it is still difficult to imagine that the U.S. will drop its objections to Soviet membership in the IMF, or that the Soviet Union will change its negative view of the Fund and its policy.[2] Prospects for membership in the Fund seem to be even less promising today for the smaller European CMEA countries (the GDR, Czechoslovakia, and Bulgaria) than for the Soviet Union, although they are supposed to have a greater interest in institutionalized international cooperation. These countries still seem to adhere to their joint declaration given at UNCTAD IV, in Nairobi (1976), in which they expressively shared the negative Soviet view of the Fund and its policy.

This chapter focuses on the experiences of two CMEA countries, Romania and Hungary, as examples of two different kinds of relationships with the Fund. Whereas Hungary's cooperation with the Fund seems to work in a mutually satisfactory way, cooperation between Romania and the Fund seems to have failed in recent years. Implications of their experience for Poland will be discussed.

IMF Credit Policies

Transactions by which a member country can make use of the IMF's resources consist of the sale of its own currency to and the purchase of foreign currencies from the Fund. National currencies must be repurchased within a set time limit against SDRs or in freely usable currencies designated by the IMF. A country qualifies for Fund resources if it can prove balance-of-payments need. The amount of resources that can be drawn is related to the country's quota, determined when it joins the IMF.

Apart from limited "unconditional" or "slightly conditional" credit drawings, the IMF provides assistance only in conjunction with a strict stabilization program, which is intended to remedy the borrower's balance-of-payments problem. As a rule, credits are extended under standby arrangements and are paid in installments. The borrower is able to draw down the credit only if the performance criteria agreed to with the IMF are observed.

In connection with the growing debt problems of many developing countries in the 1980s, IMF conditionality has been criticized as too stern and rigid. It is true that many of the affected countries had successfully improved their balance-of-payments positions through an enforced policy of austerity, but they often achieved this improvement only by a dramatic reduction of imports, at high costs, and to the detriment of other objectives. The adjustment measures typically advocated by the Fund are said to impede growth and to impair incomes.[3] Since stabilization programs contain various measures with various distributional effects, such as currency devaluations, increases in farm and other producer prices, reductions of subsidies, wage restrictions, credit restrictions, etc., the burden of the adjustment falls more on some segment of the population than on others.[4]

Have the adverse circumstances allegedly created by IMF conditionality occurred also in the cases of Romania and Hungary, both of which had concluded standby agreements with the Fund? And what do their experiences imply for Poland? In trying to answer these questions, the distinct differences between Romania and Hungary must be taken into account, namely, those involving their economic system, their economic situation at the start of the stabilization programs, and their ways of implementing the programs.

Romania

When Romania joined the IMF in 1972, the presumed reason for its entry was the intention to continue along the course toward the greatest possible economic and political independence from the Soviet Union. The country was under no pressure then to join on balance-of-payments grounds, as was Poland and, to some extent, Hungary, when they joined. However, the Romanian payments position has subsequently deteriorated dramatically. In 1981, on the verge of insolvency, Romania signed a three-year stabilization agreement with the Fund.

Romania did not unexpectedly or suddenly find itself in a position of imminent insolvency. Rather, a concurrence of factors led the country into severe debt-service difficulties:

—Its strategy of economic development had caused serious disequilibria in the investment) and consumer-goods markets, so that a worsening domestic supply situation met a permanent domestic excess demand.

—Imports from the West, which had risen consistently faster than exports during the 1970s, had led to an excessive rise in Western debts; between 1978 and 1981 the country's indebtedness doubled to $10 billion.

—Romania's foreign exchange reserves (excluding gold) dropped to $223 million by 1981, equaling the cost of less than two weeks of imports.

—At the end of the 1970s, Romania started to finance trade deficits to an increasing extent by short-term credits; from 1980 onward the

maturing of these short-term credits coincided with increasing set-
tlements of earlier medium- and long-term loans, so that the annual
repayment burden rose appreciably. In 1981 Romania had incurred
arrears of $1.1 billion.

—In this situation Romania became particularly vulnerable to adverse external developments. Rapidly rising interest rates, terms of
trade deterioration due to oil price development, and a continuing
weakness of world demand sharpened Romania's problems.

—The crisis finally broke when Western banks, responding to the
Polish shock, refused to grant new credits or to extend those falling
due.

Although Romania's difficulties were in evidence by the end of the
1970s, the IMF was unable to prevent the country's slide into default,
despite compulsory annual consultations, in the course of which the
Fund analyzed the country's debt situation (volume and growth rate of
debt-servicing obligations, maturity structure, etc.). If situations arise
that signal future payment problems, the Fund can issue warnings and
discuss measures that may help solve the problems. It is not known to
what extent this happened in Romania's case and whether such warnings were, perhaps, disregarded. In any event, the IMF's possibilities
of effectively influencing a country's economic policy are too limited
outside of standby arrangements. Romania is neither worst and not the
only example of a country having run deeply into a debt crisis. In the
Hungarian case, this is not a relevant problem because the country
already faced payment difficulties when it joined the Fund.

For both countries, however, membership in the IMF was of valuable assistance in their acute crises. For Romania, access to Fund resources was the only available credit source in 1981-82. Despite Fund
membership, which in other cases had contributed to maintaining credit
flows from commercial banks, neither private banks nor governments
had been willing to extend new credits or further guarantees on export
credits. Appraisals of Romania's economic situation and economic policy
by Western banks and trade partners was at that time pessimistic; prospects for a quick recovery seemed poor, partly as the result of the unwillingness of the Romanian government to cooperate with its Western
creditors. The 1980 current-account deficit in convertible currencies of
$2.4 billion was by far the worst in the country's history. Despite standby
credits from the IMF of SDR 1.1 billion (spread over three years), Romania had to reschedule credits due in 1982 and 1983.

Romania's three-year standby agreement came into force in June
1981. The amount, equivalent to 300 percent of the Romanian quota of
SDR 367.5 million,[5] was planned to be paid in three installments by June
1984. However, the agreement was cancelled in January 1984 because
Romania refused to observe some of the IMF's performance criteria,
such as the further increase of the domestic price of certain commodities,

the devaluation of the leu, and the abolishment of certain subsidies to enterprises. Therefore, the actual credit amount drawn was only SDR 817 million. Together with drawings under other IMF facilities, Romania faced its highest use of Fund credits at the end of the first quarter of 1984 (SDR 1.068 million). Since then, no new drawings have been made. By October 1986, Romania diminished by "repurchases" the outstanding amount to SDR 640.7 million which equaled 122 percent of its new quota of SDR 523.4 million.

The standby credit had been accompanied by an adjustment program aimed at the elimination of the external imbalance caused by excess domestic demand and structural disproportions on the domestic market. Apart from quantitative criteria, such as maximum limits for its current-account deficit in convertible currencies and minimum limits for international reserves, the program contained demand restrictions as well as structural adjustment measures that affect the supply side (i.e., price and exchange rate adjustments) in order to balance demand and supply at home and to secure a sustainable external equilibrium. The measures restricting demand sought to reduce the annual growth of investment and public and private consumption. Exports were to be stimulated by the depreciation of the exchange rate. Hard-currency imports were to rise only slowly. All of these measures were intended to bring about a positive effect on Romania's balance of payments.

Indirect instruments, i.e., prices, interest rates, and the exchange rate, were to play an important role in the adjustment process. However, there are serious doubts that these standard instruments of IMF conditionality have more than a very limited impact on the balance of payments of such traditional CPEs as Romania.[6] In fact:

—The impact on demand in 1981-83 was not achieved by higher interest rates but by a direct curtailment of the investment funds distributed to enterprises and by far-reaching restrictions on new investment projects.

—Although the leadership tried to adjust domestic prices to rising world market prices, especially of raw materials and energy, the savings were not generated by price increases but by rationing and cut-offs.

—Demand restrictions in the consumer-goods markets were also achieved by the rationing of food and certain other commodities rather than through the financial reduction of real incomes.

—Romania turned the convertible-currency current-account deficit of $2.4 billion in 1980 into a surplus of $1.5 billion in 1984. However, this spectacular performance was not achieved by the stimulation of exports through exchange rate depreciation but by strict import curtailments, implemented by the foreign trade monopoly. While hard-currency exports had remained below plan targets by 14 percent (1982 against 1981), imports were reduced by one-third in 1982 compared to 1981 and by more than 40 percent as compared to 1980.

After the rescheduling of credits due in 1982 and 1983, Romania could pay its debt service in 1984 without further rescheduling. Its outstanding debt in hard currency decreased from $10.2 billion in 1981 to $7.2 billion in 1984; arrears were eliminated, and international reserves increased to more than $700 million by 1984 (i.e., to almost 8 weeks' hard-currency imports of that year).

Hungary

When Hungary applied for membership in the IMF in November 1981, its external position, at least on the surface, was more manageable than that of Romania or Poland. Its trade balance in convertible currencies showed a surplus of $445 million in 1981; its current-account balance, however, a deficit of $730 million—almost twice as high as in 1980. This deficit was due to the rapid increase in interest payments on outstanding debts. The deficit and a highly unfavorable debt-maturity structure— one-third of total outstanding debt of $8.7 billion was short-term—pushed Hungary into a serious liquidity crisis in 1981, when Western banks suddenly refused to renew short-term loans, and access to new medium- and long-term credits was largely closed because of the Polish crisis. Nevertheless, Hungary could still service its maturing debts, though just barely.[7] The Hungarians claimed that their application for membership was not a consequence of liquidity shortages but, rather, reflected the resolute pursuance of the reform policy began in 1968. Membership in the IMF was designed to back Hungary's efforts to achieve closer integration into the world economy. Hungary's interest in Fund membership had also been determined by its simultaneous membership in the World Bank, which—after controversial discussions—classified Hungary as a developing country, thereby opening substantial additional credit sources to the country.[8]

Hungary's progress toward economic reform greatly facilitated its entry into the IMF on May 6, 1982. Hungary voluntarily implemented during the 1970s and during the early 1980s, in conjunction with the further introduction of market-related management elements, measures demanded of Romania under the standby program.

In contrast to the case of Romania, Hungary's admission into the IMF was sufficient to restart the flow of private credit. The country obtained a six-month $500 million credit through the Bank for International Settlements (BIS) to bridge liquidity bottlenecks until Hungary and the IMF could agree on financial assistance. In August 1982 it received a credit of $260 million from a Western banking consortium, thus becoming the first European CMEA country to receive such a credit after the Polish crisis.

In December 1982 the IMF agreed to give a one-year standby credit of SDR 475 million (126 percent of the then Hungarian quota of SDR 375 million),[9] which had been replaced by a second standby credit in the amount of SDR 425 million in January 1984. In the case of Hungary, too, the standby credits were accompanied by an adjustment program aimed at the further consolidation of Hungary's current-account balance. As in Romania, the measures were primarily designed to reduce overall demand. But unlike Romania, Hungary has relied to a much greater extent on indirect adjustment instruments, such as prices, taxes, interest rates, and exchange rates. To be sure, many of these market-type instruments are not market-determined, and it seems impossible to precisely measure their effects on incentives and on the behavior of Hungarian producers.

Perhaps because Hungary had been under less external pressure than Romania, its external adjustment was also less spectacular. The current-account deficit of 1981 was turned into a surplus by 1983 of almost $300 million, which was, however, only half of the IMF target. The shortfall was reportedly due to unfavorable weather conditions that kept agricultural exports below the projected amount. The surplus was increased to $331 million by 1984, roughly in line with that year's commitment.

Although the gross hard-currency debt increased to $8.8 billion by 1984 (from $7.7 billion in 1982), the country was able to considerably improve the maturity structure of debt; in 1984 only 16 percent of all outstanding credits were short-term. International reserves, which had decreased from $2.0 billion at the end of 1980 to $0.46 billion at the beginning of 1982, rose again to $2.1 billion by 1984.

Hungary, too, owes much of the improvements to a substantial reduction of hard-currency imports, which decreased by 20 percent (1984 against 1980), while exports stagnated. Like Romania, Hungary had been unable to increase exports, in spite of measures taken to stimulate exports, such as the devaluations of its exchange rate.

Effects of the Adjustments

In both Romania and Hungary, import curbs—particularly of intermediates and investment goods from industrialized Western countries—and the demand restrictions that conform to the IMF's guidelines, could not remain without consequences for overall economic growth. In 1981, Romania faced the lowest growth rate of national income of the last 25 years (2.2 percent), which rose only moderately to 2.7 percent in 1982. Hungary's national income grew by only 0.5 percent in 1983, which was substantially slower growth than in previous years. The same is true for industrial production in both countries.[10]

Therefore, the adjustment process, without doubt, had negative consequences for both countries. They were, however, less serious in Hungary because of its more stable overall economic situation. The adjustment was also felt less by the Hungarian population because, in spite of a general orientation toward austerity, Hungary's policymakers have tried to limit the effects on the standard of living.

In the case of Romania particularly, a legitimate question is whether the IMF aggravated the country's economic crisis by its enforced demand curbs, since Romania, after the cancellation of the standby agreement in January 1984, published amazingly high growth rates of national income and industrial production for 1984 and the following years.[11] The Romanian leadership refused to follow further the course of the IMF adjustment program and, in 1984, it had even reversed some important measures that were previously implemented in the frame of that program. Instead of further price increases, the introduction of so-called maximum profit rates in industry led to price decreases; interest rates were reduced to the level from which they were once raised; and the exchange rate of the leu was unexpectedly revalued by 25 percent after having been continuously devalued since 1981.[12]

Most striking is that, with or without the IMF Romania would, in any event, have been forced to adjust its external deficit to the available amount of foreign financing. Commercial credits were no longer available, the annual debt service had become unbearably high, and hard-currency exports could not be increased to the necessary extent because of the lack of competitiveness of Romanian products and the sluggish demand on the world markets. Therefore, even if not under pressure by the IMF, Romania was forced to curtail its external borrowing and, to achieve this, cut back its net absorption of resources from abroad under the competition imposed by the international capital markets. Under the prevailing circumstances, Romania had no choice but to adjust by reducing imports.

Fund conditionality, with regard to the restoration of a "sustainable" position in the current balance, had originally foreseen a smoother adjustment. But since the underlying assumptions of the program, with regard to the capital balance (i.e., the inflow of new medium- and long-term credits and the net outflow of short-term credits), proved too optimistic, the balance-of-trade adjustment had to be more rigorous. However, even the revised Fund conditionality in this area had been simply "overfulfilled" by Romania during 1981-83 thereby making the consequences of external consolidation even more painful for the domestic economy.

Certainly the financial assistance of the IMF to Romania during 1981-83 helped relieve the most urgent pressure, although it has not allowed a "soft landing," mainly because the adjustment process started too late and Fund resources were too small in comparison with the burden of Romania's annual debt service. However, it seems that Romania could have achieved the same results without the IMF, considering the kind of direct administrative adjustment its leaders have chosen. The path of external adjustment, the annual results of which had always exceeded the targets set by the Fund, would most likely have taken the same course without the IMF. Standard Fund conditionality, using indirect levers directed toward the restructuring of the domestic economy, had not worked, for the reasons stated above.

Consequently, it is hardly conceivable that IMF conditionality was responsible for the sharpening of Romania's economic crisis. Owing to the inflexibility of the Romanian economic system, market-oriented adjustment measures must fail. The IMF is thus unable to contribute to an urgent change of the country's domestic structural imbalances. Other serious reasons for the previous Romanian external disequilibrium still prevail, latent as they may be, and could cause external imbalances in the future as soon as import restrictions are loosened.

Recent Developments and Prospects

It is not to be expected in the near future that Romania will be able—or willing—to create the preconditions for further financial assistance from the IMF. Under its current leadership, the country does not seem to be prepared to expose itself once more to a stabilization program under Fund conditionality. Nevertheless, the clear improvement in the current balance, after 1980-81, and the expected maintenance of solvency with regard to debt servicing has made commercial banks and governments loosen their credit restrictions.

The forecast made in the Economic Memorandum of 1985 for current surpluses in convertible currencies in 1985 and 1986 ($1.55 billion and $1.67 billion, respectively) had indeed suggested that these amounts would be sufficient to cover Romania's hard-currency needs for the repayment of credits due. But since the country could not fulfill its foreign trade plans—the 1985 current surplus reached only $0.915 billion—in mid-1986, Romania, once again, came into serious payment difficulties. There are no signs of any new demands for IMF resources. The Romanian government instead tried to get new commercial bank credits in 1985, and in June 1986 arranged a new time table for the repayment of some $880 million, which had been part of the rescheduling arrangements of 1982 and 1983.[13]

Romania's renewed deterioration in the external situation—caused mainly by an adverse development of exports—shows clearly that the adjustment efforts during 1981-83 have not yet produced any noticeable effects on the domestic production structure and on the stimulation of exports. Romania still has to directly control imports to generate the necessary trade surplus. However, since the annual debt service, according to Romanian projections, will decrease considerably until 1990,[14] the tense payments situation may soon be eased. If and when hard-currency earnings will become available for imports rather than debt service, positive effects will be achieved in domestic production and supply.

Compared to Romania, whose relationship with the IMF has become strained, the Hungarian performance under its two standby agreements will not hamper subsequent Fund assistance, if it is needed. Hungary did not resist the stabilization program of the IMF, since the recommended adjustment measures "fit", more or less without controversy, with Hungarian economic policy. To be sure, Hungary also implemented much of its external adjustment in part by direct administrative measures.

Hungary's external situation was ambivalent in 1986. Net inflows of medium- and long-term private capital increased from $60 million in 1983 to $965 million in 1984 and to $1.6 billion in 1985. During the first quarter of 1986 alone, net capital inflows amounted to $700 million. Hungary used these credits for imports and for increasing international reserves (excluding gold) from $2.2 billion in March 1985 to $3.3 billion one year later.[15]

Recent trade developments did not meet Hungarian expectations. When it relaxed the central "monitoring" of imports in 1985, hard-currency imports started to increase considerably, while exports once again stagnated. For the first time since 1981, the hard currency current account showed a deficit of $457 million in 1985, rising to $573 million during the first three months of 1986. Net debt in hard-currencies rose to some $10 billion. To control the growing external disequilibrium in 1986, the authorities again imposed rather rigid import restrictions. Allocation quotas of foreign exchange were reduced by 50 percent in the second half of 1986. Hungary is still trying to do without additional IMF credits as was announced by János Fekete, Vice President of the Hungarian National Bank, in 1985[16] (although it is not able to finance its balance of payments deficits without imposing foreign trade restrictions). The deficits of 1985-86 are, most likely, the reason that Hungary did not, as originally intended, prematurely repay its Fund liabilities that remained from its first (1985) standby agreement.

It seems that, for Hungary (even more so than for Romania), the World Bank has always been a more important partner than the IMF. By mid-1985, i.e., within 3 years, Hungary has received World Bank commitments totaling almost $1.5 billion, of which some $1 billion was in the form of the World Bank's share of co-financings with the private sector.[17] By financing developmental projects in cooperation with commercial banks, the World Bank is able to activate long-term, hard-currency credits, which substantially exceed the Bank's own contribution. Apart from that, Hungary plans to increase its participation in Third-World projects that are financed by the World Bank. This participation would open additional possibilities for earning hard currency.

Implications for Poland

What could Poland expect from the IMF? When Poland applied for membership in November 1981, when it was under strong economic pressure at home and abroad. With net debts then of about $25 billion and a current-account deficit in 1980 in convertible currencies of $2.6 billion (Table 2), Poland had already been unable to repay maturing loans at the beginning of 1981. When, in early 1981, debt-rescheduling negotiations could no longer be avoided, several Western banks judged Poland's non-membership in the IMF as a further obstacle to a successful debt arrangement, since the Fund had proved to be of valuable assistance in restructuring the debts of many other countries. Poland was, therefore, urged to apply for membership in the IMF before refinancing negotiations took place. The banks hoped that the Poland's membership would bring more than just financial assistance; they hoped that Poland would start a comprehensive reform program under Fund surveillance.

Because of the declaration of martial law in December 1981, Poland did not become the 151st member of the IMF until June 12, 1986. Nevertheless, rescheduling negotiations with private banks were successfully settled in each year after 1981; the negotiations, with the Western governments under the Paris Club, interrupted in 1981 were reopened, and in January 1985 Poland's debts to Western governments were rescheduled (when a new arrangement with regard to the 1981-84 arrears of $15 billion—repayments and interest [see Chapter 1]—was agreed to). Furthermore, Poland announced an economic reform program independent of the Fund.[18] However, since 1981 Poland had retained interest in membership in the IMF. Therefore, consultations between Poland and the IMF took place during the entire period of the pending application, and one may presume that the blueprint of Polish economic reforms, partially implemented thus far, were set in part on the basis of consultation of the Fund, particularly in the field of price and exchange rate policy and with regard to demand management.

Up to early 1987, Poland did not draw any IMF credits. But under the guidelines of 1986, a country in balance-of-payments difficulties can draw credits in three successive years under Fund conditionality up to a maximum annual limit of 90 to 110 percent of the quota. Since Poland's quota was set at SDR 680 million, it may be allowed to draw up to a maximum of SDR 612 to 748 million per year during three years. In addition, drawings to a maximum of 105 percent of the quota might be available under the Compensatory Financing Facility to offset a fall in export receipts and increases in the cost of feed and grain imports. These drawings could add approximately another SDR 700 million. Therefore, within three years Poland could expect a maximum financial support of SDR 2.5 to 2.9 billion from the IMF. The question is whether these amounts will be granted, given that Poland has payments arrears, and whether they could mean noticeable relief for Poland.

According to a Polish projection of the balance of payments through 1992, annual interest payments alone are expected to rise from $2.5 billion in 1986 to $3.3 billion in 1988.[19] Based on rather optimistic forecasts of the hard-currency trade balance and of the balance of services and transfers, the current deficit was expected to amount to only $360 million in 1986 (in comparison: the deficit totaled almost $1.2 billion in 1984 and more than $400 million in 1985) (Table 2), and to rise only moderately to $700 million by 1988. During the same period the annual repayment of maturing credits will increase from $1.8 billion to $3.1 billion. In order to cover the projected current deficits plus the annual repayments of principal due, the same projection expects new Western credits of some $3 billion in 1987 and $3.5 billion in 1988, of which medium- and long-term credits account for $1.5 billion and $2.5 billion respectively.

However, seen from the point of view of the developments of early 1987, these projections are unrealistic. In particular, the trade balance in 1986 did not develop according to expectations. Although external adjustment efforts have led to growing trade surpluses through 1984, foreign trade plans could not be fulfilled. Instead of $1.5 billion, the surplus is estimated to have been only about $1.1 billion in 1986. Hence, the current deficit in 1986 was probably at least one-half billion dollars higher than estimated. One might add that overly optimistic and unfulfilled projections have been the rule in Poland for at least a decade.

This unplanned development of exports and imports may have been the reason that the earlier projection of the trade surplus for 1987 has been reduced by $850 million, to $1 billion.[20] This new forecast reflects the very pessimistic assessment of export capabilities by the government.[21] Compared to 1986, hard-currency exports are expected to fall by $300 million. Accordingly, this year's current deficit could run up to $1.4 billion and the total gross medium- and long-term indebtedness could rise from $31.3 billion in mid-1986—which equaled 40 percent of that year's national income—to almost $35 billion by the end of 1987.[22]

Considering the recent world economic situation, it seems unlikely that Poland could meet the expectations of the IMF, according to which Poland would have to reach a current balance within the next 3 to 4 years, i.e., by 1990.[23] On the contrary, it is possible that increasing current deficits will require even higher inflows of foreign capital than previously expected.

To realize projected credit inflows under the prevailing circumstances, Poland has to rely on the (future) benefits of IMF membership and a greatly improved credit standing in the private capital markets. Given Poland's annual burden in the redemption of principal due and interest payments—the sum total of which will have increased to about $10 billion by 1992—it seems clear that the IMF can provide only temporary and very limited relief. Poland is, therefore, in urgent need of the help of private banks and Western governments. The likelihood that those

Notes

1. For details, see the preceding chapter in this volume, and Paul Marer, "Centrally Planned Economies in the IMF, the World Bank, and the GATT," in *Economic Adjustment and Reform in Eastern Europe and the Soviet Union: Essays in Honor of Franklyn D. Holzman*, Josef C. Brada, Ed A. Hewett, and Thomas A. Wolf, eds. [forthcoming].

2. See Marer.

3. W. Tseng, "Die Effekte der Anpassung," Finanzierung und Entwicklung, 1984, Vol. 21, no. 4, p. 2.

4. V. Buttner, "The IMF's Adjustment Concept, a Strategy for a Permanent Solution to the Debt Crisis?" *Intereconomics*, Vol. 20, no. 4, p. 172.

5. Romania's quota rose to SDR 523.4 million under the Eighth General Review of Quotas, which raised quotas by an average of 47.5 percent at the end of 1983.

6. T. Gudac, "Preise und Wechselkurse in Planwirtschaften," *Finanzierung und Entwicklung* 1984, Vol. 21, no. 3, p. 40.

7. For details of Hungary's circumstances at the time see Paul Marer, "Hungary's Balance of Payments Situation," in Joint Economic Committee, U.S. Congress, *East European Economies: Slow Growth in the 1980s*, Vol. 3. Washington, D.C., 1986.

8. On the controversy involving Hungary's dollar per-capita GNP, see Paul Marer, *Dollar GNPs of the USSR and Eastern Europe* (Baltimore, 1986).

9. The Hungarian quota rose to SDR 530.7 million under the VIII General Review of Quotas.

10. The reader should be warned that intra-CMEA and East-West comparisons of growth rates have many pitfalls. It is the view of experts that Romania's official growth statistics are especially upwardly biased. See Marer, *Dollar GNPs*.

11. See note 10.

12. This see-sawing of Romanian economic policy seems to produce rather arbitrary results, but it seems to be characteristic of a country relying on strictly central management and arbitrary intervention into the economy by its top political leaders.

13. Die Erste Österreichische Sparkasse-Bank, *Economic Survey: The Present Development of the CMEA Economies*, 1986, p. 23.

14. The debt service will decrease despite the mentioned recent rescheduling of $880 million, the repayment of which will start in 1989 and continue through 1992.

15. IMF, *International Financial Statistics*, December 1986.

16. *Handelsblatt*, no. 196 (October 11-12, 1985).

17. *Figyelö*, no 17 (April 24, 1985), and no. 24 (June 13, 1985).

18. For details, see Fallenbuchl's chapter in this volumne.

19. H. Gabrisch "Polen—1984-85—Wirtschaftliche Belebung setzt sich fort," in K. Bolz (ed.), *Die wirtschaftliche Entwicklung in den sozialistischen Ländern Osteuropas zur Jahreswende 1984/85* (Hamburg, 1985), p. 145.

20. *Rynki Zagraniczne*, no. 152 (December 22, 1986).

21. *Nachrichten für Aussenhandel*, no. 74 (April 17, 1986).

18. For details, see Fallenbuchl's chapter in this volumne.

19. H. Gabrisch "Polen—1984-85—Wirtschaftliche Belebung setzt sich fort," in K. Bolz (ed.), *Die wirtschaftliche Entwicklung in den sozialistischen Ländern Osteuropas zur Jahreswende 1984/85* (Hamburg, 1985), p. 145.

20. *Rynki Zagraniczne*, no. 152 (December 22, 1986).

21. *Nachrichten für Aussenhandel*, no. 74 (April 17, 1986).

22. W. Oschlies "Polen: Noch 31.3 Milliarden Dollar Westverschuldung," in *Bundesinstitut für ostwissenschaftliche Studien, Aktuell Analysen*, 1986, no. 33, p. 1.

23. *Handelsblatt*, no. 110 (June 12, 1986).

28

What Roles for the IMF and the World Bank in Poland?

Paul Marer

In addition to the significant resources the IMF and the World Bank can provide to eligible member countries, these institutions play a catalytic role in managing the global debt problem. Both creditor governments and commercial banks look to them, especially to the IMF, to exert the right kind of pressure on the borrowing countries to pursue policies that will re-establish their creditworthiness.

I would like to discuss briefly the compatibility of IMF and World Bank programs with the operations of traditional or modified CPEs.[1] IMF programs focus on relatively short-term balance-of-payments adjustments, those of the World Bank on longer-term structural adjustments.

It takes some combination of three types of measures to improve the balance of payments of a country with any type of an economic system: (1) a reduction of net domestic absorption, which involves cutting investment, consumption, or government expenditures (demand measures); (2) a transfer of resources from less to more productive uses (supply measures); and (3) switching goods and services from non-tradable to the tradable sectors (demand-switching measures). In dealing predominantly with market economies, the Fund has developed a set of policy measures in each area that, when tailored to the circumstances of the country, generally yield balance-of-payments improvements, though not necessarily without undesirable side effects (the main reasons that Fund programs are controversial). But in CPEs, the standard policy measures often do not work as expected, for systemic reasons.

For example, to reduce domestic absorption, Fund programs typically focus on reigning in money and credit. But owing to the soft-budget constraint on enterprises, whose effects are similar to those encountered when firms initially have an excess supply of money, and to the large forced savings in the hands of the population, which can be mobilized to maintain consumption levels, a tighter control over money and credit may not constrain effective demand.[2] In CPEs, the authorities are more likely to achieve this through administrative intervention. Even if inter-enterprise credits are cut, so that *effective* excess demand in the enterprise sector is eliminated by imposing economy-wide ceilings on credits and subsidies to enterprises, the authorities, intolerant of bankruptcies, may tax the unprofitable firms to subsidize the inefficient. This means that credit ceilings will not yield the desired effects on production efficiency.

To improve the general efficiency of the economy, Fund programs typically rely on market-incentive mechanisms, such as adjusting relative prices of tradeables to reflect prices on the world market and raising interest rates to improve the efficiency of investment allocation and to promote savings. But in CPEs, such measures often do not work as intended. Given the soft-budget constraint on enterprises, the policies against open unemployment, and other system features, investment decisions—by the center or by enterprises—tend to be made not on the basis of expected rates of return (which, in any event, are difficult to estimate plausibly, given the arbitrary nature of factor and product prices), but on some mix of social, political, economic as well as bureaucratic considerations. And given the accumulated large "forced" savings in the hands of the population, the pervasive shortages of the very items that are most in demand (e.g., apartments, automobiles, foreign travel), and the prohibition against many types of investments, the impact of interest rates on savings are questionable.

The preferred instrument of the Fund to encourage switching demand into tradeables is exchange-rate depreciation. In a "traditional" CPE, where enterprises producing exports and using imports are insulated from the external sector, they will not feel the impact of a devaluation. In a "modified" CPE, like Hungary or Poland, where enterprises do feel the impact, we know relatively little about their responses to price and profit signals, given the exceedingly complex and frequently changing environment of financial and administrative regulation in which they make decisions.[3]

A further problem is that it is one thing to increase the supply of products to be marketed for convertible currency through some combination of exchange-rate manipulation and other levers, and quite another to actually sell them on the world market. The manufactures CPEs produce often lack competitiveness due to nonprice factors, such as obsolete, low-quality products or poor marketing and service. Moreover, the extent to which these economies have the capability to substitute domestic production for convertible-currency imports, especially in response to price signals, is also a question.

One consequence of the situation just described is that even through recent Fund programs in Romania and Hungary (as well as of Yugoslavia, though that country is not a CPE) have been associated with significant improvements in their balance of payments, it appears that, in varying degrees, most of the improvements were brought about by administrative restrictions on imports and mobilization of exports, rather than improved efficiency, even though the latter is one of the objectives of Fund and Bank programs. Direct administrative intervention was especially striking in the case in Romania, as was detailed in the previous chapter by Pissulla. The problem with excessive reliance on administrative measures is that they typically undermine *sustainable* improvements in the balance of payments.

The economic reform process under way in several CPEs will be helpful, but we should realize that in all CPEs the reform process inevitably is a long one. Hence, in the short-run, improvements in efficiency will, at best, be modest. The kinds of reforms measures recommended in the next chapter by Gomulka will, gradually, improve the functioning of an economy such as Poland's and thus increase the applicability of standard IMF and World Bank programs. Because there are significant differences among the reform programs of the CPEs, understanding how "modified" CPEs like Poland, Hungary, and China function, and designing appropriate programs for them, can be exceedingly difficult.

All CPEs are in "structural disequilibrium," which means that a disproportionate share of their products have become obsolete and thus not readily salable on the world market, and that much of production is excessively wasteful in inputs. The programs and policy advice of the World Bank are designed to help overcome the structural problems of members. But the Bank, too, faces difficult operational problems in CPEs. For example, in deciding the kinds of investment projects that it should endorse and help fund, it has to deal with arbitrary domestic prices and inflexibilities. Moreover, since investment projects often use inputs from, or sell a portion of output on the CMEA—a market whose supply, demand, and pricing policies are not well understood or kept secret—project evaluation poses uniquely difficult problems.

A further dilemma is whether the Bank should evaluate the fundamental investment strategy of a CPE, or whether it should focus only on investment decisions at the margin. For example, should the Bank take as given the planner's projections of a country's future energy requirements that may be based on maintaining the existing, excessively energy-intensive structure of production (in which case the Bank's chief concern would be the choice between alternative energy projects), or should it try to convince the authorities that they should alter fundamentally the country's production structure? In CPEs, investment choices even have foreign policy implications because some projects are more likely to promote trade with the CMEA, others with the West.

The systemic and structural problems of the CPEs just enumerated have many similarities with those of certain developing countries. The essential commonality is the imperfection of their market mechanisms.

Financial markets are often at infant stages of development, which calls into question the feasibility of depending heavily on financial instruments for influencing economic performance.

Many factor and product prices are arbitrary and inflexible, which call into question reliance on market-mechanism incentives.

Severe structural disequilibria are often present, which—together with the problems in the financial and price mechanisms—cast doubt on the effectiveness of currency devaluations to improve the balance of payments.

These statements are not intended to imply that the market mechanisms of the industrial countries operate perfectly, only that the extent of the problems and distortions are much greater in the CPEs and in certain LDCs.

If the IMF and the World Bank wish to promote the purposes for which they were established, they should try to convince both the more "traditional" and "modified" CPEs, as well as the LDCs that have severe weaknesses in their market mechanisms, to reform, step by step, their economic policies and systems. Are the two international organizations politically willing and bureaucratically capable of insisting on "institutional reforms" in CPEs—given that this would be precedent-setting and controversial? And would the countries so targeted accept such type of "conditionality," should it be promoted?

Be that as it may, the ability of the IMF and the World Bank to succeed in promoting policy and system reforms cannot be guaranteed any more in a CPE than in any other country. Only when the authorities in a member country are themselves convinced of the advantages of reform and of cooperation, and have a firm commitment to such a course, are the prospects of meaningful external influence assured.

The willingness of a country like Poland to cooperate fully with the IMF and the World Bank in their suggestions for institutional and policy reforms should, in my view, be the principal consideration for Western policy on granting the country new credits and other forms of assistance.

Notes

1. This section is based on my "Centrally Planned Economies in the IMF, the World Bank, and the GATT," in Josef C. Brada, Ed. H. Hewett, and Thomas A. Wolf (eds.), *Economic Adjustment and Reform in Eastern Europe and the Soviet Union: Essays in Honor of Franklyn D. Holzman* (forthcoming).

2. For details, see two articles by Thomas A. Wolf, "Exchange Rate Systems and Adjustment in Planned Economies," *IMF Staff Papers*, June 1985; and "Economic Stabilization in Planned Economies," *IMF Staff Papers*, July 1985.

3. Paul Marer, "Economic Reforms in Hungary: From Central Planning to Regulated Market." In *East European Economies: Slow Growth in the 1980s* (Compendium of papers published by the Joint Economic Committee, U.S. Congress, 1986).

29

Reforms the IMF and the World Bank Should Promote in Poland

Stanisław Gomulka

This chapter discusses how Poland may tackle its current problem of external indebtedness and restore a viable balance-of-payments position.[1] Its focus is economic reforms and related policy measures by which Poland may achieve a substantial improvement in its balance of trade in convertible currencies over the next five years *and* sustain that improvement thereafter. The broad aim is taken to be a reduction of the debt-export ratio, from about 5.5 in 1987 to perhaps 4.0 by 1992 and below 2.5 by the year 2000.

The main reason for the primary concern with reform measures is the fact that, in contrast to the situation during 1946-80, domestic supplies of primary resources and basic materials are expected to remain stagnant or increase only very slowly in the foreseeable future. Therefore, any substantial increases in final outputs are conditional on improved efficiency. The unusually poor use of inputs is, at present, Poland's most important growth reserve. The activation of that reserve is, therefore, a task that is at once economically attractive and, given the constraints to reform operating in Poland, intellectually and politically challenging. The specific measures recommended in this chapter, while paying attention to those constraints, are designed primarily to invigorate the present reform sufficently for Poland's activation of that growth reserve. The recommendations should thus be of interest to Western creditors, the IMF and the World Bank, and the authorities in Poland.

Comprehensive Reform or Selective Measures

In 1981 several alternative reform documents were proposed. The most comprehensive of these were two: one prepared by a large government reform commission and one by "Network," a group of activists associated with workers' councils from a large number of enterprises.[2] The former proposal was subsequently adopted by the communist party's congress in July 1981 and the latter by Solidarity's congress in September 1981.

The two major proposals differ in the choice of specific solutions. The Network's was similar to the labor-managed, market-based system of Yugoslavia, and the government's proposed system was similar to the Hungarian model. However, the stated principal aims of both blueprints are similar: (1) the "three-S" principle of self-finance, self-management and enterprise autonomy; (2) market-clearing prices; (3) hard-budget constraint for enterprises; and (4) central plans reflecting social preferences, to be implemented through the use of market-type instruments (central planning of the parametric type).

Much of the legislative machinery of the reform was devised by the government with these desirable principles in mind. However, in addition to the usual social, political, and ideological obstacles to reform that were discussed in the contributions by Brus (Chapter 8), Bielasiak (Chapter 11), and Fallenbuchl (Chapter 12), the actual implementation has also been adversely affected by the economic and political crisis as stated, for instance, by Kamecki (Chapter 13). In particular, the government insisted that this crisis would require a transitional period of three years, during which some essential elements of the old command system would be maintained. Since the three years have already passed, the government should insist on the full implementation of its reform program of 1981 rather than a new, across-the-board reform. The selective measures proposed here are intended to achieve that aim. But the measures must be implemented forcefully and must concern, above all, the hard core of the reform program: financial discipline for enterprises and the creation or further development of proper markets—fairly competitive if possible, oligopolistic ones if necessary. Especially important are markets for credit, foreign exchange, investment goods, and intermediate inputs. This implies phasing out quantity rationing of inputs and introducing market-clearing input prices. The latter is essential if enterprises are to be subjected to market discipline and equally essential for subordination of the government's physical planning to its financial planning, both of which are recognized as necessary conditions of any effective reform. The proposed reform measures are fairly comprehensive, so that their package may be regarded as an across-the-board economic reform. It may be politically wiser to present the proposals as a package of selective measures—a reform of the existing reform—rather than as a new reform. In any event, much of the legal structure needed has been in place since 1982.

Interenterprise Zloty/Dollar Convertibility

The retention of a part of export earnings in hard currency is, according to a governmental report on economic reform, "the principal instrument to stimulate the interest of enterprises in exports to hard-currency capitalist countries."[3] Independent studies based on questionnaires confirm this assessment. In 1985, about 2,000 enterprises (roughly one-third of all enterprises in the socialist sector) had dollar accounts. However, granting the right to a percentage of export earnings that can be retained, and the percentage itself, are prerogatives of the central authorities. As such, they are enterprise specific, subject to bargaining, and serve as instruments of central administrative control. Moreover, in the use of these retained earnings, enterprises can finance only their own imports and those of their immediate suppliers. This administrative constraint thus has the consequence of limiting the interest of many enterprises in dollar exports only to levels needed to meet their own import needs. The removal of these allocative and motivating deficiencies of the present system may soon have a considerable effect and should therefore be a priority target.

Suppose the system is reformed as follows:
a. All enterprises have the right to retain a given proportion of their hard-currency earnings in uniform proportions.
b. The initial proportion is, say, 35 percent. Also, it is announced in advance that the proportion would be increased by, for example, 5 percentage points annually over a period of 5 years, in order to induce enterprises to make longer-lasting pro-export investment commitments.
c. Enterprises are free to sell their retained hard currency, at negotiated prices, only to other state enterprises. This provision amounts to the creation of an inter-enterprise free market for hard currency. The non-retained hard-currency earnings would continue to be sold to the National Bank at the official exchange rate.

Under the present reform, state enterprises already have the right to sell most of their products or material inputs to other state enterprises but not to private enterprises or individuals at freely-determined prices. If my suggestions were adopted, retained hard currency would be just another product or input. This change would be a straightforward extension of what is already in place.

The creation of an inter-enterprise market for convertible currencies is likely to have major psychological and economic implications. Most important of these would be a significant strengthening of the incentive to increase net dollar exports, as a result of the likelihood of a much higher market exchange rate. Another advantage of such a devaluation of the zloty derives from the fact that only free-market dollars would be more expensive. Since these dollars will presumably go to particularly productive uses, this devaluation would be less inflationary than an equivalent across-the-board increase of the exchange rate. As a result, some major exporters of minerals and metals, which at present are subsidized (for example, the coal industry), would probably become profitable even before the lifting of the prices of their products to the world-market levels. By adopting a uniform retention rate and leaving the allocation of exchange increasingly to the market mechanism, the central authorities would save their valuable time while the enterprises would gain independence and flexibility. The free exchange rate would also provide market evaluation of the domestic value of imported foreign resources, thus providing very useful information for the Polish authorities, enterprises, and Western banks.

If the efficiency of resource utilization happens to remain the same in the short run, an increase of net exports would of course reduce supplies for domestic markets. By how much? The marginal resource cost of one dollar in 1985 was probably about 200 zloty. An additional annual export of $1 billion, if that would be the effect of the measures outlined above after about 3 years, is therefore equivalent to 200 billion zloty, or 4 percent of Poland's private consumption. The population may be prepared to accept such a cost in the short term, or at least oppose it less forcefully, if the implementation of economic reforms gives reasonable hope of an improvement in the standard of living in the 1990s and beyond. Hopefully, by 1990 the gain to consumption and GDP from a program of comprehensive reform may already exceed this four-percent shift toward exports. This scheme should be taken as an important part of the price reform. That reform is to rest on the general principle that all prices, including the exchange rate, should be adjusted or allowed to adjust themselves toward market-clearing levels. (See the section on prices and interest rates, below).

Suppose that our proposals were adopted in 1987, and by 1991 the authorities buy from enterprises at the official exchange rate only about 40 percent of their dollar earnings. Some 20 to 30 percent of all the dollar earnings would be used for servicing the foreign debt. The remaining 10 to 20 percent would go for domestic purposes and the accumulation of dollar reserves. The difference between the market-clearing rate and the official exchange rate would be a form of tax imposed on enterprises. Initially, a significant percentage of the dollars bought by the state at the official rate would re-enter the economy as centrally-allocated input at a low price. The enterprises receiving foreign exchange would thus be subsidized by the enterprises that earn foreign exchange. However, as the market takes over most of the allocation of foreign exchange for domestic purposes, the subsidy of this particular category would gradually disappear. Before that happens, a lower official exchange rate would increase the subsidy but lower the inflationary impact of the proposed scheme. A lower exchange rate, implying a higher tax rate, would also inhibit the incentive to export. For the two conflicting reasons, the overall size of the tax should be chosen with particular care. In fact, if inflation was a minor consideration compared to the promotion of exports, the tax could be negative and the official rate set at a level higher than the market-determined rate. In this case, some exports would be subsidized. The state could also buy its share of the dollars at a price significantly lower than the market price and sell its surplus over and above that required for debt service to enterprises, which would pay a price only marginally lower than on the market. Under the latter option, inter-enterprise subsidization would be insignificant.

There may be a concern that the proposed scheme (1) leads to excessive nonexport-related purchases of foreign exchange (2) encourages the production of import substitutes and (3) does less than a straight devaluation would to promote a more economical use of imported inputs. External purchases that are unrelated to exports are mainly inputs or final goods designated exclusively for domestic consumption. These purchases can be controlled by requiring importers to obtain a license or by the imposition of import duties. In any case, the market value of the dollar will probably be high enough to hold down most consumption-related imports. There are a few exceptions, such as coffee, electronic gadgets, and some types of cars; the authorities should have little problem in controlling their inflow.

Given that the market exchange rate is likely to be higher—and perhaps much higher in the first few years—than the official rate, the scheme will promote both import substitution and a more economical use of imported inputs more effectively than a straight devaluation. The second and third concerns are thus baseless, unless a straight devaluation can be so large that the official rate would be greater than the free market rate, which I think is not feasible because of its inflationary impact.

Will the inflationary impact of our more liberal retention scheme be significantly less than that of a straight devaluation that has the same stimulating effect on exports? Chart 10 will assist us in giving an answer.

Suppose that the initial exchange rate is e_1 This rate induces exports at a level E_1. A straight devaluation from e_1 to e_2^* would lift exports from E_1 to E_2. Suppose that under a segmented devaluation, e_1 remains the official exchange rate, e_2 is the market-determined exchange rate, and $e_2^* = \lambda e_2 + (1-\lambda)e_1$ is the effective exchange rate, λ being the retention rate. The two rates, e_1 and e_2, would induce the same exports, E_2. However, under the latter scheme, exporters would obtain fewer resources,

Chart 10. Resource Costs of Obtaining a Marginal Dollar as Function of the Level of Exports.

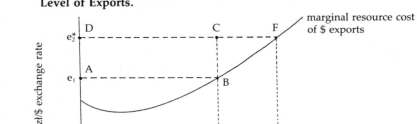

by the amount equal to ABCD, than when all E_2 has to be sold to the government at the rate e_2^*. From Chart 10 it is clear what factors decide how significant would be the size of that amount. In particular, given that ABCD $= (e_2^* - e_1)E_1 = \lambda (e_2 - e_1)E_1$, the size would be higher the steeper is the rise of the marginal resource costs as a function of exports (since the greater must be the difference $e_2 - e_1$ if the export target E_2 is to be reached) and the higher is the rate λ.

The Dollar Investment Bank

Let us suppose that our recommendations are implemented. The higher profitability of dollar exports will make export-oriented projects attractive for enterprises. An indication of this attractiveness would be provided by the interest rate that enterprises would be willing to pay to absorb a particular volume of dollar credit. If the dollar credit supplied is low, the market-clearing interest rate may well be high. In this case, it would be useful to set up an independent dollar investment bank (DIB) for channeling new Western resources to Poland, which may originate from the World Bank or private banks to partly finance, such projects.

Initially, the loans should be relatively small and for short periods of time, possibly not more than five years. The total supply of funds would be defined, up to a ceiling imposed externally, by the requirement that the market-clearing rate of interest should equal the Eurodollar rate, augmented by a commercially viable risk premium and a service charge. The DIB would serve as a market-screening device for selecting new projects that are capable of generating high dollar returns. The projects lacking external finance will thus be implemented. All enterprises—state-owned as well as private, Polish-owned as well as joint ventures, and fully foreign-owned—would be allowed to compete. The DIB itself would be Polish-owned, but foreign investors would provide much of its management. For all practical purposes, the DIB would be a joint venture of its shareholders, of which the National Bank of Poland (NBP) might be one, the net profits of which would, however, be fully Polish.

This suggestion has virtue in that it makes new loans to Poland for purposes other than servicing the debt contingent on the existence of suitable export-oriented projects. If the Polish government wants substantial loans, it must help create an economic environment in which there will be more projects capable of generating sufficient returns.

Incidentally, if the dollars were to be exchanged for the zloty on the interenterprise dollar market, the dollar loans would be less risky for both the DIB and the borrowing enterprises. The DIB should, in any case, have the power to recover its loans by seizing part of the incomes or assets of the enterprises that do not service their debts.

The Negotiated Profit-Share Incentive System and Modified FAZ Tax

Incentives and taxes are crucial levers of any economic system. Here the Polish reformers are faced with a fateful problem: how to reconcile the socialist principle of full employment with an effective control of price inflation when enterprises have the freedom to set wages. In a typical market-based economy, a certain degree of unemployment is usually necessary to keep wages and prices from exploding. The government does control the money supply, but if it decides not to validate wage inflation by refusing to increase the money supply, the ensuing shortage of liquidity will drive up interest rates, eventually causing bankruptcies and unemployment. East European reformers have for years been searching for a substitute to the capitalist tradeoff between inflation and unemployment. Their solution is a steeply progressive wage tax on enterprises, known in Poland as FAZ. The problem with this solution, however, is that it greatly limits the amount available for incentive-type payments, and thus weakens the incentive to work hard and pursue efficiency-enhancing innovations.[4] In addition, there are in Poland huge negative taxes (subsidies) which, up to a certain point, eliminate or reduce the threat of the unpleasant consequences of inefficiency. The positive incentive to work efficiently is especially undermined when the centrally-controlled component of wages and other income rises significantly (for example, by 20 percent per annum or more), creating an excess demand for goods and thus the possibility of financing all the wage and bonus increases that FAZ permits, by increasing prices alone.[5]

The profit tax, called the enterprise income tax, was also highly progressive during 1982-83. The tax is now linear, but the effective tax rate of about 50 percent is rather high; moreover, the rate is to be increased to 65 percent during the next few years. Given that profits after taxes also fund the social and investment projects of enterprises, the residual profit left to increase wages is just pocket money.[6]

Perhaps the best approach, in the long run, would be to abandon the FAZ tax altogether. However, in the short run such a step could lead to a wage-push inflation. The following changes might be considered instead:

(1) Both the subsidies and the profit tax should be greatly reduced. In 1984 the enterprise (socialized) sector received 831 billion zloty in subsidies and 294 billion zloty to cover losses, while it paid 815 billion zloty as the profit tax and 1190 billion zloty as the turnover tax. (For manufacturing and mining, the corresponding numbers were 469, 0.3, 503, and 911.[7]) A substantial reduction of the profit tax rate, for example, to 30 percent, would require a reduction of subsidies and losses by some 30 percent, keeping state revenues unchanged. To promote greater economy of capital and investment assets, a new tax may be introduced, in the form of minimum "social dividend" on capital "rented" to enterprises by the state. Revenues from this tax may also be used to finance reductions of the profit tax.

(2) Even after the reduction of profit taxes and subsidies, the profit bonus will still remain a relatively small proportion of employees' personal income. Therefore it is a mistake to think, as the Polish reformers apparently do, that the profit bonus could be used to provide a strong incentive for the average worker. This bonus is, however, large enough to serve as such an incentive for the managers and the innovators in the enterprise sector, the "entrepreneurial group." In each enterprise, the top member of that group is, of course, the managing director. The entrepreneurial employees, some 5 to 10 percent of all personnel, are the director's key staff, the research and development personnel, and some notably creative or skilled workers. The authorities may wish to consider allowing, say, half of the bonus fund to be under the sole discretion of the managing director to reward entrepreneurship, while the other half would be under the control of workers' councils to supplement wages in the usual way. Under this scheme the profit bonus has the potential of becoming an important source of income for the entrepreneurial types. To reduce arbitrariness in the distribution of the bonus fund, all employees could compete for a share of the profit bonus. The size of the share of each group or individual may become a part of the process of wage bargaining, first between the workers' council (or whatever organ appoints the director) and (candidates for) the managing director, and then between the director and the employees. This arrangement may be called the incentive system of negotiated profit-share (NPS). The fine details of proposed changes in the present system of taxes and incentives are, of course, secondary as long as they meet the need to sharply upgrade the motivation of key personnel while retaining a modified FAZ tax (see below) for the purpose of controlling price inflation.

(3) The suggested modifications of the present FAZ tax system would make the tax less progressive and would reduce (or preferably eliminate) both tax allowances of all kinds and the ministries' powers to tailor the allowances and other taxation rules for each enterprise separately. These proposed changes are designed to limit the opportunities for bargaining

between enterprises and the central authorities. The flexibility of the present system to adapt the taxation rules to particular circumstances may well seem justified in most individual cases. However, there are powerful external effects of each such case. The point is that granting benefits to an enterprise induces other enterprises to invest a great deal of effort in seeking similar benefits, consequently opening the way to the widespread perception, if not the practice, of dependence of enterprises and favoritism by ministries, hence undermining the all-important principles of self-financing and managerial independence.

The suggestion above is that the gain in the state budget from the proposed reduction of subsidies to enterprises and a new tax in the form of capital rent may be used to lower the rate of profit taxation and thereby augment incentives. An alternative, given the concern over inflation, would be to cut turnover taxes. Is this alternative feasible?

The turnover tax in the socialized sector, at 986 billion zloty in 1983 and 1,190 billion zloty in 1984, is now approximately as large as gross subsidies (straight subsidies plus losses, the latter amounting to about 25 percent of the total) and larger than the profit tax. The primary sources of this turnover tax are industry (911 billion zloty in 1984) and foreign trade (111 billion in 1983, mainly from the tax on imported consumer goods).[8] Within industry the main sources of the tax are the branches that produce alcohol and relative luxury goods, such as cars, gasoline, color TVs, household appliances, and some categories of tobacco products and textiles. In 1984, the sale of alcohol and refinery products accounted for 511 billion zloty, or 44 percent of all the turnover tax revenue.[9] The tax is a key instrument for the state to limit the demand for these consumer goods. Reducing the tax would tend to promote a reallocation of resources from exports to consumption, something we do not want to happen. The alternative must therefore be judged unfeasible.

Market-Clearing Prices and Interest Rates

Since the introduction of the reform in 1982, Poland has made welcome progress in reducing the huge price distortions that had accumulated up to that time. However, about half of the volume of all goods produced are still traded at state-fixed prices. State pricing need not be inferior to free-market pricing, especially in highly monopolistic markets, provided the prices clear the relevant markets. In Poland there are simply too many prices under administrative control—their number apparently runs into the hundreds of thousands—for the state to succeed, even if it wanted to, in finding equilibrium levels. The overriding economic importance of having prices at market clearing levels for the success of the whole reform effort may not be fully appreciated by the government or fully understood by society. The authorities tend to insist that prices should be based instead on the cost-plus principle. Although the observed substantial variation in the ex-post profitability of enterprises suggests that the principle is not rigorously followed, the authorities' insistence does slow down the needed reallocation of resources from less to more profitable uses. The various state regulations that severely limit relative price flexibility undermine the proper functioning of the price system. A great number of prices are frozen for long periods; others can be increased by not more than a certain percentage annually. The problem, therefore, is not one of a general underpricing of tradeables, which a rise in the exchange rate, if fully passed through, might correct. The problem is, rather, that of significant price misalignments within the category of tradeable goods, although it is probably much less pronounced now than it was in 1980, and of the inhibition of the forces of supply and demand to act on prices, thus sustaining and possibly exacerbating price misalignments. The suggested changes are enumerated below:

(1) The number of prices set by the state price offices must be commensurate with the offices' ability to maintain those prices at or close to their market-clearing levels. This principle is likely to require a drastic reduction in their number.

(2) The state must retain control over the prices of some key commodities and services.

(3) Only in cases when it is not clear what the market equilibrium prices are should the prices initially fixed by the state equal the average unit costs of production or the costs of imports. This situation will be only temporary, since equilibrium prices are not hard to approximate.

(4) The market-equilibrium principle would also apply to domestic interest rates on bank credits of all kinds, especially on investment credits.

In a market-based economy the price system is the crucial signaling mechanism for producers and consumers. It informs them quickly and at a very low cost of the relative resource costs of producing additional units of goods and services and of their relative value for buyers. It is for this reason that all prices, whether free or state-fixed, must at any time and as closely as possible reflect the market conditions of supply and demand. The state may wish to influence the amounts of goods consumed and produced, for valid reasons of social policy. However, to implement that policy the state should influence equilibrium prices and quantities only indirectly, by the use of taxes and subsidies.

The approach to consumer prices may be more relaxed than that to other prices. An increase of the price of a consumer good to its equilibrium level is more likely to cause an increase in its supply than a reduction, as well as reduce waiting lines and searching time. Still, any price increases reduce the potential purchasing power of individuals and, in the case of poor people, the prospect of obtaining certain goods at all. Given the apparently strong opposition of the population to con-sumer-price increases, especially to those initiated by the authorities, it would make sense to focus on producer prices in the first instance, allowing the effects to be passed through to consumer prices. In the meantime, the nominal zloty level of consumer-price subsidies may be held unchanged.

After removing all price subsidies for producers, the main concern should be market clearing rather than the alignment of such prices with international prices. However, in the case of some important, interna-tionally-traded goods, such as major minerals and metals, it would be necessary to set their domestic prices close to their international prices. In the case of freely-determined producer prices, competition between domestic and foreign buyers will insure parity between domestic and international prices. I see no reason to allow any exceptions to these rules in the area of nonagricultural goods and services.

The setting of agricultural procurement prices, however, must fol-low a different rule, since farmers do not have an opportunity to export their produce directly. The major concern here must be the maintenance of the desired level of the average real income of the farming population. At present, that income is roughly the same as that of the nonagricultural population, after decades at 25 to 35 percent lower. Given the need to promote interest in farming, it may be reasonable to maintain the present income parity. Subsidies on food mean that agricultural-procurement prices are set at levels high enough to produce the quantities demanded at those prices, taking into account the maintenance of the desired stand-ard of living of the agricultural population. There cannot be simple, clear-cut rules on the allocation of the total subsidy of this category among particular agricultural goods.

A potentially significant tool for limiting inflation is a rise in the interest rates on private savings and consumer credits. Since 1980 the real interest rates on both savings and credits have been highly negative, encouraging the population to borrow money and buy commodities or foreign exchange. A substantial rise in interest rates would increase both the desired savings ratio and the desired ratio of monetary to real assets, thus removing some of the "hot money" from consumer markets. It is both feasible and desirable to use private savings to a greater extent as a source of investment funds for enterprises.

It may be of interest to have an estimate of the potential inflationary consequences of the proposed deregulation of prices, including interest and exchange rates. Particularly pressing is to know the inflationary impact of any adjustments in exchange rates. One possibility is to keep the official (dollar-and-ruble) exchange rates unchanged in real terms at the time when these new reforms are introduced and let the market-determined dollar-zloty rate absorb and reflect the impact of all the various price and quantity adjustments. Suppose that 35 percent of the dollar export earnings, or 2 billion dollars, are traded freely in the first year of the program and that the free market rate is (for the sake of illustration) 220 zloty, or say, some 70 zloty above the official rate (based on the dollar of October 1985). Exporters would then earn 140 billion zloty more than they would otherwise. This amount would represent (in 1985), about 2 percent of the GDP. This two percent would also be the direct inflationary consequence of that particular reform in its first year. If the free exchange rate happens to be much greater, say 300 zloty for the dollar, then the direct inflationary impact would be about 5 percent. The impact would thus appear to be relatively minor. In the remaining four years of the program the impact would still be minor, about one-seventh the impact of the first year.

The amount of accumulated forced savings is not known with any accuracy. Some governmental analysts maintain it is 500 billion zloty, which represents about 8 percent of the GDP in 1985 prices, and about 10 percent of private monetary incomes in 1985. Deregulating prices over two to three years would thus add not more than 5 percent to the present rate of inflation. Including the exchange-rate reform, the direct inflationary impact would be, at most, 7 percent per annum over 3 years. However, this additional inflation may cause wages and other income to increase faster than they would otherwise, giving rise to an indirect inflationary impact. The size of that impact is difficult to judge, since it will, in part, be an outcome of the government's social policy and in part dependent on the specific provisions of the FAZ tax.

Another major problem is the uncompetitive structure of many markets in Poland. In state-owned industry there were only 2,271 enterprises in 1983,[10] about a quarter of the number of industrial enterprises, excluding very small businesses, which operate in much smaller Austria or Sweden. Western empirical studies indicate that the welfare losses due to monopolistic and oligopolistic pricing, as opposed to non-equilibrium pricing, are usually minor. However, the monopoly power of domestic producers is, in the West, greatly restrained by strong inter-industry competition and, in the case of tradeable goods, international competition. Both types of competition are particularly important in limiting the long-term welfare losses that arise if market pressure to reduce costs and invent new processes and products is low. Given that even under the reforms proposed here, import competition would at first be weak, it is particularly important to keep the concentration of Polish domestic industries at levels consistent with the need to maintain a reasonable degree of competition. (The details are discussed below).

Hard Budget Constraint

The achievement of real self-finance in the enterprise sector is recognized by the Polish government as critical for the success of the reform. But practice is far from consistent with this professed principle. Some of the key changes needed to remove this inconsistency are: first, the lifting of state quantity constraints for inputs and outputs and the de-regulation of product prices and interest rates; second, the formation of an interenterprise market for foreign exchange; and, third, the elimi-nation of all negotiated, product- or enterprise-specific subsidies and taxes. Very substantial progress in implementing these changes is nec-essary for the proper working of the reformed economic system.

In 1984, state gross subsidies (direct subsidies plus losses) for the enterprise sector, excepting state farms, amounted to 1032 billion zloty. This was as much as 80 percent of gross investment in the nonprivate economy, or as much as 106 percent of all the wages and bonuses earned in manufacturing and mining. As a percentage of added value, the level of subsidies has remained about the same since the introduction of the reform in 1982. Subsidies to the food industry represented, in 1984, 22.4 percent of the total. There may be good social reasons for keeping these particular subsidies in place. However, it makes little economic sense to have coal, energy, and basic metals priced below production costs and much below world prices. The authorities acknowledge that the use of these inputs per unit of final outputs in industry and construction is highly excessive. They take the trouble of constantly appealing to en-terprises to use inputs more efficiently, but during the years 1983-85 they have, in contrast to their policy, allowed the relative price of coal to fall significantly. Raising the price of coal to the world level would transform the coal industry into a major source of revenue for the gov-ernment, reduce incomes of the energy-intensive industries, and in-crease relative prices of these industries' products. All of these changes should, in turn, induce a beneficial change in the composition of demand and output, the choice of investment projects, and the use of production technologies. Without such a change, Poland may have difficulty in the future in maintaining coal exports at the present level. Alternatively, if coal exports are maintained, domestic supplies of energy will soon begin to constrain total industrial growth and therefore non-coal exports. Given the poor quality of Polish engineering products, coal exports appear to be one of the most profitable export lines; thus its preservation, or even expansion, would seem to be a correct policy, especially if the expectation that energy prices will increase again in the 1990s proves correct.

Finally, financing the government domestic debt through the cre-ation of money should be restrained. The issue of bonds by the central government and local authorities should instead become a standard practice. This change is important if inflation is to be controlled more effectively.

Investments and Resource Mobility

In the past, government officials have often complained, and aca-demic economists have charged, that too much investment goes to ex-pand the outputs of raw materials and basic intermediate inputs (such as coal, electricity, steel, and cement) and too little to upgrade the quality of the goods produced and to expand the quantity of final products. These complaints usually gloss over the fact that most investment decisions in CPEs are made by the center in response to recorded or anticipated shortages of particular goods. The system of (positive and negative) incentives under central planning is simply inducing enterprises throughout the economy daily to make millions of microeconomic choices on inputs and outputs, at the aggregate level, this then results in the country's observed energy- and material-intensive bias in output. The role of central planners, in this respect, may well be surprisingly modest, little more than that of bookkeepers: drawing input-output balances and noting shortages and responding accordingly. The branch composition of investment effort (but not the level) should therefore have little to do with the quality of investment planning as such. It is, rather, more an indicator of the nature of the economic system. It would be pointless to recommend any major change in the branch composition of Poland's investment effort. That change should come naturally as an end product of other, more fundamental, systemic and policy changes. This is not to deny that some investment projects, in particular those that supply public goods or have strong external effects, are initiated at the center, regardless of the economic system. However, investments of this category (roads, schools, hospitals, military projects, etc.) have been and are relatively modest; it would serve little purpose to look for savings in this area.

The economic reform of 1982 gave state-owned enterprises considerable power to initiate and finance their own investment projects. The percentage distribution of all gross nonprivate investment in 1984 was as follows:[11]

Enterprises	49.1
of which: fully self-financed	32.2
Central authorities	16.4
Local authorities	16.4
Housing associations	14.8
Other	3.7

However, in the industrial sector a high share of investment finance is reported to be spent on large and often long-term projects initiated during the 1970s. The wisdom of this strategy is unclear. In any case, in 1983 the destination of 85 percent of bank-investment credits was predetermined by that strategy.[12] Consequently, Polish industry did not and probably still does not have the resources necessary to significantly change its composition of outputs and production technologies. Therefore, changes in composition would have been limited even if they were motivated by new relative prices and incentives. The heavy investment commitments of the 1970s are also likely, over the next several years, to slow considerably the responsiveness of the economy to any new reform effort, a point which the Polish officials in charge of economic affairs often stress. According to the government plan for 1986-90:

> A considerable part of the investment expenditure will have to be earmarked, especially in the first years of the plan, on the continuation of investment projects in the priority sectors: food, the fuels and energy complex, and the social and economic infrastructure. It is to be stressed that investment in the fuels and energy complex will make if possible only to sustain the present level of output of hard coal . . . steel, sulphur and other key materials. . . . Taking into account the expenditure required to complete existing investment projects, the government takes the view that new investment projects in the processing industries can be undertaken on a wider scale only in the second half of the five-year period.[13]

From incomplete data available to the author it would appear that about two-thirds of the expected total gross expenditure on investment (of approximately 10,000 billion zloty during 1986-90, in 1985 prices) will be spent in the so-called productive sectors, and about one-half of the investment in those sectors is already committed. Moreover, most of the non-committed investment is expected to go to industries that produce primary inputs and basic materials, the processing industries being left with very little indeed. This pattern of investment allocation would be consistent with that observed in the last few years. For instance, in 1984 in all industries, as much as 74 percent of the investment in the sector was undertaken to maintain or expand the production of minerals and basic inputs, and only 10 percent was concerned with the production of consumer goods.[14] This pattern provides strong evidence supporting the view that, up to now, the reform has been ineffective, for it has not broken and is not expected to break the traditional material-intensive bias in the choice of investment projects, processes, and products.

Can a reform of the reform, as outlined in this paper, make a difference? In particular, can proposed changes in relative prices alter the economic calculus of enterprises sufficiently to lead to a significantly greater cancellation of old projects? The answer depends on two factors: first, on the speed with which the new prices for coal, energy, and other inputs are phased in; and second, on the seriousness of the government's commitment to close down consistently loss-making production units. The price reform may be expected to increase the variation in profitability among enterprises and possibly to increase the incidence of loss-making (or the scope of the losses, if the loss-making lines of production and whole enterprises are allowed to continue their operation). With such losses, the commitment to a much greater financial discipline will be put to the test. Provided that the commitment survives the test, a considerable fraction of industry, particularly that based on energy- and material-intensive technologies, should be phased out. As a result, there might be less need to invest in the sector that produces basic materials for domestic purposes and a greater scope for their exports or the expansion of processing industries using these materials. The present bias toward materials and energy is so large that the effects for the reallocation of investment could be quite significant, especially when the price reform is fully implemented.

The provisions of the present reform to ensure fast interenterprise mobility of investment finance appear also to be deficient. In principle, banks should serve as intermediaries to channel finance from enterprises with no suitable investment opportunities to those with such opportunities. A competitive banking sector, comprising at least several independent and self-financing banks, is vital for the efficiency of the process. The competition between those banks would be intended to ensure that the interest rates bring equilibrium to the relevant financial markets, that the banking charges are not abnormally high, and that banks are guided by the profitability of investment projects rather than the decisions of ministerial lobbies or party officials. However, before the establishment of a degree of competition, the service charges would have to be centrally controlled.

The mobility of resources may also be enhanced by lowering barriers to entry. To this end, enterprises should have the option of setting up subsidiaries in their own or other industrial branches. Enterprises may also be allowed to issue bonds or stock shares to attract private savings as well as the funds of other enterprises. A stock market should, therefore, be established in Warsaw at some point, but I would not regard this step as vital in the next several years.

Another important intermediary is the wholesale sector. The primary responsibility of the government in that sector is the assurance of an efficient operation of the markets for intermediate goods. At the moment, each industrial branch has just one wholesaler, clearly an inefficient market structure.[15] Two changes are needed. One is the elimination of quantity rationing in favor of price rationing for nearly all intermediate goods. The second change is to set up several parallel wholesale enterprises in each branch so that the price charged for their services is kept in check. These two changes, of which the first is vital and the second is useful, are designed to create and maintain proper markets for intermediate inputs. The existence of such markets would assist production enterprises in identifying demand and reducing their costs of distributing outputs, as well as offer services of particular importance to small-scale enterprises and potential new entrants. In the meantime, the present restrictions on the direct supply to enterprises by the producers of inputs should be lifted.

Market Structure

A particularly serious problem of high concentration is found in the state industrial sector, where in 1983 there were only 2271 enterprises, 46 fewer than in 1982.[16] The average employment in these enterprises is about 1800 workers. Guided by Western experience, it would be desirable to increase the number of state-owned industrial enterprises to about 10,000, or five times the present number. This is not an impossible task. Many of the present enterprises are in fact a collection of distinct establishments. In socialized industry the number of establishments equals about ten times the number of enterprises.[17] Planners find it convenient to fuse establishments into larger units. High concentration is also favored by aggressive enterprise managers, because social status, financial rewards, and bargaining power vis-à-vis the ministries is partly a function of enterprise size.

The new economic system requires that establishments that are financially and managerially independent be the basic units. The government should form a special task force to review the organization of all the state enterprises with a view to implementing deconcentration. This is important particularly in those industries that will remain sheltered against foreign competition, such as most consumer industries.

The Nomenklatura System

Party *nomenklatura* is a system of appointments of key personnel of all decision-making structures at all levels by appropriate executive committees of the communist party. It is, perhaps, the most important instrument of the party's powers in peace time. The lists of such posts used to be a well-guarded secret. As discussions of this issue become more open, we find that most managerial appointments continue to be subject to approval by the party committees. According to the reform provisions, most chief executives were to be appointed by workers' councils or specially-convened committees, for whom the professional qualities of the candidates were to be the deciding consideration. For example, in 1983 about 80 percent of new managerial appointments were supposedly made locally by such professionally-minded committees.[18] However, given the nature of a communist political system and state ownership of most means of production, up to now political interference has been both excessive and probably inevitable.

The best way to reduce such interference is by a large increase in the demand by enterprises for entrepreneurial talent rather than simply well-connected directors. When the welfare of the enterprise depends strongly on the allocative and other decisions at the central and intermediate levels—as it still does at present—even appointment committees dominated by Solidarity would favor candidates with good ministerial and party connections. Conversely, when that welfare depends above all on the performance of the enterprise in the marketplace, even appointment committees dominated by communist party members may find political qualifications less important. The Hungarian system of open competition between candidates for the post of enterprise director may hold useful lessons for Poland.[19] In any event, proper economic reform should automatically have a desired effect in this sensitive area. A depolitization of the economy at the enterprise level would thus be indirectly introduced. The political system would be challenged, but not openly and not provocatively.

Intra-CMEA Trade

Another related systemic problem is the wedge that is driven into the reform process by the dependence of Poland on trade with its CMEA partners. How can the government ensure that Polish producers, without compromising the decentralization of decision making, will deliver the exports to Poland's socialist partners that were promised in intergovernmental agreements?

I know of no systematic study of the problem. This may not be as serious as it first appears. The bulk of ruble exports is conducted by fewer than 200 enterprises, many of which were built for the specific purpose of supplying the CMEA markets. For them domestic markets are too small and Western markets too difficult or inappropriate. In trade negotiations government officials usually act as representatives of these enterprises, and what they agree to deliver is also what the enterprises themselves can and want to export. It is interesting that, despite the low exchange rate for the ruble—only about half of the rate implied by the official rate of dollar-ruble exchange—in recent years the zloty has been devalued against the dollar much more than against the ruble. Thus, the CMEA markets still appear attractive to Polish producers.

In the case of "hard goods"—items that would have buyers in the West at attractive prices—transactions with the CMEA partners may be conducted in dollars. The share of such dollar transactions is already significant and is likely to increase. Furthermore, the government may use investment credits or subsidies to induce a particular producer to supply a CMEA partner with what the state has agreed to supply. The government may also introduce an interenterprise market for rubles, although its significance would be constrained by limited commodity convertibility within the CMEA. Finally, the government has the option of ordering an enterprise to do what it wants and compensate it for any opportunity costs. In 1983 only 35 such orders were officially recorded, out of the total number of 358 orders.[20] However, many more *informal* orders were probably employed.

Foreign Investment and Private Industrial Activity

In many newly industrialized, capitalist countries, foreign private capital is playing an important role in the transfer of modern technology and know-how, the development of local skills, and the generation of exports. East European countries have been slow and hesitant in taking advantage of this policy option. In principle, joint ventures are permitted not only in Yugoslavia and Hungary but in Bulgaria and Romania as well. In practice, their presence is insignificant in all these countries.

In Poland, foreign capital is present but can operate on its own only in small-scale manufacture. In 1985, there were about 600 foreign enterprises, called Polonia firms, which employed 45,000 people (1 percent of the total industrial workforce), accounted for about 2 percent of net industrial output, and contributed more than their share to net exports. In 1986, legislation was introduced to liberalize foreign investment in Poland. However, given the political risks and economic constraints, it seems unlikely that Poland can attract sufficient foreign capital to make a significant difference in the overall economic condition. But the scope for improvement is substantial. Even a change from the present 1 percent of industrial employment to 5 percent would have a substantial positive long-term impact on the trade balance in convertible currencies and on the spread of entrepreneurial and competitive attitudes.

Private activity exclusive of agriculture may also play an important economic role. By the end of 1984, such activity engaged 663,000 people working in 315,000 outlets.[21] The growth of these private outlets is now severely constrained by registration difficulties, the limited allocation of centrally-rationed inputs, and a highly progressive income tax (the maximum tax rate is 80 percent; at the official exchange rate, it applies to annual incomes above about $30,000). This private activity is also exposed to risks of sudden adverse changes in policy. Despite these difficulties and risks, the sector generates high net incomes and is supposed to be a major holder of Poland's forced savings and a major consumer of luxuries. A relaxation of registration, allocative, and fiscal constraints would, in due course, channel some of these savings into productive investment and the expansion of output, thereby making the nonagricultural private sector a significant earner of foreign exchange, an important supplier of goods and services for the agricultural sector, and a useful competitor for some state enterprises.

Agriculture

Total net agricultural output doubled between 1953 and 1974, but has remained stagnant since then, fluctuating during 1973-85 from a low of 133.4 in 1982 to a high of 159.1 in 1978 (1961-1965 = 100). In per-capita terms, net agricultural output (net of inputs) increased from 1950 to 1973 by 46 percent, or 1.7 percent per annum, but during 1973-83 it declined by 11.1 percent, or 1.1 percent per annum. During 1981-84 the output per person was consequently only about 18 percent higher than during 1961-65 and only 30 percent higher than in 1950. To increase the food consumption per person in the 1970s and to "pay for" the mistake in policy (see Chapter 5 by Andrews), the government phased out net exports of food products to non-socialist countries and, since 1976, engaged in net imports. As a result, from 1977 to 1981, Poland became a major net importer of food. Net dollar imports reached about $1.4 billion in 1981 (see Chapter 4 by Boyd). These imports were reduced to $394 million in 1982, and since 1983, Poland has again become a net food exporter, though as yet on a modest scale ($66 million in 1983 and $90 million in 1984). This turnabout in foreign-trade policy has significantly reduced domestic food consumption since 1979. In fact, during 1980-84 consumption per person was some 20 percent lower than during 1978 and 1979.

Poland's agriculture has the potential of becoming a major contributor to the country's balance-of-trade surplus in convertible currencies. One way to increase net exports would be the maintenance of domestic food consumption per person at the present depressed level and an increase in domestic output at rates higher than the growth rate of the population (now about 0.9 percent). One Western forecast envisions the possibility of increasing net food exports to non-socialist countries as follows:[22]

Year	1987	1988	1989	1990
$ millions	360	505	735	983

These numbers do not seem unrealistic, especially if the government modifies its agricultural policy. One possible source of output gains would be a phasing out of the resource and fiscal preferences that are still enjoyed by the socialized sector, necessitating the closure of loss-making state farms and the sale of state land to the highest bidders, either from the private or state sectors. Such a move would make the private farmer more confident in making long-term investment decisions. Another potentially important change is the role of the nonagricultural, private sector in servicing the private farm sector. If the government decides to abandon its ideologically-motivated, punitive policy toward private entrepreneurs, well-equipped workshops and small-scale production units servicing the machinery of the private farmer are likely to increase in number.

Modifications of the present agricultural policy should bring considerable results, especially if industrial supplies for the private farmer improve. However, there are a number of factors at work that make it difficult to rapidly increase agricultural output under any policy. Perhaps the most important of these factors are those which underly the low mobility of resources from inefficient farmers to those who have the

entrepreneurial talent, knowledge, and motivation. The number of inefficient farms is apparently large and will therefore remain large. Other
factors relate to the damaging external effects of industrialization: the
drop of the level of ground water, a reduction in the area of farm land,
and the pollution of the soil, air, and water. There is no immediate
prospect for a sizable improvement in any of these areas.

Still, compared to the probable stagnation in the volume—or even
the value—of raw-material exports, sales of directly edible agricultural
products and processed food provide a more promising area for expansion. A good way to achieve such an expansion would be upgrading
the quality and expanding the capacity of the food-processing industry.
The reduction of the apparently high food losses now incurred at various
stages of production, transportation, and storage is equally important.
Investment projects in the food processing industry are usually on a
small scale and highly profitable. These projects are also quickly completed. Such projects may attract foreign capital more easily than would
larger and more risky engineering projects. There is, therefore, the potential for making Poland a more important supplier of processed food
products, and perhaps also fruit, to Western Europe.

Policy Adjustment Versus Systemic Changes

Economists often find it useful to make a distinction between policy
adjustments (changes in economic policies within unchanged economic
systems) that are designed to reduce certain macroeconomic imbalances
directly, and systemic changes (changes in microeconomic rules and
incentive systems) that are designed to have substantial, indirect, and
beneficial macroeconomic effects. The changes discussed in this chapter
are predominantly of the latter type. The fact that economic policy may
be a powerful tool was demonstrated vividly by the government in 1982,
when a drastic fall in domestic absorption was engineered to quickly
improve the balance of trade. In its plans for 1986-90, the government
hopes to increase consumption by about 10 to 15 percent and investment
by about 20 to 25 percent. These targets may be unrealistically high,
given that they require unusually large improvements in key efficiency
indicators. If the authorities insist on these plans, there is a strong possibility that the balance of trade, instead of improving, will deteriorate.
The policy of the Polish government at present seems to be guided by
the principle of maintaining the trade surplus in convertible currencies
at a level judged necessary to avoid bankruptcy. On the other hand,
something like a zero-growth policy, implying a freeze in the standard
of living and modest increases in investment, would almost certainly
bring about a further substantial improvement in the balance of trade,
possibly eliminating the current deficit within a few years. This is, however, a policy option that Poland is likely to strongly oppose. Apart from

the political implications of a stagnant level of consumption per person, the feature that must worry the government is the continuing low level of technological imports from the West. It is so low that the present technological and productivity gaps between Poland and the West will continue to increase significantly in the 1990s (see Chapter 6 by Poznański). This would make the task of reviving an expansion of engineering exports to the West extremely difficult. Such an expansion is, however, necessary if an "export-led" policy is to have any chance. Continued austerity for many years would also increase the risk of a major social upheaval.

A comprehensive reform of the kind outlined above would be much preferred, since it would make it feasible to increase simultaneously exports, imports, and domestic absorption. This option may or may not bring about a rapid elimination of the payments deficit, but it should reduce significantly the relative indebtedness, as measured by the debt-export ratio. This would be seen by Western creditors as an improvement.

For the authorities, the constraints and risks associated with the reform option are also considerable, as spelled out by Brus (Chapter 8), Bielasiak (Chapter 11), and Kamecki (Chapter 13). Still, there should be room in politics for a significant improvement of the present economic system, especially if longer-term considerations prevail. The provisions of the so-called Stage Two of the reform, as announced by the government during 1987, are not yet sufficiently radical. But they seem to indicate some new determination on the part of the authorities to move more decisively with the marketization of Poland's economy.

Notes

1. Much of the work on this chapter was done during my research fellowship at the Hoover Institution, Stanford University, in the summer of 1985. The final version was prepared at the Harriman Institution, Columbia University, in the Spring of 1986. I wish to thank both institutions for providing financial support and a stimulating research environment. I would also like to thank Keith Crane, John Farrell, David Granick, Agota Gueullette, Cezary Józefiak, Kazimierz Poznański, Jacek Rostowski, Peter Wiles, Eugeniusz Zaleski and the editors of this volume for their useful suggestions.

2. The core of that group were representatives of large industrial enterprises, and their key adviser was Dr. Leszek Balcerowicz of the Warsaw High School of Planning and Statistics.

3. RER-84, *Report on Economic Reform*, Accepted by the Council of Ministers at its meeting on June 22, 1984, *Rzeczpospolita*, August, 1985.

4. S. Gomulka and J. Rostowski, "The Reformed Polish Economic System." *Soviet Studies*, no. 3 (July 1984).

5. In industry during 1982-84, about two-thirds of the wage increases were the result of "central decisions and tax allowances." C. Józefiak, *Życie Gospo-*

darcze, February 3, 1985. p. 5. This author in turn refers to a Report by Konsultacyjna Rada Gospodarcza (KRG), *Życie Gospodarcze*, 1984, no. 14, as the source.

6. RER-84, Tables 12 and 17.

7. *Statistical Yearbook for 1985* (in Polish) (Warsaw, 1985) p. 106, Table 30 (167) B. Profit tax is reported as the income tax of enterprises.

8. Ibid., p. 49.

9. Ibid., p. 94.

10. RER-84, Table 9.

11. "Communiqués on Poland's Social and Economic Results in 1984," GUS, Warsaw, February 4, 1985.

12. RER-84, p. 12.

13. M. Gorywoda, "National Economic Plans for 1986 and 1986-90: A Speech in the Sejm by the Chairman of the Planning Commission," (in Polish) *Życie Gospodarcze*, May 19, 1985, pp. 8-9.

14. J. Szewc in *Życie Gospodarcze*, April 7, 1985, p. 1.

15. In 1983-84 there were twenty such wholesalers of intermediate goods and four of final foods. See Józefiak in *Życie Gospodarcze*, January 27, 1985, p. 5.

16. RER-84, Table 9.

17. C. Józefiak, *Życie Gospodarcze*, February 10, 1985, Table 2.

18. RER-84, p.22.

19. For details see Paul Marer, "Economic Reforms in Hungary: From Central Planning to Regulated Market." In Joint Economic Committee, U.S. Congress, *East European Economies: Slow Growth in the 1980s*, vol. 3, (Washington, D.C., 1981).

20. RER-84, p. 7.

21. *Życie Gospodarcze*, May 12, 1985. p. 3.

22. J. Vanous and C. Movit, "Polish Hard-Currency Trade, Balance of Payments and External Debt, 1980-90." mimeo, Washington, D.C., May 31, 1985.

PART VI.

POLICY TOWARD POLAND

30

Strategy and Tactics in U.S. Foreign Policy Toward Eastern Europe

Thomas W. Simons, Jr.

The purpose of this chapter is to offer my theory of change in Eastern Europe, to discuss the evolving nature of East-West competition in the region, and to identify some of the premises and tactics of U.S. policy toward the countries of Eastern Europe.[1]

The East European Situation in Historical Perspective

Looking back over the postwar period, change which has seemed massive and even cataclysmic to the peoples of Eastern Europe seems glacial to outsiders, who are more aware of the extent of change west of Eastern Europe and less aware of where the countries of the area began at war's end.[2] By glacial, I mean that it has been both slow and punctuated by earthquakes, or near-earthquakes. Change has occurred in Eastern Europe; the upheavals of 1956, 1968, and 1980—the crises that are all most outsiders know about the area—attest to that. But it is hard to say with confidence how far it has gone.

Let me state briefly my theory of change in Eastern Europe. In every country the Soviets imposed cliques which more or less successfully became parties. These parties then have created and worked through state organizations that became much stronger than anything the countries had had before. The postwar states of Eastern Europe, modeled after Stalin's USSR, in some sense have fulfilled the dreams of the area's traditional elites, in terms of the concentration of state power needed to implement a nineteenth-century ideology of economic development. That ideology, carried to its extreme by Stalinism, wants to build heavy industry based on coal and steel (and chemicals, beginning in the 1950s) paid for by the transformation of agriculture. The East European countries have gone forward with this power structure and this ideology, trying to adjust them as their advantages for takeoff have been exhausted one by one. One reason this ideology of development is difficult to move away from is that centralized state power is so attractive to the powerholders. This is not just because of the perquisites—the dachas, the special shops, the cars, and the police escorts that are so well-known. It is because the elites in these countries never before had that kind of power, for any purpose. The fact that initially the power structure was imposed from the outside and works to Soviet advantage is paradoxical, but the power is not less real and attractive for that.

The De- and Re-Politicization of East-West Competition in Eastern Europe

Throughout its postwar history Eastern Europe has been an arena of competition between East and West. The cold war started there because of that competition, and the division of Europe which the cold war produced has fueled that competition. The Soviet method of competition—the imposition of the Stalinist system, forcing isolation from the West—was an act of Soviet colonialism, involving total or near-total Soviet control of all significant aspects of life in each country. The upheavals this produced led the USSR, in the late 1950s, to rationalize and streamline their means of control.

The development of the new Soviet policy unfolded differently vis-à-vis every country. In most places the Soviets kept a full panoply of mechanisms in place, except for military forces, which they withdrew in some cases. They simply calibrated the extent to which the mechanisms were used. Overall, during the second half of the 1950s the accent shifted from political means—military forces, police, the army of advisors—to economic means. From the Soviet point of view, this was risky. They gambled that the inertial weight of the Stalinist economic model in Eastern Europe made the Soviet market the natural resting place for those economies. The risk was that the Soviets would lose the degree of control that was essential to them by depending more on indirect—economic—means of exerting it. The period from 1956 to about 1980 was a kind of test of this new policy.

Let me describe what was being tested. Heavy industrialization within a Stalinist economic structure tends to produce more and more goods that cannot sell on Western markets, but which require more and more inputs of energy and raw material resources that the area does not possess in abundance. The natural inclination of these economies is to seek the Soviet market, provided that market gives them stable supplies of raw materials and stable outlets for their shoddy goods.

All the countries of the area have tried to escape this natural trend at various times and by various means. The means have included openings to the West, barter arrangements with Third World countries, and economic reform. Since the primary incentive for economic reform has been to produce goods that could sell on hard-currency markets, even economic reform, whatever else it represents, should be seen as a device to escape the natural economic tendency of these economies toward integration with the Soviet economy. One way to write the history of this area would be to describe the dialectics of how this has worked, how much effort the Soviets have permitted, how much access these countries could gain to outside markets. In the end, however, it seems to me that, for a generation, this controlled experiment has worked out generally in a way to console the Soviets. The Soviet market has remained, by and large, the natural partner of the East European economies.

Returning to the larger theme of East-West competition, this shift in emphasis from the political to the economic arena in Soviet control has also transformed "economized" the competition from the West, which, although as keen as ever, has become primarily economic in form. In addition to political means (the regular government-to-government work of embassies, the radio broadcasts, and the propaganda), the West now has in place a variety of economic ties with the countries of the area, which began in the U.S. with the PL-480 grain sales to Poland after 1956. In the 1970s the accent shifted to credits, trade, scientific and technological cooperation, and some joint ventures.

This shift to competition in an economic form has had tremendous political advantages for both sides. It has "depoliticized" the competition for influence, making that competition more correct and less tense, though not less real. The Soviets could tell themselves that they were merely doing their fraternal duty, building the infrastructure of the socialist community; dominion was the last thing they had in mind. The West could tell itself it was only doing business, disposing of surpluses, letting its businesses make profits; rollback or liberation was the last thing it had in mind. Each side, of course, remembered its own "last things" and hoped that the other side would forget theirs. It was a convenient fiction, and it was especially useful for the East Europeans themselves because, in pursuit of their national interests, it broadened their margin for maneuver in relations with both East and West.

Has this situation changed fundamentally in recent years? Are we in an era in which the political competition for influence in Eastern Europe between the Soviet Union and the West is being "repoliticized" in some basic way? The evidence from the last decade seems to me to point in this direction.

To begin with, the negotiating process initiated at the Conference on Security and Cooperation in Europe (CSCE) in 1972 and enshrined by the Helsinki Final Act in 1975 has turned out to be primarily political in content. It is, of course, a complicated process with many purposes. Beginning as a classic Soviet peace initiative in the 1950s, it resurfaced as a way of overcoming the results of the invasion of Czechoslovakia in 1968. Then, on the Eastern side, it became a means of ratifying the postwar territorial settlement and, on the Western side, a bargaining chip for a Berlin settlement and for negotiations on mutual and balanced force reductions (MBFR). As the CSCE became a process, the West developed its human rights aspect. At the same time, the East Europeans found that it provided a wonderful cover for a whole range of new bilateral dealings with Western countries. The Soviets, on the other hand, remained hooked on their own initiative. They sought to ward off the dangers inherent in the process by various means, bilateral and multilateral, and they were partially successful. But the process itself, with its large human rights component, did not stop. All efforts to beef up Basket II, the economic component, have been unsuccessful, which registers the fact that economic relations proceed mainly on their own momentum and largely in practical bilateral channels. But on balance, the Helsinki process signals a certain "repoliticization" in East-West relations and the East-West competition for influence in Eastern Europe.

Another kind of evidence involves "repoliticization by subtraction." By a combination of facts of life and choice, both sides no longer have large economic resources available for competition, certainly not on the scale of the 1960s and early 1970s. In the West, lack of economic buoyancy since 1973 has had its impact; so have legislative and regulatory restrictions on exports and credits. Furthermore, the very experience of developing economic ties has shown Western businessmen and bankers that state-trading countries are difficult partners to work with—many have trouble paying their debts, and dealings with them produce only modest profits. In the East, resources have dried up partly because Western economic anemia shrank the markets for earning the hard currency needed to pay for imports, but mainly because of the skyrocketing costs of exploiting Soviet energy and raw materials, and the consequent Soviet preference for selling them on hard-currency markets rather than in Eastern Europe. The main result—the dwindling away of resources for economic competition on both sides—seems to me beyond doubt. So does its corollary: a repoliticization of the competition, this time by subtraction of the resources needed to give it an economic form.

Let's try to put the liberalization impulse from the Soviet Union into this context. Through the late Brezhnev years, the two transition regimes, and the early Gorbachev years, the Soviets seemed to be muddling through on a case-by-case basis. Their approach to each country involved some combination of tolerance and warning, without much of a coherent pattern. It is not clear to me that such a pattern has yet emerged. It may be that Gorbachev's statement in Prague and Ligachev's statement in Budapest in April 1987 have unveiled a new strategy.[3] It may be that the Soviets are calling on the East European countries to tighten their economic ties with the USSR and produce better goods for that market, but are substantially leaving it up to them as to how they go about it. If so, we could be seeing a reaffirmation of the post-1956 line which combined separate roads to socialism at the political level with consolidating the socialist camp on the economic level. The Soviet statement of October 30, 1956, on the eve of the recapture of Budapest, remains after all the charter for different roads to socialism.[4] It was followed by Khrushchev's campaign for integration of the "camp" on the basis of a socialist division of labor in the CMEA framework. In other words, the inspiration may be from the Khrushchev era, like so much else about the Gorbachev regime. But the evidence is not yet in.

U.S. Interests and Policy

What should the U.S. do in this situation? The answer must start with some definition of U.S. interests in the area. The first and most fundamental of these is responsibility for our security and that of our allies. It is a broad responsibility, which we exercise in many forms. In Europe, we see it as a responsibility to deal, in many ways, with the postwar division of the continent, which we perceive as an element of instability. We stand for the rule of law in international relations, and we are not calling legal obligations into question. We are not revisionists in that sense. But on a continent packed with weapons, "earthquakes" and upheavals in Eastern Europe are dangerous. Therefore, we want to work on the weapons, through the arms control and arms reduction process. But we also want to work on the reasons why they are there, the basic causes of the mistrust and lack of confidence that put them in place and keep them in place.

Second, there are 15 to 20 million Americans who have their roots in Eastern Europe, and an even greater number who identify with the traditions and cultural heritage of the region. The welfare of the people living in the area matters deeply to our public, to Congress, and to the press, continuously for some, intermittently for many. Therefore, as a matter of practical politics, we must maintain our interests in Eastern Europe.

Third, we are interested in Eastern Europe because we believe that the peoples of this area, too, have the right to freedom, peace, and prosperity. We think those rights are the wave of the future for all humanity. Humanity does not divide itself into those societies that are ready for or deserve these rights and those that do not. We believe we share the aspiration to enjoy those rights with the East Europeans. And we have learned that American foreign policy must promote American values and aspirations, or it does not work on any sustainable basis. Promoting those values is important for the future of the international system. Moreover, human rights are now written into the texts and texture of international relations. They are recognized under the UN Charter, the Universal Declaration of Human Rights, and the Helsinki Final Act. They are not contradictory to the search for a more stable peace; they are part of it. As a responsible member of the international community, the U.S. has a duty to promote and foster those rights at every opportunity, and nowhere more so than in Eastern Europe.

Fourth, and finally, we support legitimate U.S. business interests in Eastern Europe. We see nothing wrong with making money, if there is money to be made, and if making it does not impinge on our other interests—national security or human rights. In 1986, the area represented a $714 million market for U.S. exports, one which could be expanded.

How do we fashion a policy that articulates these various interests in terms that can capture sustainable bipartisan political support? The answer we have come up with, in practice over the past thirty years and formally over the past dozen years, is commonly called differentiation. It is a conceptual framework which does not determine day-to-day policy decisions very well, but does define a policy approach which is understandable and sustainable over the long run in terms of the national interest and public opinion.

The differentiation approach is based on a recognition that the countries of Eastern Europe are different not only from the Soviet Union but also from each other, and that there are potential differences even where there are no actual differences on specific aspects of policy. It says that we will seek to develop better relations with the individual countries of Eastern Europe, at whatever pace they set, and that we will be guided in these efforts by one or both of two criteria: the extent to which they are different—in the right direction—in terms of domestic arrangements and/or in terms of foreign policy.

Of course, differentiation is not an approach adequate to all the richness and complexities of the situations in each country. I would be the last to deny that it is difficult to apply day-to-day. But it is, as the saying goes, good enough for government work. The people who are interested understand it. It makes clear that we wish to deal both with governments and with the governed, and that we will take the treatment of the latter by the former into account in our dealings with them. The policy has bipartisan Congressional support, and provides an element of stability in our policy which is also important for a power with responsibilities across the breadth of the international system. One effect of this policy is to rank-order the countries in terms of domestic liberalization or independence in foreign policy. To be sure, this makes their governments uncomfortable wherever they stand on our policy ladder. But to the extent that they are interested in relations with us, they know where they stand and what their options are.

The differentiation policy framework is certainly a constraint. But I would argue that it is a good constraint; it prevents us from haring off after every tactical shift by an East European government, or every impulse from narrow interest groups active in American politics. Intemperate or precipitate moves would shatter the framework that assures public and political support for the overall policy. Thus it takes a good deal of change in an East European country for it to move up or down our ladder of differentiation, and that is not a bad thing.

An important question is whether the policy framework is flexible enough to permit us to respond to major new challenges and new opportunities. In my view, the answer is yes, and I would suggest two kinds of evidence.

First, initiative is built into the concept. Seeking to improve bilateral relations on the basis of our criteria, at the pace a given country can stand, in effect calls for us to set out "challenge programs" for each country. These are not revolutionary programs designed to turn relationships inside out. They are practical, step-by-step programs, defined in terms of our interests, on which the East European authorities can choose to work with us to the extent that they can, and to the extent that they are interested in improving relations. We have such programs in place with every country of the area except Albania, with whom the prospect of developing relations of any kind is remote. We thus have in place "dynamic yardsticks" of their political intentions toward us, and of our intentions toward them.

Second, Poland provides a case study in policy flexibility within the differentiation framework. During the 1970s Poland occupied a privileged place among our East European partners. Following the imposition of martial law in 1981 and the subsequent outlawing of Solidarity, it dropped to the bottom rung of the differentiation ladder. The imposition of U.S. sanctions made clear our intolerance for the policies of the Polish authorities and our support for the forces of democracy in the country. But our stated willingness to remove the sanctions in response to progress toward national reconciliation and human rights also provided an incentive for the Polish government to substitute dialogue for repression in dealing with dissent.

Since September 1986, we have been involved in a step-by-step process aimed at improving U.S.Polish relations. Following the amnesty of political prisoners in September 1986, we engaged Poland in November (not a bad turnaround time for a big government like ours) on the margins of the opening of the CSCE Review Conference in Vienna. We suggested a specific program of steps to expand commercial, scientific, and political exchanges. Prompted in part by the amnesty and in part by appeals from Solidarity and the church, President Reagan lifted the sanctions on February 19, 1987, as the best way to assist the Polish people.

This evidence shows that the policy of differentiation is capable of adjustment both in response to negative developments and to opportunities for progress in terms of our criteria. With Poland, we made it clear that progress had to be measured in deeds and not mere rhetoric. We were able to act appropriately, within a consistent framework which made U.S. policy both clear and effective. It was neither grandiose nor particularly elegant, but it has been effective.

Challenges of the Future

In conclusion, I would like to offer a few thoughts on the future. First, it seems to me that we have in place a policy framework that allows us to deal with change, up or down, creatively, and in keeping with the national interest. It is comprehensive, flexible, realistic, and it has the political support it needs. Second, we are equipped to deal with the "repoliticization" of East-West competition for influence in Eastern Europe.

On the negative side, I doubt that either the USSR or the U.S.—or even our West European allies—will ever again have the economic resources to engage in the kind of competition that we had from the late 1950s until the late 1970s. On the positive side, I think it was probably time to return to politics anyway, in terms of our interests and the interests of the countries of the area. Three aspects of this are worth noting.

First, the exhaustion of the Stalinist economic system's functional usefulness in country after East European country and in sector after economic sector is forcing upon each country strategic decisions that are in essence political. They are being forced to grapple with tradeoffs between flexibility in economic management and political control. Economic pressures, not Gorbachev, are forcing these tradeoffs; the fact that the Soviets are now headed in the same direction makes decisions on the tradeoffs more urgent.

Second, the international political and legal framework for repoliticization is in place, and is accepted by the governments of the area. It was not planned that way; it is, in fact, a classic case of unintended byproduct. But the CSCE process, the Helsinki Final Act, and its successor documents legitimize a focus on the peoples of Eastern Europe as an international issue. Attention to the relations of the governors and the governed is therefore not simply forced by domestic developments, or by the intrusive interest of outside powers; it is also a proper aspect of foreign relations.

Third, the U.S. has shared in the general trend within the countries of the Atlantic alliance toward a recognition that issues of morality, values, and human rights are issues of peace and war. This has a practical significance for policy vis-à-vis the countries of Eastern Europe, not simply as a constraint on what we can do but as a criterion for what we and the governments of the area should be doing if we are to improve relations. I think it responds to the way of the world, to what the Soviets call "life itself"; in particular, I think it equips us to deal creatively, and in keeping with our national interests, with the evolving situation in Eastern Europe.

If, as I believe, foreign policy is to be more and more concerned with both the governors and the governed, then there is no other area in the world where the structural preconditions for real progress are so advanced as in Eastern Europe. Despite the "glacial" pace of change (as it appears to outsiders), there have in fact been many changes in all of the countries since 1945, and especially since 1956, which make the possibility of democratic development better rather than worse. There has been an educational revolution which has produced analogues of the middle classes that these countries never had before, except perhaps in the Czech lands. There has been a revalidation of national values, and often these are democratic values. And yes, there have been in- creasing ties with the outside world, particularly with the West. Dem- ocratic developments in this part of the world, where two World Wars and the cold war began, would mean real alleviation of the consequences of the division of Europe and an international environment genuinely more conducive to stability with peaceful change. The democratization of Eastern Europe is therefore of importance to us, and worthy of our support.

Notes

1. This chapter is an edited version of personal remarks made on May 21, 1987 at a workshop on De-Stalinization II and Eastern Europe sponsored by the U.S. Department of State at Airlie House near Warrenton, Virginia. It represents the personal views of the author and does not necessarily reflect the position of the Department. The author's colleague, Robert M. Perito, contributed to developing some points.

2. By Eastern Europe, I refer to Albania, Bulgaria, Czechoslovakia, the GDR, Hungary, Poland, and Romania. Yugoslavia is not included, for both objective and policy reasons.

3. Gorbachev clearly intended to break new policy ground in his April 10 speech to a Czechoslovak-Soviet "friendship rally" in Prague. He announced the beginning of a "new stage" in relations among socialist countries. In the previous stage, "firm foundations were laid for the international socialist division of labor," and Soviet "experience was, naturally, taken as the standard." Now

the whole system of cooperation must be raised to a "qualitatively new level," with political relations based on "equality and mutual responsibility." No single party has a monopoly of truth; no one can claim a special position; each party's independence, responsibility before its people, and right to decide questions of the country's development independently are "to us absolute principles." The criterion for the "value of this experience" is sociopolitical practice, economic results, and the "actual strengthening of socialism." But on the economic side, "consistent observance of the principles of mutual advantage and mutual aid" is still necessary, with equalizing the levels of economic development the prescribed goal. (*Pravda*, April 11, 1987, reported in FBIS, *Soviet Union*, April 14, 1987, F10-11.)

Ligachev in Budapest also blessed independence, but in more qualified fashion, and he sharpened the economic requirement. In his April 25 press conference, he affirmed the sovereignty of each party in its specific conditions, but put more stress than Gorbachev had on common aims, common ideology, and common principles. Like Gorbachev, he made praxis the "supreme criterion for the correctness of the chosen course." But Ligachev bore down harder on the need to develop higher forms of production and cooperation involving direct links between entities, and in his talk with Kádár he made a special point of the need for "consistent implementation" of agreements. Most Hungarian reporting simply juxtaposed these two elements of political independence and tightening economic ties. (FBIS, *Eastern Europe*, April 27, 1987, F27; see also FBIS, *Soviet Union*, April 24, 1987, F14, and April 27, 1987, F46).

4. The Declaration of the Government of the USSR on the Principles of Development and Further Strengthening of Friendship and Cooperation between the Soviet Union and Other Socialist Countries, October 30, 1956, applied "peaceful coexistence," often reserved theoretically for relations between states with different social systems, to relations among socialist states. It proclaimed that they can build relations "only on the principles of complete equality, of respect for territorial integrity, state independence and sovereignty, and of non-interference in one another's internal affairs." Admitting past mistakes, it said the Soviet government was consistently carrying out the decisions of the CPSU 20th Congress, which "proclaimed the need for taking full account of the historic past and peculiarities of each country that has taken the path of building a new life." It of course also referred to common ideals, the principles of proletarian internationalism and close fraternal cooperation and mutual aid, so nothing was given away. But the stress was on legitimate independence, and that was a lot at the time. The Declaration is reprinted in Paul E. Zinner, ed., *National Communism and Popular Revolt in Eastern Europe* (New York, 1956), pp. 485-489.

31

U.S. Policy Toward Poland in a Global Perspective

Zbigniew Brzeziński

The dominant factor in Polish-American relations is the relationship of the United States and the Soviet Union.[1] It is within this global context that I will set my remarks, which will first address the issue of détente and how it was perceived by the superpowers in the early 1970s.

The policy of détente—as defined by Nixon and Brezhnev—began largely as a defensive response by the two superpowers to the dangers of their unchecked rivalry. By the mid-1970s, however, the Soviets had become much more assertive, a fact stimulated largely by their perception of opportunities. These opportunities were opened up by what they called "the aggravated crisis of capitalism" as well as by the *receuillement* of the U.S., which was an expression of our post-Vietnam trauma. For the USSR, the strategic goal of détente was the deterence of an effective American response to the changing political balance. Soviet spokesmen often put forth the view that "the policy of peaceful coexistence has nothing in common with the 'freezing' of the status quo, with any artificial mothballing of the revolutionary process."[2] On the contrary, détente and military parity were now said to facilitate significant political "change" in Western Europe and elsewhere.

This policy of "decoupling" the East-West agreements from the global behavior of the Soviets left the strategic choices of the USSR open. At some point, when the "objective" situation became "historically ripe," the Soviets could adopt a more revolutionary policy, exploiting favorable preconditions whenever and wherever they arose. The Soviets thus subtly combined elements of cooperation and competition; their view of détente was not to preserve the status quo but to transform it.

Our initial misunderstanding of how the Soviets perceived détente in the 1970s raised unrealistic expectations. Moreover, it is incorrect to argue that the only alternative to détente is war. In my view, Western relations with the USSR must be based on a realistic assessment of Soviet intentions and on the acceptance in our relations of both cooperation and competition.

The possibility of meaningful cooperation with the USSR will improve if the Soviet leadership realizes the self-defeating consequences of some of its actions. I believe that a Soviet thrust toward global preeminence is less likely to lead to a *Pax Sovietica* than to international chaos. The Soviet Union might hope to displace America from its leading role in the international system, but it is too weak economically and too unappealing politically to assume that position itself. I have argued over the years that[3] this is the ultimate self-defeating element of Soviet policy;[3] Gorbachev and some of the strategic thinkers on whom he relies may have begun to realize this. The USSR can exploit global anarchy, but it probably will not be able to transform it to its own enduring advantage. Therefore, the Soviet danger is of a different kind than that usually stressed by conservatives. The proper Western response should be a carefully calibrated policy of simultaneous competition and cooperation, designed to promote a more comprehensive and more reciprocal détente—one that would engage the Soviet Union in a more constructive response to global problems.

A comprehensive and reciprocal détente would mean, in practice, a scrupulous fulfillment of the Helsinki agreements; responsible Soviet behavior on fundamental issues of global order rather than irresponsible behavior, such as in Angola, the Middle East or the UN (e.g., the stimulation of extremist resolutions such as that equating Zionism with racism); and a realistic effort on both sides to reach arms control agreements. At the same time, the U.S. should move away from its excessive preoccupation with U.S.-Soviet relations, which could only breed either excessively euphoric expectations of an American-Soviet partnership (inspiring fears abroad of an American-Soviet condominium) or hysterical preoccupations with a U.S.-Soviet confrontation. Instead, the U.S. should address itself to a variety of Third World problems, preferably through trilateral cooperation with Western Europe and Japan. The Soviet Union should be included in that cooperation whenever it is willing and should not be made the focal point of American interest to the exclusion of the rest of the global agenda.

Regarding U.S.-Soviet relations, we may now be entering a phase of unique opportunity for improvement. It is perhaps the first time since World War II that the Soviet Union is on the defensive internationally and domestically at the same time. Internationally it is not in a phase of expansion, which is the product of its ideological appeal, economic dynamism, and the effective application of its military force. The case in which the military force of the Soviet Union is in current use—Afghanistan—is not proving very productive. Domestically, the Soviets are entering what I think is a period of systemic crisis. This has not only an economic dimension, which is self-evident, but also a domestic political (including restive nationalities) dimension. These problems are beginning to permeate Soviet political life and will inhibit the capacity of the country to undertake either expensive and risky global ventures or significant reforms at home. In the Soviet bloc, which one of my colleagues has aptly called the Soviet sphere of co-stagnation, there is a rising sense of uneasiness about the future and a pervasive realization that the Soviet model is not working well and that it does not provide any of the solutions that the various component parts of the bloc are now seeking. We are dealing with a Soviet world that is in a crisis which is likely to endure and which may manifest itself in very significant political instability at the top. Although I am not sure we are going to be dealing with Gorbachev until the year 2000, as so many pundits are asserting, there may now be a historic opportunity, as well as a more and more urgent need, to negotiate meaningful and lasting agreements on arms control and on a variety of other issues.

The world is becoming increasingly turbulent. The factors that cause international instability are gaining the upper hand over the forces that work for organized cooperation. Social turmoil, political unrest, economic crises, and international friction are likely to spread. In this context, a stable American-Soviet relationship is all the more important and all the more difficult to achieve. While Soviet military power is increasing, internal tensions within the Soviet system and the Soviet bloc grow more acute. There is every reason to believe that without major structural adjustments, the Soviet system will be unable to cope with the problems of modernity, that its overly bureaucratized structure will continue to stifle creativity, and that the maintenance of such a system over Eastern Europe will generate rising resentment. The contradiction between the poor internal performance of the Soviet system and the growth of the country's external military capabilities is likely to create a much more unpredictable pattern of Soviet behavior. The erratic opportunism of a world power in the context of global turmoil will pose an increasing threat to international peace.

In the Third World, demographic pressures and political unrest will continue to generate increasing upheavals and will inevitably impose major strains on the international order. By the end of this century, 85 percent of the world's population will live in Africa, Latin America, and the poorer parts of Asia. Most of them are likely to continue to suffer from weak economies and inefficient governments, while their increasingly literate, politically awakened, but restless masses will be more susceptible to demagogic mobilization. In addition, it is almost certain that an increasing number of Third-World states will acquire nuclear weapons, and some of them, or some of their affiliated terrorist groups, are likely to use them in anger.

In the past, the Soviet Union has tried, as if by reflex, to exploit these difficulties. But Soviet power, used in a shortsighted and dogmatic fashion, can intensify global unrest and stimulate increasing fragmentation of the global order. The menace confronting humanity, in brief, is not Soviet hegemony but global anarchy.

In the years ahead, the most ambitious and taxing goal of American foreign policy will be to prevent Soviet exploitation of global turbulence while encouraging evolutionary change within the Soviet orbit. The U.S.-Soviet relationship will thus continue to be a mix of competitive and cooperative elements; the question for us now is which of the two will predominate. The rivalry between the two powers is not likely to fade; it is motivated by historical, philosophical, and psychological impulses. Ultimately the competition involves different conceptions of the individual's relationship to society and the state, as well as a different notion of history. But while rivalry must be maintained, it must also be controlled and cooled. With careful management, it can also be guided toward additional accommodation on matters such as arms control and regional restraint. The expansion of cooperative links can also encourage slow internal changes within the Soviet sphere. Such evolutionary changes, however, are more likely to occur first in Eastern Europe.

U.S.-Polish Relations

During much of the postwar era, the U.S. has encouraged Eastern Europe to promote political and economic trends that are already very much in evidence. We have sought to reward those nations that evolved toward a more liberal internal political system and to call attention to the human-rights abuses in the others. Through the Conference on Security and Cooperation in Europe, we have maintained public pressure on the Soviet Union and its allies to comply with the provisions of the Helsinki Accords.

Greater diversity in Eastern Europe is clearly desirable. In order to respond effectively to opportunities to promote change in Eastern Europe, the U.S. should treat the Soviet bloc neither as a monolithic adversary nor as a group of uniformly friendly neighbors.

Turning specifically to Poland, I would say the U.S. and the West have several goals. One is to consolidate the new political condition in the country, which is detailed very well by Hardt and Boone in Chapter 32. Essentially, the most striking political condition in Poland is the existence of, for the first time in a communist-ruled state, a nearly self-sustaining and open opposition—one that would be very difficult to eradicate. Since the suppression of open opposition would be most costly for the regime, both domestically and internationally, it is likely that the existence of the opposition will continue. Our interest is, in my judgment, to assure that the opposition consolidates itself in that it becomes part of the legitimate political scene. We should encourage the progressive reform of the economy, for its own sake and because economic reform tends to reinforce political pluralism, which in turn leads to the possibility, at a later stage, of a gradual transformation in the nature of power in Poland.

There is a subtle relationship between our policy toward Poland and our policy toward the Soviet Union. Obviously, the two cannot be identical; they need not even be synchronized. But if the American-Soviet relationship becomes progressively moderated, if there is some movement toward arms control, if we enter a period of what might be called quasi-détente, without the exaggerated expectations and rhetoric of the seventies, it will be easier for Poland to make the progress I have described above. Therefore, we have to tune our relationship with Poland by how the American-Soviet relationship unfolds. I am not suggesting for a minute that our steering of the Soviet-American relationship be subordinated to our goals in Poland. Obviously, in terms of importance, it has to be the other way around. But if the American-Soviet relationship loses some of its sharp edge, then the policy that we must pursue toward Poland will be more easily sustained and is less likely to encounter manifest and effective Soviet opposition.

Our policy toward Poland should be compatible with our goals for Europe. We can neither coordinate our policy toward Poland with our European allies in the sense that we all play the same game, nor even effectively undertake the division of tasks, because such a coordination simply does not exist; there are no mechanisms adequate to attain such coordination. But our broad strategic objectives do create a degree of complementarity. In my view, the engagement of our European allies in more active economic relations with Poland is a positive development at present because it helps us in our policy objectives in that country. Beyond that, I think there is the possibility of progress on limited troop reductions in Eastern and Western Europe, either through negotiations or through unilateral actions, which would begin to relieve some of the intensity of the military confrontation in Europe. That too I find compatible with the kind of policy I advocate toward Poland. Eventually, and in the long run, American-Soviet competition, which will certainly continue, will become less centered in Europe and intensify in other regions. Certain geostrategic tendencies of this sort are already evident. If this trend continues, the disengagement of Europe from the U.S.-Soviet contest will facilitate the pursuit of the kind of policy I summarized above.

Returning specifically to Poland, and addressing myself to the three conditions of the Reagan Administration regarding the lifting of the sanctions the repeal of martial law, the release of all political detainees and prisoners, and the resumption of a dialogue between the regime and Solidarity and between the regime and the church (the wording of the last condition has varied from time to time)—it is important to distinguish between the first two conditions and the third condition. The lifting of martial law and the release of political detainees and prisoners can be satisfied by discrete, specific acts by the Polish regime. Resuming an effective dialogue between the regime and its opposition requires a process; it is the creation of a dialogue, of a process of reconciliation, the establishment of a pluralistic, institutional diversity in Poland. A single act will not bring about this diversity; a gradual process may. I am in favor of the lifting of the sanctions because martial law has been repealed and political prisoners released, and the third condition, namely this dialogue of reconciliation, is in process.

This brings me to my last point. In shaping American policy toward Poland, I think we have to take into account some of our own domestic bureaucratic and political considerations. In my view, most important is the fact that the Reagan Administration is probably the administration least interested in Poland since 1956, and perhaps Reagan and his staff are personally the most ignorant of Polish conditions. Actual American policy toward Poland has been conducted on a bipartisan basis since 1956. Kennedy and Johnson built on many of the premises that shaped the initial Eisenhower-Dulles policy; Nixon carried these policies further; and the same is true of the Carter Administration.[4]. Except for a burst of emotional sympathy from President Reagan after December 1981, through January 1987 (when these lines were written) there has been a striking absence of top policymakers who show a truly strategic interest in the situation in Poland. This does not negate the genuine, very constructive interest of several upper level officials in the Polish situation. But by and large, as a strategic preoccupation of the U.S., Poland is much less important than many issues that should not be nearly as dominant in American thinking. As we approach the presidential elections of 1988, this miscalculation may be corrected, for domestic political reasons.

Notes

1. The chapter is based on the edited transcript of a presentation the author gave at the Conference on Poland, organized by the Rand Corporation and held in Washington, D.C. in January 1987.

2. See, for example, N. N. Inozemtsev in *Kommunist*, No. 18, December 1975.

3. Zbigniew Brzeziński, *Power and Principle: Memoirs of the National Security Adviser 1977-1981* (New York, 1985).

4. President Carter, to demonstrate his administration's more forthcoming approach toward Eastern Europe, decided that his first major trip abroad would be to Poland. We arrived in Warsaw on December 29, 1977. In his formal meetings with authorities, the President indicated a willingness to increase American commodity credits to Poland. The next year's U.S. budget included the provision of $400 million in direct Commodity Credit Corporation (CCC) credits for Poland, to be administered by the Department of Agriculture. As the enormity of Poland's grain shortfall became apparent, CCC assistance was increased further. In 1979, the President approved a total of $500 million in assistance to Poland, consisting of $200 million in direct credits and $300 million in credit guarantees; in 1980, CCC assistance was increased to $670 million in credit guarantees. We regarded this assistance essential to prevent the food situation in Poland from deteriorating further. The credits reflected the Administration's assessment that it was in the U.S. interest to assist Poland in overcoming its economic problems. In retrospect, it is clear that the sum total of private and government credits extended to Poland was excessive.

32
The Effectiveness of U.S. Sanctions Against Poland

Nicholas G. Andrews

The Polish and Hungarian events of 1956 mark the beginning of a change in U.S. policy towards Eastern Europe.[1] The apparent commitment to rolling back the communist tide was set aside in favor of dealing with the regimes and normalizing diplomatic relations with them. Taking advantage of the changed political leadership in Poland, the U.S. administration launched an active policy of developing relations with Warsaw, a policy which led to the sale of agricultural commodities for Polish currency and the extension to Poland of most-favored-nation (MFN) status. The U.S. relationship to Poland was in contrast to its policy toward other East European countries, which unfolded more tentatively. In the 1970s, however, President Nixon's administration pursued a policy of détente and negotiation with the Soviet Union and activated relations with all the East European states.

American policy consisted of a series of rewards for the good behavior of the East European countries. A rank of East European states was set up, based on the willingness of each state to promote friendly relations with the United States and its desire for greater autonomy from the Soviet Union in its internal affairs.[2]

Using economic sanctions as an element of policy was not a practical option during this formative period of U.S. relationships with Eastern Europe because the level of bilateral trade was very low, although both sides (especially the East Europeans) were constantly expressing their keen interest in its expansion. At this time, if the United States wished to punish rather than reward an East European country, the available "sanction" was to discontinue a pending negotiation or to change the rank of countries to delay the development of relations with the country in question.

Until 1981, then, U.S. policymakers had no experience with the use of economic sanctions against East European countries for political purposes. Although the level of U.S. trade with these countries had risen greatly during the 1960s and 1970s, in no case was it as much as 10 percent of that country's overall trade. Hence, the application of U.S. economic sanctions against Poland was a political enterprise with uncertain consequences.

General Jaruzelski's imposition of martial law in Poland on December 13, 1981, without the participation of Soviet military forces, was unanticipated in Washington. Western governments believed that the suppression of Solidarity would involve Soviet troops. The reaction of the West was thus complicated by the fact that martial law was, to all appearances, a purely internal measure. The American announcement of sanctions was delayed for several days; the NATO countries arrived at a limited consensus after several weeks. U.S. sanctions, which came as a surprise, if not a shock, to the Polish martial-law leadership, included the following:

—a ban on the shipment of non-humanitarian agricultural goods for distribution by the Polish government;

—a freeze on Export-Import Bank's credits for Poland;

—suspension of civil aviation privileges in the United States;

—a ban on Polish fishing in U.S. waters;

—a "no-exceptions" policy on the licensing of high technology exports;

—no new credits and no support for Poland's entry into the International Monetary Fund.[3]

The following items were added later:

—on May 13, 1982, in retaliation for the expulsion of two American Embassy officers, the United States expelled two Polish Embassy officials and at the same time suspended travel under the Marie Skłodowska-Curie Fund by participants in the U.S.-Polish program of scientific cooperation;[4]

—on October 9, 1982, in retaliation for the outlawing of the Solidarity trade union by the Sejm, Poland's MFN status was revoked. The ostensible justification was that Poland had failed to increase imports by 7 percent per year as promised upon its accession to GATT.[5]

Three conditions were specified for the removal of the sanctions: the lifting of martial law, the release of all political detainees and prisoners, and the resumption of a dialogue between the regime and Solidarity and between the regime and the church.

Attributing a major share of the blame for martial law to the Soviet Union, which had exerted extraordinary pressure on the Polish party leadership, the United States also imposed economic sanctions on the Soviet Union:

—suspension of Aeroflot flights to the United States;
—tightening of the export licensing system for high technology items, including oil and gas equipment;
—closure of the Soviet Purchasing Commission office in New York;
—postponement of negotiations on a new long-term grain agreement;
—suspension of negotiations for a new maritime agreement;
—decision to allow certain bilateral cooperation agreements to lapse, namely, those on energy, space, and science and technology.[6]

These sanctions were probably designed to signify condemnation of the imposition of martial law, to levy a burdensome economic cost on the Polish and Soviet regimes, and to seek the restoration of the situation before martial law, when Solidarity played an important political and economic role in Polish affairs.

Early in 1982, the United States also considered the advantages and disadvantages of declaring Poland in default since the latter had announced, in March 1981, its inability to meet its loan obligations. In summarizing the debate, *The Wall Street Journal* listed the following arguments in favor:
—declaring Poland in default would put the financial burden of the Polish economy where it belonged, on the Soviet Union's shoulders;
—the resulting drain on Soviet resources would force the USSR to reduce military spending and foreign adventurism;
—the default would punish the Polish martial law government.[7]

The logic of the assumption by some that the Soviet Union would accept financial responsibility for the Polish economy was explained. The standard of living of the Soviet peoples is lower than that of the Poles. Soviet concern for the strength and stability of the Warsaw Pact, which may indeed be weakened by the economic difficulties of one of its member states, has never extended to the assumption of its foreign debts. The Soviet Union has, however, extended trade credits and other forms of specific assistance to Poland, in the full expectation of being repaid. In any event, it seems extraordinarily unlikely that the Soviet Union would forgo spending for defense or military purposes even if its resources were stretched thin. Moreover, American bankers did not want Washington to declare Poland in default. Thus, the benefits to the United States were questionable and the sanction was not imposed.

To a considerable extent, NATO governments supported the United States on banning new commercial credits (except for food), delaying negotiations on the rescheduling of Poland's debt to them, and tightening restrictions on the export of high technology. Some of them suspended Polish civil aviation privileges, and most of them agreed to suspend contacts with Poland at a politically significant level.[8]

The year 1982 was marked by the Polish authorities' campaign against the sanctions in which they singled out the United States as the major culprit. They particularly emphasized to Western audiences that the sanctions hurt the Polish people more than the state, which contradicted the West's belief that the sanctions would not significantly affect the people but would undermine and weaken the authorities in the eyes of the people. In that year, the Polish government also tried to draw Lech Wałęsa and Solidarity into a new role, under official auspices and control. The failure of this effort led to a ban on all trade unions. Although in 1982 the authorities released many detainees, including Wałęsa, and suspended some martial-law regulations, the West was not sufficiently impressed to remove any sanctions.[9]

In the succeeding years, Poland began to meet the West's demands. Would the Polish leadership have been more reluctant to take these steps if it had not been for their urgent desire to have the sanctions removed?[10] It seems highly unlikely that General Jaruzelski hazarded any actions that endangered his control over the Polish domestic situation.

The following paragraphs describe chronologically the interactions between Polish policy and the lifting of sanctions:

1. Following Pope John Paul II's visit to Poland in June 1983, Polish authorities lifted martial law on July 22, 1983 and released a number of political prisoners or reduced their sentences by one-half. In response, Western governments agreed to begin negotiations on rescheduling Poland's debt to them. (The Poles had already reached agreement with Western commercial banks in 1982 on rescheduling debts due in 1981.) In addition, the U.S. administration began discussing arrangements that allowed the Poles to resume fishing in U.S. waters.[11]

2. Lech Wałęsa appealed to the West to remove trade sanctions, without mentioning the ban on financial aid and credits. In response, in January 1984, the U.S. administration restored the right of Polish vessels to fish in U.S. waters and allowed the Polish airline to fly charters between the two countries.[12]

3. Poland announced a sweeping amnesty on July 21, 1984, which included almost all the dissident leaders. By this far-reaching step, Polish authorities hoped to win some good will from the population and to induce the West to drop its sanctions.[13]

4. In early August 1984, the administration reacted by allowing regular, scheduled flights to the United States by the Polish airline and agreeing to reestablish scientific, educational, and cultural exchanges. Furthermore, the administration said it would withdraw its objection to the IMF processing of Poland's application for membership if the amnesty decree were fully carried out.[14]

5. Reflecting their desire to normalize their relations with Poland, Western leaders began to resume political visits to Warsaw in the fall of 1984. The Austrian foreign minister and the Greek prime minister visited in October, while the British minister of state in the foreign and commonwealth office went in November.[15]

6. The kidnapping and murder of Roman Catholic priest Father Popiełuszko in October 1984 and the cancellation by West German Foreign Minister Genscher of his planned trip to Poland in November marked a setback for the Polish policy of opening windows to the West that had been blocked by martial law. In a press conference in November, General Jaruzelski attacked the United States, France, and the Federal Republic of Germany for demanding concessions from Poland.[16]

7. In December 1984, however, Poland released the two Solidarity underground activists who were caught the previous June. The U.S. administration then announced that it would remove its objection to consideration by the IMF of Poland's application for admission. At this juncture, U.S. authorities considered that the amnesty had been implemented and the second condition for removal of the sanctions had been met.[17]

8. In January 1985, representatives of Western governments (the Paris Club) agreed in principle to reschedule roughly $10.5 billion of the debt owed by Poland for 1982-84. Discussions had begun after the amnesty of July 1983.[18]

9. In July 1985, representatives of Western governments signed a framework rescheduling agreement with the Poles covering about $12 billion due for the 1982-84 period. The main provision of the agreement called for the repayment of the principal and the bulk of the interest between 1991 and 1997 after a five-year period of grace.[19]

10. In November, Poland rescheduled a further $1.3 billion of debt to Western governments, falling due in 1985.[20]

11. During 1985 General Jaruzelski often traveled abroad. His most significant visits, from a political point of view, were those to the United Nations in September and to Paris in December. Willy Brandt's appearance in Warsaw in December for the fifteenth anniversary of the signing of the Polish-FRG treaty was also noteworthy. Western leaders were becoming keen to resume normal relations with Poland. They realized that Jaruzelski had established a strong, personal political position, that the party and military under his leadership were in unquestioned control of the country, and that a policy limited largely to criticism and disapproval of the actions of the regime would no longer adequately serve their interests.

12. In June 1986, Poland rejoined the International Monetary Fund.

13. Addressing the Tenth Congress of the Polish United Workers (Communist) Party on June 29, 1986, General Jaruzelski offered a partial amnesty to political prisoners. Moreover, on September 11 the minister of internal affairs announced that all 225 recognized political prisoners would be released within the next four days.[21]

14. With the ball again in the American court, so to speak, the U.S. administration studied whether the time was ripe for lifting the remaining key sanctions, namely, the ban on new government credits and the

suspension of MFN status. In formal terms, restoration of MFN status was still contingent on the establishment of trade-union pluralism. From all the evidence, however, it was clear that the Polish regime was unwilling to enter into a dialogue with Solidarity leaders for fear of according legitimacy to the independent union which they had legally banned. In December, however, General Jaruzelski appointed a Social Consultative Council attached to the Council of State, which included a number of lay Catholics, former advisors to Solidarity, and nonparty intellectuals.[22]

15. The administration used a series of meetings between State Department and Polish government officials to ascertain the plans of the regime in the areas of human rights, economic reform, and bilateral relations. The American side spelled out its hopes and expectations. At the same time, U.S. officials sounded out Polish opinion, including the views of church and lay figures, Solidarity leaders, and other opposition groups.[23]

16. A notable event in January 1987 was General Jaruzelski's official visit to Italy, the first to any Western country since martial law. Even more significant was his long private meeting with Pope John Paul II. Like Solidarity leader Wałęsa, the Roman Catholic Primate of Poland, and many others, the Pope conveyed to the U.S. administration the wish that economic sanctions be removed because they deepened the suffering of the people.[24] Taking all these factors into account, on February 19, 1987 President Reagan lifted U.S. economic sanctions against Poland.[25]

Let me draw some conclusions about the effectiveness of U.S. sanctions. Despite Poland's need to have the sanctions lifted, martial law was lifted only after a year and a half, and only after the Sejm had passed a series of laws, some of which replaced martial law measures, in order to reinforce the ability of the authorities to deal effectively with any opposition.

Western pressure was probably a factor in the decision to grant a far-reaching amnesty in 1984 because the Polish leadership increasingly wanted Western sanctions to be removed. The release of political prisoners, however, took place at the convenience of the Polish authorities, not before they had assured themselves that they were thoroughly in control of the domestic situation. The pressure of the sanctions contributed to, but did not cause, the decision to release the 652 political prisoners.[26] This Polish initiative was a partial failure because the internal security authorities were too quick to rearrest and reimprison members of the opposition, and the killing of Father Popiełuszko put the Polish regime in an unsavory light.

The amnesty of 1986 became necessary because the previous amnesty had failed to lead to broader support for the regime's policies and to the lifting of Western sanctions. The authorities have thus far resisted the temptation to reimprison those they recently released. In fact, of some twenty political prisoners who did not benefit from the amnesty because of their conviction for criminal as opposed to political offenses, some have been released since the lifting of sanctions.

Throughout the period of martial law, the government held periodic talks with representatives of the church but none with Solidarity. Although the officially approved union has occasionally disagreed with the government on price policy, it is not regarded as anything other than the government's instrument for manipulating the working class; its leader, Alfred Miodowicz, was elected to the Politburo in 1986.

While trade-union pluralism does not exist, the establishment of the Social Consultative Council is regarded as a significant step toward a dialogue between the regime and at least some of its critics. It seems that the regime is trying to mollify the population; it even allows former opposition leaders to live and work above ground. Meanwhile, the Solidarity trade union continues to exist underground, more or less in cadre form, although the government remains rhetorically committed to the destruction of the union. Nonetheless, persons who were members of Solidarity before martial law can be elected to the self-managing bodies of enterprises, which are not, in many cases, completely controlled by the ruling authorities (see chapter by Holland).

We now come to the heart of the matter. Was the application of economic sanctions successful? Yes and no. The main purpose of the sanctions was to punish the Polish martial law authorities. To be sure, as a consequence the regime did have greater difficulties in dealing with the economy. It was misleading for the United States to say that the sanctions would not hurt the Polish people; the Polish authorities could blame the sanctions for depressing the standard of living.

If the Soviet Union bore a major share of the blame for martial law, the sanctions against it were mild indeed. The pressure of the U.S. farm lobby prevented imposition of a ban on agricultural exports to the Soviet Union, and within a year—before all political prisoners were even released and before martial law was lifted—the United States had signed a five-year agreement with the Soviet Union on the sale of agricultural commodities. Perhaps the sanctions against the Soviets were mild because they had not intervened militarily. There was also some muddled thinking about the effect of sanctions on the Polish-Soviet economic relationship. The Soviet leadership made credits available in 1980 and 1981 and continued to do so after martial law, but it clearly expected that, upon normalization, Poland would begin to repay them. Therefore, the first result of Western economic sanctions was, inauspiciously for Washington, to compel the Polish regime to expand its economic and commercial relations with the Soviet Union. To be sure, Soviet credits were of no great help in those sectors of the Polish economy dependent on raw materials and spare parts from the West.

The hope in the West that the Polish authorities would yield to Western political conditions in order to have the sanctions removed was ill-conceived. The survival of the Polish leadership depended on its achievement of complete control over domestic affairs; only then was it ready to begin to meet Western conditions while trying to concede the minimum possible. Moreover, because trade-union pluralism goes against the theory of the unity of the working class in communist-ruled societies, this U.S. condition, entailing a fundamental change in the Polish socialist system, was the least likely to be fulfilled by the regime, for domestic as well as for geopolitical reasons.[27]

The application of economic sanctions also had the counterproductive effect of making it more difficult for the Polish economy to generate the level of exports needed to service Poland's hard-currency debt, even though the sanctions were not the fundamental cause. Furthermore, the refusal of the West to negotiate the rescheduling of Poland's debts to Western governments meant that the resources that Poland acquired through the drastic reduction of Western imports and the accelerated increase of Polish exports to the West went toward payments to Western commercial banks. The rescheduling agreement of 1985 between the Polish and Western governments put an end to this form of self-punishment.

On the positive side, the application of sanctions did express the revulsion of the West at the imposition of martial law. The depth and breadth of feeling in the United States may have helped convince its Western allies to provide modest support for the U.S. position. The sanctions also demonstrated to the Polish authorities that they could not reorient all their economic relations towards the CMEA. Greater economic integration within the Soviet bloc was too difficult and uncertain a process. The financial hardship caused by the sanctions seemed to exert pressure on the Polish leadership to take account of Western conditions for their removal. Thus, the economic sanctions may have been effective in that virtually all political prisoners were released in the amnesty of July 1984. Some dissidents believe that they might not have been released had it not been for the sanctions.[28]

Similarly, the continuation of the key Western sanctions of a ban on government credits and the U.S. suspension of MFN status, may have provided General Jaruzelski to adopt the amnesty measure of 1986. The strengthening of Jaruzelski's personal political position at the party of Congress of June 1986 facilitated this renewed effort to have the sanctions removed.[29] To be sure, Warsaw's political need to try to bridge the credibility gap between the authorities and the people was probably the dominant factor.

The case of Poland in 1981-86 shows that the first two U.S. conditions were met only when the Polish leadership felt sure of its control over the domestic situation. The third condition, calling for a dialogue between the authorities, and the church, and Solidarity to establish a degree of trade-union and political pluralism, was not precisely met. Nevertheless, the application of sanctions seems to have contributed to what Hufbauer and Schott, in their comparative historical analysis of economic sanctions, called "a somewhat positive outcome."[30]

Finally, in considering the determinants of U.S. policy in East European countries, limited experience shows that the application of economic sanctions is unlikely to provide the United States alone with sufficient leverage because the relationship of the leaderships—ideological, political, military, and economic—to the Soviet Union is much more important than the relationship of these countries to the United States.

The dubious success of economic sanctions in achieving political ends does not undermine the previous U.S. policy in Eastern Europe—inducements and rewards for what the United States considers "good" behavior. At the same time, the withdrawal of inducements and the withholding of rewards to express disapproval of the East Europeans' behavior may be just as efficacious in advancing U.S. interests. Sanctions directly challenge the East European leaderships to demonstrate their ability to endure or to circumvent them, too often at the cost of the population. They also exacerbate the bilateral, official relationship without exempting any areas of that relationship from possible retaliation. In the context of the slow development of U.S. relations with the East European states, the imposition of sanctions can also mean a costly loss of momentum. In other words, prudence suggests that economic sanctions for political purposes should be used only as a last resort.

The removal of Western sanctions against Poland should open the door to the possibility of improved relations and an increased involvement of the West in the economic recovery of Poland.

Notes

1. Included in the term Eastern Europe are the Warsaw Pact member states of Bulgaria, Czechoslovakia, the German Democratic Republic, Hungary, Poland, and Romania.

2. See Raymond L. Garthoff, "Eastern Europe in the Context of U.S.-Soviet Relations," in Sarah Meiklejohn Terry, ed., *Soviet Policy in Eastern Europe* (New Haven and London, 1984), pp. 318-24.

3. Lee Lescaze, "Reagan Takes Economic Action Against Poland," *Washington Post*, December 24, 1981, p. A1, A8.

4. "Polish Exchanges Suspended by U.S.," *Washington Post*, May 14, 1982, p. A24.

5. Lou Cannon, "Reagan Acts Against Poland," *Washington Post*, October 10, 1982, pp. A1, A24.

6. Don Oberdorfer and John Goshko, "Reagan Orders Economic Steps Against Soviets," *Washington Post*, December 30, 1981, pp. A1, A14.

7. Frederick Kempe, "Forces Advocating Polish Default Fail To Consider Full Impact, Wharton Says," *Wall Street Journal*, February 26, 1982, p. 34.

8. For examples of supportive Western actions, see Edward Cody, "Polish Debt Renegotiation Suspended," *Washington Post*, January 16, 1982, p. A16; Leonard Downie, "Britain Curbs Ties with Soviets, Poles," *Washington Post*, February 6, 1982, pp. A1, A23; Tracy Dahlby, "Japan Imposes Sanctions on Soviets, Poles," *Washington Post*, February 23, 1982, p. A13; and "Belgium Reports Sanctions on Poland, Soviet Union," *Washington Post*, February 23, 1982, p. A13.

9. John M. Goshko, "U.S. May Relax Sanctions," *Washington Post*, December 11, 1982, pp. A1, A6.

10. Stanislaw S. Wasowski discusses the economic impact of U.S. sanctions in his article "U.S. Sanctions Against Poland," *Washington Quarterly* (Spring 1986), pp. 107-83.

11. White House press release of November 2, 1983.

12. "Warsaw Arrests 2 as U.S. Spies; Wałęsa Wants Sanctions Ended," *New York Times*, December 6, 1983, p. A8; Francis X. Clines, "U.S. Again Lifts Some Sanctions Against Poland," *New York Times*, January 18, 1984, pp. A1, A4.

13. Bernard Gwertzman, "Reagan Reported Ready to Lift some Polish Curbs," *New York Times*, July 22, 1984, p. 6.

14. Don Oberdorfer, "President Lifts Some Sanctions Against Poland," *Washington Post*, August 4, 1984, pp. A1, A15.

15. William Drozdiak, "Allies Leave U.S. Behind in Reviving Polish Ties," *Washington Post*, October 11, 1984, pp. A1, A31.

16. William Drozdiak, "Bonn Policy Set Back," *Washington Post*, November 23, 1984, pp. A1, A30; Dusko Doder, "Jaruzelski: 'No Concessions'," *Washington Post*, November 29, 1984, pp. A1, A38.

17. "Reagan Drops Opposition to Poland Joining IMF," *Washington Post*, December 18, 1984, p. A22.

18. "Western Nations to Reschedule Polish Debts," *Wall Street Journal*, January 17, 1984, p. 31.

19. Christopher Bobinski, "Warsaw Delays Signing of Debt Agreement," *Financial Times*, July 4, 1985, p. 2; David Marsh, "Poland Signs Debt Accord with West," *Financial Times*, July 10, 1985, p. 2.

20. "Poland Reschedules $1.3 Billion of Debt," *Wall Street Journal*, November 21, 1985, p. 35.

21. Jackson Diehl, "Jaruzelski Offers Partial Amnesty, But Defends Crushing of Solidarity," *Washington Post*, June 30, 1986, pp. A13, A19; Jackson Diehl, "Poland Declares Amnesty," *Washington Post*, September 12, 1986, pp. A1, A28.

22. Jackson Diehl, "Poland Forms Council for Dialogue," *Washington Post*, December 7, 1986, p. A53.

23. "U.S. and Poland Hold Talks in Vienna," *New York Times*, November 12, 1986, p. A5; Jackson Diehl, "Poland Bars Visit by Kennedy," *Washington Post*, December 10, 1986, p. A29; and Jackson Diehl, "U.S. Expands Contacts with Poland," *Washington Post*, February 1, 1987, pp. A1, A30.

24. Loren Jenkins, "Jaruzelski, Pope Air Differences," *Washington Post*, January 14, 1987, p. A18; Jackson Diehl, "Poles Ask End to U.S. Sanctions," *Washington Post*, October 16, 1986, p. A28; Robert Suro, "Jaruzelski Talks with Pope on Ties," *New York Times*, January 14, 1987, p. A7; Frederick Kempe, "U.S.

Decides To Soon Lift Polish Sanctions," *Wall Street Journal*, February 18, 1987, p. 31.

25. John H. Cushman, Jr., "Reagan Lifts Polish Trade Curbs, Cites Progress on Human Rights," *New York Times*, February 20, 1987, pp. A1, A5.

26. See "Poland's Half-Learnt Lesson," *The Economist*, September 4, 1985, p. 55.

27. See the letter to the Editor from Gary C. Hufbauer and Jeffrey J. Schott, *Washington Post*, January 6, 1985, p. A14.

28. Personal conversations with the author, May 1986.

29. Nicholas G. Andrews, "Jaruzelski Strengthens His Leadership," *Christian Science Monitor*, July 31, 1986, p. 14.

30. Gary Clyde Hufbauer and Jeffrey J. Schott, assisted by Kimberley Ann Elliott, *Economic Sanctions Reconsidered: History and Current Policy* (Washington, D.C., 1985), pp. 683-95.

31. See Jerry F. Hough's discussion of U.S. policy options in *The Polish Crisis: American Policy Options* (Washington, D.C., 1982), pp. 63-78.

33

A New U.S. Economic Policy Toward Poland

John P. Hardt and Jean F. Boone

Step-by-Step Reciprocal Engagement

Positive developments in Poland in 1986, including reentry to the International Monetary Fund (IMF), high-level Polish statements in support of economic reform, and full amnesty of political prisoners, support a new U.S. policy of "step-by-step" reengagement with Poland. Further implementation by the U.S. of the step-by-step approach will require a careful assessment of the policy statements as well as the actions taken by Polish authorities. Moreover, Poland's success in attaining the shared objectives of economic and political renewal will require the coordinated efforts of other influential actors, including the IMF, the World Bank, commercial banks, the Paris Club, the Soviet Union, and—of central importance—Polish society. As reengagement proceeds, the U.S. may ask what conditions must be fulfilled to ensure that our contributions to the process of Polish renewal are justified? What kinds of programs might be pursued that would serve both U.S. and Polish objectives and needs?[1]

For the Polish leadership, the key to economic and political renewal lies in expanding both economic relations with the West and societal support for the full implementation of the "second stage of the reform." For the U.S. and the West, the benefits of renewal would be significant steps toward the democratization of Polish society, the strengthened independence of Poland as a sovereign state, and the improvement in the lot of the country's citizens.

Poland's Uniqueness

Poland has historically occupied a special place in U.S. policy because of the country's vital role in Europe and its unique characteristics:

—Poland has ties to the American Revolution through individuals such as Casimir Pulaski and Tadeusz Kościuszko; the U.S. and Poland have never been adversaries.

—The role of the large emigré population in the U.S. with ties to the Polish homeland has been important in U.S.-Polish relations.

—Because of Poland's Western bent and record of relative liberalization in Eastern Europe, the U.S. has measured developments in Poland by a different yardstick than in the other East European countries, with higher expectations and greater determination to encourage Poland to be more closely integrated into Europe as a whole.

—The right to publicly express divergent political views is greater in Poland than elsewhere in Eastern Europe. Poland possesses a lively media, with debate on important political, social, and economic issues. The existence of some pluralism within a Marxist-Leninist system has created the potential for developing institutional bases for political participation and dissent.

—The existence of private property in much of agriculture and freedom of religious choice are further distinguishing characteristics of the regime in Poland.

—Freedom to relate to Western countries, even limited rights to emigrate from and to the West, make Poland unique; a large number of Americans of Polish extraction have returned for their retirement to Poland.

—The gap between Poland's economic performance and potential also makes it unique. Although during 1979-81 it experienced the worst economic performance of any country in Eastern Europe during the postwar period, Poland has a greatly underutilized potential in terms of natural, human, and capital resources, which could be tapped if effective economic policies were pursued.

In light of Poland's unique economic and political situation, the alternatives for Poland's future appear clearcut: either economic decline and austerity in a political environment of permanent confrontation, or significant economic and political change. There appears to be no middle course, such as a policy of "muddling through" the difficulties.

U.S. policy toward Poland has reflected these elements of uniqueness both in times of positive relations and negative relations. During more favorable periods, Poland has gained greater benefits than the other East European countries, whereas during times of stress, the U.S. has followed a relatively harsh and demanding policy.

The Evolution of U.S. Policy Toward Poland

Prior to 1982, the U.S. had more fully normalized trade relations with Poland than with any other communist country. In 1960, the U.S. restored MFN status to Poland; in 1972, the U.S. made Poland eligible for Eximbank and Commodity Credit Corporation (CCC) credits. Because it already held MFN status when the Jackson-Vanik amendment (linking trade privileges to emigration policy) was passed by Congress in 1974, Poland was not subject to Jackson-Vanik restrictions.

During the 1970s, the U.S. and other Western countries followed a policy of preference for Poland, involving the extension of government and private credits, preferential tariffs, active scientific and cultural exchanges, and political interaction at the highest levels. Support for and participation in Poland's development flourished during this period, in spite of what in retrospect were clearly ill-conceived economic policies of the Gierek regime. Total U.S.-Polish trade turnover peaked in 1979 at $1.2 billion; the U.S. maintained a trade surplus from 1974 to 1981, with its exports dominated by agricultural products. When Polish economic problems and social unrest gave rise in 1980 to the establishment of an independent trade-union movement—Solidarity—and a political process of change referred to as "renewal," the U.S. continued to extend assistance to Poland in order to encourage the development of greater openness, democracy, and respect for human rights consonant with the process agreed to at the Helsinki Conference on Security and Cooperation in Europe.

With the imposition of martial law in Poland, however, the Reagan administration responded with sanctions that severely curtailed bilateral commercial relations. Details of the sanctions and the evolution of their effectiveness were discussed in the previous chapter by Andrews. Suffice it to add that without credits or credit insurance—their denial being a part of the sanctions package—U.S. exports to Poland were drastically reduced; without MFN status, many Polish exports could not compete in the U.S.

While refusing to consider the rescheduling of official Polish debts until certain political conditions were met, the U.S. decided not to declare Poland in default. To avoid a formal declaration of default on the $71 million owed to U.S. banks in 1981 and guaranteed by the CCC, the Reagan administration issued an emergency regulation waiving the requirement for a formal declaration of default before the government made good on its guarantee. Both the manner in which the change was made and the administration's decision not to declare a formal default (which would have accelerated the maturity of all outstanding debt and would have provided a basis for seizing Polish assets) were criticized by some in Congress and the press. Senators Moynihan and Kasten introduced legislation forbidding the use of CCC funds to pay guarantees on loans to Poland without a formal declaration of default unless the President explained in writing each month why the action advanced national security.[2]

Disagreements over U.S. policy arose within the alliance, particularly when the U.S. extended sanctions to the Soviet Union in response to the perception of Soviet responsibility for Polish martial law. In December 1981, President Reagan banned U.S. sales of energy-related equipment and technology to the USSR and then in June 1982 expanded the sanctions to include U.S. affiliates and foreign companies with U.S. contractual relations. This imposition of U.S. extraterritorial reach created the "pipeline dispute" within the alliance over West Europe's alleged excessive reliance on energy supplies from the Soviet Union.

While most of the U.S. sanctions against Poland were gradually lifted during 1983-86, the U.S. maintained a policy of disengagement from Poland. This policy was designed to demonstrate that the U.S. would not conduct "business as usual" with the Polish state. However, with the emerging normalization of Poland's international relations (including those with Western Europe, Japan, and the Vatican, its readmission to the IMF and the World Bank, and indications of renewed regime commitment to reform), the U.S. began to reassess its policy in late 1986.

The U.S. abstained from voting on Poland's readmission to the IMF. While the U.S. administration voiced no economic objections to approval, the decision to abstain arose from uncertainty as to whether Poland would be able to meet requirements for loans under U.S. law. The U.S. is required by law to oppose loans by the IMF to any communist country that does not meet certain criteria, including that the loan help a majority of its people.[3] The administration was also reportedly concerned that support for Poland's IMF membership could spur opponents in Congress to reduce U.S. contributions to the multilateral institutions. But if this approach of disengagement were continued, the U.S. might forfeit its influence over developments. Active engagement by the U.S. in the process of developing IMF terms might allow it to better assure that the conditions required of Poland by the financial community are consistent with the U.S. objectives of encouraging political and economic reform.

Reflecting the move toward reengagement, Polish and U.S. government officials met in Vienna in November 1986, the first official U.S.-Polish contact since 1981. This meeting was followed by a three-day visit to Poland in February 1987 by U.S. Deputy Secretary of State John Whitehead, after which he announced that the U.S. had begun a step-by-step process of engagement with Poland. New bilateral contacts agreed upon during this visit included discussions on a new scientific and technological cooperation agreement; a meeting of the U.S.-Polish Joint Economic Commission in the fall of 1987 (the first commission meeting since

1980); and participation by U.S. firms in the annual Polish trade fair in Poznań in June of 1987. These indications of movement led to the removal on February 19, 1987 of the major remaining U.S. sanctions, diminishing further the perceived stalemate in bilateral relations.

A Propitious Time for Effective Polish Renewal

A variety of factors are likely to influence the prospects for deepening U.S.-Polish reengagement: developments in Poland toward full implementation of its stated plans; responses by the international financial institutions; the role played by the Soviet Union in encouraging or constraining Polish reform; and assessments in the U.S. of its interests and policy options. Beginning in 1986, a qualitatively new environment for U.S.-Polish relations emerged, based on a confluence of forces that may encourage developments in Poland consonant with long-standing U.S. policy objectives: national dialogue, reform, and economic restructuring.

Debt Management: From Austerity to Growth

The reentry of Poland into the international financial institutions is a singularly important factor in making 1986-87 a window of opportunity for Poland to rebuild its links with world trade and financial markets. For Poland to obtain access to new hard currency, the IMF is the primary gate-keeper. Even if support is initially provided only at a minimum level, the prospects of a reduced debt burden and the availability of significant resources (under external economic conditionality) provide incentives to Poland that has been missing in the past. There is a range of assessments among observers of the level of support the IMF might provide; the extent of Poland's demonstrated commitment to reforms could determine whether it receives the minimum or maximum variant.

While reentry to the IMF may provide new opportunities for Poland's recovery, serious obstacles remain. The growth of Poland's debt has led to debt-service obligations whose full servicing appears to be unsupportable, both politically and economically, particularly since a substantial and sustained growth of exports will be difficult without new investment (as noted by several contributors from Poland in this volume). In 1985, full debt service would have claimed 81 percent of convertible currency exports; in 1986, it was projected to rise to 93 percent. This poses a dilemma between necessary debt management and the growth of domestic output and exports.[4]

While most observers agree that Poland must do more to promote an export strategy, such a strategy may not be effective as long as the short-term debt-servicing burden falls on Polish society through further declines in the standard of living and further restrictions on new investment and imports that would be needed for modernization and generation of competitive exports, as documented in the chapter by Poznański. A debt-management policy based solely on austerity may yield short-term benefits, but is not likely to facilitate reform, restructuring, and expanded exports. However, if a long-term, innovative debt management strategy were to be put into place—combining the efforts of the international financial institutions, Poland's creditors, the Polish state itself, and the Soviet Union—simultaneous progress toward reducing the country's net debt and promoting economic growth may be achieved. This approach, effectively using the resources of international financial institutions and implementing such new initiatives as debt-for-equity swaps (involving privatization of new domestic enterprises), may be successful in Poland, as similar initiatives are proving to be in other debtor countries, notably in Latin America. The key building blocks of such an approach are:

—*A stabilization program under the IMF* would serve as the first and fundamental element in a debt management strategy linked to growth. An IMF program could include, if Poland adheres to required conditionality, a restructuring of the debt beyond the normal repayment period of 10 years (up to 12-20 years) as well as new credits for investment. Informed observers estimate that $400 to $700 million might be made available initially under a standby program. The U.S. could play a significant role in shaping the terms and scope of the agreement, should it decide to fully exercise its influence in support of the IMF process.

—Building on the assurance of increased discipline by Poland and continued IMF surveillance, *World Bank sectoral loans* may be forthcoming, particularly in agriculture, such as food processing. Opportunities to participate as suppliers in World Bank projects would improve also.

—An IMF precedent in restructuring Poland's debt could also affect the *response of the Paris Club governments* in the rescheduling negotiations to be held in 1988. One possible approach to ease Poland's debt-servicing burden would be converting government debt into local-currency projects, building on the precedent of U.S. Public Law 480. In this way the U.S. could convert some debt to support projects in Poland that the U.S. considers in its interest, such as support for cooperatively-owned water projects in rural villages. In essence, this approach would use U.S. leverage over Polish funds to benefit Polish society in specific ways. A U.S. example on debt conversion might be followed by other Paris Club creditors.

—The application in Poland of innovative approaches like those employed in other debtor nations might be considered, such as *debt-to-equity swaps by commercial creditors.* One way the U.S. could support innovative approaches by the commercial banks would be to modify the regulation requiring banks to hold collateral equal to 50 percent of debt, a requirement that banks contend constrains creative approaches to debt management.

A debt management strategy involving these elements would not, alone, ensure growth; the promise of the "second stage of reform," announced by the Polish government in April 1987, would need to be fully translated into action in order to assure the productive use of the resources made available by debt management programs.[5] In the course of reform, wider political participation in the economic process and a democratization of management might facilitate increased incentives and productivity. Polish plans to develop cooperative and private domestic enterprises and joint ventures with foreign firms might also be vehicles for private domestic investment. If they would succeed on a sufficient scale, they would facilitate growth and dampen inflation. Observers note, however, that changes in the economic mechanism must be accompanied by changes in policy, directing investment and resources into efficient industries with export potential.

Gorbachev's Reform Policy and its Implications for Poland

In general, Soviet discussion under Gorbachev of reforms in both the domestic economy and in foreign economic relations may provide an "umbrella" for Polish reformers—an indication of Soviet approval of more far-reaching change than in the past. Some analysts have argued that none of Gorbachev's reform proposals goes beyond what already has been proposed in Poland. Nevertheless, the endorsement by the Soviet leadership of a program of reform and the encouragement of debate among economists on far-reaching issues, such as a reduction of subsidies, the redeployment of labor, and price reform, helps Polish reformers in a more indirect way: it precludes opponents of reform in Poland from using fear of Soviet opposition as an argument for blocking progress.

Trends in Polish-Soviet commercial relations also have a direct impact on Poland's economy and its relations with the West. While in recent years Poland has apparently been permitted to continue to run a trade deficit with the Soviet Union (despite an avowed Soviet policy of establishing a balance with all its CMEA partners), it is likely to face increasing pressure from the USSR, particularly in light of the Soviets' need to hold down exports of oil to East Europe in order to boost hard-currency exports. Poland signed an agreement with the Soviet Union that permitted it to run a trade deficit in 1986 and again in 1987. However, trade is to be balanced in 1988, and Poland is scheduled to achieve a trade surplus in 1989 and 1990. According to one observer, Poland would have to increase its exports to the USSR by 48 percent and its imports by only 17 percent during the 1986-90 plan period in order to achieve a balance by 1990. Clearly, these demands could come into direct conflict with the need to expand exports to hard-currency markets to meet debt-servicing obligations.

Furthermore, some other aspects of Poland's economic relationship with the Soviet Union may be limiting the second stage of reform and a debt-management strategy keyed to economic growth, such as the promotion of unproductive or inefficient investments. Given these concerns, Western governments and financial institutions would likely look for assurances that increases in Poland's production and financial resources would not be flowing to the Soviet Union, to the detriment of achieving stated restructuring goals. Western flexibility on Polish debt would need to be met with a comparable degree of accommodation on the part of its Eastern partners.

Fulfilling the Promise of Socialist Pluralism

Since the Party Congress of July 1986, the leadership's apparent new commitment to moving forward in addressing Poland's growing debt has been translated into several specific initiatives, among them the formation of the State Consultative Council, the amnesty of political prisoners, the announcement of a second stage of reform, and new laws facilitating joint ventures. To some degree, these efforts are consonant with conditions for improved relations set out by the U.S. and other Western creditors on the implementation of a comprehensive strategy, one that would involve broadening the national dialogue, economic reform and restructuring, and the development of an export strategy. In effect, these conditions represent the already approved program of the Ninth Party Congress (1981), whose proponents may now include Poland's reformist economists, its foreign creditors, and the church, as well as the authorities.

A renewed commitment to reform at the highest levels of the Polish party is reflected in several studies prepared and published by official agencies, such as the Foreign Trade Ministry and PRON (Patriotic Movement for National Revival)—institutions that until now have not been advocates of substantial economic change.[6] In addition, there appear to be renewed efforts to expand the dialogue between the party and the population and to build a consensus for reform. (The church has long sought the return of the Sejm to the legal status it enjoyed before 1945.) The Sejm has become a more active forum for debate in recent months, taking the unprecedented action of reversing two government proposals submitted in November 1986 which were said to weaken the implementation of the reform. Some contend that the new assertiveness of the Sejm is merely an illusion of greater pluralism aimed at placating Polish opposition and foreign opinion; alternatively, it may reflect a recognition by the leadership that the effective implementation of reform will require broader participation of society in decision making. Besides a growth-promoting debt-management strategy, the creation of a stable structure of participatory mechanisms that go beyond freedom of expression and public debate to involvement in decision making, increased accountability by the leadership to the government, and better recourse against the restriction of civil and human rights would enhance the prospects for political and economic renewal.

Politically, Poland has become unique in Eastern Europe. Whereas in other countries, adjustments responding to macroeconomic crises may still be imposed by the party leadership and implemented by the central planning apparatus, a forced compliance is apparently not feasible in Poland. Either the authorities or society can precipitate a gridlock, but neither can effect a significant change unilaterally. Therefore, the creation of genuine socialist pluralism, as called for by the state and elements of Polish society, may represent the only way to attain effective consensus and full implementation of the second stage of economic reform.[7]

For example, in order to change the income policy to payment based on productivity, a broad basis of participation and trust among managers of state enterprises, workers, and peasants is essential. Assuring the right to influence the policy of the government through the deliberation of a democratically chosen Sejm, thereby changing this body from a debating society to a decision-making organ, would also contribute to securing society's support for economic reform. Workers would likely respond favorably to an assured and unrestricted right to organize and bargain collectively. These rights, granted in principle, need to be firmly implemented in law and in practice to provide the participatory basis for linking wage incentives to productivity.

Alternatives: Economic and Political Confrontation or Growth and Pluralism

While the factors outlined above have created an environment in which U.S.-Polish reengagement may proceed, Poland faces several serious dilemmas that have yet to be resolved that could block significant progress toward economic reform, national reconciliation, and more active participation in the international economy. Escaping these dilemmas will require determined and enlightened efforts by the Polish leadership to implement its stated reforms, together with coordinated actions by the U.S. and other actors to encourage and facilitate positive change.

Two of the crucial actors in promoting growth and pluralism are the Polish state and the U.S. The Poles, by translating their blueprints for reform and pluralism into reality, could increase societal support for their economic policies. A positive response by the U.S. would in turn be helpful for providing leadership in the West for coordinated support of Poland's economic recovery. But the opportunities may not be available for long if the Polish government fails to take decisive actions.

Notes

1. For more detailed discussion of options for U.S. policy see U.S. Congress, House Committee on Foreign Affairs, Subcommittee on Europe and the Middle East. *Poland's Renewal and U.S. Options: A Policy Reconnaissance*. Report prepared by the Congressional Research Service, 100th Congress, 1st Session. March 5, 1987. See also the Update to this study, Congressional Research Service, May 31, 1987.

2. A modified version of this proposal was included as Section 205 of the Urgent Supplemental Appropriations Act of 1982 (P.L. 97-216) enacted in July 1982. Section 205 was later included as Section 306 of the Supplemental Appropriations Act, 1982 (P.L. 97-257), enacted in September 1982.

3. Section 804 of Public Law 98-181, enacted November 30, 1983, amended the Bretton Woods Agreement to add the following: " . . . the Secretary of the Treasury shall instruct the United States Executive Director of the Fund to actively oppose any facility involving use of Fund credit by any Communist dictatorship, unless the Secretary of the Treasury certifies and documents in writing upon request . . . that such drawing" (1) provides the basis for correcting the balance of payments position; (2) would reduce the severe constraints on labor and capital supply rigidities and advances market-oriented forces in that country; and (3) is in the best economic interest of the majority of the people in that country."

4. See Witold Trzeciakowski, "The Possibility of a Solution of the Polish Debt," forthcoming in *Forschungsberichte*, The Vienna Institute for Comparative Economic Studies, 1987. See also Hubert Gabrisch, "The Perspective for Covering Western Economic Obligations by Poland," *Forschungsberichte*, The Vienna Institute for Comparative Economic Studies, no. 113, February 1986.

5. "Theses Concerning the Second Stage of the Economic Reform" (in Polish), *Rzeczpospolita*, Economic Reform Supplement no. 102, April 17, 1987. (Prepared under the auspices of the Secretariat of the Economic Reform Commission.) Translated in the *Polish News Bulletin of the British and American Embassies*, Warsaw, *Economic Review*, April 28, May 5, and May 8, 1987.

6. See "Poland's Foreign Debt Problem and Ways of Resolving It. Report of The Foreign Trade Ministry's Institute of Business Trends and Prices (IKG HZ) and [the Planning Commission's] National Economy Institute (IGN)" (in Polish), *Rzeczpospolita*, No. 222, Sept. 23, 1986. Translated in the *Polish News Bulletin of the British and American Embassies*, Warsaw, *Economic Review*, no. 78-86; and "PRON Report on Economic Reform" (in Polish), *Odrodzenie*, no. 24, June 14, 1986. Translated in the *Polish News Bulletin of the British and American Embassies*, Warsaw, *Economic Review*, June 27, 1986. The critical and frank assessment of Poland's economy contained in this new study is significant, since it comes not from individual economists as in the past, but from an official institution of the Polish government, reflecting a change in Poland's internal political environment.

7. See, for example, the statement issued by Solidarity in April 1987 on "The Situation and Directions of Polish Economic Reconstruction."

Appendix. Five Models of Macro-Management Systems

Each of the five MMS models is identified by a set of 12 system descriptors, grouped into three categories, characterizing the organizational structure, the direct regulation, and the indirect regulation of the system, respectively. The tabulation below identifies and explains briefly the parallel descriptors under each of the five models.

Descriptor	Autocratic (0 points)	Directive (1 point)	Combined (2 points)	Quasi-parametric (3 points)	Parametric (4 points)
I. Organizational Structure					
1. Organizational structure, measured by the ratio of branch ministries to functional ministries	*Linear:* large number of industrial branch ministries. No functional ministries. At each level, departmentalization by product	*Quasi-linear:* dominated by branch ministries, departmentalized by product. The only functional ministry is Ministry of Finance	*Functional-linear:* equal number of functional and branch ministries	*Quasi-functional:* dominated by functional ministries. One branch ministry responsible for all of industry	*Functional:* only functional ministries
Graphic presentation of structure*	Presidium of Government; Industrial ministries; Chief administrations; Firms	Presidium of Government; Functional Ministry of Finance; Planning Board; Industrial ministries; Main administrations; Enterprises	Presidium of Government; Planning Council; Functional ministries; Industrial ministries; Unions of enterprises; Enterprises	Presidium of Government; Functional ministries; Ministry of Industry; Enterprises	Presidium of Government; Functional ministries; Firms
2. Basic legal entity	Entire economy one large enterprise	Industrial branch ministry	Trust; hierarchically organized on the branch principle; union of enterprises	Enterprise or horizontally-organized association of enterprises	Firm as a part of enterprise

*Legend: ——— direct linkages ----- functional linkages ...... basic economic unit

3. Intermediate supervisory unit over enterprises	*Chief administration:* a part of political structure. Main function is transmission of commands from the top and monitoring implementation	*Main administration:* an intermediate, administrative organ between ministries and firms. Main function is transmission of command from above and of reports from below	*Union of enterprises:* a formally independent economic unit, operating on profitability principle	*Association of enterprises:* a voluntary union of independent enterprises. Main functions: fulfillment of common objectives or goals, i.e. purchasing, sales, advertising	*No intermediate control units over enterprises*
4. Degree of enterprise autonomy in designing internal organizational structure	*None*	*Very limited:* same structure on all levels of management system, but different numbers of personnel in the same divisions depending upon each enterprise	*Moderate.* Enterprises can develop their own structure, but must adhere to staffing instructions by superior units	*Substantial.* Enterprises can develop their own organizational structure but must obtain approval by superior ministry	*Unlimited.* The structure depends totally on the management of enterprise

II. Direct Regulation

5. Structure of the central economic plan	*No structured national plan.* Production is oriented toward fulfilling a national campaign, i.e. victory in the civil war (Soviet Russia) or sugar campaign (Cuba)	*Hierarchical plan:* similar to the structure of the MMS, divided into sectors, branches, classifications, groups and individual products. Ministry of Finance prepares own financial plan	*Hierarchical and functional plans:* the former prepared by the branch ministries and coordinated by the Planning Board, the latter by functional ministries, in cooperation with the Planning Board	*The plan is functional* and divided in accordance with the responsibilities of the functional ministries. The Ministry of Industry prepares the R&D and investment plans for subordinate enterprises	*The plan is exclusively functional* and consists of a large number of separate plans devoted to different functions, prepared by the functional ministries and coordinated by the Council of Ministers

6. Degree of enterprise autonomy in designing own plan	*No operational plan* by enterprises. The activity of all economic units is oriented toward the execution of directives from above	Enterprise *totally dependent* on the hierarchical national plan	The plan is *in part dependent* on the national plan, with a limited margin of freedom. Enterprises can start new production if this does not impede execution of plan. Can reduce plan targets if there is no demand for production established in plan.	*Independent* of the central plan, except for investments	*Fully independent* of the central plan
7. Types of instruments and their range	Differentiated commands that define the exact volume and structure of production directed to all economic units	Differentiated commands that define the minimum volume and structure of production directed to all economic units	Differentiated commands that define the minimum production volume only of enterprises producing key raw materials and investment goods	Differentiated instructions by the Ministry of Industry only to enterprises of strategic importance concerning R&D and investment	No commands and no directives
8. Scope of administrative rationing over supplies	Comprehensive	Comprehensive, with the exception of certain consumer goods	Rationing of basic materials and investment goods	Limited rationing over certain strategic investment goods	None. Auction mechanism
III. Indirect Regulation					
9. Types of instruments	No functional instruments. No indirect influence by the state	Relies mostly on variable turnover taxes and subsidies to level enterprise performance	Relies on prices, taxes, subsidies, and wage differentiation as incentive or disincentive to output	Relies, in addition, on credits to promote or limit output	Relies, in addition on tariffs, R&D allowances and investment to promote or limit output

10. Success indicators	No financial success indicators. Quantitative output targets	The leading criterion: *gross production*, supplemented by a large number of financial indicators	*Rentability:* the ratio of outputs to inputs, supplemented by a significant number of financial indicators	*"Profit":* sales minus costs, or "financial result," plus a few supplementary indicators (i.e., index of obligatory export or limits on investment)	*Net value added* without supplementary indicators
11. Bonus criteria and source	No bonus funds. Compensation in physical goods. No relationship between the amount of goods given as wages to the worker and quality quantity of work	Based on the fulfillment and surpassing of quantitative production targets established by the plan. Base salary is predetermined	*Two simultaneous sources: plan and rentability.* One depends on the degree of fulfillment of the plan targets, the other determined as percentage of "profit"	*Profit is the major source.* Bonus fund is determined by the "workers fund," which in turn is a percentage of profit fixed by enterprise or workers' council. Base salary is predetermined	*Net value added* of enterprise. Basic salary as well as bonus funds are fully dependent on the financial performance of the enterprise
12. Degree and scope of control over wholesale prices	*No money and no prices;* physical rationing	*Marginal.* Industrial wholesale prices are fixed on a "cost-plus-formula" basis	*Partial.* The state fixes prices on basic raw materials and certain protected industrial goods and services and sets "rules" of price formation	*Dominant.* Prices are fixed by the state on all goods and services in all sectors, with the exception of some strategic investment where a "cost-plus-formula" is in force	*Total.* Prices are fixed by the state on all goods and services, either directly or through "rules" of price formation